MY FRIENDLY CONTEMPORARIES

By HAMLIN GARLAND

Pirie MacDonald, Photographer

HAMLIN GARLAND

MY FRIENDLY CONTEMPORARIES

A LITERARY LOG

BY

HAMLIN GARLAND

MEMBER OF THE AMERICAN ACADEMY
OF ARTS AND LETTERS

Decorations by
CONSTANCE GARLAND

NEW YORK
THE MACMILLAN COMPANY
1932

PRINTED IN THE UNITED STATES OF AMERICA
NORWOOD PRESS LINOTYPE, INC.
NORWOOD, MASS., U.S.A.

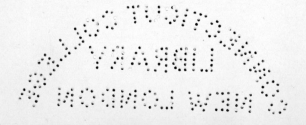

PREFACE

This volume like its predecessors, "Roadside Meetings" and "Companions on the Trail," is based upon my literary log, entries made from day to day, and like them it is designed to be self-explanatory, capable of being understood without reference to any other of my books.

Ten volumes of my diaries running from 1913 to 1923 have been drawn upon, as a mariner might thumb his log-books to furnish forth the story of his voyages. In these citations I have not only recorded the ships I have hailed and the captains I have spoken but also some of the storms, fogs, reefs and doldrums I have encountered in my devious course. In all these excerpts the moods of the moment have been left unchanged in order that the record shall be authentic.

In deference to the advice of my publishers, certain biographic lines have been repeated—an expedient which I trust the readers of my earlier chronicle will pardon. Ultimately this book will be sold in a set with its kind but it will not do to assume that its readers are familiar with the preceding volumes. Far less can I assume that they remember "Back-Trailers from the Middle Border," therefore a slender thread of family history has been used to bind the records together and to aid in tracing the author's incessant and erratic voyaging.

My original intention was to put these dated records forth in stark diary form but my advisers all voted against it. "To do so would limit the number of your readers," they said. "Bumping into dates is like motoring over a corduroy road." Recognizing the value of this warning, I have kept the dates subordinated to the narrative. Only now and again do I permit a paragraph to begin with a date.

I will confess to my readers that with each succeeding volume of my records, the task of editing them becomes more difficult and dangerous, for the reason that many of the men and women mentioned are alive and able to reply. However, I think I may say that all those mentioned are (as my title indicates) friendly critics and I am sure they will pardon any errors of judgment, and as my own comment and estimations are without malice, I hope they will be accepted as the expressions natural to a man whose long life as a writer entitles him to state his personal predilections, however mistaken they may appear to be. I have no scores to settle, no personal hatreds to voice.

Furthermore I make no claim to finality in my judgments. Their value lies in their sincerity and in the date under which they were set down. Some of them have been proved correct. Others I am less ready to endorse. Nevertheless they are included as a part of my mental history—the value of which depends upon its representative quality. If nobody agrees with me, what I print will be without effect.

The title of the book defines its scope. It does not pretend to be a book of reference. It is not a history of American literature from 1913 to 1923; it treats only of those whose acquaintance I enjoyed and whose books, plays and pictures were of interest to me. Many of the personalities mentioned are friends of long standing, men and women whom the reader may have met in preceding volumes and who come and go, as one critic remarked, like characters in a novel. Theodore Roosevelt, William Dean Howells, John Burroughs, Henry Fuller, Brander Matthews, who played leading parts in "Companions on the Trail," reappear in this volume and then pass into silence. Others of those I can fairly call my friendly contemporaries continue fellow-voyagers to the end of the period herein covered.

It is my hope that they and I may keep within hail on the charted course which lies before us. Ten volumes of later diaries are in my desk and will some time be offered to those who remain interested in my literary log.

HAMLIN GARLAND

Hollywood, California
July 15, 1932

CONTENTS

VI. CLUB LIFE AND MOTION PICTURES

VII. MOTION PICTURE PROMISES

VIII. HOWELLS' HOME AT YORK HARBOR

IX. AT SAGAMORE HILL

X. CITIZEN ROOSEVELT AND HIS SONS

XI. THE GOOD SHIP SANITAS

XXIII. ANOTHER SOUTHERN TOUR

XXIV. THE DEATH OF HOWELLS

XXV. HOWELLS' EARLY LIFE IN CAMBRIDGE

XXVI. THRONGS OF FRIENDLY WITNESSES

XXVII. "A DAUGHTER OF THE MIDDLE BORDER"

XXVIII. DEATH OF JOHN BURROUGHS

XXIX. HOUSING THE AMERICAN ACADEMY

CONTENTS

XXXVI. A LUNCHEON AT BALFOUR'S

XXXVII. KIPLING'S HOME AND BODIAM CASTLE

XXXVIII. LITERARY LIFE IN KENSINGTON

XXXIX. CONAN DOYLE AND BATTLE ABBEY

XL. WE VISIT JOSEPH CONRAD

XLI. CONRAD COMES TO TOWN

XLII. BERNARD SHAW AND HIS NEIGHBORS

MY FRIENDLY CONTEMPORARIES

CHAPTER ONE

A GROUP OF CHICAGO FRIENDS

I

ON January 1, 1913, my home was in Woodlawn, Chicago. It was a three-story brick house on Greenwood Avenue, not far from the university and within a few minutes' walk of the Midway studios of my illustrious brother-in-law, Lorado Taft. My study, a small room on the south side of the third floor hall, overlooked an ugly expanse of chimneys and was lighted by three large windows which let in the dust as well as the sun. The paper on which I wrote was often gritty with the dust which blew from neighboring roofs.

Notwithstanding its surroundings, this house was attractive, and my wife and two small daughters liked it —but they loved my family homestead in the little village of West Salem, Wisconsin, for there they played beneath trees on a generous lawn and looked away on lovely surrounding hills. Each year as May grew toward June, they demanded to be taken to "our real home"— and my wife was quite as eager as they to go. Four or five months of each year were spent in a plain, spacious old house on the edge of my native village. I mention these family conditions in order that this volume may be self-explanatory.

My fortunes were at low ebb. After a fairly successful series of novels and short stories, I had become absorbed in writing the history of a pioneering family of which I was a member. For more than two years I had been revising this manuscript, and my zest for fiction was dulled. I had published some ten or twelve fairly successful novels dealing with the mountain West, a region which I knew intimately; and while they continued to sell, they were of no great assistance. None of them were sufficiently sensual in appeal to win a large audience. They had no news value. "Hesper" and "The Captain of the Gray-Horse Troop" had gone beyond the fifty-thousand mark, but the others lagged at fifteen or twenty thousand copies. I was not in need, but I was at a point where I could no longer depend upon my royalties.

The Cliff Dwellers, a union of workers in the fine arts which I had originated in 1907, was still active, and as its chairman, I continued to give it much of my time while in the city. It was my habit to lunch there and afterward give an hour to its affairs. It occupied a kind of penthouse built for it on the roof of Orchestra Hall and its balcony commanded a view of Grant Park and the lake. To its dining room every passing artist, author, and musician was brought. I describe this club in order that the reader may understand the many references to it which I shall make. Like the Players in New York, it was a meeting place for men whose lives were concerned with literature, painting, sculpture, architecture, and music. It had only three rooms—an entrance hall, a fairly large sitting room, and a dining room with about eighty chairs.

In taking up the log of my literary career, it is necessary to go back to the date at which, for the sake of a cheerful ending, I closed "Companions on the Trail," for there are certain 1913 entries which should not be omitted.

"Chicago, January 1, 1913. Although poorer than I was in 1912 and with less power to earn money, I am rich in friends and the winter is singularly genial—a fact which I appreciate at this time, for I am far from well. Chicago is still 'assisting the drama' at this time by supporting the Horniman Players of Manchester, England, and during their stay this capable company will give 'The Tragedy of Nan' by John Masefield."

Masefield was a new name to me, and I recorded my impressions of his play. "It is a singular and unforgetable piece of poetic melodrama with a really great character in Nan, a subtle and beautiful acting part. It moved me deeply."

At the Fine Arts Theater on the afternoon of January 11, I saw Yeats' play, "The Countess Cathleen," another poetic play. "The setting was entirely a matter of curtains with a few—a very few—significant properties, but the audience did not appear to miss the canvas walls and pasteboard rocks."

That night I sat in an Orchestra Hall box with Professor Michelson, Chicago's world-renowned physicist, to hear an American composers' program.

"Michelson is not only a great scientist; he is a painter, a skillful musician, and a graceful and dangerous hand with a tennis racket. He is of Jewish descent, although he does not show it, a handsome man, small but admirably proportioned. We agreed that the musical program, while able and scholarly, was not inspiring. Pieces by

Henry Hadley, Frederick Converse, John Powell, and Arne Oldberg, and one of MacDowell's suites made up the list of compositions."

Among the visitors at the club during January, was Charles Wakefield Cadman, the composer of American Indian songs. "He is a slim, quaint young fellow, thin and dark and plain. He is by no means timid or hesitant. I do not mean to call him forth-putting, but he is fairly secure in his judgments. He has made a distinguished place for himself by way of his red Indian music. His sincerity of purpose in taking up the Sioux and Omaha songs cannot be questioned. He is, indeed, an enthusiast. He agreed to send me some of his songs and I am to reciprocate with a book or two."

During their stay in Chicago, members of the Horniman troupe came often to the club and I found them a serious and cultivated group. At the same time we suffered an invasion of "Cubists" and other faddists in painting. Several of these amazing exhibitions were open to the public and some of our artists had the doubtful honor of entertaining their projectors.

"It is incredible how much space these freaks have succeeded in winning from the press, but Bert Leston Taylor, our 'colyumist' on the *Tribune,* has routed them all with a single poem, which is too clever to leave unquoted.

> "At first you fancy they are built
> As patterns for a crazy quilt,
> But soon you see that they express
> The ambient simultaneousness.
>
> "The thing which you would almost bet
> Portrays a Spanish omelette,

Depicts with wondrous art and skill
A horse and cart upon a hill.
Now Mr. Dove has too much art
To show the horse or show the cart.
Instead—*he paints the creak and strain!*

"Another thing which would appear to show
A fancy vest scenario,
Is really quite another thing—
A flock of pigeons on the wing,
But Mr. Dove is much too keen
To let a single bird be seen.
To show the pigeons would not do
And so he simply paints—the *coo!*"

This poem set the whole town laughing, and one by one the exhibitions closed and their creators vanished, leaving the field for the "Imagists" or some other notoriety seekers.

"These esthetic rebels or discoverers (as one prefers) remind me of the coming of the Impressionists in 1890, whose landing I witnessed in Boston and whose warfare I shared. It may be that my zeal for novelty has waned, for these Imagists and Cubists seem mutually destructive. I join Bert Taylor in his ridicule of their claims. They are freakish amateurs, whereas the Impressionists worked in accordance with certain laws of light and shadow in mind. Monet's discoveries were not theoretical; they were actual, based on physical laws.

"It is natural for the young artist to claim superiority over his elders, but his claim is often justly disallowed." (The Cubists are gone; they are but a name to point a jest. They gave way to new invaders with new claims to genius.)

On April 28, Herbert Quick and Vachel Lindsay were guests at the club. "Lindsay, disregarding my suggestion, has dropped the Nicholas from his name and is now forced to explain that Vachel rhymes with Rachel. He looked older and a bit more subdued. Quick was as humorous as ever. He is now located in Omaha, but only temporarily. He is always on the move."

In spite of a severe illness and many distractions—as my diary entries show—I gave another series of lectures at the university, and during July I was in West Salem at work on two novelettes—one called, "Not in the Service Book" and the other "The Palace in the Mesquite." "The Service Book" was a story of the forest rangers' life experiences which I had been sharing for several summers.

In the intervals of my writing and lecturing, I took a father's delight in my daughters, now ten and six years of age. In reading to them, taking them into the woods of the hillsides in search of fairies, I regained my youth. Their growing appreciation of me as a writer was very sweet and altogether marvelous—as the following lines show:

"West Salem, August 18. With my wife away, I am in sole charge of my daughters. They take care of themselves during the morning while I am writing, but they depend upon me thereafter. Each night I plant in their small heads some good seed. Just before they go to sleep I read something to them in the belief that nothing stays longer in their minds than concepts given them just as their eyes are closing in sleep. Last night I read Hawthorne's 'Artist of the Beautiful,' to-night I read King Henry's wooing of Kate and they reacted to it with breathless interest. Naturally I do not write much with these small, lively creatures dependent upon my care."

On September 13, I returned to Chicago and resumed my duties as head of the Cliff Dwellers.

"Henry B. Fuller came home with me to-night and we discussed the literary situation which he finds quite as nauseating as I do—but agrees with me that we cannot complain without being called 'old fogies.' Well, at fifty-three I suppose I *am* an old fogy."

(Fuller, as I have stated in "Companions on the Trail," was my constant companion and my chief adviser while in Chicago. He was not only the author of several novels of local conditions, but a critic with international experience.)

To the reader who has not read the preceding volumes of my chronicle, it may be helpful to say that lecturing was a large part of my potboiling activities. Whenever my diary indicates a sudden journey to a distant city, a lecture engagement is the likely explanation. My "main-traveled road"—as some one said—lay between Chicago and New York with a stop at Philadelphia, where Edward Bok's beautiful home was always open to me. While I was not precisely on the staff of his *Journal* its editors were always hospitable to whatever manuscript I elected to submit.

II

While I did not record the engagements, I am quite sure that one or more lecture dates took me East in October, for on the 16th I was in Merion, Pennsylvania. "The weather is ideal Indian summer and I am once more tasting the luxury of Mary Bok's lovely home. Edward is less optimistic than usual. He is deeply concerned over the latest developments in dress, dancing, and conversation, and we gave them careful consideration. Certainly there is a distinct coarsening going on, a loosening of the bonds which women of a certain type (of all types) seem to be making much of. The animal side of life is more and more insisted upon. Many women are already claiming the right to take on the vices of men, confusing license with liberty. Men have never claimed vice as a *right*, they have merely considered it a privilege."

As a member of the council of the Authors' League, I attended a meeting, in New York City, at the Astor House, on October 21. "It was an assembly of young and vigorous men to whom literature is very largely a trade. I was the oldest man in the room, and their attitude toward me was that of kindly nephews tolerating a blundering old uncle—a new character for me.

"A depressing discontent comes over me as I go about this roaring, remorseless city, so desperate is its race for wealth and the satisfaction of its physical appetites. With a vague sense of its multiplicity of excitations, nothing really calls me. It has its quiet nooks, however. Last night I took Francis Hackett to a nine o'clock supper at the Authors' Club, and we sat at a table filled with white-haired, scholarly men. To my handsome guest they were, I fear, intolerably aged and slow. Hackett, whom I had known in Chicago, looked pale and worried, as if he had not yet found his place in our metropolis.

"A sense of disharmony between myself and the younger writers I have met in New York has filled me with uneasiness. Many of them are of small talent which they use meanly. Others are opportunists, changing with the winds of each day's sun. The city seems a wild and whirling mass of humankind, but this conception is probably due to my homelessness and to my years. At fifty-three noise is irritating."

On the train toward home late in October, I read Rex Beach's "Iron Trail," finding it an able book. "It has no charm and no distinction in its method, but it is vigorous and manly and truthful—up to a certain point. It is like him—adventurous, wholesome, and matter-of-fact."

I ended the year of 1913 in Chicago. "As I read Barrie's article on Meredith to-day, I realized more clearly than ever before how little there is in the West to link us with the past or with the East. Our young people lack the old-time respect for writers. No one in Chicago could feel such reverence for an older writer as that which Barrie expresses in this noble tribute to his fellow craftsman."

CHAPTER TWO

PRISON REFORM AND WAR NEWS

I

IN the final chapter of "Companions on the Trail," I set down in some detail my desperate invasion of New York in January, 1914, bearing a large autobiographic manuscript and two short stories. I was a limping, disheartened man of fifty-three, and the unexpected sale of these manuscripts is recorded in the following lines, written on the 15th of February, apparently while on the train —or perhaps at Niagara Falls, where I sometimes stopped in order to walk for an hour or two.

"By rising early and hustling sharply, I left New York on the eight-forty-five morning train for Chicago. I spent the day in revising and recasting the manuscript of my 'Son of the Middle Border.' I am in hopeful spirits. With four thousand dollars in sight, I can almost clear myself of debt. *Collier's Weekly* is to pay me twenty-five hundred dollars for six installments of my 'Chronicle' and four hundred dollars for 'Tall Ed Kelley.' The *Century Magazine* has already paid me for my article on James A. Herne, and Mark Sullivan (editor of *Collier's*) is considering 'The Gingham Bonnet,' my forest ranger novelette. When I remember my disheartenment in Pittsburgh two weeks ago, I am amazed at my good fortune."

Chicago presented a dark, snowy, dismal aspect when I arrived at the Englewood Station the following dawn. I should have hired a taxi but I did not do so. My faith in my future was not sufficiently strong for that, and my ride in a Sixty-third Street electric car, jammed in with strange types of workmen on their way to their daily tasks, was not cheering. My triumphant session in New York faded into a desolate drab.

Early in February Mark Sullivan wired me his delight in the first section of my story as revised and put into type. His telegram was the longest I had ever received and was correspondingly gratifying. It gave proof that I had made a successful revision of the story.

At his request I returned to New York on February 12, and spent several hours at the office of *Collier's Weekly*, proofreading section three of my serial.

"At night Mrs. Cordenio Severance took me to see Frank Craven in his play, 'Too Many Cooks,' a very original and amusing comedy, quite as true and fetching in its local color as the plays which the Irish players are presenting. It is funny without a touch of the sexual morbidity which taints almost every present-day book and play. It is a slice out of life—ordinary, decent, hardworking life. It is interesting at every moment. Insight, humor, and courage went into the writing and the performance of it. We all enjoyed it and rode home in high spirits."

"Chicago, March 22. Zona Gale having been announced to speak at Jenkin Lloyd Jones' church this morning, we all went to hear her. She looked like a Whistler portrait as she sat on the platform waiting for the signal to rise. The audience was large, larger than it seemed possible for her voice to reach; she was such a shy, gray little figure on that wide platform, and yet there was power in her reposeful attitude. When she rose and faced her audience, I perceived in her the ease of the natural orator. Her bearing was surprisingly commanding and her voice carried without effort to every part of the room. Her introductory speech was a finely proportioned performance; natural, easy, masterful.

"The story which she read was deeply moving to us all. Her manner, so singularly restrained, possessed a quality which all readers strive for and few obtain. Nothing could have been more adroit, and yet the art of it was concealed. As she closed, we wished to applaud but did not do so, inhibited by the church's traditional sense of propriety. Zona came home with us and seemed amazed at the warmth of our praise. She is a great little woman."

During March I bent to the task of preparing my "Chronicle" for *Collier's* and often found myself weary and confused.

"I am puzzled to know what to put in and what to leave out—but this has been my problem from the first. To-day is my day for feeling old and useless, but my sweet little daughters came to see me and their trust enabled me to take up the burden of my work again. I am tired of being forever humped over a desk. At times work seems futile. I have rewritten this manuscript so many times that at two hundred dollars per thousand words I would not be getting gardener's pay for the hours I have spent upon it. In a sense it has taken twenty years of my life. I am hopeless of ever getting it into book form."

On April 13, The Little Room, our literary and artistic group, had an evening meeting—a rare event—and some thirty of its members, mainly elderly folk, assembled. Some of them danced old-fashioned dances and, when they were tired of that, Henry Webster and I sang for them. I sang "The Rolling Stone," the chief number of my repertoire, and in so doing amused my fellow members immensely. Webster was much more ambitious in his selections. "It was a neighborly and informal party, pioneer in spirit. In such ways Chicago still retains something of the borderland simplicity. In truth the life we lead here is amazingly rural. Our circle is narrow, our amusements monotonous."

Early in May, I again went East to confer with Sullivan concerning my serial, and while there I saw for the first time a moving-picture company "on location."

"At eight-thirty this morning (May 14) I met Augustus Thomas at the Century Club and talked moving-picture plays with him. He said, 'There is a picture in each of your novels. Why not come with me and see how a screen drama is made? It's a superficial form of dramatic art, but I rather like it.'

"At nine we took cars for Englewood, New Jersey, where we found the company assembled at a queer little unsavory tavern. All were in the costume of Civil War time and as I mingled with these characters I was reminded of my aunts and uncles some fifty years agone. Here were soldiers in blue, hoop-skirted ladies, and gentlemen in long brown frock coats with huge cravats, high hats, and the like. Among them Augustus moved, smiling, companionable, but always dignified, the arbiter of every dispute. The weather was exquisite and the company gay.

"Loading us all into motor cars, the manager led the

way to a lovely house, which possessed a typical Southern portico, and there, with an aged darky driving an aged horse hitched to an aged carriage, a group of the players enacted a scene of parting in Virginia. Lew Dockstader, a famous black-face comedian, was the negro driver. At noon we all ate in the little tavern and the company fell into delightful groups—like illustrations from a Civil War novel. I came back to the city filled with a belief that some of my Western novels could be depicted in this way."

At the suggestion of Augustus I went almost immediately to see Jesse Lasky. The motion-picture bug had bitten me! Lasky was interested and asked me to send in some scenarios.

A few days later I accompanied Augustus to Yonkers to the studio of his company.

"It was a highly educative hour for me. The huge shed was so noisy that the director was forced to use a megaphone in addressing the actors. The blinding lights, the players moving aimlessly about, the carpenters hammering, sawing, and snarling, made the place a pandemonium."

"How can a worthy art rise out of such confusion?" I asked myself. Nevertheless I found that on the same day I wrote a letter to one of the leading companies in answer to a suggestion that I compose a scenario on the life of Grant.

During most of my stay in the East at this time, I was a guest at Irving Bacheller's beautiful home in Riverside, and on May 23, Job Hedges, a famous after-dinner orator and politician, spent the night with us. My candid estimate reads thus:

"I have never been deeply respectful of Hedges. He is almost too funny. He is the humorist, obviously and studiedly. His speeches are arranged to produce laughter. He did not change my opinion of him during this visit. He told stories and made faces all the evening. He was amusing, that I will admit, but I shall not vote for him if he is nominated for governor. Physically he is a short, ungraceful man, but able and adroit. He is not entitled to the high honor of being governor of New York, however."

The nation was suffering at this time an outbreak of pageantry, and among the towns whose citizens had awakened to the value of their local history, St. Louis held first place, for during the summer of 1914 she staged an immense spectacle in which the legendary and savage life of her river led up to the coming of the white explorer. My valued friend Percy MacKaye was the author of the first and most poetical part of this pageant, and a Chicago man, Thomas Wood Stevens, assisted in presenting the pioneer history. Reports of this program were so ecstatic that Lorado Taft and I went down to see it and to speak at a conference of community drama specialists. The dramatic conference, which took place on May 29 in a small hall, brought together a notable group.

"Chief among them was Mackaye with shining face and eager eyes. Among others whom I knew were George Pierce Baker of the Harvard play-writing school, Thomas Wood Stevens, a Chicago man, small, serious, and pale, Laura Sherry of Milwaukee, vivid and poetic, and Thomas H. Dickinson of Madison. They all applauded this aroused interest in local tradition and community theaters

as if it were something vitally important, a spirit usher-
ing in a tremendous era of self-enlightenment among
our inland towns. Taft spoke to this effect, for his own
work lay along somewhat similar lines of propaganda.
My own brief speech was, I fear, not quite keyed to the
highest pitch of enthusiasm, but I welcomed any stirring
of the Mid-Western literary consciousness.

"At night we witnessed the pageant, which was quite
marvelous in all ways, but the crowd was as impressive as
the play. Nearly two hundred thousand people were
seated there on the hillside, all facing the east, and as I
rose and looked back upon that enormous wave of humanity rolling against a sunset sky, realizing that each of
those pink dots was a face, the outward sign of an aspiring soul, I was appalled. It was, in very truth, stun-
ning. Humanity seen in mass reduces the individual to
an atom. That carpet made men and women of small
account. It reduced each of us to the weight of an in-
sect. I turned from that hill of human flesh and for relief
fixed my eyes on the stage where the individual was ag-
grandized and honored.

"The historical section was superb, but the masque
which preceded it was less effective. It was too long, like
many of MacKaye's works, but it was very much worth
while. The stage direction was masterly and the scenery
impressive. We came away with a higher concept of the
city. It has shown a noble interest in thus dramatizing
the significant events of its early history. It was all poor
and thin when compared with Warwick or Chartres but
it was not trivial. 'We must make the best of what we
have,' Taft said, 'and St. Louis has set a high mark.' "

From this most colorful and poetic celebration I passed

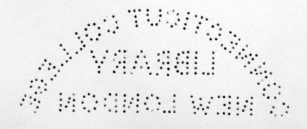

almost at once to the campus of the University of South Dakota, where I was scheduled to give the commencement address. Here again in its own small way was a civic coming together.

"At the chapel I found some five or six hundred fine young people and their lean-faced, careworn parents. Many of them were from the farms of the region and carried in their faces that serious, wistful look I had often seen while living among them twenty years before. The students were almost equally serious under their surface gayety and I understand their feeling. It was their great moment—to be followed by dull routine. How remote they all are from the nation's heart! The magic of the old-time prairie came back to me, voiced by the wind which blew fitfully through the sparse, small grove. It was a relief to go back to the Pullman car and ride away from these memories which are sadder than the anthem of the wind."

II

In "Companions on the Trail," I told of arranging a luncheon for Vachel Lindsay and of my visit to his father's home in Springfield, Illinois, but since that time I had seen little of him.

"Lindsay was at the club to-day [January 22], looking quite as rough-hewn as when he spoke here three years ago. He is even more self-confident. He has taken on the manner of a success although he admits that his work does not pay very well. He was not what I would call a timid or bashful youth in 1911 and he is now so confidently assertive that some call him truculent. However, I do not blame him for doubling up his fists. He has been forced to fight for every inch of his advance. 'Springfield still regards me as a "nut," he said.' "

On July 10 of 1914, I went to Colorado to deliver a series of lectures for the Normal School at Greeley and while there I received an invitation from Thomas Tynan, warden of the state penitentiary, to visit his "honor camp" at Boulder, Colorado. This invitation was the result of a public dinner in Chicago where he and I had been seated side by side. He had impressed me as a bluff, vigorous, and kindly man with most advanced ideas concerning the care and employment of convicts. Knowing something of me as a writer, he had said, "Come out and see what we are doing in Colorado. It may give you something to write about."

Now here I was, not far from one of his experiments, and taking the early train from Greeley on July 18 I went to Denver to meet him.

"At about eleven this morning we set out for Boulder, where I inspected a camp of convicts building a road up the cañon. A stranger would not have known that they were prisoners. They all wore dark shirts and trousers and broad-brimmed hats. They looked like cowboys or miners. They were brown, muscular, and apparently cheerful. All were on honor not to run away. There were no locks and no guards other than the one who acted as foreman of the gang. Under his direction they were blasting rock, grading soil, uprooting trees. I had no sense of being among criminals as I talked with them. One particularly handsome man of thirty-five was about to be discharged. 'I am grateful to Tynan for including me in his outdoor plan,' he said. 'I shall go out looking like a man and not like a white-faced, crop-haired, cellar-bred brute. It is a frightful handicap for a man to go from a cell into the world again, but to go from a camp like this will be an advantage. I am stronger and more skillful than I was when convicted.'

"I didn't ask him what his crime had been, but, as I recall it, he had shot a man in a sudden, fierce anger. 'Many of these men,' Tynan told me, 'are suffering the outcome of a moment's passion. They are not criminals in the habitual sense. They are not even criminally minded and should not be branded as outlaws.' "

"Cañon City, July 20. After a slow and tiresome trip over a slippery red-loam road, we reached here at ten last night. Tynan was taken ill on the road and has not been able to take me about the prison. He gave orders to his deputies, however, and I have been going freely to every part of the yard. I have talked with all sorts of officials and workmen. It is not precisely a model prison and some of Tynan's judgments of the men are biased and his punishments seem to me as extreme as his privileges. His honor camps are a success, but the more I talked with him the more I was inclined to qualify my estimate of him.

"At night I went with the night captain on his rounds and as I did so he convinced me that the cell house was a magazine of dynamite. 'It blew up twice before and may do so again.' He pointed at a certain window and said, 'That fellow is dangerous. I have warned him against showing himself. "I'll shoot you on sight," I have warned him.'

"He told me of a recent attempt at escape. 'A crowd of the prisoners having captured a guard and a visitor, used them as a shield while their fellow conspirators attempted to dynamite the locks of the outer gate,' and as he whispered this story, treading softly in the shadow, I sensed the smoldering desperation of the swarming cells. I had sentimentalized the prisoners, for I had seen the best of them. This armed guard believes in none of them. His task is to anticipate any outbreak and to kill the man who raises a hand in attack."

It was a sinister experience. I had known rough men, fighting men, dangerous men, all my life, but not desperate, remorseless men, and yet I could not blame any man for an attempt to escape!

I returned to Chicago late in July and was alone in my Woodlawn home when the morning papers brought the appalling news of the European outbreak.

"These reports are enough to make me an anarchist," I wrote. "As between the killing of a few kings and the shooting of a hundred thousand citizens, I should vote instantly for the assassination of the kings. It is horrible, incredible, that all Europe should go to war over a murder. Assuredly the outcome of such a commotion will be the setting up of republican forms of government in place of these monarchies and it is equally sure that some of these rulers will fall by violence."

(As I read this entry now, I marvel that I should have formed such definite judgments on the basis of a single day's issue of the city papers. Nevertheless I wrote these words and added, "In face of this colossal turmoil, the work I am doing seems so petty that I have no heart to go on.")

"Chicago, August 2. Sunday. War! WAR! WAR! is shouted by every newspaper. As men rise to this beautiful Sabbath morning, all Europe is swarming with marching men, and here I sit, trying to write a little story of the Rocky Mountains, while Germany is moving into Belgium."

At the club that week, nothing but war was discussed. "All talk is of this frightful, all-embracing conflict. Confusion spreads. The world to-day is so close knit that we cannot avoid sharing its hatreds in some degree. We shall all feel a real pinch and strain. Personally I am worried about the fate of my serial with *Collier's Weekly*. Sullivan does not reply to my letters or telegrams. I hope this does not mean an entire loss of interest in my story."

On August 15 I returned to West Salem.

"A wild wind roared through the trees last night. The noise of it was like the sound of a storm on an ocean beach. It seemed at times as if the trees were in battle. War news is getting scarce, but all that does filter out from the censor's office indicates the movement of titanic armies. With so much tragedy in the air I find myself unable to concentrate on my literary plans. All my writing seems petty and futile."

On October 6 I went to Des Moines to take part in an Authors' Home-coming, an event which the literary citizens of the state had awaited with keen interest. It was an attempt to do what Indiana had done so frequently, stage a round-up of all the writers who have at one time or another lived in Iowa. "I was met at the train by James B. Weaver, a son of my old friend, General Weaver, accompanied by Henry Wallace, son of the man who made the *Farm Journal* famous. I feel a little as I imagine the members of the National Institute of Arts and Letters felt when they landed in Chicago. This is just another and smaller literary outpost. In an esthetic sense, this is Des Moines' great day."

First of all, a reception on the lovely lawn of the Cowles home brought out the full strength of the invasion. Emerson Hough, Randall Parrish, Rupert Hughes, and I were the featured visitors, while Alice French, Arthur Ficke, and Colonel Byers were honored as "home folks" along with several others whose names and books I did not know. In the midst of the pleasant party, some ten or twelve young people all in costume—among them a cowgirl on a handsome horse—came around a clump of trees and ranged themselves before us. These were characters out of our various novels. The cowgirl was "Berea" from my "Forester's Daughter." This troupe was a complete surprise to us and quite delightful. At night we all spoke to a most enthusiastic audience, Rupert Hughes making the hit of the evening.

"October 7. This day has been a round of receptions, luncheons, and dinners. In fact we began the day with a breakfast at the country club. At ten I shared in a meeting at the office of Pierce's *Farm Journal*. At eleven-thirty I addressed the pupils of the high schools and at twelve-thirty joined the others at the home of the 'Successful Farmer,' for luncheon. Hough and I spoke but Hughes dropped out. At three Arthur Ficke and I hurried to the Woman's Club where we each read a few of our verses. Ficke read very well and his poems were charming. Alice French was present but did not speak. At six-thirty we all sat in at the final banquet in which nearly four hundred people took part. Parrish, Hough, Ficke, Joe Chappell, and I were the speakers. I was a rag when the chairman dismissed us."

During these two days I forgot the war and busied myself with Iowa's esthetic progress. "True, its papers are all political or agricultural, but it has produced and partly supported a considerable group of authors, many more than those who were able to show themselves, for Edgar Harlan, state librarian, has made a list of the writers who can, in some way, be related to the state. To me this interest is highly commendable, even though I find among them names of men whose work is of no value to me. That the people of the state should care to enroll its writers is significant of progress."

Within ten days of my return to my home in Wisconsin, my father, a veteran of Grant's army, was "mustered out" and took his place beside my mother in Neshonoc, the little burying ground on the bank of the La Crosse River.

CHAPTER THREE

LITERARY PIONEERS AND EASTERN ARTISTS

I

THE death of my father caused a profound change in my way of life. For more than twenty years I had made my home in the West in order that I might be near him (my mother had been dead many years) and now, no longer bound to this Wisconsin valley or to my house in Chicago, I began at once to think very definitely of taking my family to New York City, where most of my literary friends lived and from which all my income was derived. I argued that my wife and daughters could live as cheaply in a suburb of Manhattan as they could in Woodlawn, and that I would have the advantage of more frequent contract with the editors of the metropolis.

"I am aware of the risk involved," I wrote at the time. "Every week makes my lectures and stories of less value to the public. I am too old to adapt my style of fiction to these new readers even if I were minded to attempt it —which I am not. My only hope is in retaining the support of my own generation and that elder diminishing one to which my father belonged."

All questions of this character I discussed with my friend, Henry B. Fuller, whose intellectual stories were more completely out of demand than my own. He was a small, alert, gray-haired man two or three years older than I, a strange, elusive, homeless being—a native of Chicago. As one of the wisest and keenest of my critics, I carried all my problems to him for analysis rather than for solution. He hated his environment, but was unable to escape his obligations to his family. Essentially pessimistic of all attempts to raise the level of Western culture, his biting phrases were at times rather hard to bear. Although widely known, he permitted few intimates. With me he was entirely frank.

"Why stay in this town if you can get out of it?" he demanded. "No writer can earn a living here except on the newspapers. If I could get away I would go to Italy and never return."

He was right. Not one dollar of my income came from Western publishers and it was always with a sense of weakness and dismay that I reëntered Chicago from New York. The source of my income, such as it was, lay in the goodwill of Eastern editors and in this stormy time I felt the need of supporters like Mark Sullivan, Edward Bok, George Lorimer, Frederick Duneka, and others of my friends who directed the policies of great journals and established publishing houses. Then, too, I enjoyed frequent meetings with Irving Bacheller, Albert Bigelow Paine, Brander Matthews, Ernest Seton, John Burroughs, William Dean Howells, and others of my long-time friends and literary associates.

It may be counted a weakness, but I was no longer content to live the life of a literary pioneer. I came to Chicago in 1893, at the time of the great Columbian Exposition, and I had aided, in so far as I could, to build up the esthetic and literary side of the city's life. But now, feeling my years and alarmed by the increasing war-time psychology, I was restless and unhappy. Looking round my poor little study and thinking of the spacious homes of my fellow authors in the East, sumptuous, rich in books and pictures, I saw myself only a camper in the literary field. "For the sake of my wife and children I must get out of my rut," I said to Fuller.

II

"The Players, New York City, November 14, 1914. At luncheon to-day I sat with Robert Underwood Johnson and John Lane, the London publisher. Lane, who is over here on some secret mission, asked me many questions concerning the attitude of the Central West toward the war. He had heard that the German-Americans were disposed to favor Germany and that they would oppose any aid to England and her allies. I did my best to reassure him. 'The old people naturally sympathize with their fatherland, but the young are wholly American.' "

I had never met Lane before and was struck by his resemblance to Henry Arthur Jones, the English playwright: both were small, gray-bearded, and alert.

"Lane, who has made a great reputation with his Bodley Head publishing house, professed a desire to bring out some of my books. 'This war can't last long—it's too destructive,' he said, voicing the general opinion of the historians, but he was so deeply concerned for England's future that he could talk of little else. 'I am appalled by the power and precision of Germany's war machine,' he said."

In calling on the editor of the *Century Magazine* I was aware of a sadly disturbing change.

"The fine old magazine is passing through a time of

trial—Gilder is gone, Johnson, his successor, is out of control, and Douglas Doty, its temporary editor, is plainly in doubt of his future. As I walked its familiar corridors lined with portraits of renowned writers and paintings by equally renowned artists, I recalled the awe with which I first entered the inner office where Gilder received his favored writers.

"I had a moment of sadness also. This publishing house has been a source of encouragement and guidance to hundreds of authors and illustrators, and with sorrow I now learn that these rooms, this treasure house of memories, is about to be dismantled and transformed. 'Perhaps, after all, the magazine will not pass,' I wrote. 'It is too high in price and it is too dignified, too thoughtful, to find a large public, but there should be a way of being vital and at the same time noble. Some editor will discover and use this method.' "

I fell at once into the city's literary current.

"At a reception given last night [November 18] by President Butler of Columbia, I met Eugène Brieux, who is in America to give an address before the joint meeting of the American Academy and the National Institute. Butler's beautiful house was filled with members of both organizations and with other distinguished guests. Brieux made a fine impression on us all. He looked like an Englishman or an American, not at all the Frenchman I had expected to see. He is blond, smoothly shaven, and of good stature. Nothing about him but his speech set him apart from the other guests.

"Butler presented me to him with a pleasant word of introduction and left us together for a chat. Brieux said, 'I speak bad English'; and I replied, 'I speak no French.'

Nevertheless we had a few minutes' talk. He understood me very well till I dropped into certain idiomatic Western expressions, then he laughingly interrupted. 'You go beyond me. I cannot follow.' Whereupon I revised my speech."

At the meeting in Aeolian Hall next day he was guest of honor and, as a representative of the French Academy, wore the handsome green uniform of its members. This amused some of my fellows but pleased me. I defended it. "I believe in anything which indicates the honorable distinction of art and literature. Why should the writer or painter be held a mean, drab fellow? I believe in giving to learning, to esthetic eminence of all kinds, all the pomp and circumstance obtainable."

Howells was brief but graceful in his introduction. "He and Burroughs are both deeply moved by the war. They had both grown into a belief that no great war was possible and both are shocked and alarmed. Burroughs frankly said, 'I hope some one will shoot the Kaiser,' for all our papers are accusing him of having brought on the conflict.'"

At the club one night I had a long talk with General Hawkins, a tall old man of eighty-five or six—who told me that he was one of those who used to meet at "Pfaff's" in the good old days before our own war. "I knew Whitman, Aldrich, Stedman, and other young Bohemians of that time," he said. Then with profound melancholy he added, "I have outlived them all. I come and go here with no one to talk to. No one knows me or remembers my friends." He is in truth a tragic figure. Length of days is only partial compensation for this loneliness.

III

On my return to Chicago on December 9, I was still sufficiently at home to meet with a committee to organize a society of Western writers for which I suggested the name "The Midland Authors." There was no association of this kind in the West and in the normal course of development such a society was due.

"Edith Wyatt, Harriet Monroe, Clara Burnham, Maud Warren, Douglas Malloch, Hobart Chatfield-Taylor, and I were present. Hobart acted as chairman and Malloch as secretary. By reaching out into Iowa and Wisconsin and back into Indiana and Michigan a very respectable list of eligibles was made up; but I am only half hearted in the attempt, for I have seen the literary section of the Cliff Dwellers dwindle to a small group. Furthermore I have fully decided to transfer my headquarters to New York as soon as I can sell my Woodlawn home. 'Some time Chicago will be an important literary center,' I said to Chatfield-Taylor, 'but not in your time or mine. Without a first-class publishing house or magazine how can it hold its writers and artists?' 'It can't and it won't!' he replied."

Among the Western authors included in this list but not yet a member was Arthur Ficke of Davenport, a scholarly and graceful poet whose sonnets had won him recognition in New York. I was his guest at luncheon not long after this meeting and we talked this question of a Midland Authors' Society and the lack of "literary atmosphere" (detestable phrase) which he felt less than his neighboring poets, for he was able to travel at will. "He is the farthest removed from the slap-dash newspaper men now coming to notice, a man of training, taste, and skill. He is a little like Fuller in his critical judgment."

Hobart Chatfield-Taylor, who had written several novels of Chicago, had won election to the National Institute of Arts and Letters by two capital books on Molière. One of these, "Fame's Pathway," I greatly admired, and when Brander Matthews proposed him for membership I gladly seconded his nomination. Though a man of wealth and a social leader in Chicago, Hobart worked with amazing pertinacity at his desk.

In his ability to concentrate on his task he always reminded me of another Chicagoan, Frederic Bartlett, a mural painter who took his wealth as a warrant to spend all his time in decorating the University Club and other public buildings. "Fred works as hard and as steadily as any hungry artist in the city, and everything he does is beautiful. He is like one of Henry Fuller's characters. As the son of a rich hardware merchant he turned with smiling resolution to creative art. Such men as he and Hobart Taylor help to redeem Chicago."

Some of the Midland authors were connected with the Chicago University, but they were few. That vast and growing caravanserai had been weak on the literary side from the first and it still remained so, for William Vaughn Moody and Robert Herrick were no longer there. Northwestern University was equally barren of writers.

"It is all rather pitiful to me, now that I am set free to go East. Fine and earnest as most of our Midland authors are, they form only a small nucleus in the midst of a ramshackle, ripping, roaring metropolis. Only the paragraphers, reporters, and poets of the daily press are able to survive in this bleak and noisy town."

In preparation for my removal I resigned the presidency of the Cliff Dwellers, a club which I had organized some seven or eight years before.

"It has proved a pleasant meeting place for the men engaged in some form of art, but it is now mainly used as a lunch room by painters and musicians. Few men of letters are to be seen there. The truth is we have been forced to scrape the town to keep up our membership, voting in beginners in the arts and hard-working newspaper men—all admirable in their way but not very distinguished—just as similar organizations in other cities have been forced to include reporters and space writers. Chicago is only a larger town. Architects and music makers are increasing in power, but our workers in creative literature are diminishing in number. I shall return to New York immediately after the holidays."

For more than fifteen years I had kept a diary (on which this volume is based) and on the first page of 1915 I find this entry:

"We took down our Christmas tree to-day and burned its branches in the fireplace, with our usual prayer to Santa Claus, 'Come again next year.' Constance, now seven years wise, clings to Santa Claus, although her illusions concerning him are gone. This makes me sad. Life must broaden, and yet!— We begin our new year in good health and fairly comfortable circumstances, although the war is becoming each day more terrifying. I am eager to go East. I hate to leave my wife and daughters, but I must go if I am to make any sales of manuscript. I am at a disadvantage here."

As I stood on the station platform in Englewood, I saw my highly successful brother-in-law Lorado Taft also waiting for an Eastern train—but as he held tickets on a twenty-four hour Pullman and mine were good only on a much slower train, we met only to part. It is worth recording, also, that I rode all the way to Pittsburgh in the day coach. I couldn't afford the Pullman fare. The war had carried me back to familiar measures of economy. There is something amusing to me, now, in the further fact that I spent some hours reading Thorstein Veblen's "Theory of the Leisure Class."

My dated comment on this book reads: "Here is a big idea but not entirely carried out. The author's style is poor—repetitious and heavy. The irony of the theme demands a tone of scientific, passionless, and generalizing accuracy which Veblen couldn't quite sustain. It starts off well, but is not worth while all the way through. I changed to Mary Austin's 'Woman of Genius,' a good book of its kind filled with a certain lofty femininity. It is masculine in handling, but betrays the elderly woman in its context."

Another book which I read the following day was "The Midlanders," a story of the Mississippi Valley by Charles Tenney Jackson, "a novel of mellow charm which deserves to be reprinted and reread. Beginning in Louisiana, it ends in a small Iowa city—much of it is fine and true. I know nothing of its author."

IV

"New York, January 6. On arrival at the Players about two, I found a message from Mrs. George Barr Baker inviting me to dine at her home to meet Martin Egan and his wife. This I accepted. I like the Egans immensely. They are broad-minded, traveled folk, of that cultivated Irish type which always appeals to me, musical of speech, gay, a bit irresponsible, yet essentially fine.

"In calling on Augustus Thomas, I found him reading Henry Holt's two big volumes of psychic material and we spent the evening in discussing these and certain dramatic subjects. Augustus told me that in his youth he had acted as advance agent for a mind reader, and that ever since he had been interested in such matters. His most successful play was 'The Witching Hour,' a psychic subject."

At the club I learned that our club librarian, Volney Streamer, had been taken to a sanitarium.

"For a year or more he has been trying to keep up his work, but it had become evident that his usefulness was ended. . . . I shall miss him, for he was one of the most authentic features of the club. In him all the traditions of Edwin Booth were preserved. He loved the library and everything connected with it, and many of the members had a genuine affection for him. There is something cruel about a club. A man—any man—no matter how notable or how essential, can drop out of it without leaving a ripple. In a few days, Volney Streamer will be forgotten. One or two men will ask, 'Where's Streamer? Haven't seen him around lately.' Another will say, in a casual tone, 'I hear Streamer is down and out. What a pity!' That will be all! This is the end of Streamer—an end to which we are all liable."

January 12, the night of Bessie Potter Vonnoh's reception to Lorado Taft, was one of the worst nights I ever experienced in New York. The rain fell in slashes, the wind blew like a West Indian hurricane, and the streets were littered with umbrellas which had been blown inside out.

"Notwithstanding the storm, a charming group of people assembled. Ben Foster, William Armstrong (formerly of Chicago), Fosdick, the Roulands, the Jones brothers, Fraser (who told me he was from Winona, Minnesota), and Carl Akeley, whom I had never met before. Lorado made friends as he always does and the affair was voted a success in spite of weather conditions. Carl Akeley made a vivid impression on me by reason of his resemblance to John McCutcheon the cartoonist. His rugged face, slow and rather wistful utterance, and his humor quite won me."

Another of the institutions with which I had been concerned as an organizer was the Authors' League. As a member of its board I met with a committee having its annual dinner in charge.

"In this activity I find myself in touch with the business end of authorship. I find myself associated with a group of young men who not only hold writing to be a trade but are disposed to safeguard their interests by affiliation with a trade organization. Some of them argue frankly for joining with union labor, all of which is rather disturbing to men like Burroughs and myself. We are honored by the officers of the League, but in our hearts we resent the implication that we are merely day laborers with the pen as other men are workers with hammer and chisel. We have been nurtured in an elder school of thought. While not much in sympathy with those who consider writing something inspired I do hold it to be an art and not a trade."

Among the most active of the workers in this League

were Winston Churchill, Rex Beach, Gelett Burgess, Ellis Parker Butler, and Jesse Lynch Williams—all good friends of mine and excellent craftsmen.

"Many of the members are pleasant companions at the club, but I grow weary at times of their endless discussion of the financial side of authorship. I acknowledge the altruistic aim of their league and I advise all my young writer friends to join. 'In so doing you will have the advantage of the secretary's advice and the services of an attorney when you are in need of legal aid,' I assure them. Although Burroughs says, 'I have no need of such a membership,' I know that he has suffered from lack of just such guidance as the League could have given him, which is another evidence of the growing power of authorship."

One night at the Century Club I met William Morton Fullerton, whom I had known thirty years earlier as the boyish editor of a Boston paper. At that time he was a slender youth with a dainty mustache, a George Meredith enthusiast.

"He went abroad as the Paris correspondent of his paper and has lived there ever since. He is now an elderly exquisite in appearance, but an able and pleasing talker. I was particularly interested in his 'inside views' of men and measures in London and Paris. When he spoke of Theodore Roosevelt's liking for Ambassador Myron Herrick, I said, 'If that is so, Herrick has a good chance to be President.' We had a pleasant visit, albeit we were both a bit saddened by the changes which the years had brought to our friends as well as to ourselves. I must have been as great a shock to him as he was to me."

On January 13, agreeably to my promise, I met Professor Fred L. Pattee of Pennsylvania State College at the Franklin Inn Club of Philadelphia to discuss with him certain phases of American literature.

"I found him to be a tall, lean New Englander, very able but with the manner of a man whose life goes on a long way from the city. He told me that he had made the fullest use of my 'Crumbling Idols' in his forthcoming volume (a history of the short story in America) and that he wished to talk with me about some of the early writers whom I had personally known. He has the same admiration for Mary Wilkins that I have, and the same dislike for the tricks in O. Henry's tales. I found that he has read every one of our leading short story writers and that his opinions are based on firsthand knowledge. We parted with a mutual and very genuine liking."

v

"January 14. Washington was deliriously springlike when I landed here at about one o'clock. It often happens that I find the air of this city delightfully and surprisingly mild, for I usually come to it from either New York or Chicago. I hardly remember a single visit to this place which has not been a pleasure, notwithstanding the fact that it is almost barren of literary activities and associations.

"Irving Bacheller was at the Cosmos Club, and in accordance with a promise given some weeks before, I accompanied him to the theater where he was to speak, and acted as chairman. In my introduction I facetiously described his absent-mindedness, his disregard for trains, baggage, and clothing. 'If forgotten overcoats, overshoes, valises, and canes were capable of sprouting, they would produce a fine crop from Maine to California.' I told of one occasion when Mrs. Bacheller and I rescued his bag from the railway platform in Riverside, after he had put it down and forgotten it, and of his sheepish look when, at a point about halfway into the city, he suddenly wondered what had become of it. The audience enjoyed these jests, but I ended up by saying, 'Irving Bacheller is one of the finest types of American manhood I have ever known; and what he will say to you this afternoon will be an expression of the truest and finest Americanism.'

"When he rose to reply it was in the character of old 'Socrates Potter,' one of the chief exponents of his criticism of American social life, and he made a fine plea for right living and high thinking. After the lecture he and I rode out to dinner in the home of Lynn Haines, an old friend of Irving's from the 'North Country.' At the close of the meal we returned to the library fire and sang old-fashioned songs, and talked of old-fashioned things till eleven o'clock."

I went back to my hotel in the mild, sweet, Southern air, happy with the whole experience. It was all so much more gracious, so much more in the open air than my life in Chicago could possibly have been.

"January 15. In a call on Secretary Franklin Lane this morning, we had a great deal of talk on all kinds of subjects, except politics. He reminisced of experiences in the single-tax crusade, of Henry George, and of various men who were our mutual friends. He was delightfully cordial and very plain spoken. One thing he said sticks in my memory very much as he said it: 'Washington is a most benighted place, so far as literature is concerned. It is a *hollow* place. I go out to dinner a great deal, and suffer almost intolerable boredom, for I am usually obliged to talk all the evening with two hen-headed women who have nothing whatever to say. That is the trouble with a formal dinner—at least in Washington.'

"In dining to-night with Winston Churchill, I became really acquainted with him for the first time; for although we had met many times before, it had always been at some public meeting where we had little opportunity for talk.

"I found him like his books: earnest, sincere, and noble of purpose, but lacking in precision and grace of phrase. He made no claim to being either subtle or precious in his diction. He confessed that he had been too much the man of action to give proper thought to the use of words. 'I have no ear for niceties of rhythm, or the overtones of prose.' Like Rex Beach and many others of the journalistic school, he is fine and manly but lacking in distinction and in charm. He is very successful and lives handsomely, both in the city and the country. His home in New Hampshire is said to have almost the dignity of an English country seat.

"I do not begrudge him or men of Bacheller's type the success they have won, for their work is essentially noble. They have the gift of expressing for hundreds of thousands of people the thoughts, the relationships which they could themselves put into words if they would."

My glimpse of Congress was disturbing. I had not been in the lower House for a long time, and only once of recent years in the Senate, and the action of both Houses was so desultory, so lacking in dignity, that it would have been ludicrous, had it not been for a consideration of the matters of world-wide importance awaiting their decision. They were discussing "pork barrels," busied with getting something for their selfish little inland constituencies. America in the mass, humanity in the mass, is impressive, but our senators, when seen individually, like Europe's kings, lose their bulk.

VI

"New York, January 19. At a luncheon to-day William H. Bliss, one of our members, brought ex-Ambassador Myron Herrick to our table, and for more than two hours we listened to his stories of Paris and the war in France. While not a profound thinker, nor a man of any commanding power, he is a fine, upstanding citizen. In comparison with Roosevelt he is almost commonplace, but he has charm, and a simple, wholesome manliness. He told some very amusing stories of a very celebrated newspaper correspondent who had been asking him for permission to visit the front. 'There came a day when the sound of the German cannon could be heard in my office. I called in several of these pestiferous journalists and said, "Gentlemen, it will not be necessary for you to go to the front, the front has come to you." ' Here he smiled and added, 'Two of them turned very pale and disappeared. I haven't seen them since.'

"On invitation of Ray Baker, I accompanied him to a performance of 'Children of Earth' by Alice Brown. It was, in many ways, an original and powerful drama, entirely New England in spirit and expression, and extremely well played. It deserves the Pulitzer prize."

At Orlando Rouland's studio one night, I heard a young Mohawk sing a program of American Indian melodies.

"He made his appearance in costume, approaching from another room with slow step, beating a small drum and keeping time with a deep humming chant. Like most of the red men I have known he was perfectly composed, not at all embarrassed or hesitant. He explained that this was the way an old man would approach the fire. His voice was powerful but musical, and for all his training remained characteristically Amerind. Mrs. Rouland told me that he is acting as usher at one of the big music halls, and that he is studying to be a professional singer. His stories and interpretations of the songs were interesting and concise."

Later in the evening, the Setons came in and took me down to the home of Eva Ingersoll Walton-Brown (the daughter of Robert Ingersoll), a gracious personality, greatly given to civic reform and deeds of charity. Her mother, Mrs. Robert Ingersoll, was present, an alert and vigorous woman of eighty or thereabouts. The house was filled with portraits and memorials of the great agnostic orator and the company presented various phases of liberalism in several directions.

On January 26, in company with Mrs. Haggin, I sat in the orchestra of the Booth Theater and listened to Beatrice Herford in one of her programs of monologues. Although I knew her brother Oliver very well I had never met her, and up to this moment I had never happened to hear her recite. "She is mistress of a very rare and dainty art. Her comic spirit and her keen perception of character enable her to do what very few women are able to do. She renders the most familiar and, in a sense, commonplace things delightful. It was astonishing! Here was one small person furnishing an evening's dramatic entertainment, with no aids, no costumes, no scenery, and yet she was applauded as if she were a theatrical star of the brightest sort—which she is."

Three days later, Juliet Wilbor Tompkins and I saw Harvey O'Higgins' play "Polygamy" and found it interesting but not "convincing."

"It is too remote, too improbably dramatic. I can not credit such tales of Mormon power, such instances of the cruel subjection of women, and so the play, admirable as it is in some respects, fails to move its auditors. Chrystal Herne was appealing but not moving in the strong scenes. Mary Shaw alone touched our hearts. As a detail, the men seemed altogether too well groomed. Indeed the whole cast were New York citizens in masquerade."

On January 31, Grace Seton and I, with Doctor and Mrs. McLane and Mr. and Mrs. Hutchinson, dined at the National Arts Club and afterward listened to Samuel Untermyer speaking on the railroad situation. "At the close of the talk we all rode up to A. A. Anderson's studio at the top of the Beaux-Arts Building on Fortieth Street, where a musicale for the benefit of the families of the French artists now fighting in the ranks was being given. This studio is one of the most spacious and richly decorated 'workshops' I have ever seen. Anderson occupies the entire upper floor of this building, and his studio glows with lights and decorations. The music was especially good. A Russian choir in native costume sang some very strange songs, of which I could make little musical sense. They all seemed of a piece, like hymns and street songs mingled."

On February 2, at the invitation of the chairman of the

lecture committee of the MacDowell Club, I presented my illustrated talk on the life of the forest ranger.

"My audience was small, the room was cold, and I, the speaker, lacking in spirit. Augustus Thomas was there, together with several others of my best friends who did their best to cheer me up. Juliet Wilbur Tompkins introduced me neatly, and I tried hard to interest those who were kind enough to sit through my talk. Augustus came up to me afterward and said, 'It's all right'; but I had a sense of failure and disappointment. It all seemed a part of my dwindling power and failing fortunes.

On the day following I lunched with Mr. Howells at the St. Hubert, and afterward we retired to his study, where he read to me from his latest manuscript, a short story intended for *Harper's Magazine*. At the close of it he smilingly said, "This is like old times, my reading manuscript to you." And as he said this, my mind filled with memories of the many delightful hours we had spent together in similar literary reminiscences and discussions.

"At the close of our hour he gave me the manuscript of his new novel, 'The Leatherwood God,' and asked me to read it and tell him what I thought of it. This I gladly promised, and came away. He is looking very well these days, but seems a little uncertain on his legs. I hate to see him grow old."

"February 5. I have studied this day two publishing plants so widely separated that they may be said to represent the opposite poles of modern journalism. First of all I lunched at the quaint home of the *New Republic* on West Twenty-first Street, where, at a round table in this transmogrified old New York house, I met seven bright young people who talked of high things, while eating a very plain omelet. I felt something very like London radicalism in the serenity and gracious consideration of this journalistic home. These editors were as remote from the noise and movement of New York as if in Soho and yet in a sense they are ultra-modern.

"At dinner I met Charles Lincoln of the *World*, who invited me down to his office. I accepted, realizing that in doing so I was traveling toward the opposite pole of journalism. In the World Building on City Hall Square, I felt the stir of the universe—not the intellectual stir so much as the emotional stir. Under my feet the floor quivered with the passion of enormous presses, and one by one others awoke as the evening advanced. Telegrams from the four winds of heaven came pouring in and ranks of linotype machines clicked like mad. Hearing all this, I sensed, imaginatively, not merely the active politics of the country, but the crimes and accidents of every state and territory; and, under it all, ran the stress and strain of the great war in France.

"Mr. Lincoln advised me to stay on till one o'clock in the morning. 'Things are just beginning,' he smilingly said. But I decided that I had seen enough to build up a contrasting body of experiences, and so, thanking him for his courtesy, I came away, understanding as never before the feverish charm which held several of my friends to the never-ending 'newspaper game.'"

CHAPTER FOUR

WAR EAGLES, POETS, AND LECTURERS

I

THEODORE ROOSEVELT in 1915 was still the most distinguished citizen in America and his office at the *Metropolitan Magazine* was called the "New York White House," for the reason that its anteroom swarmed with lawmakers, military men, writers, artists, and politicians from England, France, and Belgium. Reporters waited there quite as if he were some high official, whereas he was only a private citizen working hard to earn a living, coming and going each day by street car like any other hard-working editor. "He is too young, too vital to retire even if he could afford it."

One day (February 7) a note from him invited me to come in and have a chat and naturally I lost no time in accepting.

Several people were waiting to see him in the outer office, but I sent in my name and at last was admitted. I found him at his desk looking much better than I had expected, for he had been very ill from the effects of his exploration on the Amazon. He was distinctly older, however, and for the first time used the tone of age. He mentioned his fifty-seven years, and when I said, "You should take things easier," he replied, "My financial condition will not permit me to take things easy. I must go on earning money for a few years more."

44

I had not seen him since his South American trip and it was plain that the River of Doubt had left its mark on him. He admitted this. "I came very near remaining up there on the edge of the jungle. I am not the man I was before I went in."

We talked a little of politics and he frankly confessed the complete failure of his Progressive party. "Americans are a two-party people. There is no place for a third party in our politics." That he was hard hit by the failure of this movement was apparent, but he concealed it under a smiling philosophy.

The longer I sat with him the more he showed the ill effects of his frightful experiences in the Brazilian wilderness. The fever which he had contracted there was still in his blood. His eyes were less clear, his complexion less ruddy. I came away with a feeling of sadness, of loss. "He will never run for President again. For the first time in our many meetings he acknowledged his years and forecast the end of his activity. I cannot understand why he should say, 'I must go on earning money,' for he is supposed to be a rich man. 'That he may never lose his sense of humor is my prayer.' "

He was very serious during this entire interview, more subdued than I had ever known him to be.

Granville Barker, the English dramatist, was at the club for luncheon February 17 and Clayton Hamilton made a place for me at his table. "I liked Barker, with whom I had corresponded while secretary of the Chicago Theater Society. He looks the fine, clear-eyed boy— candid and humorous. He is not only physically power- ful but his face is unusually handsome. He talked quite freely of the theater, and frankly acknowledged his mistakes and his failures. Al Thomas joined in the conversation, which was highly technical and very able. I took occasion to invite Barker to the Authors' Club dinner as guest of honor and a speaker. He consented readily and Clayton and I made out a list of special guests. I decided to go home on Friday morning. My lameness is very discouraging."

II

"Chicago, February 20. Feeling about ninety years of age, I crawled home this morning at nine o'clock. My little daughters welcomed me with a thousand kisses. They do not despise me because I am old and sick. They hung around me all the forenoon, and the clasp of their arms made me forget my troubles—for the moment. I tried to do some writing, but the pain of every movement was so intense that I gave it up. All this is a warning that the gate is closing for me. Only a few more years of work remain. Whatever I am to do must be done quickly. 'I am a failure all the way round,' I said as I went to my bed.

"On February 22, at eight o'clock in the evening, Wallace Heckman came around with his car and took me over to the Quadrangle Club, where I listened to a very witty, balanced, and thoughtful address by Paul Shorey. He was quaintly amusing in his attitude toward his job, and toward himself. His formal English made his occasional witty excursions into the vernacular very telling. I enjoyed it intensely, and came home in a fine intellectual glow, quite stimulated by this contact with a very exceptional mind.

"Nashua, Iowa, February 24. This town is very like

West Salem, Wisconsin, and just about as big. I could not understand how I came to be engaged to speak in this little town till Wade Burley, the chairman of the committee, came in. I suspect that he alone is responsible for my engagement. He is a native of Yankton, Dakota, and one of my most loyal admirers.

"A subtle, reminiscent charm is in the air. It is a day of glorious, dazzling winter sun with dripping eaves; and I enjoyed the street and the people, for they bring back my youth in Osage."

As a matter of fact, very few of the citizens were interested in me, or knew anything about me, and my audience was small. I felt rather sorry for Burley, who was forced to meet what criticism the town uttered with regard to me and my lecture.

"March 12. Mary Isabel and I went downtown to buy some presents for her mother. The book department proved a strong attraction for her. I could scarcely drag her away and in her enthusiasm I caught a glimpse of the wealth of romance and poetry, the wonder and magic, which these bookshelves represented to her. I recalled my own book-starved youth on the prairies of Iowa. What magic the printed page had for me in those days! It is impossible for any city child to have the reverence for a book which I had between the ages of six and twelve."

III

Returning to New York about the middle of March, I met Mark Sullivan at the club and discussed with him the corrupting effect of advertising on magazine editors.

He said, "I exist and *Collier's* exists (like all other editors of popular magazines) to make certain commercial products known to the American citizen. We standardize everything: food, clothing, fiction, poetry—everything. It was not so thirty years ago when you were starting in life. It is a question of numbers. As *Collier's* takes on new multiples of subscribers, its field of choice narrows to subjects which appeal to the many."

At four-thirty in the afternoon of March 20, the council of the National Institute of Arts and Letters met and discussed the question of a memorial to be sent to the European nations, but on learning that Howells, the president of the American Academy, was opposed to it, we decided to refer it back to the Institute membership. "Mr. Howells said, 'Such a memorial might very properly be considered an impertinence by the European powers,' and I guess he is right."

Jesse Lynch Williams, Lincoln Steffens, and George Creel sat with me at dinner one night and Creel amused us all by confessing his "genius for controversy."

One of his stories was very neat. It was to this effect: "On one of my camping trips I had for a companion a genial, absent-minded character, who was always willing to help but was of no practical use. One day as we were camping in the Arizona desert, I said to him, 'You may make the coffee.' Delighted to be of service, he filled the pot with water and looked about for a fire. Seeing a bunch of dry sagebrush, he poured the water of the pot into a long-handled saucepan and, after setting fire to the brush, held the pan on the blaze till it burned out. He then lighted another bunch and repeated the process, but by the time the coffee was cooked he was a mile and a half from camp!" Here he made the application. "Lincoln

Steffens in argument reminds me of that man. When he has finished his argument, he is out of sight of his starting point."

Steffens received all this with an absent-minded smile, not disturbed by Creel's amusing characterization. He was at this time a stout advocate of Carranza, the Mexican revolutionary leader.

IV

Some manager having professed an interest in a revival of Herne's play, "Margaret Fleming," Katharine Herne asked me to come down and help her rewrite the play from memory. The burning of "Herne Oaks," Herne's summer place on Peconic Bay, had destroyed every line of all his plays. No record of them remains except in the possible piratical versions of "Shore Acres." As I had much to do with the first production of "Margaret Fleming" in Boston, Katharine was certain that I could be of use to her in recalling the lines.

We spent the evening at this work, she reading and I making suggestions from time to time. Happily, my memory retained most of Herne's exact intonations, as well as many of his phrases, and together we got the first act pretty nearly exact. There was a melancholy pleasure in this, for it brought back to us both those wonderful days, more than twenty-five years ago. I thought of my first meeting with Katharine Herne, as Mary Miller in "Drifting Apart"; and it was disturbing to see her wearing glasses and to note the gray in her hair. Nevertheless, her voice took on that familiar musical chuckle which she had so often used in real life as well as on the stage, and for the moment we were both back in Boston, producing this play. I hope sincerely that the work we have done is not lost.

On the way to Syracuse, March 25, where I was scheduled to give my talk on "The Life of the Forest Ranger," I read Irvin Cobb's "Back Home" and found parts of it very moving indeed. "There are some traces of a formula here and there, such as making the old judge too heroic, too astute (under his Horace Greeley make-up), but it is good work all the same."

My life in New York had fallen into a routine. I rose from my bed in the Park Avenue Hotel at seven every morning. At eight I breakfasted at the Players' Club, and at nine was back in my room at the hotel. I wrote till noon quite comfortably, for I had an inside room which was quiet and comparatively roomy. At twelve I knocked off and walked to the club for lunch. During the afternoon I visited my friends at tea or went for an airing in the park. Sometimes I got in an hour of two of revision.

"To-day, March 29, Bacheller and I had a talk with Rex Beach, who is in the thick of the moving-picture business and is a friendly adviser to us all. He advised us to hold on to our material. 'It will be in demand some day,' he said. Although grateful for his advice I have not much faith in the screen value of my fiction; it is not sufficiently 'red-blooded.'

"David Bispham and Francis Wilson sat with me at dinner and we had an interesting talk on all kinds of subjects. Bispham asked me to write a Cromwellian play for him. He would make a gorgeous Cromwell and I wish I could do the work. He and Wilson are charming dinner companions. The opportunity of dining with men of such wide experience and delightful humor is one of the joys of the Players."

Upon invitation of my good friend Edward Wheeler I attended a meeting of the Poetry Society at the National Arts Club; and a lively meeting it was. "The toilets of the ladies were varied and some of them were beautiful. Many of the guests were not, by the most liberal construction, fashionable, but I saw few signs of poverty. Many writers of distinction were present. Wheeler is an admirable presiding officer. He kept the meeting from degenerating into a mutual-admiration society or a general slaughter. His smiling face and his native good sense enabled him to check excesses of any sort.

"Richard Burton spoke, and spoke to the point as he always does. Cale Young Rice recited like a poet, but effectively. Anonymous unpublished poems were read by Mrs. Richard Mansfield, as the official reader, and the whole company then fell to a remorseless discussion of these poems. Later a vote was taken on the poems as read and the ones receiving the largest number of votes were announced.

"The discussion, led by Amy Lowell, was quite frank—too frank for the complacency of the poets whose verses happened to meet with the caustic criticism of some rival. Wheeler kept things well in hand, however; he kept it from becoming a Donnybrook Fair.

"Never having seen Amy Lowell before, I was astonished at her huge size and masculine air. Her name had not suggested to me a burly woman smoking a six-inch cigar and apparently aching for a fight. She was very able both as critic and poet, but her *vers libre* argument had no weight with me. The meeting was still in lively session at midnight when I came away."

Katharine Herne and I, on April 8, resumed our attempt to rewrite "Margaret Fleming" from memory. As she read I listened, stopping her at points where it seemed to me she had gone wrong. The second act we got very well, but when we came to the third act I perceived that she had departed widely from the text as I recalled it, and she then admitted she had done so designedly. "I must make it more acceptable to the modern audience," she said. As she read, all the familiar inflections and subtle melodies of her voice came back to me.

At Mrs. Ripley Hitchcock's literary luncheon to Cale Young Rice, I was fortunate enough to sit beside Corinne Roosevelt Robinson, Theodore's sister. "She is great fun; with something of her brother's ability to tell a story. She has a very wide acquaintance, and made a delightful seat mate. She is herself a poet of unusual gift and is often at the meetings of the Poetry Society."

Lincoln Steffens having induced me to attend a meeting in aid of Mexico at Cooper Union, I made him promise not to call on me, and to this he agreed; but Fred Howe who presided saw me in the audience and forced me to come to the platform. I was not in a state of mind to make a valuable contribution to the discussion, and what I did say aroused the antagonism of one Fonaro who had been in prison under the old régime and was not disposed to listen quietly to any praise of Diaz. In describing the conditions as I saw them on my two visits to Mexico, I made no claim that Diaz was an ideal ruler; I merely said (or implied) that it was better to have a ruler of his sort than one of the sort of Villa. Fonaro could see no good in any program except that of Carranza, and as it turned out neither of them knew very much about the situation: Fonaro was embittered and Steffens idealistic.

During my stay in New York, Hopkinson Smith died, and I attended his funeral April 11. Many of the Institute members were present at the ceremony in a lower Fifth Avenue church. To me it seemed perfunctory and lifeless, one which "Hop" (so full of life and humor) would have resented. "If he could speak," I said to Augustus Thomas, "he would say, 'Here, one of you fellows get up there and speak a candid word. Say that I was a live wire and had a good time.'

"Roosevelt was there, looking sad and stern. Like the rest of us he was fond of Smith and I wondered if he too did not resent the perfunctory character of the service. Notwithstanding his recent illness, he appeared rugged and vital. He walked like a young man. Hardly any gray showed in his hair. Power was in his face and in his compact body. He is a wonder."

My address on Whitman and Lincoln at the Arts Club on April 13, had a very important effect on my future work. W. C. Glass, my loyal lecture manager, was present, and at the close of my talk confronted me. "No more of these Forest Ranger shows. You are a man of letters. People want to hear Hamlin Garland discuss his fellow authors. Throw away your manuscript and tell about 'em as you did to-night."

All this chimed in pleasantly with what I had been thinking for some time. I decided to drop all my forestry propaganda. I was tired of playing announcer to a box of colored slides.

For several years I had used "The Life of the Forest

Ranger" for my chief lecture topic and I had accumulated a box of fine slides. I had enjoyed giving this talk for a season, for it carried me back into the high trails of Colorado and Wyoming; but the public had lost interest in the subject and my slides were pale and inert by contrast with the motion pictures which other speakers were using. Furthermore, as my manager had said, the committees wanted me as a man of letters and not as an advocate of the Federal Forest Service. I then and there authorized Glass to discard my old circular and issue a new one featuring my literary acquaintances and opinions. As a veteran, I began to reminisce.

V

The Authors' League dinner at the Waldorf on April 14 was largely attended. Augustus Thomas presided with grace and precision and the speeches were all short and to the point. Each writer wore a button with his name printed on it and some of the waggish guests traded buttons with the result that when admiring readers from the inland crowded to greet them, Ellis Parker Butler was taken for Rex Beach and Beach for Will Irwin. This led to amusing situations.

I sat between Kate Douglas Riggs and Corinne Roosevelt Robinson and had a lively time. Mrs. Robinson told me much about her brother and surprised me by saying that he had not been able to save anything out of his salary as President and that he had never been a money-getter. "He has never earned any money at all except as a writer or as an officeholder," she said.

She told a very funny story about him, one of the most amusing I have ever heard.

"He came in from Oyster Bay late one afternoon to attend a public dinner. He had arranged to dress at my house. In preparation, I had sent his evening suit to be pressed. It did not return till the last minute, just in time to start for the dinner. Upon attempting to get into it he discovered that the coat was not his. It was so small that he could hardly squeeze himself into it. It had a tendency, whenever he raised his arms, to slip up and cover his ears. Furthermore the sleeves were so short that his cuffs were entirely exposed. It was Saturday night, the tailor shop was closed, and we were unable to locate the owner, so Theodore decided to make the best of it.

"He got along very well in it until the time came for him to speak, and even then his outfit was not especially noticeable, so long as he stood quiet; but as he began to gesticulate, the collar almost went over his head. He was in the midst of his speech and in the thick of his trouble, when a boy with a box in his hand entered the dining room. A waiter brought the box to the speakers' table. He stopped and looked down at it. It was his coat which the tailor, or some one else, had discovered and thoughtfully sent to him. Theodore then did what no other man in public life would have dared to do. He told the story of his mishap, and, begging the indulgence of his audience, took off that wretched, misfit coat. Slipping on his own, he resumed his speech in perfect self-possession to thunderous applause from his amused and admiring auditors."

On the following night at the Cosmopolitan Club, while dining with Jesse Lynch Williams and his wife, I met his brother-in-law, Doctor Vaughn, a surgeon who had been all over the Northwest and knew many of my trails. We revived experiences in a glow of reminiscent pleasure. He told one story which was painfully poignant. He said, "When as a youth I was working on a ranch in Colorado, I one day visited Denver and carried back with me a box of candy for the poor little wife of my ranch boss. As I gave it to her I was astounded by her emotion. She broke down and cried. 'No one ever thought of me in that way before,' she said. This gave me a partial realization of the sordid drudgery and neglect she had endured during all the years of her life on the ranch."

I felt a sharp pang of the same resentment which was in his voice. There is so much useless suffering in this world.

One day B. O. Flower, my old Boston friend, and Walter Elwood, the author of a Philippine novel, "Guimo," lunched with me at the club. I had not seen Flower for several years, and when he confessed that he was nearly at the end of his rope, I was shocked and saddened. "My wife is still in a sanitarium, and my powers for earning money are almost at an end," he said. He looked thin and worried. The war and other changes had made his services of no marketable value.

"I owe him a debt of gratitude for his aid at a time when I needed it most and I shall do all I can to assist him now. Elwood turned out to be a big, awkward, boyish fellow who improved with acquaintance. There must be a good deal to him, more than he indicates in conversation, for his book is really colorful, and very well written in all respects, my main criticism of it being one which bears upon his too frequent use of Filipino words and phrases."

VI

Returning to Chicago, April 25, I dined with the Midland Authors, meeting Zona Gale, Clarence Darrow, and several others of my literary friends. They all spoke of my "abandonment of Chicago," and expressed regret that I had found it necessary.

"There was nothing for me to say in reply to this, for each time I return I feel more keenly than ever the fact that my life in Chicago is almost rural by contrast with my life in New York. My Chicago home is comfortable, my way of life peaceful and easy, but I am walking in a circle. I am making no progress. There are no surprises here, no stimulation to effort. If I were forced to live here I fear I should very soon cease to produce anything at all. No doubt this is a sign of weakness, but such is my psychology."

"Ordway, South Dakota, April 30. At Aberdeen, the county town, I was met by two old acquaintances, James Pond and Charles Kimball, who drove me out over the road toward Ordway, the road I tramped in 1881. The little farmhouse which I helped my father build was still standing, and I took my seat on the doorstep, precisely where I began to write 'Prairie Songs'; while Kimball made a snapshot record of the event. The country is at its green and tender best, and I am glad to remember it so, for I shall never see it again. The house in which I began 'Main-Travelled Roads' is unchanged, and the garden quite as forlorn and treeless as when I saw it last."

"Chicago, May 2. Having been notified that the Cliff Dwellers had planned to present to me a silver bowl, I went down to the club for the first time since before the holidays. The dining room was filled and the fellows cheered lustily as I came in. The speaking was agreeably brief, and on receiving the bowl I read a few lines of humorous verse in appreciation of the gift, and the ceremony ended."

VII

"New York, May 7. Upon meeting Duneka, down at Franklin Square, I learned that George Harvey is out of the firm and that his place has been taken by Charles P. Brainerd, all of which was very disturbing. I confessed to Duneka that I was hesitant about publishing my Forest Ranger novel, and that I had decided to hold it up. 'It will be better to wait,' I said."

"May 8. The destruction of the *Lusitania* last night is the sole topic of conversation at the clubs and on the street. The German Government has outraged the world by this deed. I tried to write, as usual, in the morning, but could not succeed in doing anything. Lunching at noon with Herbert Adams and Ernest Peixotto, we discussed the effect on Germany's future. The whole club was deeply stirred.

"At three in the afternoon I took the train for Greenwich. Grace Seton met me at the station, and as we rode out through the most glorious spring landscape, it was impossible to imagine such a horror as the sinking of the *Lusitania*. I found Ernest in his study and we had an old-time session, discussing the Indians, the sign language, and other Western subjects. Later he read to me part of a manuscript on which he is at work. We then went for a little trip around the lake he has built and which he has named Lake Peko."

The following morning was very beautiful, so beautiful that I dared not look out of the window, for fear that it would tempt me to neglect my work. All about were blossoming cherry trees, lighted with exquisite sunshine.

"During the afternoon, appalled by the *Lusitania's* fate, we gave up all our plans for recreation, and sat on the lawn, or strolled about the garden striving to counteract the horror of it. There is every indication that the nation will act, but in what way, no one seems to have the slightest notion. One suggestion is that we should open our ports to the Allies, and abandon our neutrality, which has been only a form. In this way we might make Germany repent her international crime."

"May 14. I spent the day helping Grace and Ernest Seton improve their new cottage in Greenwich. Among other chores I painted some big vases on the gateposts, and a part of the garden fence, greatly enjoying the warm spring air. Charles Eastman, the Sioux physician, and his daughter Irene came to call, and we all went boating on the lake. During our visit, Eastman and I discussed the work which he is doing as special agent for renaming of the Sioux, a position which I had secured for him by presenting his name to President Roosevelt.

"In describing his method of procedure, he said: 'I call a family council, and get a vote on the family name.'

"At night we all attended his lecture at the little church in Greenwich. At the close of his fine talk, his daughter Irene sang the songs of her people delightfully. She is an attractive, clear-eyed, and graceful girl with a captivating smile. She won her audience instantly. Together they gave a singularly clear and noble concept of the Sioux, a concept which few were able to accept. Eastman is very proud of his daughter, as he has a right to be. He stood beside her to receive the praise of her auditors."

Eastman came to town next day, and we spent the afternoon in talk concerning red men.

"I respect him as a Sioux and admire him for his force of character. He is a mine of information, but he lacks the power of construction. I doubt if he will ever succeed in writing the big book that is in him. He read to me two acts of a huge historical pageant called 'Pontiac,' a very ambitious piece of work indeed with enormous pictorial possibilities. He is hoping to have it done this summer."

At the end of our talk I set this line down: "For all his knowledge of white man's ways, he is a Sioux. In spite of my respect for him and my interest in his people, I cannot overstep the racial barrier which rises between us."

"As I went to the club to-day, I found Mark Sullivan and Richard Burton there, and soon after Henry Arthur Jones, the English playwright, came in with George Creel. After dinner a group of us lingered at the table while Creel told the story of his life—and a curious story it was. He began life in Kansas and had been a newspaper man and politician in Denver. He was at one time an amateur prize fighter. His unterrified political experiences in Missouri and Colorado, as he related them, were highly amusing. He has the true American humor, which involves self-ridicule and exaggeration. No one else would dare deride his career as he himself does. He is a valiant defender of President Wilson, and especially of Daniels, Secretary of the Navy. In this I cannot take him seriously. Austin Strong, a fine, clean-cut, serious-minded young dramatist, and Gerald Stanley Lee were among the group. Lee is a curious type, a playful Emerson, pithy of phrase and wholesomely radical.

"Brander Matthews still maintains his Sunday evening at home, and there I met Henry Arthur Jones again, and heard from him much caustic criticism of Bernard Shaw, Granville Barker, and other of the younger dramatists. It was, I fear, the resentment of age. I took no part in this discussion, but my sympathies remained on the side of Shaw and Barker. At the close of this pow-wow, somewhere about half-past ten, we all went down to the dining room where, according to time-honored custom, our host served a peculiar kind of cake along with apples and various light drinks. So far as I know, none of the older writers keep this kind of open house, and I sincerely hope that Brander will be able for many years to continue his charming custom."

One of the notable events of my stay in New York was the May Day annual outing of the Poetry Society.

"For several years Mrs. Samuel Untermyer has generously invited the entire membership to a supper at her home in Yonkers, and on May 25, the appointed day, I, as one holding a card of invitation, took myself to the Grand Central Station, where, according to our cards, a special train was awaiting us.

"The promise of free transportation and a meal had brought such a smiling mob of poets around the gate that I marveled at the number of them. In less than an hour we were streaming up the beautiful drive of the Untermyer estate. Mrs. Untermyer looked anxious. The throng of guests was quite evidently much larger than she had counted upon, and there was some delay in providing for the feast, which was an eagerly anticipated part of this very delightful entertainment.

"The garden was in glorious bloom, and all the poets were enchanted. I observed Richard Burton, Ella Wheeler Wilcox, Florence Wilkinson, Edward Wheeler, Alice Brown, and many other of my friends on the terrace. Nothing could have been more delightful than to sit, as we did, at tables overlooking the Hudson, eating ice cream while watching the moon lifting grandly above the trees. It was only afterward that we learned how the many unexpected guests had taxed the resources of this great house."

Irving Bacheller's home in Riverside remained my refuge. Whenever I could get away even for a night, I ran out to "Thrushwood." I usually found Irving in tweeds, milling about the place, like an English squire, superintending a gang of workmen. He loved activity of this kind. Not at all disturbed by the expense involved, he went on improving his garden and his harbor.

At night, we always sat about the fire and often we sang old songs.

"Sunday, May 30. Irving's home is flawlessly beautiful. As I looked out of my chamber window last night upon the Sound, the trees, the islands, the shimmer of the water, and the rising moon united to make a picture of noblest composition. I have a guilty feeling, however, for while I am enjoying the comfort, the beauty of this home, my wife and children are living in a dreary Chicago street. As Irving was lecturing in Plainfield to-day, I walked over to Seton's house, finding him as full of plans for improving his place as Irving is of his. It was heavenly on Lake Peko, and as the day faded, and the night came on, clear, cool, and sweet, we recovered something of the spirit of those days at Wyndygoul some fifteen years ago. We took on the quality of youth—or at any rate early middle age."

"May 31. We were up early this morning mixing paint and getting ready to work on the addition for the use of his little daughter Anne. (He calls this building 'the Anne-ex.') I nailed or painted nearly all day. After priming the walls, I shellacked four of the gates. We had a glorious lobster dinner and at nine-thirty in the evening they took me to the train. I reached my hotel lame and weary, but feeling very happy over the lovely week-end my good friends had provided for me."

"June 1. John Alexander died this morning. He was one of the finest painters and one of the most useful citizens this city has ever had. He was my friend, one that I am proud to name. Sunny in disposition, helpful of spirit, he was at the same time so distinguished in his art that his friends and admirers moved in every walk of life. Like Edward MacDowell, he uttered nothing but beauty. He never did an ugly thing, or expressed an ugly thought. His humor was unfailing, yet kindly, and his sympathies broad. His home was one of the most harmonious I knew, and it is a pleasure to remember how cordially he welcomed me to it. He should have the highest honors paid him, now and hereafter.

"His work for the MacDowell Club has been of the highest value; and it was in committee work for the welfare of this club that I have been associated with him for several years. I have known for a year or more that he was not well, but even in the midst of weakness and pain, he retained deceptive sweetness and brightness of humor.

He explained to me once the peculiar affliction under which he worked. 'I feel as if an iron ring were tightening about my brain,' he said—and yet, a few minutes later, he uttered a pleasant jest, and put away with a wave of his hand all discussion of his pain.

"His paintings were like him, distinguished, graceful, beautiful; even when treating of Pittsburgh and its perilous trades, these qualities were maintained. He put charm and distinction into the smoke of the chimneys and furnaces of Homestead. He saw beauty where other people see grime. He was essentially the poet."

CHAPTER FIVE

NEW YORK IN WAR–TIME

I

ALTHOUGH I spent the summer of 1915 with my wife and daughters in the peace and beauty of my native valley in Wisconsin I have only torturing memories of it, for the reason that I suffered the most acute, cramping pains in my shoulder and across my chest almost every waking hour. None of my doctors could tell me what caused these agonies. I was able to write only for a short time each morning. My worst suffering came just before dawn. Often I was forced to rise and sit in a chair and wait for daylight.

During the heat of August noons I was a little less affected, but as September brought cold winds and frosty nights, I became so much worse that my local doctor advised me to return to New York and consult a famous specialist in such disorders. "I can do nothing for you," he ended with discouraging candor. I took his advice and began to pack.

I cannot say what my wife's feelings were as she watched me crawling up the steps of the sleeping car, but that I was leaving the old home forever was my own unspoken fear.

"En route, September 14. My fifty-fifth birthday was

spent on the train rereading, after many years, Bret
Harte's 'Tales of the Argonauts.' I find some of them
poor stuff. In 'The Fool of Five Forks,' for example,
coincidence is employed to save the situation, and muddles
up what would otherwise have been a good story. 'How
Old Man Plunkett Went Home' is better, and a part of
'The Episode at Fiddletown' is capital, but they all seem
less important as American fiction than I had esteemed
them to be. I also read Sidney McCall's 'Dragon Painter,'
but found it rather artificial."

"New York, September 16. Lincoln Steffens, who was
at the club for breakfast, remarked to a group of his
friends, 'Garland is the link between Howells' generation
and the present,' and Mark Sullivan, who was sitting near,
added, 'And he is a friend of both.'

"It is homelike at the club. The waiters attend me as if
I were an honored master. The spirit of fine servants
(such as these men are) is altogether admirable. It is respectful without being obsequious. They have the spirit
of service. They are not working for tips. Walter, who
has been here so long, comes in every day from his chicken
farm, eager to be of use.

"Francis Hackett, who is now connected with *The
New Republic*, sat with me and talked of editing, fiction,
and the like. He appeared vividly Celtic, a spirited young
artist, as he bent across the table toward me, his handsome but rather careworn face hawklike for keenness.
He is Irish in all his sympathies, naturally, and it is hard
to say just how he is going to adjust himself to the developing situation in Ireland. I said very little, but to whatever I did say he listened with the same sort of respect
which Sullivan shows. I fear they both regard me as not

merely venerable but of no vital concern, in which they are entirely right."

Charles R. Crane, who had been so helpful to me in Chicago, had taken an apartment in New York, and one evening Sullivan and I went to call on him. I made this notation of our interview:

"Crane is an amazing character. He is very close to the source of national power just now. The President is making use of him in an advisory capacity. As we came away, Sullivan suggested that I do a character study of him as 'The Modern Vidocq.' I may do it, for I have had many opportunities for seeing him in action."

Although I had returned to New York with full intention of finding a home for my wife and children, I did nothing definite in way of renting or buying.

"The closer I study the publishing situation the less confidence I have in my ability to maintain a suitable apartment in this city, and my increasing infirmities make the thought of a suburban residence intimidating. The war shows no signs of ending and each week renders my kind of writing less acceptable to the bustling editors of rapidly expanding periodicals. No one has time to consider the sober pages of my manuscript. While maintaining a fairly confident exterior I am inwardly a defeated man. The honor and the ease which writers of my years are expected to enjoy have been changed into care and unrest."

Coincident with the growing fury of the war, the market price of manuscripts of a certain popular sort had risen to astonishing heights. Stories of a sensational type, or of easy-going humor, and tales of adventure, brought enormous sums—or so they seemed to me.

"High-salaried war correspondents swarm about the club—Will Irwin, I. F. Marcosson, Frederick Palmer, and many others. They are like homing pigeons, glad to get back. They are all garrulous with the joy of it. Irwin announced that he was 'fed up' on the horrors of war. 'No war ever had so many sordid and disgusting features,' he declared.

"Marcosson, less the war correspondent and more the student of the financial situation, is full of talk concerning his meetings with McKenna, Lloyd George, and other of the leaders of England.

"Listening to this talk I am made ashamed of my aches and pains. What are my twinges of rheumatism when contrasted with the agonies of millions of men and women in Europe? I shall make no more outcry. I shall go on with my work as best I can, but these tales of young lives being thrown away in myriads make the writing of fiction impossible. How can I interest myself in imaginary characters when air raids are being recorded in the daily press? There is only one thing for me to do, and that is to take up and complete 'A Son of the Middle Border.'

"Although the war has been raging for a year the people of New York are going their accustomed routine and the government in Washington still lives. Printers and publishers are bringing forth new books, periodicals are multiplying, and schools and colleges are proceeding on their accustomed way."

"We have the habit of war," I wrote. "We are grown accustomed to battles. We accept reports of carnage as a part of our daily entertainment. We buy newspapers at hourly intervals and discuss the horrifying details of trench warfare without any real emotion. What will the newspapers do for headlines when peace comes?"

"That the past year has raised the war correspondent to high power, I know; but that the competition of editors has given him audience with kings, I am only now aware. All poets, novelists, and philosophers are subordinate to the reporter. His comings and goings are news. His reports are headlined. Members of my clubs whom I had considered rather commonplace are now honored like ambassadors. I am not saying that these honors are illogical or undeserved. For the moment, at least, the reporter is far more important, so far as the daily press is concerned, than any novelist or historian. As war eagles they come and go and they must be forgiven if they confuse the interest of the public in their news with an admiration of their art.

"Even before the war, the age belonged to the reporter —the war has but increased his tribe. All the best paid novelists of 1915 are essentially newspaper men, writers of breadth, not depth, who study their moment and boldly advance upon it.

"In most cases their education has been acquired at the editor's desk, in the crowd rather than in college halls or libraries. All of which (up to a certain point) is admirable; but a shallowness of appeal, a note of commonness and flippancy, runs through much of their writing. Written for the moment, their books are forgotten like any other newspaper story."

As the days passed I studied these men and my own relationship to them with care—and some anxiety.

"They have the laugh on us," I said to Howells. "They are not concerned with lasting honor; 'posterity has done nothing for us,' they say. 'Our honors, our acclaim are here and now!' I am hoping—from their standpoint foolishly—to be read ten years hence, possibly after I am dead, but they are confessedly content with a wide, hasty, unthinking present-day acclaim."

"Yes," replied Howells reflectively, "and theirs, after all, may be the better part."

At the Players, Bacheller, Paine, and I discussed, one noon, this submergence of our generation.

"If this war goes on for three years," said Paine, "we old fellows will be dead ducks. We're too old to get into the newspaper game even if we wanted to. The world in 1920 will be a different place for our generation."

"The editors still respect us," Bacheller added, "but they can't print our manuscripts—the public interest is elsewhere."

"Some of these war correspondents respect us," I contended. "They speak to us kindly and tolerate our presence in their groups. Some of them remember when they, too, were mere novelists; they patronize me, but they are not offensive about it. I suppose I should be grateful for any sort of notice."

II

Our group at dinner one night included Frank Cook and Harris Dickson. Dickson and Cook had a story-telling contest which kept us chuckling with appreciation.

"Dickson, whom his friends call 'the Judge,' is a Southerner. He told two or three negro stories, which I suspect he uses on the platform as a Chautauqua lecturer. One of these, which he dramatized as an incident of his life in

Vicksburg, involved his study of an up-country negro at the circus.

"The negro, a timid, wordless, awkward type, had never before seen a town and of course knew nothing of a circus, and Dickson decided that here was a rare opportunity to gather material for a character study. He took the black in hand. He fed him. He showed him every wonder of the parade, the side shows, and the circus, ending up with a second visit to the menagerie, expecting him at some point of his progress to express his appreciation in a distinctive way. He said nothing whatever until the end of the day. As they came out of the animal tent reeking with the odors of sweating negroes, Harris said: 'Well now, Sam, this has been a marvelous experience for you, and I want you to tell what you enjoyed most. What of all you have seen and heard seems most wonderful to you?'

"With a hesitating stutter, the darky replied, 'Dem camuels—dey sho' is got a noble smell.' "

Another of Dickson's yarns concerned an escaped lion whose presence in the swamps had thrown the entire country into panic. Schools were closed and bands of armed men were out looking for the dangerous beast. People were fleeing to towns or gathering in strong places in order to be safe from him. A band of hunters volunteered to go out from Vicksburg and Dickson was in the posse.

"Along toward sunset," said Dickson, "as we were sitting on the porch of a little hotel in a village waiting for supper, a tall, thin negro woman dressed in faded calico, and wearing a limp sunbonnet, came into view leading a huge dog by means of a rope tied around its neck. As she

drew near we were amazed to find that the beast was a
lion. While we all sat in a stupor of amazement, she approached and said, 'Ha; ha! Has any of you gemmens los'
a giraffe?' "

The use of the word "giraffe" in place of "lion" added
just the right touch to this fantastic yarn which I
accepted at its face value. Dickson's "Old Reliable"
was among the first to treat the negro as a comic
citizen.

"October 10. For the first time in my life I attended
the morning service of a Christian Science organization,
the one which meets in Aeolian Hall. I did this at the suggestion of Mrs. Ben Ali Haggin, who was quite sure that I
could be cured of all my rheumatic pains if I would yield
myself to her philosophy.

"Certain phases of the service pleased me. I liked the
kindly, hospitable air of the hall. The ushers, each with
a flower in his lapel, moved about with striking grace and
dignity, offering a cordial greeting to every one, even to
curious strangers like myself, and the audience, extremely
well-dressed, was noticeably benign of expression. The
service consisted for the most part of alternate readings
from Mrs. Eddy and the Bible, which is a bit shocking
to some people, but the general effect of the service
was helpful and essentially fine."

Mrs. Haggin, encouraged by my interest, invited me
to attend an experience meeting on Wednesday. This I
did.

"Some of the experiences given at this time were very
difficult for me to take seriously. Not merely did members report cures, they told of accidents prevented in
ways which seemed to me illogical—to put it mildly; but

the large audience present accepted each of these statements without a smile."

"October 12. One of the first encouragements I have received since coming East is an invitation from John Finley, State Commissioner of Education, to address a teachers' convention in Albany in the State of New York, and as I rode up the valley, I acknowledged once again the satisfying beauty of the Hudson River. It is ungracious to compare the surroundings of any other American city with those of New York; but as I think of Westchester's woods and lakes, of the Ramapo Hills, Bear Mountain Park, and the West Point Narrows, all other cities seem poor in their environment. I want my children to grow up in this beautiful country.'

"Finley presented me to several hundred teachers gathered from all over the state, and my paper, 'The District School,' drew forth both laughter and applause. As I told of the bare little schoolhouses of my boyhood, and spoke of the menacing changes which were taking place in the Middle West, they were interested. 'It is no longer a question,' I said, 'of rooms filled with German and Scandinavian children taught by an American teacher; it is a question of foreign teachers and foreign pupils. What becomes of the American tradition in such schools? You may say it is well to abandon American traditions, but I cannot do so.'

"Finley was pleased with my address (so he said) but at certain parts of it I caught a gleam in his eyes and a movement of his lips which said, 'Aren't you over-emphasizing the shortcomings of the school in which you and I were educated?'

"Many at the close of the session came up to tell me

how deeply moved they had been, and tried to describe the memories I had aroused. Their expressions reassured me of the value of the material I am putting into my Middle Border chronicle, an assurance which I sadly need."

On returning to Bacheller's home in Riverside, October 23, I found John Burroughs lying at ease on a couch in the wide inglenook, basking in the light of the fire. He was amazingly like Walt Whitman, as he glanced at me over his shoulder; and a noble picture of Anglo-Saxon age he made! Although a small man in fact, he produced an effect of largeness and dignity.

"Irving had sent out cards to his friends, and at three o'clock people began to arrive asking for Uncle John. During the afternoon he met nearly one hundred people. He greeted each of them with the same genial handclasp, but admitted, when it was over, that he was tired. The tributes rendered had done him good. 'When at home I spend most of my days alone,' he said. 'It is a good thing for me to get out once in a while and meet my readers.' Although shy, he was companionable and his admirers found him delightful."

We spent the evening in the light of Irving's grand fireplace, with a few belated admirers, among them Albert Bigelow Paine, who had not been able to come in during the afternoon. Uncle John toasted himself in the fire glow and said little, but loomed grandly in the firelight. He looked the poet and philosopher that he was.

He was up early the following morning, eager for the fishing trip which Irving had arranged for him. I pretended to be horrified at the thought of his fishing on Sunday, and while he admitted that it would have shocked his father and mother, he went away with Professor Curtis of Columbia and a clam digger hired to operate the power boat. They were gone for several hours, and, on his return, Uncle John was sadly crestfallen.

"Where is your catch?" I inquired in that irritating tone which one always uses in addressing the unsuccessful hunter or fisherman.

"The other men caught several," he ruefully replied, "but I had no luck at all. The brutes seemed to know and avoid my hook."

Seeing that he was really disappointed, I said no more about it.

After dinner Irving again "set me across" to Seton's, where I dined on lobsters at seven o'clock.

"At eight, Ernest, in a fine new buckskin suit, led the way to his council rock, where nearly a hundred adoring boys and girls had assembled. Their adoration of 'Black Wolf,' as they call him, is something like that which the young Sioux feel toward their chieftains and medicine men. He took charge of the games and dances, which appeared very picturesque and poetic under that clear sky and in the light of the campfire."

The prosperity and peace of these two homes, to which I was admitted almost as one of the family, added to my desire to live near them. I renewed my search for a cottage and a piece of Connecticut soil.

On my return to the city, I heard a program of violin music by Maud Powell, a long and very beautiful program. Luis Mora, the painter, and Thomas Walsh, the Irish poet, were seat mates in the box in which Bessie Potter Vonnoh was hostess.

"Mora is one of the happiest and most attractive young

men of my acquaintance. I knew his father in Boston when Luis was a little boy. Mora senior, a big, bearded, scholarly Spaniard, was a teacher in Cambridge. He had a deeply sonorous and beautiful voice, and Luis has inherited something of his father's charm.

"With an excited city roaring around me, I am living as quietly as a man in a village. My room at the Park Avenue Hotel is of good size, and as it overlooks the inner court, I am not troubled by noises. I have my typewriter and my books and papers spread out quite as if I were at home. Three times a day I hobble down to the club for meals, unless otherwise invited out; but for the most part of my time I work.

"The charm of the great city more and more asserts itself. Friends of power and influence greet me. Strangers arrive at the club with messages from far-off lands. I hear music. I dine with people who stimulate me. I see plays. I enjoy here some of the honors I have earned by a lifetime of labor as an author. It is to share these pleasures with my wife and daughters that I am planning a home somewhere in this metropolitan area.

"At times, the city appeals to me overwhelmingly on its material side. Last night, as Jesse Lynch Williams and I were walking up Fifth Avenue together, I suddenly found it profoundly impressive. The wind was brisk, and the sky, deep blue, was scarved with light clouds. Against this dome the towering buildings loomed, touched at their tops with sunset light. They were like mountain crags, their caverns humming with life. The throngs in the street formed two endless purple rugs laid along the bases of these towering cliffs. At such moments human beings sink to the stature of ants."

"November 1. I was greatly heartened to-day by Mark Sullivan, who said in his quiet way, 'I have decided to print in *Collier's Weekly* the remainder of your "Middle Border Chronicle," but I want you to put it back into the first person. The people who read it are interested in *you*. They want to know that it is a history of Hamlin Garland and his people. I shall begin the publication very soon.' "

This was a peculiarly fine and brave decision, for the lack of interest in the parts he had already published was disappointing. We had both expected many letters from our readers and only a few had written. "I cannot believe that it has been without effect," said Sullivan. "I shall publish at least four more installments."

Dropping all my other writing, I set to work on the remaining sections of the narrative.

In dining with William and Mary Roberts on the 3d, I met Hildegarde Hawthorne, daughter of Julian Hawthorne, and had a very frank talk concerning her father. She told me that he was in good health and earning a living as a journalist in Boston. I spoke of my early friendship and admiration for him. "I shall never forget the last time I met him. It was on the street in Philadelphia, and as he came striding towards me, I thought him one of the finest specimens of manhood I had ever seen. I recall also his story of the time when lost in a fog in a rowboat on the Atlantic off Gloucester, he rowed all night in a struggle to keep his frail craft headed against the wind. Only his superb strength and endurance enabled him to get in."

Although I did not say so to Hildegarde, I think she knew that I believed her father to be innocent of the de-

ception with which he was charged and which ended his
career. I sent my best regards to him.

His case was similar to that of Elwyn Barron. Knowing very little of business and trusting to the honesty of
others, they had been tricked into writing the articles
which placed them in the position of conspiring to de-
fraud. Hawthorne's punishment was almost destructive.
Lowell and Howells both thought him one of the most
brilliant novelists of his generation. "It was tragic business—that branding of a young man as a felon. My sympathy goes out to him in his brave attempt to keep afloat.
I know none of his children but Hildegarde and for her I
have a high regard. She, too, is making a brave fight."

Mark Sullivan took me to dine, November 4, with
William Allen White and his wife at one of the hotels.
I had never met Mrs. White before and I found in her
something wistful and lovely. William was wholly admirable in his care of her.

To Sullivan he said: "Garland is an old acquaintance of
mine."

"Yes," I said, "our first meeting was in Kansas in 1891."

I had been attending a Populist convention in Topeka
and was in the train on my way East when William, a
short, smiling, sandy-haired youth, introduced himself
to me as a reporter for the Kansas City *Star,* and asked me
if I objected to his sitting beside me. I made a place for
him beside me and we talked all the way to Kansas City.

He confided to me his ambition to be a writer and invited my advice. I repeated to him my usual phrase:
"Write of those things for which you care most and of
which you know the most."

"How much it meant to him I cannot tell, but his point

of view, his loyalty to Kansas, amused me at the time. Looking back on our interview from this dinner I should like to believe that I influenced him, in some minute degree, for he is one of the most eminent authors of his region and is nationally known as an editor and politician. He enjoys the friendship and the confidence of the great and is respected even by his enemies. He has made a more than comfortable living, partly as a man of letters, but more as a successful newspaper publisher. The Emporia *Gazette* is a power in the land. His short stories are true and wholesome, and his novel, 'A Certain Rich Man,' is large in concept and noble in feeling."

A few days later, my good friend Cosgrave invited me to dine with him. "Upon entering his reception room I found the center of interest to be Herbert Hoover, General Manager of the Belgium Relief Fund. His name is in every newspaper, but he looks like a youth. I could hardly relate him to the man concerning whose doings and judgments the American people are almost lyrical. He is of good size but has a round, boyish face. His smoothly brushed hair is dark and he has fine, serious eyes."

"At table his voice was not heard, but after the ladies rose, Cosgrave drew from him a candid statement of the situation of the armies and the conditions of the people of England, France, and Belgium.

"His talk enthralled us. He spoke very quietly without a single gesture and without raising his voice, and yet he conveyed to us all a sense of his mastery of facts and figures. He said that the Belgians were most grateful to us. 'The women often kissed the little American flag which graces the automobile in which I go about the streets. All salute as our car passes, but they turn their backs when the German staff rides by.'

"His mission is to obtain food and clothing for the Belgians in order that they shall not go hungry and cold this winter. He will get what he wants, for he is a most persuasive advocate. Cosgrave's dinner, which was quite perfect in its cooking and service, must have been in violent contrast with the conditions on the other side of the water."

In accordance with my custom I made a call on Howells one afternoon, Sunday, November 7. "I found him at work on a manuscript which he said was descriptive of his boyhood. 'I find it hard work,' he said. 'It is more difficult to recover that life than I had expected it to be.'

"When I asked him to lunch with me at the Players and meet some of the young men, his reply startled me. 'I hate young men.' He smiled as he said this. His tone was whimsical and yet there was a trace of bitterness in it. Perhaps he finds himself entirely out of key with the youth of to-day, or it may be that he feels that their indifferent comment would be at once useless and painful. It is the natural attitude of an old actor—one who feels that youth is crowding him off the stage. That I, too, am being pushed aside, I know, but I manage to keep on good terms with most of my younger contemporaries."

One night, as a relief from the war tension, Mark Sullivan took me to see Gillette's revival of "Secret Service," and as we waited for the curtain to go up we discussed the probabilities of its pleasing us. Said Sullivan: "I thought it one of the greatest American plays when I saw it for the first time."

After the curtain rose we were both absorbed in the action. Although a bit theatric in spots it was tensely interesting, and the audience heartily applauded it.

"Gillette gave a very good imitation of a young soldier while on the stage, but afterward, when we went in behind to see him, he was not in the least youthful—any more than I am. He, too, is losing the center of the stage. He is a shy, seclusive man whom very few people see. I recalled to him the place of our first meeting in a suburb of Boston, at the home of James A. Herne. What a handsome fellow he was in those days, quite the most distinguished of our actors, and he still retains that distinction."

III

In following out a policy to make the Institute a national affair, the directors decided to hold the annual meeting in Boston this year; and as I had been asked to read a paper, written by Brand Whitlock from his post in Belgium, I took an early morning train.

On the way over I read Jack London's "Sea Wolf," finding it a work of some imagination but boyish and disappointing in its general effect. "His formula is apparent, his method poor, and his characterization weak. It is the work of a man of adventure, one who has seen much of wild scenes and wild men, but who has little sense of values or proportion. It is worth while only in its descriptive passages."

The morning meeting was a failure. Only a handful of people came out to hear our program, but the turnout of our members was excellent—nearly fifty reported.

Lunching at the Tavern Club with De Wolfe Howe, I met a number of my old acquaintances, handsome Frank

Benson among others. Afterward I set out to see something of Boston and to look up old friends. It proved to be a melancholy expedition—such ventures always are. "In America no man and no thing endures for more than a generation. The sun shone with unusual splendor, but the ravages of time were so depressing that I gave up and went back to the luxurious Harvard Club where the present rules."

"At the second session I read the address which Brand Whitlock had written for the occasion. Several of my friends, notably Percy MacKaye and Brander Matthews, came up to say that I did it well. I hope they are right, for I have a high regard for Whitlock and desired to make the most of his paper. I made them all hear, which was a comfort to the many elderly people who were sitting in the chilly, sparsely peopled room.

"I left the city in a tempest of cold rain which came in over the roofs on a ferocious east wind, just the kind of storm which I remembered as characteristic of Boston. It seemed mighty good to be headed for New York, which is coming to be more and more my home. Boston belongs to my past, New York is my future. I could not live in Boston now, and yet at one time it was the center of America for me."

"November 20. Booth Tarkington was in the club to-day, looking big and burly and highly prosperous, but not in the least the subtle and highly imaginative literary man he really is. We rarely see him since his second marriage, for his summers are spent in Maine and his winters in Indianapolis. 'I seldom get to New York,' he said, with a glint in his eye, and when I spoke in high praise of his Penrod stories, he remarked with a chuckle, 'The material came directly from my nephews. All I had to do was to watch their antics and report!' "

On entering the club November 22, I saw E. W. Deming dining with a fellow member named Keggeris, and at their invitation I took a seat at their table.

"I seldom meet Deming these days, although we have a good deal in common. He was born in northern Illinois, but has roamed all over the mountains and plains of the West very much as I have done, except that he has actually shared the teepee life of his friends the Crows and the Blackfeet. He takes his family on these trips and is assigned a place in the camping circle, precisely as if he were a member of the clan. He illustrated my 'Boy Life on the Prairie' for Macmillan's in 1898, and that work brought us together and forms a link of association which still holds.

"His personal knowledge of wild West history is greater than that of any man of my acquaintance in New York City, with the exception of George Bird Grinnell, and I doubt if Grinnell knows more of certain phases of Indian camp life. He is better able to write of it, however. Deming not only knows the life of the red men, but he knows the other men who know it: scouts, squawmen, pioneers, and the like; and yet his home is a studio in Macdougal Alley!

"As we talked our minds took wing to the plains. He spoke of 'Yellowstone Kelley,' of 'Kip,' of Jack Munroe, and we discussed Custer, Forsythe, Miles, and many other famous plainsmen. Some of these squawmen and half-breeds I met, but Deming's knowledge is enormously more detailed than mine. He told me that he had made notes of his meetings with red chieftains and had many slides and phonograph records of them, together with a vast mass of material which his wife had recorded. He is a treasure house of mountain lore, and yet I fear will never make full use of it. He needs some one to help him put it into final form. When he goes, this valuable material will go with him unless some skilled hand can arrange and record it."

Claude Bragdon having been announced to speak at the MacDowell Club on "The Language of Form," I was interested to hear what he had to say.

"His name has been familiar to me for years, but I know little of his work. His talk was thought-provoking. He argued that the war would necessarily make a change in ornament, 'which is,' he said, 'psychological.' We cannot borrow our decorative ideas quite so handily now that the war has set up a barrier between us and the Old World, and as a result we may be able to develop something native in the way of design. We may achieve a mind of our own.

"He then argued for geometric design as being less derivative, and showed some very beautiful ones; rigidly formal, however. One of the demonstrations which interested me most intensely was his attempt to convey to our minds a notion of the fourth dimension. I succeeded, for the first time in my life, in getting a momentary glimpse of it, but it was only a flash. I was unable to recover and retain the concept."

His reference to the barrier which the German submarines had set up between Europe and America joined itself to a somewhat similar remark made by Dr. Van Eden, the Dutch writer, who said: "It would be well for American art and American literature if an impossible reef should rise in mid-ocean and make communication with the Old World impossible."

"November 27. Brand Whitlock, who has just arrived from Belgium on leave, spent the morning with me discussing the war and its probable effects upon American literature. He was paler and thinner than when I saw him last, but is quite recovered from his recent illness. He outlined a scheme for introducing American books to European readers and asked me to coöperate with him in the work, at least to the extent of suggesting typically American books. Although essentially unchanged by his own experiences, he was very definite in his statement that we who write must face an entirely new world hereafter. He has had an exciting year, but still more tremendous experiences are to come! To have a man of his ability and a writer of his skill in such a center as Brussels is our good fortune. His training as a novelist fits him to observe and record.

"I said: 'Your scheme is somewhat along the lines of one which Mark Sullivan and I have been shaping, and when I see Mark I will quote your suggestion about having our best fiction translated into French.' "

This I did, and the plan appealed to Mark, who asked me to make out a list of possible books. "Let's make 'a six-foot shelf' of American novels." "I'll do so at once," I replied. "I should like nothing better than to act as the editor of such a collection."

"He then asked me to go out to Chicago and do some editorial work for him there. This commission I am glad to undertake, for it will enable me to spend the holidays with my wife and daughters."

In carrying out this contract with Sullivan, I returned

to Chicago, December 10, and visited The Little Room for the first time in many months, hoping to meet some of the authors whose work *Collier's* might use. The moment I entered the door of the studio in which this little club met, I had the feeling of having never been away. "Fuller was there, along with Clara Laughlin, Elia Peattie, and several others of the original members. No young writers were present, and, so far as I know, none are being taken in. Each year the circle narrows. The city augments in many other ways, but its literary colony lessens and all my friends grow old."

That night I took my little daughters to see "Androcles and the Lion," which they greatly enjoyed. They were also amused by "The Dumb Wife," which served as curtain raiser. "Their delight communicated itself not only to me but to my neighbors. People all about us smiled at the radiant faces beside me, and when we came out, tired but happy, my joy in their comradeship led me to say, 'How would you like to live in New York City?' 'We want to go,' they said. But their mother is not so ready to leave her home on Greenwood Avenue."

"Elia Peattie came to dine with us on the 14th, and in talking over the past, told me something of my father which I had never known. She said: 'When in 1892 you and your father were in Omaha attending a convention, your father happened to sit in the audience near me; and when you came on the platform to read "Under the Lion's Paw," he appeared surprised and deeply touched by the splendid greeting which the audience gave you, and when at the close of your reading the audience "rose at you," I saw that gray-haired sire of yours put his head down on his arms and weep. He was overwhelmed with emotion to think that his son could win such an ovation. It broke down all his reserve.'

"This emotional outbreak on the part of my stern old father was a surprise to me. I knew that he had a certain pride in me, but I did not suspect him of being so affected by the response of my audience. I do recall, however, the confidence in my judgment which he showed as we went about the city together."

It was during this convention that I first saw Elia Peattie in her home; and I shall never forget the picture she made, when with a babe on her arm she went to the telephone and talked with her husband, Robert, who was the editor of the *World-Herald*. Her advice on the make-up of the paper was highly valued, and her pen was much more effective than his. She was at once wife, mother, housekeeper, and literary editor. I remember smilingly watching her, and thinking, "There stands the latest type of modern womanhood." It was a revelation to me of what a really fine woman could do. This was in 1892. There were not many woman editors at that time.

That this visit to Chicago marks a very decided change in me is evident in the following page of my diary:

"December 16. I now see that for many years I have been making the best of a bad bargain. I shall put this house on sale as soon as my wife will consent. She is greatly troubled by the thought of it, and I do not intend to bring pressure to bear upon her. If she will not go, it simply means that I must spend most of my time away from her and the children. My work is all in New York and it is absurd to think of remaining here. Furthermore, I hate to think of my daughters growing up in this sordid neighborhood and getting their schooling in a ratty and dangerous building which has already suffered from fire."

The day before Christmas closed in the most delightfully typical way. "It was snowing softly as the dusk fell, and the city, white and still, was really beautiful. The children applauded it as if it had been done entirely for their satisfaction. We worked till nearly one o'clock getting the tree ready; but as this is the last of our holidays in this house, I want it to be particularly successful."

The morning came, hushed and still, and white with snow. An ideal Christmas morning. All the ugly walls, all the filth of Woodlawn were covered by this exquisite mantle, and for the moment the city seemed a peaceful and pleasant place in which to live.

CHAPTER SIX

CLUB LIFE AND MOTION PICTURES

I

RETURNING to Manhattan on New Year's Eve, I found the Players bustling with preparations for the customary celebration of Founder's Night, which involved a midnight supper, a tribute to Edwin Booth, and a reading of his speech of dedication. I sat with three of my most valued friends, Irving Bacheller, Richard Burton, and Stewart Edward White, but the rooms swarmed with acquaintances from the ranks of other professions. Some distinguished members had come on from Washington, Boston, and other distant cities and for a few hours 16 Gramercy Park was a national center of the fine arts.

"Usually this ceremony at midnight is a fine and solemn hour, but in the midst of the program one of the speakers advocated moving the club uptown, a plea which brought on a debate and disturbed the harmony of the meeting. Most of the men felt as I did, that to move the club would be to destroy the Booth tradition, an inheritance which gave the club its distinction—and the speaker had few supporters."

The attendance was smaller than I had ever known it to be, because, I suppose, so many members were absent in France. I had secured another room at the Park Avenue Hotel and so I went home early to bed, escaping the customary New Year tumult with which the city was afflicted.

One of the most powerful advocates of "preparedness" was General Leonard Wood; and on learning that he was to be the principal speaker at the National Arts Club, January 3, I secured a seat at the dinner. I had not seen the general since Roosevelt introduced me to him at a luncheon in the White House and I was eager to know what kind of orator he would prove to be.

"He was in evening dress, a strong, handsome figure, and his forceful, blunt speech reminded me of Grant's concise use of words. He employed no preliminaries, had no graces, and expressed no fine shades of meaning. We knew exactly what he had in his mind, and his humor (he had some humor) was as rugged as the remainder of his message. He told us the exact truth about our past wars, and met with a strong response. He is the man who should be Secretary of War to-day, or the Chief of Staff, instead of which he is (like Roosevelt) on the outside, and his advice is not welcomed at the White House.

"It interested me to observe as I took his hand that his evening dress was not in present-day mode. He wore a shirt with only one gold stud. I liked him all the better for his indifference to change. 'He is the ideal soldier,' I said to Irving Bacheller. 'He is one of the great characters of our day. He is a lion. No wonder Roosevelt admires and trusts him.' "

In the midst of a throng of secret agents, reporters, ammunition experts, bankers, and political leaders which England was sending to us, literary America was suddenly called upon to welcome an English poet.

At luncheon one day I saw Brett of Macmillan's entertaining a tall, fair, serious man very evidently a stranger in the club. His face, faintly familiar, was interesting, and when Brett invited me to sit at his table and meet his guest—John Masefield—I was delighted, for I had been strongly moved by "The Tragedy of Nan," which had been produced in Chicago. I knew some of his verse and had been especially pleased by the "Dauber," a piteous and tremendous autobiographic fragment. Of his other work I knew nothing.

My comment reads: "He is a modest, almost shy man, serious, high-minded, and rather slow of speech and movement. His voice is peculiarly rich in tone, almost organ-like, and his accent markedly and pleasantly Oxford in quality. He quite frankly told us that the story about his having worked in a saloon in New York was true. 'I ran away to sea when I was a boy,' he said. 'I left my ship here in New York harbor and for two years made my living in and about the city. I did not tend bar—nothing so responsible as that—I only acted as scrub boy and sweep. I was only a lad.'

"Brett has become his publisher and is about to issue several volumes of his verse; and Masefield is grateful to him. 'My books have not sold in England and I cannot hope for any great sale here,' he said. He made a noble impression on me and when I said to Brett, 'I shall now read all his verse,' he replied, 'Let me send you a complete set.' "

I thanked him and when the books came I set to work on the six volumes with keen appetite. "When I meet him again, as I hope I shall soon, I want to speak of his work from sympathetic knowledge of it," I wrote Brett in my letter of thanks.

That I was moved by Albert Paine's "Life of Mark Twain" is evident from the following record:

"I gave the entire evening to the fourth volume of Paine's life of Mark Twain, finding it a tragic story. In speaking of it at the club, Paine (in response to some remark of mine concerning its gloom) said, 'The man who writes biography has *got* to be tragic, unless he is a liar. The novelist may shift the scenery and lighten the drama; the biographer must stick to the facts, and the facts of life are tragic.'

"As I read on, I discovered more and more of the hopeless melancholy which settled upon the old Missourian in his later life, a despair which had been expressed in some of his words to me at our last meeting. The scene in the book where he sends the body of his daughter out into the snow with a death march sounding on the organ is tremendous."

Masefield's reading at the MacDowell Club on the 16th, his first appearance in America, was successful. "He was obviously somewhat embarrassed, but made an eloquent introductory speech, although it was a bit too elementary, like a lecture to a group of students. Dealing with the development of English poetry, a subject to which most of us had given considerable attention at school and elsewhere, it was not entirely called for. We were not there to be informed concerning English literature. We wanted to hear him read.

"Once started in his reading, he lost all notion of time and the interest of his auditors waned; many became restless. He read very well, however, with a rich and beautiful voice, and, I'm glad to say, regained the attention of his audience. Certain favorite ballads were called for and he ended triumphantly, and went away, tired but happy. His reception was in fine contrast to the days when, as a run-away sailor boy, he scrubbed a barroom on Sixth Avenue, in Greenwich Village."

On the invitation of Robert Ely, I attended a lunch in honor of Masefield at the Astor Hotel, and found myself among friends. Augustus Thomas, Zona Gale, Clayton Hamilton, Rann Kennedy, and his wife Edith Wynne Matthison, Joyce Kilmer, Kate Douglas Riggs, Mary Johnston, and many others were there. A number of good short speeches were made, and Mrs. Kennedy read "The West Wind," one of Masefield's loveliest poems.

Masefield when called upon responded briefly and with some humor, supporting the excessive praise manfully, thus deepening the fine impression he had made on me.

Two days later, at the request of the Authors' League officials, I called on him at the Knickerbocker Hotel and escorted him to the City Club where the luncheon in his honor was to be held. We had some talk on the way over, and I drew from him other facts concerning his life in New York in 1895. He told me of his search for work in Katonah. Just why he should have ventured to Katonah he could not say. "I finally found work in a harness factory in Yonkers," he said, "and worked there for nearly two years." He spoke of his humble boarding-house keepers with affection, and said that he had tried to find them, but had not yet succeeded. "They were kind to me, they gave me a home."

Winston Churchill presided at the luncheon and his words were few and appropriate. Miss Tarbell and Dr. William M. Sloane were at my table. Masefield who sat beside me was deeply interested in "Red Indians" and asked many questions concerning them. His attitude in the midst of so much adulation was admirably modest.

At the Poetry Society dinner on the 25th, Mark Sullivan, Juliet Tompkins, and I sat together. It was a jolly dinner. Edward Wheeler presided with humor and tact and the speaking was particularly good.

"Corinne Roosevelt Robinson was a hit, making one of the best short after-dinner speeches I have ever heard from any one. Among other interesting stories she told a quaint tale of her brother and of his sufferings on being fulsomely introduced to audiences. She quoted him as saying, 'Whenever I am introduced by a flamboyant chairman as "the greatest man in the world," I always try to look like an absent rabbit.' " Mrs. Robinson then added: 'Whenever my poems are being read, I always try to look like a *disappearing* rabbit.'

"Louis Untermeyer was an interesting speaker, and so was Robert Frost, although his utterance was rather too deliberate. His expressions concerning poetry deepened my regard for him and his work. He is a man of quiet power and wholesome outlook, notwithstanding his insecure health. There is something nobly New England in his sober humor."

On the following day, in accordance with an arrangement with Burgess Johnson, I spent a day at Vassar.

"Johnson met me at Poughkeepsie, and took me for a walk around the College grounds, which were attractive even under their burden of snow. At four I confronted a 'press bureau' of young lady students who interviewed me for an hour. I had expected to meet a few of these amateur journalists in a classroom, and was somewhat appalled by the meeting, which took place in a small hall, with seats rising in circular rows, somewhat like the operating theater of a hospital, a fact which caused me to confess that I felt like a patient being cut up for the benefit of fifty critical young surgeons. It was, in truth, a good-humored party and I had no real grievance against them." What they got out of me I never knew.

The authors' reading at the Waldorf (in aid of The Mary Fischer Home on January 27) drew a large audience, and called out a number of favorite poets.

"Angela Morgan, one of the first to read, looked the poet. She is very handsome, handsomer than any real poet has a right to be. She read well also and her verse had eloquent emotional sweep. She made a strong appeal. Kathleen Norris, another attractive personality, read a story and read it well. So did Josephine Dodge. Corinne Robinson showed her serious side in several admirable poems. It is not often that so many good readers are assembled; and the audience quite properly applauded them all with fervor.

"After this program, I went to Orlando Rouland's studio, where I met Viola Allen, Beatrice Mansfield, Alice Fisher, Henrietta Crosman, David Bispham, and Mrs. Rouland, acting as a committee to arrange a tribute to William Winter, the old dramatic critic. I imagine the idea came from Mrs. Rouland who greatly admires Winter and is given to these altruistic enterprises."

"In running over the literary magazines at the club to-day, February 3, I was sickened by the cheapness, the insincerity of the announcements of new books, and by the slovenliness of the writing by reviewers. I find myself wondering whether there is any worthy criticism being published in America. I say 'published,' for it may be that all the finer writing is begging for the light of print. Most of the reviewers I meet are lacking in that high respect for their art which is an essential of lasting work. Many of the critical notices sound hollow or mechanical. Most of the favoring notices read as if they had been made up in the office of the publisher, and copied by the over-worked scribe who acts as critic."

The Authors' League reception confirmed me in my distaste for most of the work being done in the magazines and in the daily press. "Few men and women of distinction were in the throng of writers at this function. They were for the most part negligible amateurs or hard-working space writers hoping to find leisure some time to do a best-selling novel or a 'smashing' play. Some of them belonged to the atmosphere of the Press Club or the reporters' room. Few of them gave evidence of a cultural background. The women showed up better than the men. Quicker to take on manners, they appeared a little less crudely commercial.

"Something has gone out of American literary society. I cannot believe that these writers are the analogues of Emerson, Lowell, Howells, and James. It is not that they are young and raw—they are in totally different relation to their work. Their talk is not so much of excellence as price. I have no wish to be unjust to any sincere worker and it may be that my impressions are wrong; but they are here honestly set down."

I have no intention of misrepresenting these writers: I am merely making plain the fact that they are the products of our inescapable provincialism. Their lack of standards, or comparative concepts, is a part of our pioneer heritage. That is what Henry Fuller meant when he said, "Our soil is thin and sandy"—whereas a man like John Masefield who suffered more from poverty than any of the men in the Authors' League and with even less of a college education, possesses a beautiful voice and carries himself like a gentleman. It is largely a question of environment. We who are the sons and daughters of pioneers must labor long and hard to lose our strident voices and uncouth habits, qualities which spring from early association with illiterate farm laborers and mechanics.

In other words, we have the defects as well as the excellencies of pioneer ancestry. We are forced into gainful arts. We keep in mind the money to be won. With no backing, no secure footing, we are of necessity wage-earners even in our art—and there are those who argue that this is a more inspiring condition than that in which Old World writers compose. Perhaps it is, one way, but it does not produce gracious and cultured men of letters—not in these days.

II

"February 4. As I was walking up Fifth Avenue this afternoon, I met Bliss Carman swinging along in stately promenade like a figure out of the past. He was dressed in a long, dark coat with a high-pointed linen collar and black stock, and on his head was a wide-brimmed black hat. He was a poet of the time of Emerson's day rather than of ours—entirely alien to the crowds and commerce of the avenue. His pale face, wide, pleasant mouth, and grave eyes reminded me of Henry Clay. He was the original of a daguerreotype of 1850 come to life—a gentleman and a poet of noble dignity.

"When I stopped him, he peered down at me from his lofty tower with genial but absent-minded consideration. In answer to my inquiry he said, 'I am living in a small town in Connecticut, and very seldom come to town.' I carried away an impression of serenity and nobility which comforted me. 'Here is a writer who has *not* cheapened his wares in order to sell to the half-educated European peasants with whom he is surrounded. The motion picture has not succeeded in wresting *him* from his narrow path.' "

One day (February 5) I happened to have as seat companion at the long table at the Players an old friend of my brother, an actor by the name of North. During our dinner, he told me that he was in the employ of the Vitagraph Company, a huge moving-picture concern with studios in Brooklyn. "Come out and see us. Our studios might be of interest to you. We might be able to use some of your work," he added. Although I considered this merely being kind, I promised to go.

Up to this time I had given little thought to the development of the moving-picture industry, although from time to time the subject had been brought to my attention by the action of my friends. Almost every day some novelist staggered into the club weighed down with money which had been thrust upon him by some rapid-fire president of a "movie" company. This had amused me, but for the most part I had remained unmoved. I did not consider my stories suitable material for the screen. My virtue was not assailed.

All this aloofness on my part vanished during my visit to the Vitagraph studios in Flatbush, for young North not only showed me about the place but introduced me to Stuart Blackton, the president of the company, and also to Colonel Brady, the head of the scenario department.

"Brady was not only cordial, but professed an interest in me. 'I was a soldier on the plains,' he said, 'and the scenes of your stories of Montana and Wyoming are familiar.' He appeared eager to talk of these books, but North insisted on taking me on to see some other part of the plant. As I was leaving, however, Brady called out, 'Come again. I want to talk with you about "The Captain of the Gray Horse Troop." Send me a copy of it; it should make a great picture.'"

Perhaps my elation was justified, for the Vitagraph Company was one of the outstanding producing plants at that time, and its army of actors, its acres of studios, its photograph apparatus, and its general air of bustling prosperity deeply impressed me. I was most favorably influenced also by Blackton, its president, a low-voiced, thoughtful Englishman—not at all the type of moving-picture magnate I had been led to expect.

How little I knew of the situation! At this time there was not much talk of California and none, so far as I can recall, of Hollywood. Pictures were being made in Flatbush, Philadelphia, and Harlem. Mountain scenes were being "shot" in the Jersey hills and Civil War scenes in Englewood. The business was expanding with the swiftness and vagueness of a steam jet. Stuart Blackton had made his great picture, "The Birth of a Nation," and David Griffith was planning new and gigantic war effects. Enthusiasts predicted that the screen would displace the spoken drama.

"The financial backers and directors of this harum-scarum business are mostly Jews who are ready to gamble largely on almost any spectacular theme. No one can tell from day to day what the next development of the silent drama will be. No theme is too grandiose, no expense too great, for these wild companies. Such confusion; such ignorance; such vulgarity!"

That the head of the scenario department of the Vitagraph, one of the greatest producing companies, should chance to be an ex-cavalryman, a rider of the plains and sympathetic with my work, seemed almost providential; and when Blackton, as a member of the Salmagundi Club, invited me to a private showing of one of his lesser pictures, my doubts vanished. I met him and Colonel Brady and signed a contract which gave to them the right to produce four of my stories each year for five years, a contract which my friends Mark Sullivan and Rex Beach considered fair and highly promising.

Brady was more than reassuring. "You'll be riding around in your own automobile," he said to me, and I thought he meant it, until I heard him say the same thing to another wide-eyed author. He was a natural optimist —as a man should be in his position—and while I never came to doubt his liking for me and my work, I was somewhat chilled by this discovery of his professional jollying. Blackton remained kindly but discreet, and Smith, the treasurer of the company, was distinctly uninterested in my work. He was a Canadian and favored the work of James Oliver Curwood who was specializing in stories of the Great North.

I met Curwood in Brady's office one day and thought him a pleasant young man of essentially non-literary character. He was just beginning his immensely successful career as the writer of adventure fiction. And while I did not patronize him (I was not in the mood to patronize anybody), I did not consider him a man of letters, even after he had become a millionaire from the sale of his highly romantic stories of the wilds of Canada. Like Zane Grey and Rex Beach he was a purveyor of fine, outdoor heroes. I may have been wrong in my judgment of him, but that was my feeling then. I liked him but I could not respect his work.

Meanwhile, many other of my fellow members of the Players had gone into pictures: Rex Beach, Will Irwin, George Barr McCutcheon, Emerson Hough, Joseph Lincoln, and scores of others. The dining room resounded with the talk of dollars. The producers, I was told, were eager for the rights of books. Having bought titles, they used as much or as little of the stories as they pleased. In many cases the "adaptations" were vulgar as well as silly, and many authors professed to be shocked and disgusted by the distortions which their work had suffered.

My own understanding of this situation was clarified by a meeting with the hack writer who worked under Brady. He had been ordered to coöperate with me in preparing the scenario of my plays; and when I met him, I was amazed. He was a small man on a small salary with no literary or dramatic standing, who stood in fear of his superiors. Filled with conventional motion-picture concepts and capable only of stereotyped phrases, he disheartened me. I did not blame him, but I saw no chance of securing from him or his kind any adequate pictures of my books.

This was not the worst of the situation. No matter how fine the scenario, I discovered that it could reach the actor only through the man chosen to direct the rehearsal. The players knew little or nothing of the text; in many cases they didn't know even the outline of the story. They were dependent on the words which came from the mouth of the director. A rehearsal went something like this: "You are a young New York business man. You enter your office feeling fine. You've just put over a big deal. As you come in here you see your stenographer taking a package of letters from your safe. You register surprise, fear, rage. You rush toward her, then check yourself." And so on and on.

Some of the directors bawled at their actors through a megaphone, cursing and complaining, vulgarizing every scene which they mouthed and fed to their scared automatons. Instead of the action proceeding, as I had expected it to do, from the first scene to the last, like a play, the directors often played the last act first—if it happened to be more convenient—and the scenario was in effect a loose-leafed notebook whose scenes could be shifted at will of the producer. Augustus Thomas who had devised such a loose-leaf book gave me one as a model.

All this seems very crude and childish now, but such was the garbled mess which most producers put before their patrons in 1916. They were indeed pictures and not plays, and my vision of a logical scenario of my story, "Hesper," was shattered at the very first rehearsal, although Blackton and Brady were both sincerely desirous of having the picturization satisfactory to me. The director was intelligent and affable, but I had expected too much. Three of the scenes were exactly as I had hoped they would appear, but on the whole it was disappointing; and though according to my contract I was to attend rehearsals, and lend my advice and suggestions, I did not go again. The confusion, the lack of preparation, and the nondescript costuming chilled my hope of "riding in my own limousine." I couldn't see myself owning a Ford!

Hearing that John Burroughs was at an uptown sanitarium, I set out to call upon him. I found him in a small hospital on Park Avenue, sitting before a gas-log fire; and when I jested about this he boldly replied. "It is a make-believe, but it is better than a radiator." He was looking thin and old, but characterized his trouble as "only a case of autointoxication. Man is a creature built around an alimentary canal like all the rest of the world beneath him. When things go wrong there, the proudest of us show it."

After confessing that my life in New York was a continuous round of committee meetings, dinners, and theaters, I ended by saying, "I am not very well myself, but I keep going."

"I don't see how you do it," he retorted. "A few weeks of the city and I am worn out, ready to go back to my farm."

The dinner of the National Institute on February 21 was one of the dullest we had ever had. "The speakers were mainly painters, all so lame and bald in their English that I suffered with them, but when Clayton Hamilton and Augustus Thomas rose to take a hand in the discussion, we all sat up and smiled. Augustus was particularly clean cut, dignified, and, at the same time, delightfully humorous. [William M. Chase, a picturesque figure, was especially maladroit in his expressions. He hardly uttered a straight-away sentence. Alden Weir was almost as bad.] Hamilton and Thomas saved the day —or night. Their trained voices and their crisp, idiomatic phrasing fell upon my ear in solacing music."

Ernest Seton, whose "Woodcraft League" was his chief care at this time, had rented and fitted up a very interesting headquarters in the city and his reception to the members of the "Authors' League" was well attended.

Winston Churchill and Ellen Glasgow were gracious enough to take places in the receiving line and many distinguished authors were among the guests. "Laura Jean Libbey was almost the first to arrive. She came, indeed, before her hostess. Ella Wheeler Wilcox was almost equally prompt, and each created a stir. Their gowns were resplendent, far beyond my ability to describe. I had never seen Laura Jean before, and shall not soon forget her colorful personality.

"Ella Wheeler Wilcox I have known slightly for many years. She is a native of Wisconsin, and her childhood home was in, or near, Madison. She has become a good deal of a mystic in these later years, and writes much upon esoteric subjects. One of the most charming figures among the guests was a Miss Ross, a Cherokee girl from Oklahoma, a strikingly handsome figure in her beaded buckskin gown and graceful headdress.

"As I sat through Seton's ceremony so suggestive of the outdoor life, I could not put aside a sense of the fact that it all sprang from him and that when he dropped out the League would end. The Boy Scouts, a rival organization, is more in harmony with the growing war spirit and less dependent on any one personality."

The room, whose canvas walls were painted to resemble a stockade, and Seton with his buckskin leading in the games, made a powerful appeal to the boys and I could not fail of admiration for "Black Wolf," although I knew that he was fighting a losing battle. "He is but reviving memories of the heroic past—memories which will die with our generation."

CHAPTER SEVEN

MOVING PICTURE PROMISES

I

A GREAT deal of my time during March was given to the consideration of the moving-picture possibilities of my novels. Each visit to the office of the Vitagraph Company left me in a state of mingled elation and doubt. Colonel Brady was so confident that my stories were valuable and was so enthusiastic and so friendly, that I permitted myself to dream of large returns. "Even if only a small part of what he thinks my book will earn comes in, I shall be able to bring my family East," I said to Sullivan, and at the end of our computations, I wired my wife to put our Chicago house on sale.

In the midst of my negotiations with Brady, I was one of the guests at a luncheon given to Sydney Brooks, a visiting Englishman, by Mrs. Roland Conklin at the Cosmopolitan Club. The Conklins were friends of Lorado Taft and Mid-West in origin.

As I entered the reception room I came upon Brooks— a handsome fellow—talking with Irvin Cobb, who freely confessed to being the ugliest author in New York City. They made a striking pair. Poultney Bigelow, who looked the intellectual aristocrat that he is, was also a guest. Cobb I had met only once or twice. Bigelow I knew only as a classmate of the Kaiser for whom we all professed at this moment a ferocious hate. To us he was a war lord dreaming of world dominion, and Bigelow, who was known to have been his friend and confidant, was a bit under suspicion. However, I did not hold this against him. He interested me. For all his wide culture and his New York family, he affected a blunt speech which amused me. "He is the aristocrat who can afford to wear corduroy."

Brooks surprised me by saying, "I once lived in Chicago," and proved it by asking after Henry Fuller, Elia Peattie, and other of my friends. That he was in the city on some war mission I strongly suspected. All visiting Englishmen were held in that estimation then, but he gave no hint of it. He was a charming fellow.

All the following day I wandered restlessly about, deliberating on the sale of the motion-picture rights to my books and the possibility of moving my family to New York—all of which was highly important to me.

"As I sat among my fellow authors at the club, I felt a little foolish for having believed in Brady's figures. Sullivan is true blue. He feels sure there is something in my novels. But it has been a bad day for me. Mark is like a younger brother to me. He is kind enough to devote an afternoon to the task of seeing the Vitagraph people and helping me to a contract. While he was over in Flushing, I lunched with John Agar, the president of the Arts Club, who offered me a life membership in the hope that I would aid in building up the literary side of the club. Edward Wheeler was present and together we outlined a plan."

"April 1. A visit to the studio of the Vitagraph left me with a bad taste in my mouth. The direction was all so confused, so feeble, and so commonplace. I don't see any distinctive drama coming out of such factories. No matter how fine the scenario, the play cannot be finer than the director, for the director is the medium of its expression. They had rushed a scenario of 'Hesper' into type, and as I read it I found it so poor that I was disgusted and depressed. It was hopelessly bad. I can't let them bring out a play of mine with such scenes in it. I will not sanction this scenario." (I was but suffering the disappointment which every author of that day experienced when his book or play was adapted for the screen.)

II

Another of the reforms in which I was interested was that of simplified spelling, a cause which Roosevelt had endorsed. As a member of the board of directors, I met with them.

"They are all a group of aged folk. Starr Jordan, Henry Holt, and Brander Matthews all appeared feeble. Matthews is not only gray but in bad condition. He can scarcely hobble. Dewey struck me as a vigorous hawk-like type. Grandgent, the president, is also a fine-balanced, humorous character. Dunn, a handsome fellow, was the only young man in the room. I believe in this reform and see no way to serve it other than by adopting some of its rules. I shall do this hereafter."

The moving-picture business continued to claim the most of my time during April and I did little but ponder and write letters. Blackton reported that he was greatly pleased with "The Captain of the Gray Horse Troop" and wrote, "We will do it in Montana in September. We will make it a tremendous feature film and bring it out here next fall just as a play is brought out," which was most encouraging.

Dining with him at the Salmagundi Club, I gained still greater confidence in him, for after dinner we all retired to the hall where his screen version of Hopkinson Smith's little play, "Kennedy Square," was shown. It was charmingly done and the members applauded the art with which it had been directed.

"At the Players, Albert Bigelow Paine and Frederick Opper make a pair. No one sees one without inferring the other. Opper is a small man with a round face, whereas Paine is tall, resembling an elderly judge. To-day, April 11, I joined them, and in the course of our talk discussed the going out of holograph letters. Paine said, 'No one writes literary letters to-day. We are in the typewriter age—typewriters and telephones have destroyed epistolary correspondence.' 'We old fellows are survivors of an age of longhand. We can maintain some sort of position after the war, but I can't define just now what that position will be,' I remarked. 'We can reminisce, at any rate.' With customary humor he retorted, 'Yes, we can reminisce—if anybody will listen to us.'"

My visit to the Vitagraph Studio on April 12 was disturbing. "As I entered Colonel Brady's office he was in the midst of 'jollying' James Oliver Curwood, using precisely the same phrases he had employed in jollying me. I was instructed. I saw that it is his job to jolly authors. I respect Blackton all the more for the reason that he has not once jollied me. He has the reserve of a poker player. He is willing to gamble, but winces when a financial nerve is struck. The whole business is a gamble for them and for the author."

"April 13. The deed for my Chicago house came this morning and I signed it, returning it to my lawyer. This closes the chapter of my life in Chicago. For twenty-three years I have endured its dust and winds and I am glad to be free of it. My pioneer work is ended. At fifty-six I intend to have some part in the beauty and comfort of the East. For years this Woodlawn house has been a burden to me. It stood in a depressing region, our neighbors were noisy, and we had no yard. I breathe easier now that it is off my shoulders.

"That night Curwood dined with me, and as I listened to his enthusiastic accounts of what the Vitagraph Company had promised to do for him I sang small. His home is in Michigan, but he specializes in stories of the Canadian wilderness. His fiction does not interest me, but it fills large space in the popular magazines and has made him rich."

"April 16. A note in the *Times* settles that Harper & Brothers are to move. This is another sad change in American book-making. Harper's have been in Franklin Square for over seventy years. I spent most of the day working on a prison article but had lunch with Louis Betts in his studio. Orlando Rouland came down to see the portrait which Betts has made of me. We then went up to Robert Underwood Johnson's home to meet Ellen Glasgow. Alden was there, looking very old, old as time. Johnson was jubilant over the passage of the bill incorporating the American Academy. It has a clear field now."

Meanwhile the producer was going ahead with "Hesper," but I had lost interest in it. "The cast is not good enough and the sets and costumes are false to the scene.

Whether I can get the others done as I want them or not is a problem."

Following a promise made some two years before, I gave a sitting to Henry Hubbell, another portrait painter. I found him in an old house on Fifty-ninth Street, surrounded by carpenters remodeling the rooms, but he set resolutely to work and by noon had a good likeness. I stayed on till nearly six. "Mrs. Hubbell brought us coffee and sandwiches so that no time was lost. The outcome is a lively sketch."

One night I called on George Bird Grinnell to discuss Blackton's scheme of doing "The Captain of the Gray Horse Troop" in the field. I had not seen Grinnell for several years, but he looked quite the same as when I saw him last—lean and brown and alert. I said, "We want to do this picture play in Wyoming with Cheyennes as actors in their own land. Do you suppose I can get permission of the commissioner to do this?"

He agreed to help. "It's all up to Secretary Lane. See him."

At Mrs. Ingersoll Brown's, April 22, I met for the first time Thomas Mott Osborne, the prison reformer, and was greatly interested in him. "He is a big man, reminding me of Clarence Darrow, but is of a gentler and far more optimistic nature than Darrow. His rugged face is kindly and his habit of mind constructive. He told us of the Welfare League which had grown up among the convicts. 'The idea came to me while at work as a volunteer prisoner in the basket shop of the penitentiary. I set out to organize a league of "good" prisoners. Later on I included all the prisoners, reserving power to expel the bad members. Later I advocated self-government within the walls, with courts to try all cases. In time a completely democratic ideal was shaped up and tried out. The results are amazing. The change in prison psychology is beyond my wildest imaginings. The league is established. Nothing can overturn it now.'"

About six P.M. on April 28, Blackton called me on the phone and greatly excited me by saying: "Join me in a box at the Hippodrome at eight to-night. Irving Couse, the Indian painter, will be there and we will discuss plans for producing your novel, 'The Captain of the Gray Horse Troop,' which greatly interests me."

I found him and Couse in a balcony box and while the rather boresome program went on we held a disjointed conversation. It was plain that Blackton's mind was busy with a big scheme, and after the performance had ended we went round the corner to the little Green Room Club where Blackton ordered a welsh rabbit and some coffee.

He then opened up his plan: "I want to make a big feature film of your novel. We'll stage it in the Cheyenne country with the Cheyennes themselves as actors. We'll make Sheridan our base of operations, and we'll locate our mountain scenes in the Big Horn Range. I have brought Couse into our conference for the reason that he can help us in arranging our scenes of Indian life and also in our costuming."

All this was too good to be true, but I seized upon it with delight. "I wish we could do a few pictures of Cheyenne life before the white man came," I said. "I have in mind three great introductory pictures. One, the coming of the explorers; second, the arrival of the treaty makers; third, the breaking of the treaty and a declaration of war; fourth, the imprisonment of the Cheyennes on the reservation. This final picture would lead directly to the beginning of my story of modern reservation life."

To this Blackton agreed and Couse and I went away together, our brains boiling with ideas. Couse said, "I have some sketches already made which will make a start on your plan." We arranged to meet in his studio the next day and set to work.

(This plan was never carried out by us, but the production of a play of the Southwest by Zane Grey made use of a similar sequence of prehistoric pictures preceding a modern play.)

On May 3 a note came from Roosevelt in which he mentioned the Writers' Syndicate which Hagedorn and others had organized. "I am grateful for what you have done and I would like to have you keep on." Knowing that his estimate of what I could accomplish was too high, I nevertheless agreed to do what I could.

"A letter from my wife saying that she could not come on till the first of June threw a cloud over my sky and I spent the afternoon walking in Van Cortlandt Park whose beauty made me long to share it with her and my daughters. The club has lost interest for me. Few men of distinction turn up there now. The war has taken distinction out of the individual. Human dignity is of small account. When I vision these millions of warriors running to and fro like frantic gnats, I am appalled."

CHAPTER EIGHT

HOWELLS' HOME AT YORK HARBOR

I

THE coming of my wife and children to New York brought me face to face with the problem of establishing a home for them. The Hudson River was my Rubicon—and, having crossed it, I began to realize that I had drawn my family into a tremendous whirlpool of human life, one which the war had made frenetic and appalling. "Still suffering from my strange malady, I have moments of doubting my ability to maintain even a tenement flat in this colossal town."

This depression is recorded in these lines written on Decoration Day: "My daughters love the life of the river. Each night we go down to the pier at Ninety-sixth Street and watch the colors come over the water and the Palisades. They find it very beautiful—and very far from the life they led in West Salem and Chicago. I wonder if we shall ever know the peace of the old homestead? Can I find a quiet home in this over-crowded city?

"This morning we walked down to Ninetieth Street and there stood for some hours while the parade of soldiers, sailors, and policemen went by. They made a brave showing. The Grand Army men were very few—only seven hundred in all; and as they tottered by, graybeards marching toward their near-by graves, I recalled standing with my father to watch his comrades pass. Now he is gone to his eternal bivouac, and these his younger comrades are soon to follow. The khaki-colored ranks followed the veterans like waves of powerful new life, and behind them hundreds of boys—row on row—all marching in the war spirit which is reaching down to the children."

At half-past three on May 31 I went down to the Brevoort to address the Whitman Fellowship. Horace Traubel was there looking quite as picturesque as Mark Twain—a white-haired, quaint, and remote individual. I pointed him out to the chairman, saying, "There sits the man who really knew Whitman," and at our urging Horace rose and came forward. "Tell us how you came to write the Whitman book and the manner in which Walt worked," the chairman said.

This Horace did—a very personal and amusing tale. Nevertheless, I came away with a bad taste in my mouth. There were so many intellectual "come-outers" present, each one trying to bend Whitman to his particular theory of life.

We spent June 4 with Lee and Eve Summers, two of our valued Chicago friends. "They have bought a Long Island house surrounded by big trees and shrubs and vines. The Sound is in front of it and great steamers pass and repass almost hourly. Lee, who was looking tired, told us that he is employed by the War Department as an expert on high explosives. He looks like a boy of eighteen, but he is a man of wide experience in his field—chemical engineering."

At the club on Monday I fell in with Royal Cortissoz and Don Seitz who talked of O. Henry (Sydney Porter) with vigorous directness. I agreed with Cortissoz, who said, "Porter is a tricky newspaper fictionist, amusing but not important." Cortissoz knew him very well, it seems. So did Don Seitz, for whom Porter wrote his daily stories. Seitz said: "It was almost impossible to get Porter to deliver his stories in time to revise them. They came in at the last moment carelessly written but always interesting."

I said, "Porter is essentially the humorist, the newspaper man. His stories vary in scene, but they all carry the same exaggeration, the same comic tricks. Such criticism, however, is unimportant to those who like him."

A second meeting with Thomas Mott Osborne, the prison reformer, reawakened my interest in the subject, and one fine day in May I went up to Sing Sing to study its methods. Dr. Kirchwey of Columbia University was the acting warden. He knew me and at once invited me to lunch. Later he called in one of the "trusties" and said, "Take Mr. Garland anywhere he wishes to go."

The prisoner, who was a quaint little East Side gamin, talked freely of conditions in the prison and took me into all the shops. The sight of the convicts strolling about the yard reminded me of a camp of railway hands loafing away a Sunday afternoon. I had no sense of their abnormality as I went among them. Their faces were cheerful and their glances frank. "We are entirely self-governed," they said. "We have our own judges and police."

I sat in the court which meets each day to try offenders against the rules. The cases which came on were mostly petty but they were treated seriously by all concerned. "The whole effect of the prison and its system of government is hopeful. It seems civilized and I shall write of it and do my best to advance it."

Early in June the political convention pot was boiling, but my interest in it was not intense.

"The political game now seems rather boyish to me. It is, after all, a kind of mimic warfare, the one big interest in many commonplace lives. The present row is less absurd than formerly, I suppose, but it is absurd enough. I am glad Roosevelt is keeping away from it."

For some obscure reason, the president of the State University of Maine had scheduled me to make the commencement address, and on June 13 I visited Portland on my way to Orono. I had not been in the city for some years, and with only three hours to spare I went at once to the Longfellow Home, where I found four or five elderly women sitting in the hall waiting to display their treasures. "The rooms all had a damp, cold, decaying atmosphere. It is so hard to maintain such a shrine—nothing in America endures for long."

At eleven I went on toward Orono. Although I passed some lovely lakes, the country as a whole was disappointingly commonplace. As I neared Bangor, however, the hills began to show, and the wide green stretches were starred with white farmhouses of the Colonial type.

I reached the State University in time for supper at President Aley's house, a noble mansion on a lovely lawn. "Aley's family is Western. His students are all American."

"June 14. The commencement exercises were impressive by reason of the fine student body, native and physically powerful. The day was glorious and the dinner in the gym, the speeches, the faces of the guests, and the graduates carried me back into an America which is at once native and buoyant. This corner of our land is still Yankee and close to the northeast border."

One of the considerations which led me to accept this invitation to speak was the opportunity it offered to visit Howells in his summer home at York Harbor. On my way back I left the train at Portland and took an electric car which ran along the coast to Portsmouth. "Yawk Hahbah," as the natives called it, was delightfully typical of this region, and as I left the station and set off up the winding street to the north I passed groups of old salts sitting in the sun wholly concerned with boats and nets and fish. One of them knew the Howells place. "It's that red brick house in that grove o' hick'ries," he said.

I had phoned Howells from the village and as he came to meet me, I was shocked to find him leaning on a cane, a small, bent figure, with uncertain feet. He had aged swiftly since our last meeting.

"In spite of his weakness he led me for a tramp about the point of land on which his house stood. Our last walk had been in Central Park and I recalled our first one in Auburndale—and also the one in the neglected estate at Watertown, nearly thirty years before. As we entered his present garden, he displayed an unfamiliar phase of his character. He was interested in every plant and tree—pathetically interested, it seemed to me. I recognized in this the final employment of a dying man. He admitted that he seldom left the place. 'I have a new Ford car,' he said, 'but I use it only to visit John and my grandchildren at Kittery Point. I cannot drive it—and, if I could, Elinor would not ride with me.'

"He then told me with quiet humor of its acquire-

ment. 'In going over some boxes of old papers, I came
upon two bankbooks each of which indicated an unused
balance—quite forgotten by us both. I verified these
records and drew the money which in most marvelous
manner exactly equaled the cost of a car! I took this as
a kind of providential windfall and—there stands our
chariot.' "

His house was a plain and unimposing structure and
his study was equally unimpressive, but it was quiet and
comfortable; and I, who had seen him in so many city
flats, rejoiced to find him here in what he regarded as his
final home—in summer, I could not imagine him living
here when the no'theast gales of winter sweep across "the
p'int."

On June 28 I took my daughters over to Flatbush to
see "Hesper" run, an exciting experience to them, a depressing experience for me. The producer had thrown
into it some low comedy, and the woman who represented
my heroine was a "dimpled blonde." I was deeply disheartened by the cheap and uninspired way in which the
story had been filmed. Instead of the great peaks of the
Rampart Range for background they had used a row of
Jersey hills. In place of my bold Rocky Mountain gold
seekers and free miners, the producer had used Pennsylvania coal miners whose lamps and blackened faces were
ludicrously out of place. My feeling is indicated in these
lines:

"The outlook for my picture plays is dark; I fear I have
been led into a 'pipe dream' by Brady whose sanguine
nature and friendly interest have led to over-statement.
His talk of 'feature productions' and large sales no
longer convinces me. I am bitterly disappointed. Smith

is coldly indifferent, and Blackton himself has lost interest even in 'The Captain,' which he greatly liked when he read it in May."

We had a very quiet Fourth of July.

"The warfare in Europe and Mexico has put a damper on all mimic warfare—even the boys are subdued. I have never seen so quiet a Fourth of July. At night we went out on the river bank to see the fireworks in Jersey, a superbly beautiful panorama of cloud and river, hill and crescent moon. The rockets bursting into bloom against the great wall of cloud were very impressive."

The serious business of finding a flat near the school in which my daughters were entered occupied my afternoons for a week or more; and I finally settled upon one on East Ninety-second Street.

"It is at the top of a seven-story building on the corner of Park Avenue and only two blocks from Central Park. It is only an ugly, out-of-date, seven-room apartment, but it is in a good neighborhood and the windows of the sitting room look away to the south over the roofs of other buildings. At night the Queensboro Bridge is a series of airy loops diamonded with lights."

My confidence in the future had been shaken by the failure of my first motion-picture play; and as the war was increasing in fury, I did not feel justified in assuming a larger monthly obligation. To have a decent flat in New York was all I had any right to expect, but there were moments when I despised myself for my inability to support something better.

An outbreak of infantile paralysis drove us from the city in July and we spent the remainder of the summer in Canton, New York, where Irving Bacheller had a house.

"Irving is at work on a novel of Silas Wright's time, and to-day he took me to call on a citizen who knew Wright. The house was old, the man was old, and the 'relics' were old. Indeed the whole household was morbific save for one fair granddaughter. We came away gladly and spent the evening on the porch of Irving's house reciting bits of Shakespeare. No young person quotes anything these days—no one has the memory for it. Hourly editions of the papers and innumerable moving pictures are destroying memory. From the silent places must come the thinkers of the future."

Returning to New York, August 21, I had a conference with Brady, who was a little less sanguine than when I saw him in July. He admitted that changes in the company were going on.

"The firm looks a bit shaky to me, but Brady insists that our program will all go through as we planned. At dinner David Bispham and I had a long talk. He again urged me to write for him a play concerning Cromwell. He would make an admirable Cromwell. His face and voice are precisely right. I wish I could see my way to writing such a play."

Mark Sullivan had leased for the summer the home of J. N. Marchand in Westport and at his invitation I went out to see him. The little house was in vivid contrast to historic Chatham, but a very livable place for all that.

"We started out one afternoon, August 22, to find Mark Twain's 'Stormfield' and motored for an hour among the hills and deserted farms, unable to locate it, but we found Ida Tarbell's house under a gigantic elm.

As she came out to greet us, I saw her as an alert, intellectual 'elderly lady.' We had known each other long and I greatly valued her friendship. I hate to think of her getting old, but there is no cure for that in her or in me."

Late in August all my records and personal belongings were assembled in the apartment at 71 East Ninety-second Street. "The place is empty of furniture and I am writing this sitting on a box with my typewriter on a trunk, but I am at home in New York! At the club, Sullivan, who had Henry Allen of Kansas to lunch, invited me to join them. I found Allen a man of wide experience and a powerful personality. I have never heard him speak, but he is said to be a 'spellbinder.' He is a friend of William Allen White and also of Victor Murdock, three vivid and vigorous Western types—men Kansas is proud to own.

"Brian Hooker was at a near-by table, a serious, refined, and thoughtful young man. He, too, is trying to 'get into the motion-picture game.' Having finished the book of an opera, he has come to town with a motion-picture manuscript! In this way literature is being wrought to the level of the unthinking mob. The spoken play *is* in danger."

During my summer in Canton, I had been motored over to Wilmington and Mount Marcy, and had been greatly impressed with that region as a "location" for my Rocky Mountain screen plays. I wrote Blackton to this effect, asking him to consider the production of "Cavanagh" there.

In calling on him, I was somewhat encouraged by his agreement. "We will do 'Money Magic' next and I favor a locality like Mount Marcy. I am sure we can make a fine, heroic picture from this book—and also from 'Cavanagh.' "

One night Don Marquis came into the club and we talked poetry and free verse for an hour.

"He is a fine Illinois product, a frank newspaper man whose talk is as distinctly rural as his verse is clear and graceful and polished. I found in him a sense of beauty which comes, perhaps, from his Huguenot ancestry. Though a little too fleshy he is a singularly handsome man. His gray hair and his fresh-colored face are in striking contrast. Some of his poems are very beautiful —and sad. I consider him one of the ablest of our columnists."

"September 13. I resumed work on the 'Middle Border' this morning, and, dining at the Players, sat with Lincoln Steffens, George Barr Baker, Charles Camp, and Mark Sullivan. The members are getting back from the country and from France, and the club hums with life. Sullivan suggested that I take some part in the campaign for Hughes and I promised to do what I could. I suggested a syndicate letter or round robin.

"The strike continues, making us all choose our time for going downtown—if at all. I don't trust the populace. I don't like the kind of people who ride on the elevated or in the subway. Abstractly I grant their right to life, liberty, and the pursuit of happiness—concretely, they are a problem. They have small respect for women and no religion. They possess, I fear, little patriotism and no idealism of any kind. They may develop into something, but at present they are an uninspiring lot."

In a visit to the Vitagraph office, I found my little hack scenario writer in a state of flutter. Blackton had turned

over to him another story to "picturize" and he was off
with mine and on with the new. Understanding his predicament I took my manuscript away to finish it myself.
Brady said, "It is suggested that you go to California and
help film the 'Captain,' " and to this I replied, "I will go,
but it will be a wrench!"

That night as I unwrapped some pictures and hung
them on a wall, I had a painful sense of change, of dis-
loyalty. Mother's smiling portrait (faded by time),
father's youthful visage in an enlarged ambrotype, Herne
as "Uncle Nat," my wife as she was when I married her,
Mary Isabel as the sweetly solemn cherub—all seemed
somehow to reproach me for abandoning the West. "The
separation is greater than a thousand miles of soil. The
world to which father and mother belonged is gone. It
does not exist in the West or anywhere on the earth. The
babyhood of 'Mixobel' and 'Majory Christmas' is gone;
and I am gray. I must make a new home here with my
family, and finally I must accept their world in exchange
for mine.

"A powerful wind from the south has been complaining all day in my ears, filling me with memories of the
past—memories vaguely sweet and sad. Voices of the
plain—of my boyhood. What does life mean? Where do
we land? What is the value of the cargo we carry? Fiction seems futile in a time like this. What will come after
this slaughter ends? For forty years, from 1868 to 1914,
our nation enjoyed a steady, quiet advance. It cannot expect another period of the same tranquillity and prosperity. We have 'The Habit of War!' News of battles is
our recreation."

Ian Hay, author of "The First Hundred Thousand,"

who was at the club, surrounded by the fellows, chortled gayly of the campaign. To him it was a fine subject for humorous drama.

None of us care much about the thousands slain or captured. It has come to be merely a dramatic daily story. The truth is we are getting accustomed to slaughter. We shall miss it when it stops. It will leave a sad vacancy in our morning program.

"As I look round my poor little sooty flat and regard our slender stock of battered furniture, I admit my failure, and confess that I am too old to do better. I ought not to feel so, but I do. I am the least successful of my fellows. Seton, Bacheller, Tarkington—all possess handsome homes, and live as authors should, surrounded by books and pictures. I would not care if I were alone, but my daughters are growing up. I don't like to think of them living in this little cell, seven stories in the air; and yet a home in the country might mean poorer school facilities. It is a sad problem, one which I see no way of solving unless our film plays succeed. It is a curious reflection upon my standing as a writer, but the mere *possibility* of succeeding on the screen causes my friends to respect me!

"This is one of my sorrowful days. Lame and lonesome, I went up to Bronx Park. The delicious woods smell and the splendid colors of oaks and elms did me good. I need contact with dirt and grass and trees. The old trailer in me is dying hard. Can I stand city life? What will this riding about in cars, this work for committees, do to me? To bring my wife and children into this noisy, dirty, dangerous town seems a crime. Manhattan will be still more dangerous next year."

"October 7. War is at our own doors! Yesterday a German submarine appeared at Newport, and the captain, with debonair grace, stepped ashore, presented a handful of letters to the German ambassador, and withdrew. A few hours later he had sunk six ships and disappeared like a ghost!

"This destroys the illusion of our 'splendid isolation.' We are in the world stream. It is hard to write stories when such actualities are taking place. I find myself devouring bulletin after bulletin during the day, and all my friends are similarly engaged—to what purpose?"

"Greenwich, Connecticut, October 15. Walking all the way from the Greenwich station to Seton's place, I sampled every apple tree whose branches hung over the walls. I found Ernest deeply engaged with a new story, and Juliet Tompkins, a week-end guest, was also at work on a novel. The war has not checked her output. We went for a stroll about the place and minutely inspected the new barn, which cunningly reproduces in its swaying lines the thatched roofs of Surrey. It is a quaint adaptation but really charming. In the afternoon several people called, among them a Dane, who humorously boasted of having twenty-one decorations. He did it so charmingly that it was only after he was gone that we discovered how barefaced his bragging had been."

At the Players next day Eric Pape and I had a good deal of talk. He is a man of refinement and a most enthusiastic collector of books as well as of pictures. His boyish face was rather wistful and his confidences concerning his domestic affairs touched me. They were delicate and wholly without the complaining note.

"My 'cattle' are now two goldfish, and my 'chores'

consist in changing their water and feeding them cracker crumbs. I am living seven stories from the street and without the sight of a tree or an open field. All this is entirely out of character but (I hope) temporary. I shall get back to earth again next June. It is partly on the children's account that I am here, to finish their schooling. To keep my place in the literary world is also for them. To go to the country means dropping out of all my clubs and societies—in short, to retire, and I am not ready to do that even in my present state of health. So long as I can earn a living by writing and lecturing, this is my place. I rejoice, selfishly, in the knowledge that my daughters are going to orderly and harmoniously colored classrooms, attended by teachers who show them every consideration. All this may be 'undemocratic' in me; but if to hate dirt, lice, and disease is undemocratic, I am just that.

"What a vivid contrast Mrs. Cosgrave's school offers to the one in which I was educated. At Mary Isabel's age I was going each winter morning to a rude little box of pine boards, set on the bare Iowa prairie. Drab benches, uncurtained windows, bleak walls—these were my surroundings. Often the thermometer was twenty below zero and the north wind bitter."

CHAPTER NINE

AT SAGAMORE HILL

SHORTLY after the election in which our candidate was defeated, I received a letter from Roosevelt inviting my wife and me to lunch—"a consolation lunch," he called it; and on the day appointed we took the train for Oyster Bay. In our car we found Hermann Hagedorn and his wife and also Julian Street and his wife—all on their way to lunch at Sagamore Hill. Hagedorn laughed when I quoted Roosevelt's phrase, "a consolation lunch."

"He said the same to me, but between ourselves I don't think he expected Hughes to win."

The colonel received us at the door, dressed in a riding suit of khaki, wearing boots and spurs as if just in from a ride.

"Burly with strength, he seemed on the point of bursting through his jacket; but I discovered gray in his hair. He was in gay spirits and we had a delightful talk before lunch. Among the other guests was the young Englishman Sydney Brooks for whom I had taken instant liking. He is a handsome fellow and an able journalist."

At luncheon my wife was honored by a seat beside the colonel, while I sat beside Mrs. Roosevelt at the other end of the table. "Our host was in high spirits and full of stories. I could not hear them all, but at times he addressed the entire table and talked most delightfully, although it seemed to me that his words came a little slower than usual. He related with great humor his experiences in England at the royal ceremonies where the French minister became quite furious when put in a carriage just behind that of a certain Oriental prince. He protested to Roosevelt. 'Do you not object to being placed behind a colored petty Eastern potentate?' . . . 'To this,' said Roosevelt, 'I responded, "I don't care whether the man ahead of me is ring-streaked, brown, or spotted—it doesn't affect my comfort in the least!" A reply which appeared to pain as well as to mystify the Frenchman.' "

Although so gay in public, Roosevelt said to me privately, "I am of no use, Garland; I feel my years"—a weakness I had never before heard him put into words. It made apparent to me the fact that he still suffered from the effects of his Brazilian trip. It hurt me to hear a word from his lips which hinted at decay.

During the talk in the library, Sydney Brooks, who had been studying up on some particular phase of the commercial treaties between England and Denmark, instanced a very ancient and curious maritime law. Quick as a flash Roosevelt came back with an accurate quotation of this law, another astonishing revelation of his wide reading and his absolutely faithful memory.

For the first time I sensed decay in Sagamore Hill. I was aware of its worn carpets, over which so many feet had passed. I discovered on the furniture the marks of childish hands. I perceived with sorrow that this mansion —spacious as it was, historic as it is certain to be—is only a flimsy frame structure likely to go up in smoke at any moment.

"It has nothing of the solidity, the time-defying elements of English country 'halls'; it is merely an unusually dignified suburban home built in the style of the eighties. Exteriorly it is commonplace; within, it is rich with trophies and mementoes."

On November 16, as I came into the coat room of the Ritz Hotel, where the meeting of the National Institute of Arts and Letters was to be held, I heard a voice call out to me clearly and with humorous assumption of command, "Garland, come over here!"

It was Roosevelt, who said to me at once, probably in reference to some previous talk concerning his writing, "I have sent you 'My Holidays in the Open' and I hope you will like it. It is one of my best books."

He was in fine spirits, mingling with the members with delightful informality. He was on the program that morning and his speech saved the day; for Winston Churchill (who was scheduled for the principal address) was delayed by a snow-bound train and did not reach the hall until the speaking was over. The audience was large and friendly, and Roosevelt's vigorous and well-delivered essay was the event heartily applauded. His very presence gave distinction to the meeting.

On November 23, Mark Sullivan gave a luncheon to Frederick Palmer, just recently returned from the front, and the company included several other war birds.

"Palmer's talk was only fairly interesting, but he has had many exciting experiences. He has flown across the Channel and has dined with French and English officers on duck and champagne, close to the battle line. 'Everybody jokes on the front,' he said. 'No one, apparently, takes it seriously. New York is much more anxious in expression. The men at the front can't afford to be serious.' His talk put a bitter taste into my mouth. War lets loose the beast in men."

Barton Hepburn, the kindest of all my financial friends, called me up the following day and asked me to lunch with him at the Bankers' Club. Accordingly I went down to the Equitable Building and up to the fortieth story, where I ate a delicious meal amid swarms of bankers and brokers. "I see no signs of war here!" I said to my host.

"Hepburn, whom I have come to know through Irving Bacheller, is from St. Lawrence County, and essentially of the same stock as myself. He began as a school-teacher, as I did, but turned toward finance early in his career. To-day he is one of the greatest financiers of the city. He remains kindly and unassuming despite his millions."

At the Lotos Club late in November I was a guest at a dinner in honor of Booth Tarkington, a most elaborate affair, with George Ade, Julian Street, Montgomery Flagg, John Finley, and Chauncey Depew as principal speakers. Tarkington confessed that he was badly scared, but having committed his speech to memory, he came through neatly. Ade's address was written out, and so was Street's.

My own address which was entirely offhand was notable only for the response which it drew from Tarkington. In speaking of the growth of the local color novel, of which Tarkington was a leading representative, I alluded to Riley, to Kirkland, to Howe, and said, "But, gentlemen, we must not forget that Edward Eggleston was the father of us all." As I said this, Tarkington looked up at me with smiling, sidewise glance and said, "You are perfectly right. He was."

I went on: "It is easy to criticize 'The Hoosier School-master' or 'The Mystery of Metropolisville'; but we must not forget that when these stories were written nearly fifty years ago, no one had found the Mid-West a subject for fiction or poetry. Eggleston was a trail maker in this rude field and it takes courage to be a pioneer in letters—courage and perception. Once he had blazed the way, we who came after him found easier going. In honoring Booth Tarkington we must not forget Riley and Eggleston, who led the way into the West."

Chauncey Depew, who sat at my right, was in fine form—confident and ready. "We had much talk. Seemingly he has not begun to think of being old. George Ade looked pale and gray. I felt my own years as I noted the changes which time had wrought in him. He is prosperous as ever, apparently, but is not well. I seldom see him now."

Following the lead of other clubs, the National Arts announced a reception to Tagore, the East Indian poet and philosopher, and I was one of the guests.

It was a large affair and some interesting folk gathered. Tagore, looking a little like an aged Christ, stood up and read some of his poems.

"I found his humorous lines mildly interesting, but there was something in his manner which repelled me. As a speaker he is too illusive, too platitudinous. He represents the old and the worn-out in human life.

"America wants to be young. There is fun in *not* being finished, in not being introspective and philosophic. His very dress and attitude appear artificial. He is earning a great deal of money—and taking it. His lofty, impersonal philosophy does not debar him from carrying off our filthy gold. His manager, young Pond, told me privately that the poet was as 'pernickety' about his robes as a prima donna. 'He has a trunkful of them—one for every occasion.' . . . This is a curious quirk in a man who is reproaching us for our materialism!"

After dinner at the club with Edward Wheeler and John G. Agar, I wrote: "This is the last of our evenings in connection with the annual book exhibit, and ends my work on the committee. The outlook for books this year is not very good. It is a question whether ten years from now we will see any improvement in our literature. The present stage of public taste is low—no question of that. The moving picture is below the general level. Our public is made up of peasants or the children of peasants and they buy to their taste. The war has cheapened individual effort in many of us and diverted the stream of production."

CHAPTER TEN

CITIZEN ROOSEVELT AND HIS SONS

I

"WE begin the year [1917] out of debt and with several thousand dollars in the bank, so that as a family we have no reason for complaint. The war has made us uneasy, but it has not seriously interfered with our way of life. Food is increasing in price, but rents remain low —at least in our building."

At a reception given by Orlando Rouland at his studio in honor of the Irving Bachellers and the Garlands, we were greeted by many old friends: Buell, once assistant editor of the *Century*, Mrs. (General) Custer, Mr. and Mrs. Peixotto, Mr. and Mrs. Franks, Frank Seaman, and others. "Irving came home to supper with us and my daughters helped him decide on the title of his new novel, 'The Light in the Clearing.' His manuscripts are in high favor despite the war."

President Butler having invited us to another of his formal dinners, my wife prayed for pleasant weather— we could not think of driving so far in a cab—and fortunately the sky cleared just as we started and we were able to walk over to the Fifth Avenue bus.

At the end of the line we chartered a taxi and rolled up to Morningside Drive quite as impressively as any other taxi-delivered guests.

"At this dinner I met Dr. Helio Lobo, secretary to the Presidency of Brazil, who is visiting America. I found him a pleasant young man, not at all Spanish or Portuguese in appearance. He speaks English fluently and has written certain articles concerning America. I was greatly taken with him."

I spent several hours at the Vitagraph office next day where "Money Magic" was being tried out on the screen.

"It was done very well but not as well as I had hoped it would be. The owner of the Rialto Theater was there and found a great deal of fault with its reserve. It was not 'sexy' enough for him. Several other satellites of the moving-picture world were present and their comment produced in me a mental nausea. They are all so openly pornographic in their pandering to the morons in their audiences."

"January 5. I sat in at lunch with Edward Wheeler, Marsh of Macmillan's and Louis Ledoux, who were honoring Wilfrid Gibson, a small, rather unimpressive young Englishman, who said little and seemed to wonder just why he was being fed. Pond, his lecture manager, who came in a little later, told me of his efforts to 'boom' Gibson, who is his latest importation."

"January 6. A day at the moving-picture shop! At ten I met Colonel Brady in his new office. He has been moved into smaller quarters and is a bit subdued. That he is about to be 'let out' was my impression. He took me to lunch at a little near-by restaurant where I sat opposite an actress who talked nothing but shop. This 'star' is being greatly advertised at this time, but I found her not only rather plain but ignorant and insignificant. 'It is amazing that such a woman can draw a salary,' I said to

Brady on returning to the office. The man who did the 'cutting' ran 'Money Magic' for us and we passed upon it once more. It is very well done."

Among the most notable of the literary events of the city at this time were the luncheons given by Robert Erskine Ely in honor of the speakers for his League for Political Education. I never understood how these were financed, but I was frequently a guest and often a speaker. Each luncheon had a distinguished group of writers. At one given in honor of Wilfrid Gibson and Walter de la Mare, I saw Padraic Colum, Witter Bynner, Joyce Kilmer, Louis Anspacher, Eleanor Gates Moore, Corinne Roosevelt Robinson, and several other of my friends.

"Some very good speaking followed, all too laudatory of course, but the sauce was gracefully labeled. Gibson himself was modest enough; indeed he went so far as to intimate that his friends were overstating his merits. Colum was interesting in his quaintly Irish way and a certain Father Clifford, abandoning Gibson, let himself go in a general diatribe on the subject of Democracy. My private opinion is here set down. I doubt whether such a honeyed dish as this program of praise has any value even as publicity. It is a polite fiction on the part of our cities and clubs that all our overseas brethren deserve it and that they profit by it. I doubt both propositions. Gibson and De la Mare are minor figures in England and no luncheons of this kind can enlarge their fame at home. It may help them to a few lecture engagements here."

One night while my wife and I were dining with Mr. and Mrs. S. R. Guggenheim in their gorgeous apartment in the Plaza Hotel, I met my old *Chap-Book* friend, Harrison Rhodes, and we talked of Herbert Stone and of Chicago's literary boom in '93. After dinner we all drove to the Metropolitan Opera House to see and hear Caruso in "The Elixir of Love."

"As an actor Caruso was only fairly amusing, but he sang the one great aria in the last act with marvelous skill and passion. The audience forced him to repeat it. In trying to avoid this encore he made a comical figure. An immense audience applauded him. 'No sign of war here,' I said to my hostess. For the time we were among the secure folk. Each month makes the city more astounding in its growing wealth and power. 'All the great musicians of the world are here,' say the critics."

January 11 was the date for Mrs. Douglas Robinson's tea. "When my wife and I entered at five o'clock, we found the long drawing-room crowded and in the center of it stood Colonel Roosevelt, the center of a throng of poets and novelists. On seeing me he called out a jovial greeting and taking me by the arm drew me into the circle, saying to the group with a chuckle, 'Now, here we are—two old plainsmen surrounded by residents of the 'effete East'—a remark which produced a ripple of laughter. His arm was like the limb of a white oak tree.

"He was in perfect health,—a human dynamo. His swelling chest, his firm biceps, and his shoulders (bulging like the corners of a piano) gave every evidence of recovered power. Turning to his circle, he resumed a jocular diatribe which my coming had interrupted. Gertrude Atherton stood before him, short, blonde, intense, looking up into his face, determined to make her point. It seemed that she had written in criticism of his action in the Venezuelan matter, and in this article, which I had not seen, she had accused him of violating international courtesy in order to carry out his ends.

"He answered her humorously but vigorously, and in the course of his talk described a number of very extraordinary executive orders, revealing, it seemed to me, official secrets. However, knowing that he never spoke without care, I was not disturbed. He told of sending Admiral Dewey to the Caribbean Sea, and of the German minister's recall, then passed to a discussion of the Alaskan dispute. He admitted sending a regiment of soldiers up there. 'I am willing to assume all blame for it,' he said. Realizing that I was hearing unwritten history, I listened closely, marveling at his freedom of speech.

"At the same time I rather regretted his attempt at placating this circle of authors. His explanations should have been addressed to a group of historians. He remained perfectly good-tempered through it all, jesting in the midst of what amounted to an attack on his policies by those who knew nothing of the State Department records of the case.

"As I moved along through the throng, meeting many of my friends, I saw a quiet little lady in sober hat and gown seated modestly against the wall talking with another elderly woman; and it was only upon a word from my wife that I recognized in this retiring brown thrush the woman who had been mistress of the White House for seven years. It was Mrs. Roosevelt herself, so modestly inconspicuous that only a few of the guests realized her presence.

"We tried to put into our greeting the admiration and the affection we had for her; but it was with a feeling of regret that I passed on, marveling at her attitude which was at once retiring yet quietly secure.

"In his own way Roosevelt was equally democratic. He moved among the guests like any other writer or artist. He assumed no authority, no honor. He expected only ordinary courtesy from those who thronged about him. Radiating good humor and bubbling with reminiscence, he turned from one to another with instant quip or comment. He knew what each of us had written, and was interested in what we were at work upon. I felt once again the world-wide sweep of his knowledge and his interest."

II

"January 15. Stuart Blackton called me this morning and told me that my 'The Captain of the Gray Horse Troop' had gone before the camera in California. This disturbs me greatly, for I fear it means a cheap and hurried production. It is not possible for a director out there to give it the proper setting. I wrote Blackton at once asking him to substitute 'Cavanagh.' It all seems very casual and indifferent and adds another phase to the process of my disillusionment."

Dining one night at the home of John Henry Hammond, my wife and I met a number of interesting people of the true-blue American sort.

"The dinner moved on schedule time, and at eight we motored down to a meeting of the Parents' League at the Cosmopolitan Club. Here again we found ourselves in the midst of New Yorkers, some of them of great wealth; Mrs. Hammond presided charmingly and Hadley of Yale spoke wisely and wittily on educational matters."

"January 19. As a guest at a dinner given by the Social Science Institute in honor of E. H. Sothern, I heard Julia Marlowe read for the first time in many years. I didn't like her method; it was too strained, too theatrical. My hostess was Mrs. Robert Franks, wife of Carnegie's financial secretary. Irving Fisher of Yale presided and John Finley made a short speech in presenting a medal to Sothern. Commissioner of Police Woods spoke and spoke well. Ernest Seton was there with a wounded leg. He explained that he had hit himself with an ax. As I rode uptown with him he said, 'I'm going to England in February. I'm going to the front.' He was very deeply stirred by the situation in England. After all, he is an Englishman."

As one of the volunteer readers at a benefit for the Mary Fisher Home, I went to the Waldorf a day or two later.

"Clinton Scollard, Joe Lincoln, Mollie Best, Joyce Kilmer were on the program. Lincoln's reading was quaint and true, and Kilmer's delightful in another way. Mollie Best, of whom I knew nothing, gave an up-to-date monologue, and Scollard read a poem. The audience was largely from out of town, and the chairman entirely Newark! There *is* a suburban type! My daughters were greatly interested in Joe Lincoln, who read very well and pleased the audience by the flavor of his homely humor. Authors' readings are often painful exhibitions of individual vanity—each reader concerned only with himself—but this program was comparatively free of that fault."

On the following Sunday, for the first time in my life I visited the Ethical Culture Society to hear Felix Adler preach.

"His church, a handsome meetinghouse on the west side of the Park, was filled. I had never seen Adler before and I was greatly surprised to find him a wisp of a man— entirely bald, an almost fantastic figure, but he had the orator's magic. He contrived to hold a large audience silent for nearly an hour. He spoke as if thinking aloud, and his English, clear, concise, and apt, was an intellectual delight. I met him afterward along with John Elliott, his handsome schoolmaster, the son of a New England pioneer. Adler at close range was even more frail than on the platform, but he is an intellectual power; that is evident."

Among my other activities of this war period, I suggested and helped to organize the Joint Committee of the Fine Arts, which was composed of the presidents of seven clubs connected with the fine arts, intended to serve as a reception committee whenever distinguished citizens from other shores came to New York. Edward Wheeler was my chief aid in this organization. It was just another agency in the program of conciliation to which the city was committed. When I learned that a number of distinguished writers from South America were temporarily living in New York, I suggested to John Agar, the president of the National Arts Club, that a dinner in honor of these authors and artists would have a beneficial effect; he not only consented but put the office of the club at my service. The secretary, Mrs. Crine, entered into the plan whole-heartedly and was of the greatest aid.

In arranging for a program of speeches, I secured from Kermit Roosevelt the promise of a paper on literary conditions in Brazil as he had observed them on a recent tour of that most important South American republic.

Representatives from some eight or ten of the Spanish American republics were expected as honor guests and speakers.

At the dinner, which was furnished by Mr. Agar and Archer M. Huntington, some twenty-five guests were lingering over their coffee at half-past eight on the evening of the meeting, when an excited messenger came to Agar and whispered, "Ex-President Roosevelt has just come in!"

Agar, who was bitterly opposed to Roosevelt politically, turned hastily to me and said, "I turn him over to you, Garland. I can't manage him. You can. He is a friend of yours."

I was not so sure of my ability to "manage" Theodore Roosevelt, but I knew I could rely on his goodwill.

An eager throng was pressing through the doors and clattering among the camp chairs, and as I entered the lower door I saw Roosevelt, the best known, most powerful citizen in America, calmly, quietly sitting in the midst of an excited audience, all eager to speak to him and hear his voice. It was an incredible situation. The hall was hardly larger than a drawing-room and the seats were jammed closely together so that his prodigious personality, no matter how modestly he carried himself, was oppressive by reason of its sheer weight of historic association.

He smiled and waved his hand at me. As I reached his side he said in a low voice, "You see in me the doting father whose son is about to speak a piece. I am here to hear Kermit. Do not call on me for a speech." I assured him that, as I was the presiding officer, his wishes would be respected.

The program went through without a hitch. The speaking was good and Kermit's paper admirable. The applause with which he was greeted pleased his father—that was obvious. The audience two or three times called for Roosevelt, but I ignored their demands.

It touched me to find in Roosevelt so much of the fond father. He sat upon one of our hard, narrow camp chairs for two hours, listening to all the speeches with alert interest. He stayed on till we put our resolutions of goodwill to vote, and congratulated me afterward on the success of the meeting.

"It is a good message to send to our sister republics in the South," he said. "The news of it will go to every capital."

III

"February 11. I took up and revised chapter twenty-four of 'A Son of the Middle Border.' This is the twentieth time I have gone over it, and still it does not entirely please me. I must get more into it. It is still too bare.

"At three I met a reporter for the New York *Sun*, who wanted help in getting up an article on Howells. She said, 'There are so few anecdotes about Howells'; and I replied, 'Howells is a very dignified man—dignified without being pompous—and does very few things that give rise to picturesque stories such as are told of Riley and Joaquin Miller. I have known him for many years, but I have no anecdotes of him. His life, like his fiction, is without sensationalism; and so far as quoting him is concerned, I always do so with an apology for my failure to report his delicate and incisive phrasing.'"

On January 19, 1917, in answer to a note of invitation from Roosevelt, I went down to the Langdon, a small Fifth Avenue hotel, in which he often stayed while in the city.

Mrs. Roosevelt was with him, and while we were chatting, two other guests came. They were young Mr. Bowman, connected with the American Geographical Society, and Professor Patterson, an expert on rhythms in speech. —both fine young fellows. Upon taking seats in the public dining room, another guest, a woman friend of Mrs. Roosevelt, whose name I did not catch, came in and sat with us for a while.

The first hour of luncheon was given over to a discussion of geographical matters, for Mr. Bowman had come to notify the colonel that, on a certain date, a medal was to be given him in recognition of his discovery of the "River of Doubt" in Brazil.

This naturally led Roosevelt to talk of the River of Doubt and to explain why he went down it rather than up it. With a characteristic chuckle he said, "I was fifty-six and I decided that it was easier for me to climb down than to climb up." He spoke of his illness while on the river and said, "I came pretty near staying up there—but I'm all right now." He treated this event lightly, but I knew that it was a very serious moment for him and his companions.

After this trip was fully talked over and some very interesting reminiscences drawn from him, he turned suddenly to Patterson and said, "Now let's talk about rhythms of verse and speech." To me he remarked, "This young man Patterson is from Columbia and has been doing some remarkable work on the subject of rhythms, in verse and in nature. I have taken a particular interest in his latest book, and want him to talk of it."

In the course of the discussion which followed, he said: "The fact is the lion utters a coughing note which is usually called a 'grunt,' in rhythmic succession like this." Whereupon, to the amusement and amazement of the other diners in the dining room, he reproduced the lion's deep-toned challenge. He also imitated the bark of the antelope, and described the howl of the wolf as being substantially a rhythmic song. "You know that, Garland."

"Yes," I replied, "the morning note of the coyote is a musical wail."

This led him to say: "The conflicting rhythms of a Sioux drummer and a Sioux singer often produce a curious intermingling of syncopated rhythms." Again he turned to me and said, "You have heard the criers and singers of a Cheyenne camp? Give Mr. Patterson a notion of it."

Seeing the other luncheon guests staring at our table I begged off. They were doubtless saying, "It's Roosevelt, riding some of his hobbies," but this gave me an opening. I called to his mind the fact that parts of Carlyle's "French Revolution" were magnificent blank verse. I quoted a few lines to prove it: "Shrill Fredegonda, shrill Brunhilda, have had out their hot life—scold and lie silent. Charlemagne sleeps at Salzburg, truncheon grounded, nevermore to wake."

To this he replied quickly, "You're perfectly right," and quoted other passages to sustain his contention.

He outlined the differences between the rhythms of archaic French and the French of modern poets, and to the profound astonishment of us all, quoted a long passage from the "Song of Roland" and then, in order to prove his point, recited a modern French poem. At the end of this he demanded agreement: "Don't you see how much stronger, how much manlier, the archaic French verse is?"

We could not fail of applause, but Mrs. Roosevelt said to me with a smile, "Now you know what I endure when Theodore insists on reading French to me."

His keen ear overheard her, and instantly, with his peculiar falsetto chuckle, he retorted, "Oh, yes, I'm perfectly aware of my Oyster Bay accent."

He then quoted a passage from the "Nibelungenlied," in German. "I like the German rhythm—that rhythm— better than I do the French," he said.

He was perfectly delightful throughout the entire luncheon, and left me with a deepened sense of his enormous reading and the tenacity of his memory.

IV

As Howells was soon to be eighty years of age, I began to plan an evening at the National Arts in honor of his birthday, a program which should present the various phases of his work. I believed that his fellow craftsmen in England as well as in America would welcome an opportunity to pay him tribute and I set about writing them. Edward Wheeler was glad to second me in the plan and the officers of the club not only granted the use of the hall but offered me the assistance of the secretary, Mrs. Crine. With her aid I sent out a large number of letters outlining my project. John Howells and his sister Mildred expressed pleasure in it, but left the management entirely to me.

On February 25 Alfred Noyes was at the club and we had a short talk. "He is a big young man, blond, bald, rather heavily built, but is a handsome figure. Like most of our visiting Englishmen, he is connected in some way with the British Secret Service."

"February 26. The President this day proposed an armed neutrality toward Germany and went before Congress to ask for unlimited power. These are dark days, days of horrifying war news. England is in the midst of a life-and-death struggle. Her stranglehold on Germany seems broken by the submarine patrol. She will make a most desperate fight and will bring about an entirely new order of world economy. Her fate will affect us.

"Gentle Ray Baker, who is just back from Washington, feels this deeply. His fighting blood is stirred. My mail is heavy with calls for meetings, for subscriptions, and for the use of my name in all kinds of enterprises. A tremendous force is roiling our great melting pot.

"General Wood is saying: 'Japan if she wished could take the West, from California to the Rocky Mountains! We have no first-class gunboats on the Pacific and no adequate guns here. Our guns are obsolete.'"

"March 6. Lunching at the Harvard Club with the 'Vigilantes,' I joined their new organization. Hermann Hagedorn, Julian Street, Charles Towne, young Monroe Robinson, and several others whom I did not know made up the luncheon party. The purpose of this association is to give aid and support to the Allies.

"The war cloud darkens over the horizon and the President is now in the position of fighting his own pacifists, who refuse to vote him the power and money he needs. I have moments when I lose all faith in the future—and in life. Why live or let your children live to enter such a hell as that in which Europe now welters?"

"March 14. Lorado Taft came in on his way to a lecture at Columbia. The day was sloshy and dark. Marsh of Macmillan's cheered me by his praise of my manuscript. He insures a good chance for the book—as good as the times will allow.

"Lee Summers called, full of interesting talk concerning the secret service—and various other matters of preparedness. He was looking pale and tired, indeed we resembled the inmates of an old men's home.

"Lorado seemed to enjoy our house, and as he was going said to me: 'It is a hard thing to say, but you have done more for me than any one else. You told me long ago that I might just as well be a national character as a local celebrity. Your prodding from time to time has kept me "walking like a man." ' This was a curious remark to make, for I had done little except to criticize and argue with him from time to time. Fuller has done more for him in certain ways."

The Howells meeting on March 21 came off handsomely in all respects. The crowd was a record breaker, too large for comfort; and this fact worried me and my committee. Many people stood all through the program and hundreds could not get seats.

"It was a sincere tribute to Howells and the program gave something of the poetic as well as the humorous side of his work. One of his farces was played in a corner of the room. The general effect of the evening was gracious and pleasant. It was, in a sense, my personal tribute to him. I sent out all the letters, and arranged all the replies, which will have great value in his autobiography. Wells of *Harper's Magazine* has arranged with his firm to put all these letters into a handsome book to be presented to Howells by me, when he returns from the South. It is a generous offer and I am certain Howells will appreciate it."

"March 28. These are monotonously exciting days. Each hour has its sensation, and none of them count! Nothing means anything now. We all go about saying the same thing. Our minds move in either the pacifistic or the militaristic rut. Each and all use the same similes, the same threadbare arguments, the same uninspired logic. Caught in the world's whirlpool, we go round and round, with no aim and no purpose. I am sick of it all, yet am helpless to cure myself of my disease. The club is wearisome with discussion and so are the teas to which I go now and again. As a nation, we are shambling sidewise into war. No real plunge, as Roosevelt would have caused. To go in now is to go in without preparation, for no one knows what Congress will do when it meets next week.

"A visit to serene Irving Bacheller was a relief. His garden showed green leaves and we found him out burning brush and basking in the sunlight. My daughters were enchanted with the house, the water, and the rocky ledges, and with the big old fireplace around which we sat after dinner singing and telling stories.

"Irving and I walked over to visit Owen Young who is living in Lincoln Steffens' house. 'Owen is another St. Lawrence County boy,' said Irving. 'He and Bart Hepburn came out of the same hole with me.' Young, an extraordinarily handsome man, not so old as Irving, is the head of the General Electric Company. 'He commands an army of nearly twenty thousand men,' Irving said, as we were coming away. 'He would make a good man in the White House.' "

(I was greatly impressed with Young at this meeting. He is the finest type of American. Although I met him but once or twice after this, I rejoiced when, in 1929, he was appointed financial expert on the German problem.)

"April 6, 1917. To-day Congress spoke—only fifty in opposition—and the President signed the resolution and seized all the German ships in our ports, a momentous day in American history! We are going into the struggle ill prepared but in a large way, a way so large that twenty years ago the whole nation would have shuddered at thought of it. One big event follows another with benumbing effect, and men in the street move with solemn faces."

CHAPTER ELEVEN

THE GOOD SHIP SANITAS

WHILE the nation was clamoring for soldiers and every college had its band of students and professors drilling on the green, I was crawling about so crippled by arthritis that I could hardly walk to the street car; and early in April, yielding to the advice of my local doctor, I consented to go to a famous sanitarium in the Middle West. I didn't want to go. I had no faith in the plan, but my wife, greatly alarmed at my condition, urged it, and to relieve her mind I packed my valise and set forth like a man condemned to a six weeks' term in jail.

Arriving at my destination at eleven A.M. the following day, I left my bag at the depot and walked to the sanitarium, which loomed above the town like a big hotel. It suggested an ocean steamship and as I entered it I found its rotunda swarming with porters. In less than an hour I found myself in a mob of invalids, all taking their turn at being inspected. The doctors, absorbed, deft, business-like, treated me as a problem. All that I had gained by years of study and writing vanished; I was merely a case of "Arthritis deformans" and the doctor to whom I was assigned examined me in the way of a bored and tired man. He looked like one who abhorred the institution's vegetable diet. He appeared one who could "do" with a cigar over a whisky and soda.

Luncheon was a cheerful affair of "nuttose," "wheatena," and cereal coffee, and I went to my room like a convict to his cell, leaving the doctors to study my record and decide upon my regimen.

That night, after a throng of us had gathered in the parlor, the far-famed director, a short, bustling, genial man of sixty-five or seventy, gave us a rambling, complacent, genial talk. His audience, numbering about three hundred (all patients), listened respectfully but rather tepidly. Some of his talk was wise, and some of it was faddy. He was dressed entirely in white and looked ruddy and well.

"April 10. The food bores me, but I may get hungry enough to like it by and by. The inmates interest me. They are a curious mingling of sectional types—scarcely a man or woman of what would be called the fashionable or even of the literary world. Some few well-dressed business men are among them, but none that have an air of coming from homes of distinguished taste."

"April 11. The essential, grisly tragedy of this place becomes more apparent each day. The pale, weary faces, the slim, nerveless hands, and the shuffling feet of the sufferers are everywhere in evidence. It is true a certain number of them play tennis and others joke about the food; but in the midst of their strenuous cheerfulness, move those who are death-stricken. We are all the farthest possible remove from our soldiers who are going into battle in France, sacrificing their splendid lives to conserve ours."

The air, the confinement, and the rules of the institution, as well as its long and narrow shape, led me to call it "The Good Ship *Sanitas*," and to regard the porches as decks, and the patients as passengers convalescing after a period of storm. All that could be done to cheer us up was done. We had music while we marched and concerts after dinner, but to me it remained a prison ship, and I was restless in my tiny cabin.

"I spent the evening reading 'Clipped Wings' by Rupert Hughes. In some ways the book is admirable, but parts of it are tawdry. He does not rise above his subject as James or Howells would have done. It is true, too true, for it reports the cheapness and vanity and boasting of the stage without distinction of method. Perhaps to another this book would have charm; to me it is adroit but essentially inartistic."

At the end of the week I decided to go home.

"My decision to leave started things going. My physician phoned the chief, and the chief told him to bring me out to his house. A young assistant, elaborately considerate, conveyed me to the doctor's house, an atrocious example of flamboyant suburban architecture, standing in a fine yard. An air of neglect was over it, but my host, clad immaculately in white flannels, met me at the door with effusive respect and hospitality.

"He began talking at once and hardly ceased during the two hours of my stay. He boasted of his wonderful health, wholly due to the avoidance of meat. He asked me to feel the muscles of his arm, his leg, and called my attention to the firmness of his tongue. He brought in some huge dumb-bells and gallantly strove to put them up. He succeeded with one but not with both, and hastily laid them away. He talked incessantly, precisely as he lectures, against eating meat, and drinking and smoking. He presented me with four of his books—also with a bottle of grape juice. He brought me back in his car and found a better room for me. His courtesy was almost oppressive. He 'worked' me into staying another week.

"As I was going through the grand march that night (I really liked this), a woman left her place and came to greet me with a clasp of the hand. It was Theodore Roosevelt's sister, Mrs. Douglas Robinson. Later I saw her wheeling her daughter down the aisle. It moved me to see this brilliant society woman and poet engaged in such duty, but she did it so sweetly and so entirely without self-consciousness that I admired her the more because of it. She invited me to sit at her table, which included a lively and intellectual group.

One morning as I stood watching the man put notices on the bulletin board, I was surprised and pleased to see the name, "James W. Bashford, Bishop of China," appear.

"At breakfast I met him, a tall, stooping, venerable figure—a shocking change from the man I knew. I introduced myself and we talked of other times. I reminded him of his visit to Dakota in 1884 and told him that his words at that time had started me on my literary career in Boston.

"He is a rather disappointing character to me now. Essentially fine, he is so given to the cant terms of his religion that he repels me. It seems absurd that a man so large as he appears to be should retain so many time-worn phrases. Nevertheless he is a man of power and wide experience. His talk on China was good but not good enough. He sees everything from the standpoint of a Methodist bishop.

"It is plain that the Chinese trusted him, and I can

understand the reason: his frank blue eyes, his genial smile, and his homely good sense were disarming. He was not an official and they could talk with him without committing themselves too far. He could say things to them without in any way involving the United States. Hence he came to know the inside workings of the Japanese and Chinese governments, and stood for China against the demands of the war party in Japan. Some of these conferences were of the most dramatic character; especially so was his interview with Count Kumi, who spoke English perfectly. 'Out of it all China has been saved from the spoiler,' he said."

In the midst of my boredom, Douglas Robinson turned up. He came not as a patient but as a husband and father, to see how his wife and daughter were getting along. He was a huge, plain-featured, but delightfully humorous person, an irrepressible objector to the rules and regulations of the place. After one or two meals he began to plan what would now be called "bootlegging" in the matter of food. "I hear that there is a chicken-pie joint down the street and that some of the boys slip away at intervals for a spree," he said.

"I have heard of this business," I replied, "but I have not yet been down there. I sneak out to the home of a friend, now and then. It is the only excitement this place affords. To plan and carry out a chicken-pie spree is one of its secret rituals."

The cereal coffee especially enraged Robinson, and he fell into the habit of stealthily bringing a can of concentrated coffee to our table. "Waiter!" he would call. "A pitcher of water, boiling hot," and while the girl was gone he would spoon into our cups the proper amount of his

illicit caffeine. In this way, shielded by the bland uncon-
sciousness of his manner, we all shared his beverage, until
the supervisor, sniffing something deliciously contraband
came over to our table one day just as our hot water was
being brought to us. He knew that something forbidden
was going on, but, as a group, we were too powerful to
permit reproof. He greeted us pleasantly and stayed long
enough to see us all add cream and sugar to our hot water!
If he suspected Robinson of having bootleg coffee in his
pocket he did not quite dare to interrogate him—and
soon moved away.

Mrs. Robinson laughed at her intimidated husband
with all the gusto of her famous brother. "I never knew
Douglas to be so bullied," she said, and his look was irresistibly comic as he replied, "No wonder I'm timid; if I
stay here another week feeding on grain and grass and
lettuce, I'll be a rabbit."

One morning as I was coming across the courtyard I
heard a low whistle. Looking up I saw him sitting at a
wide-opened window in his undershirt, surreptitiously
smoking a cigar! With a comical gesture and a twist of
his lips he silently conveyed to me an appeal. "Don't betray me!" and I replied in the sign language, "Certainly
not. Trust me."

He returned to New York a few days later and I soon
followed him, in worse condition than when I arrived.
The regimen, so helpful to others, apparently did not fit
my case.

CHAPTER TWELVE

"A SON OF THE MIDDLE BORDER"

I

GENERAL JOFFRE, the great French general, was the guest of the city on the day of my return to New York, May 9. He was the hero of the hour. He filled the press, he filled the streets, he almost filled the sky with acclamation. All the avenues were gay with the mingled flags of all the allied nations—an effect which had inspired Alfred Noyes' noble poem. "The day was fair and great crowds assembled on Fifth Avenue to see the general pass. My wife and I took our daughters down to meet the procession, which came up as far as Seventy-second Street; but the general's car moved so rapidly that I had no time to observe his features. His progress had nothing of the old-time, leisurely progress of the open barouche with its occupants gracefully bowing from side to side. He swept by as if in fear of bullets.

"In the afternoon I went up to Columbia University to see Dr. Butler confer degrees upon both Joffre and Viviani.

"The crowd was enormous, and the pressure, even in the reserved-seat section, was so great that chairs were overturned. It was a well-dressed and amiable crowd, but so intensely eager to see Joffre that it surged to and fro hysterically. The police were lifted and carried away on

157

these waves of humankind like swimmers in the surf, vainly shouting *'Push back there!'* Those in front were helpless, nothing could be done. The clothing of the throng was rich in color—greens, purples, and yellows."

In the midst of all this promise of victory my friend Edward Wheeler, like many another, was suffering defeat. As we sat at luncheon on the day following the Joffre parade, he said, "I have just returned from burying my wife, and last night I saw my only son start for the military training camp at Plattsburg. This means that in a few months he will be in the French trenches. I feel like a lonely boy. We old fellows must brace one another up hereafter."

I sympathized with him, but could say little to comfort him.

Dining that night with Bessie Potter Vonnoh, I met for the first time Carl Akeley and his wife, both famous as African explorers and elephant hunters. "She is a tall, graceful woman, just beginning to get gray, whilst he, a plain, low-voiced man, is bald and wrinkled. He spoke with a wistful, nasal drone even when describing his battle with a she leopard. 'She weighed only ninety pounds,' he explained with a faint smile, 'but she was all cat! I had no gun or knife and there was nothing to do but throttle her.'"

He told of being struck down by an elephant's trunk and of the animal's attempt to pierce him with its tusks. "I lay unconscious for several hours in the rain, while my black warriors ran to my wife's camp some twenty miles away in a race to bring her to me."

He pictured huge bands of elephants, describing their silence and celerity of movement. He defended the lions from the charge of cowardice and told many stories of them. "He loves the African desert, its sounds, its air, its primeval quality, and is planning to go back to it. This I could understand, for the photographs which he showed reminded me of the old-time Western prairie. I was greatly drawn to the man. He made me think of John McCutcheon the cartoonist. Though born in central New York, he is Mid-Western in type—a modified 'Hoosier.'

"I cannot see in this quiet, gray-haired man an explorer who has been mauled by leopards, hunted by lions, and charged by elephants, and Delia Akeley's case is even more incredible. Slender of form and low-voiced, she seemed loath to confide her own experiences. She did recount, after much urging, the events of a night spent in a hut built of thorns, with a roaring wounded lion a few feet away, and hyenas howling on all sides. 'It was too dark to shoot the lion, and there was nothing to do but wait. When dawn came I was a wreck!' she confessed. 'I wanted to go right home—back to my mother,' she added with a smile. We came away from these delightfully unassuming explorers filled with admiration of their skill and courage."

(The Akeleys seemed to us a devoted and happy pair, but in less than a year they separated, much to our surprise and sorrow, and we saw no more of Delia. She became an explorer on her own account and won still further renown. Akeley himself continued to live across the park from us, and will come again into my record.)

One Sunday, in late May, Edward Wheeler came round in his car and motored us out into White Plains through an exquisite spring landscape. "Dogwood blossoms white as snow lit all the forest shades and the apple trees were clouds of bloom. The lawns were bright with dandelions, and the larks and bobolinks filled the meadows with joy. We lunched under a tree opposite a beautiful orchard, then ran over to Rye Beach, where we clambered the wave-worn rocks and watched the breakers. It was a part of Rye which I had never seen. We came home by way of Pelham, and Wheeler stayed for a piece of home-made shortcake. It was a satisfying day, one of those outings which compensate in some degree for war and sickness."

On Decoration Day I took my daughters across the park to Riverside Drive and there watched the parade, which was decidedly more warlike than a year ago.

"The men marched like disciplined soldiers, and the presence of nurses in khaki testified to a wider spread of the martial spirit—and yet how far all our preparation is from the precision and force of the German armies! My daughters were deeply interested in the pageant, especially in the marching girls. Mary Isabel found in them something especially admirable. Her attitude enabled me to understand how the daughters of my friends had been drawn into the adventure. The crowd psychology now is all for war.

"I have just finished rereading 'Uncle Tom's Cabin,' which I had not seen for forty years. In some ways it is still vital, with far less of a one-sided assault on slavery than my Southern friends still consider it. In fact I found it quite fair. It presents the proper proportion of gentle slave owners, and it pictures the patriarchal system with charm. Naturally, to make out her case, the author depicts one of these lovely groups broken up by death, and the tragic events which followed. But on the whole the book is singularly just, considering the times in which it was written. The workmanship, in the main, is good, although somewhat too preachy in spots."

At the club, Mark Sullivan and I discussed Frederick Duneka's illness and the possibilities of a new manager for Harper's.

"Reports are that he is completely out of the running. If this is true, it marks the tragic end of a bright man, one who gave himself to the work of carrying a heavily burdened ancient and honorable house through its period of depression. He came to the firm when it was on the point of bankruptcy and for seventeen years he has given his best thought to the job of keeping the firm afloat." (I did not say so, but I had heard that Mark might be asked to take Duneka's place.)

Meanwhile my manuscript, "A Son of the Middle Border," had gone to the printer; and as soon as it had reached the stage of page proof, Marsh of Macmillan's, without my knowledge, sent to several of my best friends sets of the unbound sheets. For nearly five years I had been carrying this manuscript about with me, ceaselessly revising it. It had all been rewritten five times and some of it ten times; but a sense of its incompleteness troubled me even after it had departed out of my control.

"I cannot plead age and sickness; it must go to the public without explanation of its author's disability."

"July 23. I was made very happy to-day by two letters, one from Fuller and one from Howells. Both had read the advance sheets of 'A Son of the Middle Border,' and found little or nothing to change in it. Howells is especially commendatory, and his judgment is of the greatest possible comfort to Marsh as well as to me. Brett, the head of the firm, now predicts a very large acceptance of the book. He promises a strong campaign for it. 'We will start the season with a rush,' he declared. 'We are certain to sell thirty thousand copies.' I hope he is right, but I have had so many disappointments during the last three years that I shall not count too confidently even on a moderate success."

II

As July deepened, the necessity for a summer refuge became acute. And with the plan to visit Orlando Rouland at Onteora, John Burroughs at Roxbury, and Frederick Dellenbaugh at Cragsmoor, I took the Hudson River boat for Kingston, hoping to find on this triangular outing a small cottage in which my family could camp for the summer.

The boat was uncomfortably crowded, but the day was unexpectedly cool and I thoroughly enjoyed the glorious river scenery. At Kingston, however, I took a small and rather grimy train for Tannersville, a train which was even more crowded than the boat had been. But in ten minutes after leaving the station, I found myself in a very charming hill country. Soon the Ashokan Lake on the left, running toward high blue hills, presented such beauty that I marveled at its neglect. Glorious with color, it had something of the charm of Lago Maggiore. As the train went higher the hills became more and more like mountains and the air took on a delightful coolness.

In ten minutes after arriving at Tannersville, I was knocking at the door of Rouland's picturesque, broad-roofed cottage on the side of the hill. It was about five o'clock in the afternoon. Mrs. Rouland, after greeting me, said, "Here are some good friends of yours."

These good friends were Mrs. Ben Ali Haggin and Mrs. Edward MacDowell, who had come down to greet me. This cordial interest was not only unexpected, but very grateful. It made Onteora less remote.

"As night fell, Orlando built a fire in the huge chimney, and the air was keen enough to make the blaze enjoyable. Evidently he considered me an ailing man; for when the time came for me to retire, he took down an old-fashioned copper bed warmer which stood beside the fireplace, filled it with embers, and warmed the sheets of my bed. I protested against this luxury as unseasonable. 'It is not called for by my physical condition.' Nevertheless it was an attention which I thoroughly appreciated."

On the following afternoon, the Roulands gave a little tea for me, and I was surprised to find that several other of my friends had cottages here. All were very kind and expressed such an interest in my coming to the park that I began to consider it. Under Mrs. Rouland's guidance I inspected a rude little cabin near by which was for rent; and I immediately decided to take it for the remainder of the summer. It was hardly more than a hunter's shack, but it offered shelter.

While waiting for my wife and daughters, I visited Mrs. Alexander, who lived on the side of Onteora Mountain.

"Her windows command a superb view of the southern Catskills. John's studio is pathetically complete, ideally right, but he never used it. He was already death-stricken, even while it was building. Mrs. Alexander worships his memory, and I can understand that, for he was one of the most delightful men I ever knew—humorous, loyal, self-sacrificing, and a great painter."

"August 2. My wife and daughters came at six and were delighted with the cabin, the blue hills, and the apple trees. 'The heat in the city was dreadful!' my wife reported. 'We can scarcely believe in our good fortune in getting to this mountain home.'

"There is great charm in a location like this. The view of the Rip Van Winkle peaks across the fields of buckwheat to the south is most satisfying. This morning we saw the mist in the valley below us. The sun-lighted range can be seen as we lie in our beds."

"August 15 a busy day! At one we gave a luncheon with John Burroughs as guest of honor and at four Mrs. Rouland held a 'Recipe Party' at which Uncle John wearing a long apron acted as cook and baked a huge pile of slapjacks. He was as deft as a woman at this task. At night he came over and sat by our fire while my daughters and I sang some of the old-time songs of the border. He made a grand picture dreaming in the light of our chimney, which brought out the elemental quality of his face."

He told us much of his youth in this region and of his life in Washington during the war. "I went to Washington intending to be a soldier," he said, "and if I could have gone straight to the front as a scout or as a gunner, I would have done it, but I dreaded the everlasting drill. The hustling of men from place to place as if they were cattle disgusted me. I knew I couldn't stand that." He told of his first meeting with Whitman, who appealed to him as if he were "the first man." "I wrote 'Wake Robin' while acting as a guard in the treasury, with nothing before my eyes but an iron door," he said. He described General Grant, who came to inspect the treasury. "He was a modest, quiet man—sturdy of build."

(I have on my mantel a photograph of him sitting in the firelight glow, craggily strong and weather-worn, his face wrinkled, his hands knotted. He was nearing the end of his path and I saw his fate in the ashes on the hearth. He loved the good old earth and was loath to leave it.)

Up to this date, as my readers have no doubt discerned, shadows predominated on my trail from West Salem to Onteora. Now came a lifting of the clouds. One Sunday morning, August 16, I limped up the pathway to our gate and brought back the New York *Times*. As I opened the Book Review supplement, I was amazed to find its first two pages filled with an analysis of "A Son of the Middle Border" written by William Dean Howells. Quite overwhelmed at this beautiful tribute to my chronicle, I set down my feeling at the moment in these words:

"This review undoubtedly marks an epoch in my literary life. Howells is old, I am passing to middle age, and this book represents the past, hence this tribute undoubtedly marks the highest point of my achievement. I began life as a farmer and school-teacher, and to have won a certain place as a Western novelist ought to have satisfied me; but it did not. This review leads me to hope that I can do better work than anything I have yet done. Howells is too kind in his judgment; I am still the learner, but his praise helps me to go on."

"August 17. The book of tributes to Howells which came from Harper's this morning, surprised and delighted me by its sumptuousness. It is far handsomer than the volume I had in mind. 'There is a deal of Garland in it,' I wrote Howells, 'but for this I shall not be held accountable. I designed the program and gathered most of the tributes—there is no concealing that—but I had no expectation that the men would write to me in just that way. It can't be changed now.' "

"August 20. A review of my book in the *Evening Sun* adds to my sense of security concerning its reception, for in this case the critic is unknown to me. To have both the *Tribune* and the *Sun* find the volume worth while is reassuring. My friend Brett of Macmillan's, who is greatly interested in the book, writes to say that he is placing it among his ten best books; and as he is considered one of the shrewdest men in the business, I take this to heart as another encouragement. The Garland fortunes are on the mend!"

"September 14. This is my fifty-seventh birthday and from my window I am watching some men reaping a field of buckwheat. One of the harvesters is swinging an old-fashioned cradle and another is raking and binding after. Their action carries me back fifty years to a farm in a little Wisconsin coulee. I recall my father and uncles cradling wheat in just this way. As I watch these men I am moved as by some noble poem."

My daughters brought to me their presents and at dinner Mary Isabel proudly set before me a birthday cake of her own making. It was a merry birthday dinner notwithstanding my years and lameness. My daughters, gay as crickets, waited upon me as if I were a king.

CHAPTER THIRTEEN

MY MIDDLE BORDER CHRONICLE PLEASES

I

ONE afternoon as I was walking up the road to the Onteora Inn, I passed a barn door from which a rhythmic, throbbing sound came—a familiar sound—the beat of flails. On looking in upon the scene I discovered three old men threshing buckwheat, something I had not seen for half a century. I had imagined it a lost art.

"Could any scene be farther from modern warfare? In Europe they are killing one another with new guns, new gases, new bombs, and the latest designs of tanks and flying machines; whilst here, in the infinite peace of a September day, three middle-aged farm hands are threshing grain out of straw precisely as their ancestors did it a hundred years ago. The threshers were of that faded, left-behind type which I have discovered in the high, lonesome valleys. Some of these backwoodsmen bear fine Knickerbocker names, degenerate scions of their family trees."

Notwithstanding our isolation in a cabin on the slope of Onteora Mountain, we now and then came in contact with some of our soldiers on leave for some cause or other. Our neighbor Dr. Edward Jones brought his brother Paul to see us one evening, and from him we drew a stirring account of the tragic retreat of the Serbians, a movement which he shared and has written about. "I am now trying to get into our army," he said.

It was difficult to believe that this smiling, handsome boy had shared in such epic experiences. (Later he put them into a book, a vivid and powerful narrative which is valuable historical material.)

On my return to New York in October I found myself in the position of a literary "comeback." All my acquaintances, even those who had only read the reviews, congratulated me somewhat as the friends of a prize fighter felicitate him on having recovered his "punch." This was pleasing but a bit shocking, for it clearly revealed how definitely some of my best friends had considered me a "dead duck." An old Chicago friend and fellow craftsman, Will Payne, expressed this change of attitude handsomely by saying, "Yesterday I paid you the singular compliment of buying your 'Son of the Middle Border.' No writer ever buys another writer's books, unless forced to do so. I congratulate you."

Another friend, John Phillips, remarked with mock resentment, "You beat me to it! I ought to have done that book myself."

Admitting that I had come back mentally, I was still far from a physical rejuvenation. Nevertheless on October 24, I started in to edit all my diaries and notes, with intent to put them into permanent form. I found in them much valuable material, but on many pages I discovered to my dismay that the spirit of the event I had too briefly recorded had vanished utterly. The line which was to serve as a chain to drag up a whole sequence of recollections came up, in many cases, disappointingly bare.

"Whether this is due to my depleted condition or to the fact that the impressions on my brain are hopelessly dimmed, I cannot say. If I go on with the story of 'A Son of the Middle Border,' these records are essential. It may be that I shall publish the diaries as they stand. They go back to 1898 and, while very condensed, every page offers something to think about."

Irving Bacheller, who had been in Europe all summer, came to dinner late in the month and related many incidents of the battlefields. He had been under fire on several of the front lines and was filled with admiration of the Allies. "He has lost flesh, but is in good health and spirits. It is always a pleasure to have him with us. We are all fond of the big, gray-haired poet; for he is, in spirit, a poet."

Dining at the Roulands' with the Bachellers on November 1, we found John Burroughs there. It was an intimate party and "Oom John," as some of us call him, enjoyed it keenly.

"I've been living alone at Riverby and cooking my own food all the fall," he confessed, "and I'm tired of it. It's a little like living in a tomb. I shan't go back unless my son Julian comes to live with me. A house like that needs young life in it."

The picture he drew recalled my own father's later years—a lonely old soldier, cooking and house-tending, and I said, "John, I don't like your doing that, you're too old to live alone."

"I begin to feel that," he replied.

At the home of Dr. Fenton B. Turck, on November 3,

I met Cochrane, the Minister of Railways in Canada, a fine man of large frame.

"Turck showed us all through his amazing house, which is filled with paintings, carved furniture, ancient vases, and Chinese curios. His career is another American fairy story. As the son of a Milwaukee financier he early went into biology, then into medicine, retaining, however, his scientific bent. He is a lover of research. I learned that his ancestors were Dutch and had been pioneers in the Hudson River Valley. I had met him as a physician in Chicago but could hardly call him an acquaintance. Archeology appears to be his 'recreation.'"

Dining with Mrs. Pottle, we met Elon Hooker and a Mr. Baker, an Englishman, and heard much talk concerning the war.

I had met Hooker when he was the treasurer of the "Bull Moose Party," but this was my first intimate talk with him. He quickly won my friendship and my admiration. "He is a handsome man in the prime of life, tall, dark, and smiling. His lineage is as American as my own, going back to Pilgrim times. Enormously successful as a business man, he manifests ideals aside from his business. Although a Republican, he is not violently partisan, and yet the administration cannot rise to the point of making use of him. Apparently it is still a 'Democratic' war. Hooker could be of enormous service, but is set aside as of no account, probably because of his friendship for Roosevelt.

"He spoke confidentially of the recent discovery of a most terrifying gas. 'It is possible to destroy whole cities with gases,' he said. 'Undoubtedly the use of poisonous vapor will play a dominant part in this conflict and in all the wars of the future.'

"There was something appalling in these statements by a cultivated and charming man whose faultless evening dress and smiling face made his grisly prophecies incredible. In fairness to him I must record that we drew these predictions from him by persistent questioning."

II

For nearly a hundred times and in much the same fashion, I have called on Howells in one or another of his many New York homes, always to the effect of finding him just having arrived, or just about to go away. "What a strange, wandering, nomadic life he and his daughter have led in the years of our acquaintance. He seemed more at home at York Harbor than in any other place, and yet that did not seem to be permanent. It is only his summer place. He looked old to-day [November 10], old and sad. Nevertheless, he jested: 'I have had, lately, a disturbing irregularity in my heart action. It goes along very well for a time, then skips a beat, and I, being mortal, am reminded of it, and cannot sleep; nevertheless I pretend to write each morning,' he added, and in his tone was an admission that writing had ceased to matter very much. In all that he uttered I detected a substratum of despair. Once he misspoke. 'I read it to my wife,' he began, then paused, 'I mean my daughter.' And the correction was especially significant to me."

Still concerned about his condition, I called on him a few days later. "I fear my heart is more deeply affected than I realize," he said, and in certain lights he was hardly recognizable.

"From one point of view his failing is tragic but from another it is but natural," I said to my wife. "He is full of honor as well as of years. His children and his grand-children live near him and he is free from anxiety concerning income. He wants to see you and our daughters and has arranged to come to-morrow afternoon."

He came, looking much better than the day before. "He seemed to enjoy my daughters who were at once attracted by him. He jested with them and appeared to renew his youth with them. Mary Isabel showed him the original illustrations for my book and expressed her love for West Salem. In return he described his summer home in Maine. Unspoken, yet in his mind (as in mine), was the fear that this might be the last time he would ever come under my roof; and as he was leaving he stooped to kiss each of my daughters, a gesture which touched me deeply.

"So long have I known him—thirty years—and soon he will be only a gracious memory. A tragic thing to think of! No, not tragic, for his life is lived."

Although I had written Howells immediately after seeing his review of my book, and had attempted to voice my grateful thanks, he would not listen. He was interested, however, when I described the many letters I was receiving from my readers. "They all urge me to write another volume. They want to know what followed. 'Did your mother get her new daughter? What became of David and Burton?' they ask. I am inclined to meet this demand."

"Why not?" replied Howells quickly, decisively. "You distinctly hinted at a sequel."

"I know I did and I should like to go on with the story but I am doubtful of my powers. My readers expect too much of me. If the second volume could be a continuation and not a sequel, criticism of it might not be so severe."

I did not say so, but my physical condition entered into this mood of hesitation. While each day revealed to me more clearly the fact that in telling the stories of the migrating families, I had told the stories of thousands of other pioneers, I realized that as I came nearer the present, my task would grow in complexity. Nevertheless I was minded to attempt it. "What better work can I do?" I asked myself.

Mark Sullivan when I saw him next added his word of encouragement. "Go ahead on a second volume," he said. "All your readers expect it. The horror of the war will make the times you write about all the more alluring. You should lose no time. Work while you are in the mood for it."

This advice, joined with my own feeling that the work must be done soon or not at all, sent me back to a study of my notebooks and diaries, and the following morning I wrote the first chapter of "A Daughter of the Middle Border," taking up the story at the precise point where the first volume had ended. As I wrote, I saw the two books bound in one cover, a continuous narrative, so that as the reader finished the first part, he had but to turn a page and begin upon the second and concluding part.

Each morning I reëntered the past. I forgot the war. I heard again the gay voices of my fellows. I saw their faces unlined of care and my hair untouched of gray. Again my world was vigorous, hopeful, and serene. Dreaming of those glorious days I forgot my pain and my disheartenment.

Unable to sit at my desk, I propped myself on a couch

and wrote on a pad with a pencil. To make composition still more difficult, the court on which my window opened was both noisy and odorous. However, these conditions had their value. They gave me perspective on my material. I saw the period of my marriage and the coming of my daughters in sun-lit vistas, and this sense of remoteness—a feeling which the war had deepened—enabled me to write of intimate things with a detachment which gave them historical value.

"As my 'Son of the Middle Border' chronicled the life of a typical family of Western settlers, so the story of my Chicago life must have something equally representative. In relating my own domestic joys and cares, I shall be delineating the lives of other families in the West and elsewhere. As the first volume dealt with the centrifugal forces of American life—the era for exploration—so in this volume the centripetal forces, the passion for cities and crowds, must find expression."

III

"November 26. Feeling more like work than for a month, I went ahead all morning on my new volume. At night we all went down to see John Drew in 'Lord Quex.' It is not an inspiring play, but as a carefully carpentered piece of comedy, it had one big acting scene which Drew thoroughly enjoyed—although he is getting old, like the rest of us. As I met him at the club wearing thick lenses, I wonder if he is not suffering serious trouble. His eyes have always been a little abnormal; now he frankly worries about them."

My loyal friend Edward Clement of the Boston *Transcript* lunched with me at the club one day, and we had much talk of "the good old days" when he was editor and I, a youth in the street, came climbing timidly up the long stairway to his office. It was strange and a little sad to have him look up to me as a famous and successful author. He said, "You have immortalized me in just the way I would wish to be recorded, as one who aided young and struggling genius." He seemed old, almost as old as Howells, but he is still writing a daily column. He had (to a perceptible degree) the timidity and the deprecation of the octogenarian, and this hurt me. We parted with a feeling that we might not meet again. "I too, am in the zone of the problematic in human life."

Dining that night with President Butler, I found Brander Matthews among the guests. After dinner Butler, who had been to England, told us many interesting things about the war and showed us some of the ferocious posters which the Germans had put up in Belgian towns. They were incredibly harsh. "I find Butler a delightful host. He is able, keen, and resourceful. His executive ability is amazing. He is doing four men's work, yet never shows weariness or depression. He is fitted for the largest public office. He would make an admirable minister to St. James'."

At Mrs. Haggin's I met Poultney Bigelow again. "Bigelow is an intellectual tonic. No one can predict what he will say next. Professor Harvey Robinson was in the party, a small, silent man whose manner is repellent. He has the reputation of being a savage iconoclast but does not look it. Bigelow on the contrary is unexpectedly delightful in his cynical comment. He has had a most amazing career and his judgments are as unconventional as they are amusing. He was very friendly and expressed pleasure in the fact that we were neighbors in the Cats-kill country. I enjoyed his racy talk immensely. His violent prejudices do not shock me; they interest me."

After a luncheon with the League for Political Education at the Astor on December 8, my wife and I rode home with Mrs. Shanewald.

"Dr. Lyman Abbott was in the car and we found him charming though weighted by the burden of his years. Like Howells and Burroughs he knows that his life is going out at a time of world disaster. He spoke of Howells and I said, 'He went South to-day. I am glad he is out of stormy New York. It hurts me to see him take on the timidity of age.'

"Ray Stannard Baker (David Grayson) came to supper and quite won my daughters who love his 'Adventures in Contentment.' He talked about the war—it is impossible to keep from doing that—and admitted that the outlook is especially depressing. 'The signing of a truce with Russia will enable Germany to transfer a million of her troops to the Western Front,' he said. 'This may mean the giving way of the Western line. No one can predict what is to come, but our responsibility increases week by week.' "

In spite of the war and my disablement, we had a happy Christmas time. "It is useless to assume the world's woes. We end the year in fair condition, happy in the success of my 'Middle Border' chronicle, which seems likely to keep on selling in a moderate way."

CHAPTER FOURTEEN

MY ELECTION TO THE ACADEMY

I

NOTWITHSTANDING a cold wind and a sense of diminishing vitality, I got down to the club on January 2 (1918). Mark Sullivan, who met me there, said, "I am no longer the editor of *Collier's Weekly*, although I am writing for it."

"He did not seem in the least depressed by the change in his status and I expressed my gratitude once more. 'You were a wondrous help to me just when I most needed it. Your acceptance of my "Middle Border" chronicle not only put several thousand dollars into my hands, but prepared the way for its publication as a book. Your belief in it and your determination to print it serially are facts which I shall remember gratefully all the days of my life. You may pass from *Collier's* altogether but you are certain to step into something larger. You are fitted to be the editor of a great publishing firm, and I hope to live till I see you in such a chair.' "

We discussed the growing use of the woman libertine in the novel as well as the play. I said, "Our young writers call it liberty; I call it license."

"Have you seen Jesse Lynch's play, 'Why Marry?'?" he asked. "If you haven't, do so. Jesse is poking fun at the free-love theorists. It is very deft and amusing."

Shortly after this, Williams invited my wife and me to see his play. My comment reads: "I value this work by a friend and fellow craftsman. Jesse is a neat workman. His piece is compact, clean cut, witty, and essentially fine. As a father and as a decent citizen, he resents the pornographic obsession of the day, and in 'Why Marry?' takes a whack at it. It is a highly diverting and well-written comedy, a little like Bernard Shaw, human as well as humorous, presenting a real problem without obvious preaching.

"Nat Goodwin, who played the old Judge, was but a ghastly effigy of his former self. He made me feel aged, for I remembered him as a star in the eighties.

"Jesse, who was called behind the scenes between the acts, returned to say, 'Nat is in tears because two or three of his lines have been taken away from him. He is childish now and difficult to manage.' The thought of Nat Goodwin in tears rather took away from my pleasure in the final act of the play. He is old and poor and at the end of his career."

On January 8, though hardly able to walk, I went down to the Women's University Club and gave a talk on "The Middle Border." Many Western people were in the hall and at the close of my address they thronged about me, each one eager to tell me how much she had enjoyed my allusions to things deeply buried in her memory. There was something inspirational in this. "No one else has voiced these homely facts of Western life in the same way," they said.

"There is something almost sacred in the deep-laid memories which my words call up. There is a source of power here if I can lay hold upon it."

While we were at dinner on January 11, a telegram came from Brander Matthews announcing my election to membership in the American Academy. I was delighted to have the announcement of this honor come to me by way of Matthews whom I had known so many years. He wrote: "You had the largest number of votes of any candidate. You went in with a cheer." Later, Robert Underwood Johnson, the secretary, called me and said: "Your election comes as a result of your latest book, 'A Son of the Middle Border.'"

In the glow of these and other messages I set to work with fresh resolution on the second volume of my chronicle, a sequel which my readers were already demanding.

At the Poetry Society dinner on January 31, John Masefield (looking very serious and worried) was the guest of honor. The program was varied. Padraic Colum spoke with wistful intonation, as usual, Grace Hazard Conkling read a nice little speech, and Vachel Lindsay chanted a poem. Edward Wheeler was presiding officer, gracious and tactful, and the program moved off pleasantly.

"Lindsay became almost comical as he stood on the platform ecstatically chanting his 'Chinese Nightingale.' Swaying rhythmically with closed eyes, as if blissfully swimming in the mist of his own conjuration, he provoked smiles. I like his earlier work, but some of the pretentious lines of his later verses are rather cheap. He seems a very real poet gone wrong. I prefer his smaller poems—those which show care and genuine artistry."

"February 2. Taking my courage in both hands I got out early and went down to Macmillan's carrying the

signed contract for 'A Daughter of the Middle Border.'
While there I discussed ways and means with Edward
Marsh and Harold Latham, both of whom are disposed
to take the future of these two books very seriously. 'Go
on,' they said, 'and with all possible speed.' This I shall
do."

The date of the "Vigilantes" dinner was February 5
and as Roosevelt was expected to be present I went down
to meet him. He was too ill to appear, however, a fact
which deeply disturbed us all. "Augustus Thomas presided and Mayor John P. Mitchel, looking very handsome in his uniform, made a stirring speech. Julian Street
was quietly amusing and Hermann Hagedorn eloquently
earnest. But the meeting was not what it would have
been had Roosevelt been present. It scares me to have
him admit to an illness.

"As I went down Madison Avenue, I passed two close-
packed masses of soldiers, several regiments of them, all
pink-faced and stalwart, standing in the fleecy, falling
snow, awaiting orders to march. This picture brought the
war very close to me. These superb young men are on
their way to France—to fill the trenches, to fight mud,
lice, and rats. Many of them will never return. Their
ability to endure cold and hunger and toil is marvelous to
me now, and should go to some better purpose than killing Germans."

II

One of my friends and literary coworkers, Fred Lewis
Pattee of the State College of Pennsylvania, had booked
me for a lecture before his students on March 1, a trip
which I dreaded, for I was obliged to leave the sleeper at

five in the morning and drive for several miles across country.

"Pattee in a car with his daughter as driver met me at Lemont and took me to his home at the college—a surprisingly modest home for the head of a department employing seventeen teachers, but it was a bookish home. I found the school pleasingly rural. It lies off the main line of railway and has a decidedly back-country tone which I like. I am in the real America.

"Pattee who specializes in the history of American fiction has read all the books of all the authors he treats —a tremendous task. In the main, his judgments are sound. At night some twenty-five or thirty of his friends came in to meet me and I talked to them informally of Clemens, Riley, Kipling, Joaquin Miller, Harte, and other of my acquaintances. They were nearly all teachers of history or English and seemed to find pleasure in my reminiscences. 'You brought the world of letters very close to us,' some of them said. It may be that addresses of this kind should be a part of my work hereafter. In the privacy of our talk Pattee admitted that he had made large use of my 'Crumbling Idols.' I am pleased to have this forgotten volume salvaged in this way."

III

Taking an early train, I went on to Washington. Soldiers were everywhere, and the trig figures of men in khaki uniform, mostly majors, gave an air of military authority to the Cosmos Club, where I took lunch. I saw Robert Millikan there, handsome and debonair, his work at Chicago temporarily abandoned. "Edward Deming, Herbert Quick, and I ate together. Mark Sullivan came in a little later. Quick resembles an elderly and somewhat garrulous country lawyer. 'The success of your autobiography,' he said, 'stimulates me—I'm going to try something like it myself. I lived through many of the same experiences.'

"Mark Sullivan, who has moved to Washington and is writing news letters for a press syndicate, said, 'I have a high valuation of your friend Leland Summers, who is assistant to Bernard Baruch. He is head of the Raw Materials Department. He is a great little man, an indispensable man to Baruch—so much so that Baruch has taken him into his house. He calls him "Buster" on account of his youthful appearance, and he wants him at his elbow every minute, day or night. The President is reported to have given Baruch greater authority than any other American ever possessed—and he in turn has passed this authority on to Summers.' "

Through Lee's influence, Mark and I were invited to lunch at Baruch's house, a handsome house with a noble dining room, and as we four sat at table I had opportunity to study the man on whom the President had conferred such illimitable command.

"He is a Spanish Jew, tall, handsome, genial. During the luncheon he took from his pocket the letter of the President and gave me an opportunity to read it. It was all in Wilson's rather commonplace handwriting, almost as commonplace as print, but the content of it was appalling. It made Baruch assistant dictator. 'To what far region have we come when power so vast is granted in a brief letter?' I thought as I handed it to Mark.

"Baruch is plainly feeling the weight of his job. He

seems more like an artist or a literary man than a big
business man and presents little evidence of the power
and decision which his position demands. He does not
appear the man for the job. 'I don't know why I am
here,' he admitted. 'My mind is not orderly; it is in-
tuitive.' There is something gentle in his voice. He is a
strong man, but not strong in the sense that General
Wood is strong. He is no Roosevelt. He does not impress
me as being as able as Julius Rosenwald. He is likely to be
sharply criticized. He was plainly despondent and so was
Summers."

On our way home I said some of these things to Sullivan,
who disagreed with me. "Baruch is a bigger man than
he seems at first sight. He needs Lee Summers, however.
Summers is a wonder. Baruch can't afford to be out of
his reach, not for an hour. Summers has an encyclopedic
knowledge of minerals and gases."

On the following day, while visiting Summers at his
office in one of the temporary buildings down on the flat
land, I spoke of his position and he retorted with a smile,
"I *have* no position, no title, no salary—and all the authority in the world, so long as Baruch and the President
back me up." While I sat there I heard him commandeer
(by way of the phone) all the iridium in the market.
"We need it for the tips of our carburetors," he explained,
and as he spoke he looked like a boy of nineteen, small,
blond, round-faced, and blue-eyed.

He had been my neighbor in Chicago and I knew him
as a very able "consulting engineer," whose wife, Eve
Brodlique, was a member of our literary group. Lee's
knowledge of minerals and their by-products, and of
electricity, gas, and high explosives, had made him an

authority in such matters and Baruch was very properly taking advantage of his skill.

Washington was wholly official, military, or scientific, and I felt set apart, an old fellow speaking a different language from all these young bureaucrats. "It is of no use to stay here," I wrote. "Nothing presents itself to me as worth writing about; that is to say, reporting is not my lay. I leave this war to the younger men. My business now is with the past. I shall return to New York and go on with my chronicle."

A letter from Brand Whitlock concerning "A Son of the Middle Border" confirmed me in this decision. He spoke of his entrance with me into the Academy and suggested that my "Middle Border" should be translated into French.

IV

Shortly after my return to New York I met Basil King for the first time.

"He is tall and plain-featured, with no eyebrows at all. He wore a pair of dark glasses. I found him attractive and not as repellent, physically, as had been reported. He was rather ministerial in manner but affable. He interested me. He is a Canadian, but has lived in Cambridge for many years. 'I got rather suffocated there,' he confessed, 'and so I am settled here. I was in Washington for a time, but found it too crowded and too intensely political.' . . . There was a time when King's novels had a vogue; but they are losing place."

At six, on March 20, Edward Wheeler came for us, and took us to his lovely apartment where he had provided a delicious dinner. After dinner he read to us several

letters from his soldier son, letters which not only gave
vivid pictures of the war zone but rang high and true
in their loyalty. "I am passing from one gorgeous experience to another," he wrote, "and seeing the good in
each."

His lines gave more of the wonder and the adventure of
overseas service than any correspondence I have seen.
Wheeler was admirable in his comment on them. "They
make me feel the bigness of our campaign over there," he
said.

The first of April brought almost summer heat, and
the buds suddenly started to unfold. "In the midst of
this spring ecstasy, Florence Easton, one of our Wisconsin
friends, came to call with her little boy and told us of
the wreckage of her home by the war. Her husband is
'Over There' as a surgeon, and her brother Clark sailed
yesterday. Her case is typical. She has no home now and
no plan of life. Altogether the day was filled with emotion, making writing impossible. The war spirit clouds
even this glorious sky."

Lorado Taft came in on April 18 and we lunched together at the Century Club. He came to dinner and
spent the evening talking of Chicago and of a scheme
for civic clubs in small towns.

"Together we saw a performance of Tarkington's play,
'Seventeen,' a very amusing and faithful picture of a
well-to-do Western family. We enjoyed it keenly. Mrs.
Gregg, a Scotch woman from Paris, who sat with us,
said, 'This is the first play I have ever seen in my whole
life'—an amazing statement. She has had one son killed
and two others are on the firing line. Her drawn and
tragic face brought the war very close. I was glad to

see that the play enabled her to forget her sorrows for the moment. 'It makes me think of my own boys when they were at that age,' she said.

"What a curious combination of experiences for her! To see a play for the first time, in one of the most beautiful of our theaters, in the company of friends she had known in carefree days, surrounded by people untouched by war!"

Charles Elmer, an Onteora neighbor, came for me in his car on the 22d, and took me to Horace Mann School, where I repeated my talk on "The Middle Border" to great applause. Being in a facetious mood, I went so far as to sing "O'er the Hills in Legions, Boys," to the delight of the audience. "It was all on a dangerously intimate plane, but my auditors liked it, and with no reporters in evidence I permitted myself to be almost as funny as I could. The people crowded around me at the close of the talk to tell me how much it had meant to them, and their enthusiasm made me feel more deeply than ever the historical value of this material. In it lies something of growing appeal to a Middle Western public."

On April 24, I met Howells and his daughter in a Madison Avenue car. He was looking feeble and white. He said, "We are just up from Carolina." When I asked him how he liked the South, he replied with something of his accustomed humor, "I like it better the farther North I go." As he started to leave the car, Mildred steadied him with her hand. He walks uncertainly, although he moves with vigor.

"He cannot stay with us long. He has never been an outdoor man, never a farmer like Burroughs, and his powers of locomotion are less enduring. Burroughs reports himself boiling sap in the open on his eighty-first birthday; but Howells, I fear, will not even walk in the park this year. They are the two historical figures in our literary world—our landmarks. We can hope to have them only for a few years, perhaps only for a few months."

V

Early in May, Albert Paine took me in his car and carried me out to Redding where he owned a little bungalow. It was a glorious ride and I enjoyed every moment of it. I was surprised by the beauty of the Westchester lakes created by the city water system. All along the road the trees were coming into bud, and some of the shrubs were in flower. I rejoiced in the sense of being once again in the country. I cooked both luncheon and dinner, but Albert helped in the dishwashing. That night, as we sat about the fire, I read to him several chapters of the manuscript of my autobiography and was greatly encouraged by his comment. "You have handled the chapter on 'Choosing the Daughter' with taste and candor," he said.

He told many stories of Mark Twain, and after luncheon drove me up to "Stormfield," Mark's last home. I found it a bleak spot, not at all the home I had imagined it to be.

"It stands on a barren ridge with a wide view to the northeast, and is rapidly decaying, a melancholy monument to the homesick folly of a great man. Albert was in large measure responsible for its building."

May 7 was the night of the big Roosevelt meeting in Carnegie Hall. Fairchild presided and Senator Owen spoke. It was all pretty dull and slow till the colonel himself came in, walking across the platform with the stride of a youth of thirty. He not only appeared entirely fit but spoke with fire and humor. In fact he spoke un-usually well, and his voice reached every ear in the vast hall. "I am all for putting the war through if it takes ten years," was his message.

On June 5 the Edwin Markhams came to dinner.

"The old poet was delightfully naïve and hearty. His appetite was keen and my daughters enjoyed feeding him. He explained, 'I go without breakfast as a rule, and as I had but a light luncheon, I am ready for a full meal.' He shared heartily in it all—the meat, the vegetables, the salad, and frankly asked for a second helping of dessert. As he ate, he talked of his poverty as candidly as a child. He spoke of his son as a proud father should. He ad-dressed my young daughters as if they were pupils and he a lecturer on 'The Development of Poetry' and withal they found him delightful. In some ways he is a farmer, in all ways he is the diametric opposite of Howells, who never lectures, never monologues, and never utters a random word.

"Markham is a poet, and conscious of it. He is a poet all the time. He thinks and lives the character. He is as didactic as a college professor in some moods and in others quite humble and receptive. He gives out power, but not with discretion. He is poor, but does not permit that to cloud his shining face."

VI

In Onteora, June 10, I worked nearly all day at repairs about our cabin and succeeded in laming myself most successfully without doing very much else. In fact there was very little to do but write or sleep.

"Our neighbors are not yet in residence and our evenings are intensely still and peaceful. The war, which increases in ferocity every day, reaches us only when the paper comes at eleven each morning, black with horrors. I read it and discuss the war with detachment. As a man of fifty-eight and crippled, I am out of it. I intend to aid in every way possible, but I cannot agonize over it—to do so would end my writing. The cool, rainy weather continues, making work difficult for me. I succeeded in getting in an hour or two early in the morning, but for the most part I sit on the porch in the sun. At night I read to my children before the fire.

"A very moving letter from Augustus Thomas concerning the 'Middle Border' came this day—one of the warmest tributes I have yet had and one which I deeply appreciate by reason of Augustus' long friendship and the candor of all his previous criticism. It came while I was busy with carpenter work about the cabin, thus offering another violent contrast in my life. I am making revisions on Volume II. We are very quiet here now, with no neighbors of any sort.

"In my spare time I am rereading 'Lorna Doone.' To speak candidly, I find it clumsy, long-winded, and dull, but the author has ready powers of characterization. It could be made a better book by blue-penciling. The writers of that day did not (apparently) practice compression —or revision. This story slouches along interminably, making much of little things and too little of large things. It has no proportion or 'drive,' but it has style. It begins on a gravely sweet tone and maintains it to the end. It is this 'quality' (as the painters call it) which unifies the picture."

Young Paul Jones, who has been for some months

studying aviation in Toronto, came to call June 12 and we were all greatly interested in what he told us of the art of flying. "I failed," he told us, "because of some lack of coördination between my feet and my hands. It is all a question of balance." He spoke of the brutality of his commanding officer whose attitude made the men unfit to fly. "He should have steadied us rather than put us in a nervous rage."

Dr. Jones asked me to drive with him to look up some cattle. I accepted and in an hour found myself among a kind of degenerate hill-billy people, very like the poor whites of the South, only here the faces were swarthy as well as lean.

"They appeared to be a mixture of degenerate whites and Delaware Indians. I suspect that all this high country is filled with just such offshoots. The tradition is that during the Revolutionary War many Tories fled into these lonely valleys to avoid conscription."

Thomas B. Harned sent me a bundle of portraits of Whitman and a copy of the booklet recording the Camden tribute of 1889. "It is hard to realize that Harned is almost an octogenarian and Traubel an old man sick unto death. So passes the world to which I belong, while the sun shines on my back and the good green grass continues its unfaltering cheer.

"My second volume begins to take shape and I think of sending it away to Sullivan. I have fitted up a little shack below the cottage, a kind of wooden tent under the trees, and am working there. The concentration which this isolation permits is beginning to show in my manuscript. My shoulder is now so lame that I cannot lift my pen to the ink bottle; but by dipping the pen with my left hand and passing it to my right I am able to keep going. It is as though my right hand were a separate, feebler entity. In this desperate spirit, I toil. I *must* get this record in readable shape this summer. There are good pages in it, but I can see a thousand places which need revision. I have not succeeded in keeping my pain out of it. It reads fairly well, but needs enriching here and there. Certain parts which are too trivial or too personal must come out.

"Each evening, I read a chapter or two of Joe Lincoln's 'Obadiah' to my daughters. They keenly enjoy his humor. It is true they detect his formula and anticipate his endings, but his imagination is so faithful in the handling of small events that he enables us to mix with the characters of Trumet and Denboro quite as if we had known them. I read lying down for the reason that I am in less pain than when sitting up. We are grateful to Lincoln. His books keep us either laughing or quietly smiling. He means much to us in these depressing days.

"Last night the harvest moon rode high in the sky above the misty hills and we sat out on our porch untroubled by gnats or flies or mosquitoes. Nothing could be more perfect. At times I have a twinge of guilt. To think of our living here in peace—with neither noise, dust, heat, nor flies to annoy us, eating the best of food and driving about in shining cars, while millions of sweaty, bloody, tortured men are fighting in loathsome trenches in France—makes our life appear selfish and trivial. Yet what can I do? Most of my neighbors have sons or nephews at the front and these warriors would not have us grieve over them, or uselessly curtail our pleasures. They would share our pleasures, not forbid them."

Late in August, Dr. Fenton B. Turck and his wife came to Onteora, and dined with us one night. Our cottage, hardly more than a pioneer slab shanty, must have seemed a poverty-stricken place to the Turcks (whose house in New York is a palace in the eyes of my daughters), but the doctor did not seem to mind our rawhide chairs, our unplastered, unpainted walls, and our rough-hewn porch. To him I said, "This whole establishment is not worth a thousand dollars, but it is a refuge from the noise and heat of the city and we love it."

No doubt I cut a sorry figure creeping about the lot, and I could feel Turck's appraising glance as I settled carefully into a chair, or rose from it with painful deliberation. On the following day, when he met my wife at a reception, he said, "I know what is wrong with your husband. Tell him to come to me and I will help him."

Knowing that he was a specialist of high reputation, I hesitated. I said to him when next he called, "I can't afford your services, doctor." To this he bluntly said, "Never mind about that. We'll talk of fees when I have brought you back to full efficiency."

Reading in this reply an understanding of my desperate desire to finish my manuscript, I accepted his generous offer.

CHAPTER FIFTEEN

THE RETURN OF PEACE

I

THE Liberty Loan drive came on in September, 1918, and although still crippled I responded to the call. I returned to the city on the 11th. My good neighbor Edward Jones called for me at noon, and I forgot my stiffened joints as we rolled away down the hill in the velvet ease of his great car.

"This is what money does for a man," I said to him. "It gives him wings. It enlarges his horizon—also it enables him to share his pleasures and his powers with others."

The doctor delivered me at my door at five that afternoon a little stiff with cold but not tired, and in half an hour I was at work. "It is pleasant to be at my desk with all my literary tools about me. Country life gives zest to city contacts and conveniences."

"September 12. At the Salmagundi Club last night I heard Bairnsfather, the English cartoonist, whose book of illustrations called 'The Better 'Ole,' softened the rigors of the French battlefield, and delighted many thousands of civilians. He is a small, pale man of thirty-five, a most unassuming speaker. He has made a great name for himself, here as well as in England, but remains unspoiled by praise. His humor is almost American in quality."

As I came up Fifth Avenue, I found it swarming with soldiers, sailors, foreign visitors, bond salesmen, and sight-seers. "It presents each day the fever and the fervor of our intensifying war spirit. Orators clamor from booths, pictures fill the windows with scenes of conflict, and posters flame with patriotic fury, a display which represents a roused nation, a miraculous regeneration. America is fully awake at last."

"October 12. At noon to-day, a fleet of airplanes, some fifty or sixty, moving like flocks of high-flying geese, swept in battle formation over the city; and from our roof we had a clear view of them. For an hour they maneuvered and at last formed into a long lane and moved away. It is astounding to see them sustain themselves apparently at a standstill. It seemed as if they hovered over one spot for long periods of time. They kept three regular formations in platoons like cavalry troops, with officers at one side. It was a marvelous demonstration."

After a treatment by Turck, I went down to the Players Club on the 14th. Joe Lincoln came in and I had an hour's talk with him.

"He is like his books—plain, modest, and manly. He has a quiet humor and his opinions are sound. His stories would not interest an Englishman, but they are natural products of his environment. Born of seafaring people, he has been able to use his near-at-hand material successfully—and that is not easy. All that he has written was inspired by contact with his neighbors or with the judgments and experiences of his forbears. Although his face is as impassive as that of his 'bankers,' he has a shrewd, bright, quick-moving eye. He writes well, too, clearly, flexibly, and with kindly humor. It is easy to criticize his plots, but his characters have the accent of real people. Something of this I said to him, to his evident embarrassment. 'Joseph Lincoln, you are a public benefactor'—and I meant it.

"As I was leaving the club I met William Allen White, another man who has remained loyal to the place of his birth and to the traditions of decency, plain living, and high thinking. He said, 'I am here to help on the Liberty Loan drive.' His wife, pretty as a girl, was with him and I insisted that they should come to lunch with us. 'My wife and daughters want to see you.' I felt once again the singular melancholy which finds a partial expression in the wistful tone of William's voice. He is humorous yet essentially sad. He reminds me of James A. Herne in this Celtic quality."

"October 16. Although we are in the midst of enormous military preparations, my wife and I have little to do with it. All the marching and the 'speechifying,' all the band-playing and cheering, go on below and afar from us. My own weakness and a fear that the prevalent influenza may get the children, keep us pretty closely to our flat and to the school. I had a glimpse of Fifth Avenue again to-day and felt once more its exotic character. Flags of all nations flutter there. Soldiers of all countries are on parade, while impassioned orators plead for money, giving the street a color and a life which are almost frenzied; but closely studied the throngs appear frivolous. It is hard for me to visualize the actual war. I have only a theoretic or literary sense of it."

On the 18th, Albert Bigelow Paine and his daughter came to lunch with us and afterward we all rode out to Redding through a gorgeous autumn landscape. Nothing could be more colorful than the aisles of oaks and maples in the lake region of Westchester County. We had a good dinner and a quiet evening in Albert's cottage. His humor and his fine spirit of hospitality make his fireside a delightful place. It is a fact worth recording that he and William Allen White, two of my most valued friends, began their literary careers at the same time in Kansas City.

Albert and I were up early next morning, and while I made the coffee the family assembled. We spent the forenoon at Mark Twain's "Stormfield." At one we had a Sunday dinner in which Hoover and his economics were forgotten. Roast veal, sprouts, sweet potatoes, bread and jam, with royal pumpkin pie to end the feast. War did not exist. At three we started for home, gathering pumpkins and apples along the way. The weather was perfect golden October. No wind, exquisite sun, and radiant foliage.

II

At the suggestion of James Gannon of *Everybody's Magazine* I took the manuscript of "A Daughter of the Middle Border" down to Honoré Willsie, the editor of the *Delineator*.

"Mrs. Willsie, a tall, dark girl, told me that she was a native of Iowa. She professed a keen interest in the manuscript which I remorselessly unloaded upon her desk. If anything comes of this visit it will be another of those 'rescues' with which my life has been filled.

That this young editor should know my country and my people is a piece of wholly unexpected good fortune."

(Nothing came of it. Mrs. Willsie found the manuscript unsuited for serial publication. This did not surprise me, and I gave up any further attempt to market it. Mrs. Willsie made no mention of her own work, but at a later date she published a novel based on the life of Marcus and Narcissa Whitman which won my sincere admiration.)

On October 28, President Wilson in a letter sent out to his supporters, called in question the efficiency and sincerity of the Republican leaders and openly declared that only Democrats should be reëlected to Congress. This made Roosevelt the center of the whirlwind. The papers reported that in a rally at Carnegie Hall he would close the campaign which had been organized to rebuke the administration for its slur of Republican patriots; and every one of his friends looked forward to this speech with eager interest.

It happened that he had asked me to lunch with him on the very day of this great speech; and upon my arrival at the Harvard Club I found him entertaining Dr. Dillon, an Irish clergyman, and a man from Colorado by the name of Dodge. Roosevelt was genial, with nothing in his manner to indicate that he was about to make a final and savage assault on the administration, and I was puzzled to account for my inclusion in his party. The significance of the other guests was not disclosed.

The talk was not especially interesting. Dodge was rather wordless, and Dillon, a small, elderly man who knew Russia and Turkey very well, contributed little to the conversation. Roosevelt questioned him closely, but

did not succeed in getting much out of him. In fact, I
don't think he got very much out of any of us. I confess
that my own mind was filled with speculation concerning
the meeting in Carnegie Hall. The colonel himself was
uncommonly serious. He told very few humorous stories
and while he made no direct reference to the political
struggle in which he was involved, he was, I perceived,
subconsciously engaged upon the theme of his scheduled
address.

Just as we were about to rise from the table, he turned
toward me, and his face had in it the grim lines of an
African lion as he slowly said, "We're going to win.
We're going to down the administration in this fight."
The bitter intensity of his mood and the power expressed
in his level voice boded ill for those who had accused his
followers of being unworthy of public trust. In parting
he said, "Garland, I'm sorry, but I can't offer you a platform ticket. I hope you'll succeed in getting one."

I did not hear the address, but to judge from the newspaper reports of it, he made a remorseless analysis of
the President's narrow partisanship all through this war.
My record reads: "It will have far-reaching effects. Wilson has had the best of it up to now; but from this time
on, he will find the going hard. He opened the fight himself and he will live to regret his slur of the opposing party.
Nearly all the men I meet are against him. This is no
time for party politics. 'Does he think this is a war for
the glory of his officeholders?' the editors are asking."

III

"November 7. I have just come in from upper Fifth
Avenue, which is a seething mass of shouting, singing,

rejoicing people, dancing, drumming, clamoring under a glittering shower of paper falling like snow from the windows of office buildings. Peace has come, swiftly and dramatically. As the news reached the club, the men began to laugh and sing. One man, a sober, scholarly fellow, leaned back in his chair and emitted a series of lugubrious howls one after another, at measured intervals, like a mechanical foghorn. He was momentarily mad. Edward Wheeler and I went out into the streets and walked all the way up to Forty-second Street. The crowds were mainly of European blood—young working people. Girls were banging skillets, pans, and metal waste-paper baskets. Boys were sounding horns and ringing bells. Paper filled the air like snow. Trucks moved slowly up and down, packed with shouting, laughing people. All the busses were loaded to the guard rails with happy citizens. Motor horns, whistles, sirens, everything which would make a noise, were sounding as I came away."

That night, although there was some question of the news, I went down to Forty-second Street in order to be a part of the rejoicing pageantry. It was still a mad mixture of horn-blowing, pan-beating, shouting, singing men and women. The only citizens not rejoicing were the young men in uniform, the new recruits, who realized that their chances for getting overseas were gone. They stood gloomily on the corners and took no part in the celebration.

"November 8. This celebration was premature. The Armistice is not yet signed, although Germany is in such mood that the papers all predict the end. The Kaiser cannot stand out long, for his fleet is seized and his big towns are reported in the hands of the Reds. All despatches indicate that a revolution somewhat similar to that in Russia is taking place. I do nothing but buy papers and read and surmise and wait for the next edition.

"We are living on the edge of tremendous change. I feel this so intensely that writing is impossible, and yet there is a sense of unreality about it all. It is so remote from us! We have hardly been discommoded by the war. None of us have gone hungry, only a small part of us have suffered the loss of a soldier son. In a sense it is all 'academic.' We shall begin to realize it later when we are paying taxes for the billions we have spent."

"November 11. We were awakened this morning a little before six by the blowing of whistles—a long, continuous blast. This was the signal announcing the actual signing of the Armistice. It was nearly half an hour before the motor horns began to sound. By seven the whole city was humming, throbbing, sputtering with the news. At ten a thick black stream of humanity was flowing down Fifth Avenue. By noon it had become a torrent. At three I met my daughters and we walked slowly down the right-hand middle of the avenue, and back on the other side to Fifty-ninth Street. The floods of people found horns, rattles, tin cans, and whistles inadequate to express their joy. Dancing sailors and girls (a singular mixture of crude and refined types) joined in a carnival of mad rejoicing."

IV

At three o'clock the next day the American Defence League called me on the phone and asked me to go to Babylon, Long Island, to speak for the men in an aviators' camp. I went.

"It was a small cantonment of four hundred recruits in the midst of a flat, sandy plain, three miles from the town. The men who assembled in the Y. M. C. A. hut were all singularly silent, almost morose. No one laughed, no one joked, no one spoke to his neighbor. In this surly silence they reminded me of the gloomy inmates of an asylum. They resented my address as an interruption to their letter writing. I could not bring a smile to their glum faces. I wonder if all the camps are of this gloomy and cheerless silence. The officers are all young and without experience or background. A fine, serious lot— mighty serious—with no enthusiasms, no interests, except those which they had left at home. 'Out of four hundred men,' said the major, 'one hundred and eighty write a letter per day! This means homesickness. Those who are not homesick are in despair of ever going "Over There." ' "

Notwithstanding the excitement which the Armistice had brought, we had our usual dinner at the National Arts Club and stayed for the opening of the Book Show. At dinner, Charles Towne, Irving Bacheller, and Alfred Noyes were the special guests.

"I find Noyes very companionable. During the evening he read his fine poem, 'The Avenue of the Allies,' and deepened the good opinion we all had of him. Towne read two poems and Irving was, as usual, very amusing —in his quiet way. The audience was small but choice and the room looked very well indeed. Everybody spoke of the program with pleasure and very well they might. Any one of these speakers is capable of filling an evening."

"On November 17, Ernest Seton took me home with him to see his new house, which I inspected, marveling at his skill and his resource. He makes my own powers seem feeble. At night up in his big study we discussed his new book. It was a warm, rainy night with the wind roaring wildly in the trees. This hour was a revival of our good friendship which began over twenty years ago. The newspapers seem very tame now—no big battles, hardly any mobs or riots to record. 'Reconstruction' is now the word."

"November 21. Hearing that Roosevelt was at a hospital scheduled for an operation, I went down this afternoon to see him. I found him in bed propped up against a mound of pillows. He looked heavier than was natural to him and his mustache was almost white. There was something ominous in the immobility of his body. That he is a very sick man was evident to me, although he greeted me smilingly and almost as vigorously as ever.

"With outstretched hand he cried, 'I'm delighted to see you, Old Trailer!' and we began at once to talk of our common experiences in 'the short-grass country,' and of our mutual acquaintance with the men who had lived there. We named and discussed Stewart White and other novelists who had written of the Wilderness West. We talked for some time of the changes which had come to the land of our youth, and then, at last, I came to the purpose of my interview. I said, 'Colonel, there are some of us who feel that your son Quentin's grave in France should belong to America; and after taking counsel with two of my editor friends, I want your consent to our plan to buy the land around Quentin's grave and make a little park of it, planting it with shrubs and flowers so that when you and Mrs. Roosevelt go there next summer, you will find it cared for and secure. At present it is almost neglected.'

"His eyes misted as he comprehended my plan, and after a pause, and in a low tone, he said, 'That's perfectly lovely of you, Garland, and I'll talk with Mrs. Roosevelt about it to-night and let you know her decision when you come again—and you *must* come again, for I like to recall the life which you represent.'

"At this moment, his sister Corinne, Mrs. Douglas Robinson, came in, bringing a particular kind of cake which he loved as a boy and which had been made especially for him. I rose to go, but in mock sternness he called out, 'Sit down!' and for half an hour longer I remained while he talked to us without a particle of self-pity, although beneath his jesting ran the dark shadow of his approaching operation.

"As we recalled other meetings, I secured a perspective on the friendly relationship which this marvelous man had sustained with me for a quarter of a century. Only once did he refer to politics. He said, 'I am satisfied. I wanted to see this war put through and I wanted to beat Wilson. Wilson is beaten and the war is ended. I can now say, "Nunc dimittis," without regret.' He spoke of his other sons. 'Archibald has been wounded and Theodore gassed; but they are both recovering and will soon be well.'

"During the remainder of the visit he spoke of some books he was reading and we fell into a discussion of the lasting quality of Dickens. This led to a mention of the delicate humor of Jacobs, and the good, wholesome humor of Joseph Lincoln. Once when I started to go he said to me, with the menacing inflection of a Western sheriff, 'Will you put down that hat!'

"Glad to obey, I resumed my seat and he continued his delightful literary reminiscences. At last I took my leave, asking permission to come again to hear Mrs. Roosevelt's judgment as to my plan."

I called on him again four days later, finding him propped up in bed precisely as when I had seen him on the twenty-first, but he appeared stronger. He had gained in vitality. Nevertheless, I was forced to acknowledge that he was both old and sad, and in his voice (when speaking of his sons) I heard something indicative of decay. That he was in worse condition than the bulletins stated was evident to me. He lay like a man who could not move. His feet were covered thickly with blankets and when he reached his right hand to me he did so without moving his shoulders, a motion which alarmed me. It suggested immobility. For a moment I could not control my voice, but he spoke of his condition as though it were only a temporary disability.

"He had many callers, but during a moment when we were alone he said, 'Garland, Edith and I are both deeply appreciative of your kindness in planning to build that monument to Quentin, but she is opposed to the plan for the reason that Quentin was, after all, only an ordinary airman, not even an officer, who fell doing his duty. It would not be quite fair, we think, to the other brave fellows who did their best and died in the service. Quentin was no more the hero than they, and should not be honored above his merits because he was our son. You understand, don't you?'

"To this I replied, 'I understand your position, but the

fact that Quentin was not an officer and that he was an ordinary airman makes him all the more typical. A monument to him is a monument to all the airmen like him.'

"He considered this a moment. 'That is true,' he replied, 'but Mrs. Roosevelt thinks it might be misinterpreted and so she has voted against it, and I am inclined to think she is right. Nevertheless, old man,' he said with a note of tenderness in his voice, 'we appreciate and understand your motive.' "

Never were we closer than at that moment. But when I took his hand at parting, I had a clear premonition that I should not see him again, and even after he had returned to his home at Oyster Bay, my anxiety persisted. I rejoiced in the fact that he was to spend the holidays at home, but the bulletins were all ominous by reason of their vagueness. No one knew precisely what his ailment was.

CHAPTER SIXTEEN

THE PASSING OF ROOSEVELT

I

STRANGE to say, my homely chronicle of pioneer life had found not only readers but advocates among the teachers of the public schools in New York City, and several of the principals invited me to address their pupils. One of these was School 42, at Seward Square; and one morning in November I went down to it. Nearly two thousand pupils of from fourteen to eighteen years of age filled the auditorium, a singularly suggestive and not wholly reassuring audience, for the principal said, "Their parents are all from Poland, Russia, or Galicia." They sang the "Star-Spangled Banner" vigorously, however, and saluted with military precision. The words "land where our fathers died" did not seem comical to them.

They were all black-haired. Not one Nordic blond met my eyes, and I confess to a sense of uneasiness when the principal said, "All our teachers are Jewish."

"So long as our teachers are carrying on the traditions of the republic, there is a possibility that the pupils can be made over into Americans, but when instructors as well as pupils become alien, there is danger that the principles and policies which hold our great nation together may be weakened. In our fury of hospitality, we have opened our doors to the criminal as well as to the indigent and the illiterate, and our schools cannot take care of the aspiring children of these European peasants. It is fine that they are all so eager to become educated, but to what end will their education tend?"

Our Thanksgiving Day was not in the least like that of a New England homestead. We had no wide rooms, no blazing fire, no whirling snowflakes falling through naked trees—but we had a jolly time nevertheless. We carved a small but handsome turkey and drank "to the soldiers and sailors who made our Thanksgiving possible," and the hour was joyous. "We have no time to muse on the past. We are in the present, and to our children belongs the future."

My daughters were devotees of the movies and were pleased when Dr. Turck offered to take them to see Charlie Chaplin in "Shoulder Arms." Afterward I expanded my conception of Chaplin's art.

"He is always the Italian marionette. His flat, ghastly make-up, his staring, stupid yet pathetic eyes, and his rule of always facing his audience are characteristic of the clown in the puppet booth. He is always the victim, always the foolish creature, sexless and ageless, who is knocked down, trampled upon, tossed aside, and reviled. He blunders into danger and escapes by a miracle. He performs every silly or dangerous action with blank, unchanging countenance like a Punch and Judy character. Wistful and pathetic, he remains outside all human relationship. He does not comprehend ordinary motives. He gets in the way of normal action and if he falls in love it is in a dumb, appealing elfin fashion. He is the 'goat' of every act. His clumsy feet and small hat (which he derived from a London tramp) are merely to add grotesquerie—in essence he is the puppet clown."

On December 1, I began a series of lectures at the Brooklyn Institute. My audience was small and composed mainly of gray-haired men and women.

"Youth is not interested in my themes of the past. I am now the historian treating of a vanished epoch. To the present generation my gods are vague and uninteresting shapes on far-receding hills. I hope that those who sat before me felt more keenly than they made manifest. They remained oppressingly silent. No one smiled and only a few applauded, and yet they listened! It was a revelation of the swift change which has taken place in my world. My name is now associated with the historic figures of our life and literature. Howells and Burroughs are fading out. My turn comes next—a natural course of development."

At Robert Ely's invitation, my wife and I went to lunch at the Astor Hotel, where Jane Addams was the guest of honor.

"I think Ely was a little worried about this meeting, for Miss Addams has been 'in wrong with the government,' but it came out very well. The audience, while coldly quiet, was not hostile. John Eliot spoke and so did George Foster Peabody and Edwin Markham. My own short talk did not mention the war nor Miss Addams' peace program. I merely recalled her noble work at Hull House. In her reply she was plainly on the defensive. She acknowledged that she had been 'batted' by the government. The guests were tolerant, but nothing more. They remembered her comments on the French and British soldiers." (I do not recall this comment and shall not dig it up. Since this meeting Jane Addams has again become one of the most highly honored American women.)

My lecture on Mark Twain at Columbia University, December 5, brought out a large audience, one of the largest I have thus far had, but again I observed that it was composed of men and women of my own age—the men gray-haired, the women no longer in their bloom. "It is evident that from this time on my audiences are to be of this character. My only way of reaching the young people would be to speak and write of moving pictures and books which do not prove themselves worth while to me."

With a box at the Playhouse, I took my daughters to see the Riley play which was running there. "The Turcks joined us and we were all delighted by the play, which is quite the kind of thing Riley would have liked. It is filled with his spirit and many of his characters and verses are skillfully employed. It is not a great work of art, but it delighted us by reason of its homely quality. It gave us the sweetest and best of rural Indiana—as 'The Old Homestead' and 'Shore Acres' gave us the best of rural New England."

"December 9. Getting back to the manuscript of 'A Daughter of the Middle Border,' I revised the first chapter for the fifth time. At the club I found Albert Bigelow Paine, Booth Tarkington, and Sam Adams. It was quite like old times, and Francis Wilson, passing by, beamed with pride of the group. Albert, rosy as a boy, seemed prosperous, and Tarkington, big and burly, and, as he said, 'yappy,' spoke of his growing dislike of the city's traffic. He seems quite weaned from upper Broadway. We seldom see him now. It is amazing to find him not merely 'coming back' but going on toward finer work. There was a time when I thought him finished, but he is more skillful to-day than ever.

"At five I called on Alfred Noyes at his apartment on Fifty-ninth Street and, after discussing the growing anti-British propaganda, I suggested a kind of 'Vigilante organization' to aid in bringing about a better understanding between the English and ourselves. Noyes is a man of unusual ability quite aside from literary affairs. His poetic talent is essentially noble in character. Some say his books offer more of eloquence than of poetry, and there is a measure of truth in this criticism, but many of his ballads are both musical and moving. All that he does is of high purpose and technically fine in its working out."

On December 18, in accordance with my agreement, I went out to Pelham Bay to address a soldiers' camp.

"It was dark when I arrived at the gate, and the sentry, a rather stupid youth, pored painfully over a letter which was to serve as a pass. He finally let me in and at the 'Y' I found a civilian of middle age, a Mr. Foster, who knew me and took me in charge. I ate at the officers' mess and then spoke to five or six hundred men on 'The Work of Great Britain in the War,' a tribute to England which was well received by the boys. They cheered lustily when I praised the British fleet.

"Some of them were getting off for home, glad to get away; others, restless and eager, were seeking to be discharged. Those who had been honorably discharged went off carrying their shining new bags. One of them said, 'We are to keep our valises. We may be called out for drill a short time each year.' I was tired when I reached home. The strain and distraction of such work are decidedly against composition. I cannot afford to do much more of it. I must finish my chronicle soon, for the night approaches."

II

"December 27. One night (the day after Christmas) we all went over to Carl Akeley's apartment on Central Park West, to hear Stefansson talk on 'The Friendly Arctic,' a deeply interesting and revealing talk. He made out a good case for that region. Akeley followed him with a description of 'Brightest Africa,' thus bringing the ends of the earth together. It was amusing to hear these rugged explorers bragging of their opposing climates with proprietary fervor. It was a rich harvest for us who listened, an example of the wealth of experience my daughters are getting. I sometimes feel that they are getting too much and that they will make no use of the material thus secured.

"Stefansson, for all his marvelous experiences, is to me only Willie Stevenson of North Dakota, very like the Norwegian boys with whom I played on the Iowa prairie, and Akeley is equally typical. He, too, was born on a farm, in central New York, and his earliest interest, like mine, was the study of birds. He went farther, however. His ambition was to stuff and preserve them. 'This,' he said, 'led me to taxidermy, and at sixteen I told the world that I was a taxidermist. I had a card printed on which I stated that I was prepared to do artistic taxidermy in all its branches.' Here he smiled a slow, wide smile which lightened the habitual gloom of his rugged face. 'And so I was—in all the branches I knew.

" 'At nineteen I left Clarendon for a wider field. I

went to Brockport to see an interior decorator named Bruce, whose hobby was taxidermy. His office was filled with stuffed birds and small animals and I regarded him with awe. He was my master. He took me into partnership. My prospects became so bright that I was scared. However, Bruce decided that I needed more than he could give and advised me to go to Rochester where a professional taxidermist named Ward had a studio and supplied the museums of the country.

" 'No young artist approaching the studio of Van Dyck could have been more grateful than I was when the professor offered me three and a half dollars per week. My board cost four, but I had a little money saved and so I went to work. At the end of four years I knew my job.' "

Stefansson's beginnings were equally humble and quite as typically American.

"My people came from Iceland and my early schooling was in a little cabin on the Dakota plain," he said. "I worked my way through Harvard, specializing in Latin as well as in the Scandinavian languages and literature. It chanced that a scientific expedition to Greenland needed a man who could read early Norwegian and decipher the Latin records of the Catholic missionaries. I applied for the position and got it. That was my start in Northern exploration."

"Akeley's books give but a faint idea of his quaint humor and his command of witty phrases. He has the humorist's gloomy impassivity of countenance, combined with a monotonous musical drawl, which have made him a success on the platform. He relates the most thrilling anecdotes of lions and elephants with a mournful and cautious understatement. He explained again just how he came to kill a leopard with his bare hands in this fashion: 'I knew there was only one thing to do to stop her jaws, so I rammed my fist down her throat. I didn't know at the time that my bullet had cut off the toes on one of her hind feet, but I did know that her mouth was dangerous and that I must throttle her before she tore me to pieces.' All this he related with a listless and bored expression. I will not say that he was designedly dramatizing his cool-headed warfare, but he succeeded in holding our breathless interest as he droned along describing the dying struggles of the cat."

January 3 brought me a letter from Mark Sullivan, who wrote, "I have read the manuscript of 'A Daughter of the Middle Border' but do not think it suitable for serial use."

I replied, "You are right about it—it is at present scrappy. I shall go all over it again and raise it to a higher power. The nation is moving on to other things and I am one of the 'has-beens.' A swarm of soldier authors is settling down over the publishing field and soon nothing will remain for writers of my kind. All my material is now history. It has no news value and small contemporary interest. I see nothing ahead of me but another reminiscent book."

III

On January 6, 1919, the morning papers carried these fateful words: "Roosevelt died at 4.15 this morning." I could not believe it until it was confirmed later, for it was reported that he had been greatly benefited by his return to Sagamore Hill. More than this, he and death

did not rhyme. He was so aboundingly alive, so filled with
vital forces, that I could not imagine him lying cold and
silent.

That day I wrote these lines: "He was the biggest, most
interesting, and most versatile man I ever knew. He was
in fact five great personalities in one. As I think back over
the long term of our acquaintance, I rejoice in our many
pleasant meetings. I recall no discordant moment. He
was of my generation. His life and history involve much
of mine. Unknown to each other, yet as neighbors we
had lived on opposite sides of the Missouri River in the
early eighties. In the nineties we had met frequently in
New York and Washington. At our last meeting in the
hospital where he lay on his bed, alert and vigorous in
many ways, I had a definite premonition of the change
which had come to him. He was nearing the end of his
trail and yet was willing to cross the wide river. His
work was finished. 'I am ready to say my "Nunc dimittis," ' he had said to me, and for the first time in all
our intercourse I had sensed a mood of resignation, of renunciation in his voice.

"The papers are filled with eulogies of him, many of
them belated, some of them perfunctory, and a few obviously insincere. Small men who violently opposed him
are now profuse in their praise of him. He is no longer
a menace to their political ambitions. His enormous capacity for work, his catholic interest in every phase of art
and life, are brought out in sonorous sentences by those
who once vilified him.

"He has been a dominating figure in my world for over
a quarter of a century and his going leaves a vacant place
in my horizon something like the sudden sinking of a

mountain peak. He was an American, an intense patriot to the very last moment of his life. His final letter to his fellow citizens was an appeal to their loyalty and showed an undying love of everything for which our republic stands. Everywhere I go I hear people praising him. The mechanic in the street, the colored man in the elevator —every thoughtful man acknowledges that a colossal and beneficent citizen has gone out of our world.

"He went away beautifully and his funeral is to be as simple as possible, almost private as he himself had planned it. He is to be buried in the little neighborhood graveyard near his home in Oyster Bay. A vast memorial meeting will come later."

I spent the whole day in putting together my memories of him, going over in detail our long acquaintance. "It gratifies me to find the nation's love going out in praise of him, for he was right on most points of his contention. He did not always say it as tactfully as some of us desired him to do, but he had vision and faith and a patriotism which nothing could embitter or destroy."

(Out of all the poems which appeared in praise of Roosevelt, the one which most moved me and which came nearest to being his adequate epitaph was written by Edith Wharton, a free flowing yet proportioned utterance, original in quality and emotionally sincere, entitled "With the Tide.")

CHAPTER SEVENTEEN

ROOSEVELT MEMORIAL PLANS

I

CARL AKELEY was held in high esteem by the Roosevelt family, both as explorer and as sculptor; and when, immediately after the funeral at Oyster Bay, I walked across the park to his studio in the east wing of the Museum of Natural History, I found him at work on the sketch of a lion. "This is to be," he explained, "the crowning part of a memorial monument to Roosevelt. I caught the idea from a cable message which Archie sent to his brother just after his father's death, 'The Old Lion is dead and his brood must carry on,' and I am modeling this lion as a symbol of his power.

"I have just returned from Sagamore Hill. The funeral ceremony was private and very brief. Archie was in charge of the details and bravely greeted every one who came. He is only a slender boy with one arm shattered by a piece of shell, but he is adequate—a true son of the Old Lion."

As Akeley described the ceremony, it all seemed too casual, too hurried. I said: "Roosevelt was too great to be privately buried. He was our greatest man. He belonged to the nation, not to Oyster Bay. I suppose his family felt that, as the administration had ignored him in life, it should have no opportunity to weep crocodile tears at his funeral; but in my opinion he should have had something more than a private burial in a crowded village cemetery." (I still feel that this tomb is unworthy his great fame.)

Akeley then outlined his grandiose plan. "My lion is to be of colossal size and lie on a low tower built of gigantic blocks of granite—so vast and so defiant of time that it will be magnificent in ruin a thousand years from now."

Thereafter, almost every afternoon I walked across the park to see the progress of this design which involved a forty-foot lion and a colossal tower. Akeley was obsessed with it. He could think and talk of nothing else. His idea was tremendous—no discounting that; and yet I had my doubts. How could he, an explorer and taxidermist, successfully compete with nationally known sculptors and architects?

On Sunday morning, January 12, I was surprised by the sudden irruption of Cordenio Severance and Franklin Lane, Secretary of the Interior. "We have been up to the Russian Church just above you," Cordenio explained.

"We had a deal of talk on national problems: Immigration, Bolshevism, Anti-British propaganda, and the like. Lane has few illusions concerning President Wilson, though he admires certain phases of him. He outlined a plan to aid in the Americanization of our polyglot population and drew from me a promise to help."

Carl Akeley came to dinner next day, and in the light of our gas log related other stories of African lions and elephants, especially elephants. He described one herd of over seven hundred feeding and trumpeting all night long close to his camp, held at safe distance only by the fires which the black men kept burning.

"In that plaintive, slow-spoken way which he uses, he vividly described the night-long chorus of monkeys, hornbills, elephants, and chimpanzees which went on around him. 'That was Africa,' he said.

"His face was sad and his voice more than usually plaintive, for the reason that Delia, his wife, who has been doing war work in France, has not written for many weeks. Then, too, he feels the death of Roosevelt as keenly as if he had been a brother. He is confident of getting the commission for his lion."

While Dr. Jones, Edmond Quinn the sculptor, and I were lunching at the club on the 20th, Joe Lincoln came in and we had a few words of pleasant banter. He was amusing and we all remarked, after he went out, "He is like his books." . . . Percy MacKaye, who joined us later, was (as usual) full of a lovely idealistic scheme. As I was leaving, Quinn gave me a large photograph of his statue of Booth, which I greatly prize. We then went out into the park to look at the statue which is nobly fine. "The air was like that of early April, and we lingered about the memorial, studying it from every angle. It is a true portrait."

I was struggling with a short story at this time and making little progress. "The war has destroyed my interest in fiction. My daughter Isabel (aged fifteen) is busily composing a miracle play in verse on the typewriter! Here again I acknowledge a world's difference between her youth and mine. At her age I was reading, writing, and figuring in a bare little schoolhouse on the prairie, at the corner of our Iowa farm. I had never seen a play and I had never even heard of a typewriter. It is a very pretty sight to me—this girl, my small daughter, picking at the typewriter, so deeply engrossed that she can hardly be diverted from her task."

On learning that John Burroughs was at a doctor's home over on the West Side, I called on him.

Although looking very old, he was hearty and sane and cheerful. He spoke of his years and his growing infirmities in the straightforward way of a philosopher. He was deeply affected by Roosevelt's death, and talked of him for the most part. As I was about to go he said, "I am going to California. It seems a big undertaking for a man of my years, but I am willing to assume the risk and Henry Ford is willing to pay the bills. I hope to finish another book out there."

I urged him to dictate his Washington experiences and his English visits. "Put down every incident of your experiences with Roosevelt. Do it before you go to California."

"You're right," he said. "I'm an old man and I'm taking chances. I may not survive this trip."

Despite his brave attitude I could see that he was losing power in mind as well as in body.

Ely's luncheons at the Astor Hotel continued to be significant. At the one given to Maurice F. Egan, Edna Ferber was the most appealing speaker.

"She came up to me after the luncheon and said something in praise of my 'Son of the Middle Border.' This surprised me. I had not expected a writer of her stamp to care for my 'stuff,' but she assured me that she did. She said, 'The war and family worries have so distracted me that I have produced but little.' I had never met her before. She is a very able novelist and speaks unusually well. She is American in all her work. Later I met the Wrays at the theater to see another Dunsany play, 'The Laughter of the Gods,' which I liked immensely. It had many noble lines and its sardonic humor is unlike that of any other writer. His English is delightfully unworn."

On February 1 Dr. Jones called and took us all over to Akeley's flat, where we again saw his African pictures.

"He looked tired and his voice was more than common wistful. Jones said, 'He is the last man of my acquaintance to be selected as a lion hunter,' and yet he is a most successful one. He told his stories as usual, with a melancholy cadence in his utterance, but brought into his discourse many quaint figures of speech—and many witty turns of thought. He is a great deal more alert than he gives out at first, and is amazingly versatile. He is a taxidermist, a zoölogist, an inventor, a sculptor, and an author. He writes unusually well and is an excellent shot with a rifle."

On Sunday (February 2) the Wrays came to dinner and were as gay and lively as ever. Later in the afternoon, Percy MacKaye called and we walked across the park.

"It was a glorious evening, and as we reached the northeast corner and looked across the water toward the south and west, we both exclaimed with delight. Over the golden sheen of the pond, the dark-blue masses of the buildings rose dimly in strange beauty. They seemed the walls of some far-off alien city, not just commonplace New York, and above them hung the moon, a thin yellow horn. It gave even my cold heart a thrill of admiration and delight.

"MacKaye interests me. He is a very real poet and a genuine dramatist, but remains so much of the idealist that he falls short of success. His never-ceasing efforts fail of profit. He writes with very little regard for the taste of the public. He has the face of a dreamer, and at times looks like a man without sufficient sleep. Nevertheless he goes on from one high unprofitable enterprise to another. All his friends love him for his unselfish quality, but all wish him to be a little more practical in his plans."

II

"This day, February 4, was given to advancing the plans of the Roosevelt Memorial Association. Going down to the office I handed in a letter and a small check, and then took up the work of forming a committee for the collection of Roosevelt material. Hagedorn, who is acting secretary of the association, worked with me and we succeeded in getting eight or ten men to serve. My letter, which will appear to-morrow, makes a call for 'stories of Roosevelt,' and the announcement of the committee is to follow a day or two later. This may lead to something very much worth while. 'What is done must be done at once,' I said to Hagedorn. 'Men's minds are filled with memories of him and we must secure these memories before they lose their glow.' "

The announcement of the plan for a "Roosevelt Story Book" was made that day, and my letter appeared February 5.

"After a hard forenoon's work, February 6, I met Mrs. Russell Wray and my wife at the theater where three of Dunsany's plays were given. I found them all of high imaginative appeal, rich in imagery and graceful in phrase, quite outside the ordinary current of modern drama. I do not know anything just like them. Sexual passion does not enter the plot. Rulers, ambitious advisers, beggars, all sorts of singular and riotous characters, come and go, but no lovers. His plays, essentially humorous in spirit, are all fantastic allegories of life and government filled with lines which give a smart fillip to the imagination. They make me smile at the same time that they make me think. Written long before this war, they seem to be satiric comments on it. Such work is highly stimulating to me. My letter on Roosevelt was widely copied. The 'Roosevelt Story Book' is started."

"February 9. To-day is Roosevelt Day all over America, and I spoke twice: first at the Naval Y. M. C. A. in Brooklyn, and again at the Madison Street Methodist Church. The first meeting was not important, but the second at the church was highly successful. The clergyman, as he looked over the crowded pews, said, 'Well, the writer is certainly more popular than the preacher.' My talk, which was entirely colloquial and somewhat humorous, pleased my auditors."

As I entered Akeley's studio at the Museum of Natural History on the 10th I met Archibald Roosevelt and his wife. "Archie is a tall, thin young fellow with a bright, eager face and fine eyes. He looks the poet rather than the soldier, but his mind is surprisingly positive. Jealous of the fame of his father, he expressed a dislike of portrait statues, but approved Akeley's lion. How much this will mean to the committee I cannot say, but it made Akeley happy."

A young Jew named Max Ravage, who had written a

thoughtful book called "The Making of an American," interested me, and I had him down to lunch with me.

"He turned out to be a small, dark man of thirty, foreign in appearance, but with a clear concept of what it means to inherit America. He made a very interesting suggestion for a 'Roosevelt National Scholarship' which would take young Jews from their city ghettos and educate them in the atmosphere of Western college towns. He was very earnest in this. 'I am a "new American" as you are an "old American,"' he said, and his plan showed a sympathetic understanding of our problems in 'Americanizing' the Jewish East-Sider."

III

John Galsworthy, who had been chosen to represent the English Academicians at the spring meeting of the American Academy, arrived on the tenth, and I as acting secretary was instructed to call on him at his hotel. I had read his stories and plays with interest, but had never met him, although he had been in Chicago to see one of his plays produced.

"He is taller than I had expected him to be, and far less robust. A fine, sensitive Englishman, modest and kindly, not in the least aggressive. He seemed a man of sorrows, smiling to hide his essential pessimism. We did not talk of his books, but of the Academy and of the city. He was very friendly and I went away with a decided liking for him. He is much more refined than his books —a quiet, serious man of little humor. I saw in him nothing of the spirit of social outlawry of which he has been accused.

"At the University Club I lunched with Joseph Bucklin Bishop, who has been chosen to write the life of Roosevelt for *Scribner's*. I found him to be not at all the man for the job. He is seventy-one and a son of the farm like myself. 'I have sawed wood to help pay for my schooling, hauled manure, and milked cows,' he declared. He knew Roosevelt for many years and it is evident that Roosevelt trusted him. 'I am not literary,' he admitted, 'and do not intend to put myself forward as an author. I feel the enormous difficulties of my task. The Roosevelts have given me the right to use all their father's records and I shall go through them with the utmost care.'

"This is a tremendous commission and a most valuable privilege. I cannot understand why a man of his age and training has been chosen for this most important work. What he will produce cannot be in any sense a biography. His book will be a treasure house of material, but it will not be authoritative."

Calling at the Roosevelt Memorial Committee office, I found Raymond Robins seated at a desk. "He is one of the main supports, or rather one of the forceful engines, of the committee. He has grown older and more sedate since our last meeting, but his Southern accent remains."

At a luncheon to Galsworthy on the 14th, Elihu Root and William Gillette were chief figures.

"Root surprised me. He is not so old as I had fancied him. His words came slowly and he seemed tired, but his mind is still keen. His manner is gentle and considerate. His vital force is ebbing. His active work in politics is substantially over. He will advise, but he declines to carry forward any large project. It was disturbing to have him speak to me as if I were of his own age and rank."

IV

Although for several years I had done no writing or public speaking on psychic research, my interest in the subject was keen; and when one day Mrs. Riddell invited me to have tea with her at the Ritz and to meet Mrs. Curran, whose "Patience Worth" stories were much read in psychical circles, I accepted with pleasure.

My impression of Mrs. Curran reads thus: "She is a Western type. Her home is in St. Louis, but she has the look and tone of a lively Kansas girl. She is humorous in conversation—not at all the kind of 'medium' I had expected to meet. She introduced me to her husband, a short, blond newspaper man who acts as recorder of her inspirational material.

"She receives her stories (so she said) through the medium of a planchette or 'telebord' and claims them to be of spirit origin. 'Patience Worth,' who speaks through her, is the spirit of a girl who lived in Shakespeare's day, or thereabouts, and her work shows her to be a highly endowed ghost.

"At Mrs. Riddell's request, Mrs. Curran got out her board and resting it on her lap invited me to sit facing her and to support the other edge of the board, which was about sixteen inches broad with letters arranged in a semicircle. In the center was a pointer on a pivot. On this her hand rested.

"She said: 'When I began to record these messages I spelled the words with the pointer, but now I am almost free of it.' Her hand began to move about aimlessly, while she partly spelled and partly chanted the words which came to her. Her husband took them down on a pad. They made incomplete sense to me, but took shape under Curran's practiced pencil. 'Patience' used a quaint vernacular which Mrs. Curran declared was Old English. The poems and sententious paragraphs which followed, 'Patience' called 'whimsies,' and whatever their source they were not in the least like Mrs. Curran's own speech, which was rather commonplace—and at times harsh and slangy.

"She said: 'Give Patience any subject and she will make a whimsy upon it.'

"Mrs. Riddell suggested 'A Cup of Tea'; and immediately, without a moment's hesitation, Mrs. Curran (as Patience Worth) spun a delightful little poem on tea-drinking. Thereupon I gave a title and she produced another 'whimsy'—better than I could have done with a morning's meditation—all in the same curious jargon which is supposed to be English of the sixteenth century, but in which the word 'quirt' and other Kansas cowboy phrases appeared.

"Her claim that these lines were dictated by some other entity or by a parasitic personality was supported by the fact that she could stop in the middle of a line, wait for her husband's pencil to catch up, and resume without a break. She gave no evidence of being in a trance, and yet these graceful lines were swiftly, unhesitatingly composed. Some of the figures of speech were really beautiful. 'I have received nearly a million words,' Mrs. Curran said, 'and I am still receiving novels—just now a story of the time of Christ.'

"It all seems a marvelous case of subconscious cerebration, a skill built up by long practice."

(Just why "Patience Worth," a peasant girl of Shakespeare's time, should picture life in Palestine in the time of Cæsar, I was unable to understand; but I afterward read some of these novels, finding them prolix, shapeless, and factitious. I had several opportunities of later years to study this singular character, and while I could never achieve a belief in "Patience" I was quite convinced of the reality of Mrs. Curran's amazing endowment. The poems were all vaguely good, just missing that definite quality which first-class work displays. They ran just a little below the publishing standards of the best editors— as she herself admitted.)

V

As a result of this tea, I accepted Mrs. Riddell's suggestion that I should get in touch with the Woman's Club in Cleveland. "They want you to give a series of talks on psychical research," she said, and I arranged to go on February 16. My account of this trip follows:

"February 17. Cleveland appeared very drab and raw and depressing, but a comfortable room at the University Club and a lunch with Mrs. Simeral and Mrs. Rogers (who were instrumental in bringing me here) put me right with the world. My first lecture came at eight and the small 'lounge' of the Woman's Club was crowded to the walls and many were turned away. I spoke without manuscript. My auditors were mostly women. I made them smile now and then. 'I am speaking as an investigator and not as a religious devotee,' I explained. The spiritualists were disappointed because I was too scientific, and the skeptics considered me too credulous. Again, as in my book, 'The Shadow World,' I fell between two stools.

"Nevertheless, at my second lecture the place was again filled, and men as well as women crowded around me at the close. It was hard to get away from them. They were interested, no question about that, and on the whole I think they felt that I was fair-minded. That a strong wave of interest in this subject has risen out of the war's bereavement is evident, and those who can ride it skillfully will ride high. A scientific attitude is not demanded. However, I shall not follow up this lead."

VI

The Academy dinner in honor of James Russell Lowell's Centenary was a pleasing event. I sat between Lewis Hind, an English writer, and one of the Canadian delegates.

"The talk was good, very good. John Galsworthy was admirable and so was Elihu Root. Brander Matthews was neat and clear and concise. The social part of the dinner was delightful. Mrs. Galsworthy, who sat at my table, was charming in manner and most intelligent. We were greatly taken with her gentle and serious character."

A lunch at the Union League Club next day brought me in touch with "The Pilgrims," who were toasting and dining the Canadians and the English. It was a jolly luncheon with some very good speaking. Sir Henry Babington Smith was quite flawless in tone and manner, and Stephen Leacock very amusing.

"At night, on the Academy's invitation card, I took my daughters to the theater to see a performance of Barrie's 'Dear Brutus.' I was greatly moved by the play as well as by Gillette's acting as the star of the piece. Several of my friends remarked that the picture of my daughter's eager face beside mine in the box made the theme of Barrie's play the more poignant, for Gillette, like the chief character in the play, is childless. To have such a daughter is one of the compensations of growing old. I felt for the man who had only a dream child."

The morning session of the Academy was notable.

"As one of the 'Senators' I sat between Gari Melchers and Dan French. The speaking was good on the whole, but Edgar Masters' poem made a poor showing in comparison with that of Alfred Noyes, who read his 'Avenue of the Allies' with fine effect.

"After the meeting came a very jolly luncheon, a kind of cafeteria function which brought us all together in exactly the right spirit. We had the Galsworthys and Alfred Noyes at our table. Walter Eaton, William Phelps, and Albert Paine were near neighbors. Altogether it was a delightfully informal function. We have too few such parties in this town."

CHAPTER EIGHTEEN

A SOUTHERN LECTURE TOUR

I

My good friend Irving Bacheller, who had become interested in Winter Park, Florida, was sure that a touch of Southern sun would do me good; and early in February I left New York with its snowdrifts six feet high and started for Sweet Briar College in Virginia where I was scheduled for a lecture. I had not been south of Washington for nearly fifteen years and I studied Virginia with new interest.

My general impression is indicated in these lines set down in my notebook: "It is an unkempt, empty land, a land of tiny cabins with outside chimneys, and ugly, unpainted houses set in disorderly lawns—a region almost as hopeless in appearance as it was fifteen years ago. The train is filled with soldiers and sailors returning from France. Some of them are negroes, strangely grim and silent. I wonder what is in their minds as they return to the coaches set aside for 'colored passengers.' Will they accept such conditions now?

"Sweet Briar College is on a hill several miles from the station, a lonely spot in a wooded tract. After my lecture, I was carried on a wild ride through mud and darkness to the railway at Monroe. Here I filled in a long wait for the train by reading 'Yasha,' a horrible picture of the Russian people."

"Winter Park, Florida. All the way through the Carolinas I looked for 'the Sunny South'; but did not find it till I reached this town, a New England village in a subtropic setting of palms, live oaks, and mossy sycamores. Here are lawns, flowers, and radiant orange trees.

"I found Bacheller living comfortably in a spacious rented house, but planning the building of a Spanish bungalow on a piece of ground he has just bought."

My stay in Winter Park was short, but it was long enough to fill me with desire to have a winter home there, a desire which Bacheller was careful to foster. "I want you for a neighbor," he said. The weather was like early June in the North, and the air filled with the scent of flowers and fruit. I seriously considered buying a house and garden.

As I rode north a few days later, I marveled at the brave skill of the Southern novelists—writers like Thomas Nelson Page, Hopkinson Smith, and others of the romantic group who had conspired to maintain the fiction of a "Sunny South" dotted with stately mansions and odorous with magnolia blooms. Augustus Thomas, although from Missouri, has contributed to the same illusion in his "Alabama."

"Actually the landscapes which I have visited and those through which I am now riding are without beauty. They have no smooth lawns, no vine-clad porches, and no bloom. The pine forests are scraggly, the swamp lands unpleasantly suggestive of reptiles, and the villages mainly collections of unpainted shacks. And yet out of these unlovely surroundings a school of writers has risen whose loyalty has translated the sluggish 'Swanee River' into a stream of dreamlike beauty and filled the air with a sweetness born of the myrtle and the ivy when in bloom.

"I make mention of these disappointments not in the spirit of criticism but of wonderment. Lanier, Timrod, and Hayne did much to glorify their native land before the local color group of novelists arrived. Now (I made note) it is the duty of the men and women who see this land with present-day training to picture it as it really is, an unlovely time of sorry transition."

At Chapel Hill and Raleigh I saw something of the literary South, and heard occasionally the accent of "Colonel Carter of Cartersville," but at Harrisonburg I discovered a complete change of speech and manners.

"The accent of the Highlanders is sharp and clear, their tones strident, their vowels and r's Scotch-Irish in quality. Here are no more soft 'ahs' and no drawling, cadenced sentences. The negro has not influenced the speech of the young people at this school. They are almost as Mid-Western as those in Ohio. No one so far as I know has put them into fiction, for even Joel Chandler Harris selected his characters for their picturesque qualities. He was at his best in 'At Teague Poteets' and 'Trouble on Lost Mountain.' It may be that some of the students who crowded around me after my talk last night (children of the men and women Harris so vividly characterized) are to be the novelists of the future."

The professor of history at this school, a young man by the name of Wayland, who had made a special study of the Lincoln family, assured me that the ancestral homes were still standing at no great distance from Harrisonburg; and at his invitation I stayed over a day in order that he might drive me to see these houses.

This he did on March 10. "I visited this day the ancestral homes of the Lincolns (a group of spacious farmhouses) and I visited the little graveyard in which John and Jacob Lincoln are buried. The stone farmhouse which they built gave evidence that they were men of substance and worth. It is a lovely country—not so much Southern as Mid-Western, a place of orchards and wide grain fields very far from the mossy trees, magnolia blooms, and swamps of the lowlands. It was from one of these fine farms that young Abraham Lincoln pioneered into Kentucky as so many of his friends were doing. There was good blood in these Lincolns."

After six weeks spent in traveling through Virginia and the Carolinas, I was able to say, March 10, "I have seen much of the New South but nothing of the romantic South. No doubt there are elderly folk in the small villages still clinging to the past and recounting the wrongs of Reconstruction, but I did not meet them and they had no comment in the press. The South through which I passed is young, vital, buoyant, and American. I found myself back among the Leonards, McConnells, Dudleys, Carrolls, and Colemans. It was like revisiting my home town. After the heterogeneous mixture of New York, it was a pleasure to meet once more the men and women who know what pioneering means and what our history has been. I am a philanthropist—in theory—and should have no race prejudices; but I like my own kind—at least I enjoy meeting a blond, gray-eyed citizen now and again. I grant the black-eyed people the same prejudice regarding me.

"In my tour, I addressed many thousands of college students, and their eager faces and quick responses to the best I could say have left a very pleasant impression on my mind. They are being schooled very much as the boys and girls of my time in Iowa were schooled, without show and without undue ceremony. They are earnestly trying to be a part of modern America, and their teachers are awake to the absurdity of local textbooks and sectional judgments. The New South is an integral part of the Union, and in that I rejoice.

"The South of 1919 is prosperous. I saw more new houses, more new hotels, and more new automobiles, proportionately, than in the North. Cotton and tobacco are joint kings in the Carolinas, and their subjects are happy. The cafés were crowded with people who think nothing of a list of foods as costly as at the chief hotels of New York City—even in a small city like Greensboro or Raleigh, a carriage in the midst of long rows of motor cars is a curiosity. In towns where only a few years ago oxcarts—or carts with one mule and one ox hitched to a wagon—were common, throngs of mud-bespattered motors filled the streets or lined the curb.

"The negro is being divorced from his mule! Beside hundreds of little shacks with only wooden shutters for windows, I observed automobiles patiently enduring the rain and sun. The streets of Spartansburg and Columbia were packed with these people in their weather-beaten, clay-covered, but serviceable cars. The mule is considered now only as a means of dragging the plow. He has a pathetic look as he watches his master ride away to town without him. Soon he will be as extinct as the dodo—and the horse."

II

Almost immediately after my return from the South I went over to Akeley's studio to see what he had done with his Roosevelt monument. I found him highly excited and entirely confident. "All the Roosevelt family are strong for my lion," he announced, "and we have gone so far as to look for a site on which to place it."

My own feeling was still dubious. I could not believe that a commission so important would go to an unknown architect and to a sculptor known only as a naturalist and African explorer. Furthermore, I was in doubt about the use of a lion as the symbol of a man who had always insisted on the American quality in our art. "It is a noble figure, this lion of Akeley's, but it has been used so often in history that it is less appropriate than the eagle. We have eagles in America, but our only lion is a big yellow cat called a cougar."

For all these reasons I was only half-hearted in my advocacy of Carl's grandiose plan which involved the largest lion ever sculptured—a lion forty-feet in length crouching on a low tower built of enormous granite blocks calculated to outlast the Roman Colosseum. I felt the mass and dignity of the design, but I could not see the memorial committee accepting it; and I wondered whether the Roosevelts had not been overborne by Akeley whom they greatly loved. "As for the lion itself, I admire it greatly and wish to see it guarding the tomb in Oyster Bay. It would be appropriate there. If Akeley expects the commission to come to him without a competition, without a jury of award, he will be disappointed. It is amazing to find this gentle, sorrowful soul so persistent in his plan, but according to his report, Mrs. Roosevelt (whose wishes he regards as law) has encouraged him from the very first exhibition of his sketch. Nevertheless I cannot see the committee awarding the commission without a competition."

The Roosevelt memorial committee held a meeting March 24, and a very distinguished group it was. Senator Root, General Leonard Wood, Gifford Pinchot, Colonel Thompson, Hermann Hagedorn, Lawrence Abbott, Carl Akeley, and several others of Roosevelt's personal friends were there. Although not a member of the committee at this time, I was invited to be present. I sat beside Akeley who was (I could see) tensely expectant. I think he expected his design to be named and commended. Root, Wood, and Pinchot were the big men of the committee.

"Root's speech was the deciding factor in the meeting. It was graceful, full of feeling, and very direct. He put the memorial in the place where it belonged and acknowledged the power of art as the interpreter to future generations of a great man's life, but he did not touch upon Akeley's design or mention any specific method of selection. Young Theodore also spoke briefly, but without alluding to Carl, who was, I felt, deeply disappointed; to him delay is fatal."

At the Players (April 2) George Barr McCutcheon fell into reminiscence of our literary life in Chicago. He again impressed me as a fine, slow-moving personality, sincere and dependable, all in sharpest possible contrast with his romantic novels. "He spoke of being 'poor,' but is in fact a rich man, living at ease and in luxury. His books have had wide sale, but I cannot think they are of lasting value. He has little humor and no grace of style, but his romantic notion of European kings and queens is precisely that which pleases the American girl. There is a kind of magic in this Hoosier's pen. He is not altogether absurd. I like him personally. He is intelligent, friendly, and quite unassuming, notwithstanding his immense success."

One of my "cares" at this particular time was a plan for a testimonial dinner to Edwin Markham, who had lost his place on the Hearst newspapers and was suffering from a bad investment.

My second concern was the book of "Roosevelt Stories," which was languishing for the very good reason that every man with a Roosevelt anecdote had designs on a publisher who would pay him for it. "Many contributions have come in, but not as many as I expected, for General Wood, George Cortelyou, William Loeb, and many others who were most intimate with him are, very naturally, reluctant about surrendering their valuable material. Nevertheless, Hagedorn, who is acting as secretary of the committee, is disposed to carry on with me.

"That a mass of material exists which will die with the men who possess it (unless it is drawn from them), is certain. With no criticism of those who say they intend to write their reminiscences, I have not much faith in their doing so. Most of them lack the time and the training to write. I hope Loeb and Cortelyou will record their impressions while they are vivid, but I have no confident expectations that they or General Wood will ever bring themselves to the task."

(The collecting went on, however, and Hagedorn was finally delegated to visit Dakota and gather up the material there. This he did and wrote an admirable book on

"Roosevelt in the Bad Lands." For several years he gave his time and fine talent to the building up of the Roosevelt Memorial Library.)

Henry Watterson and Julian Harris were at the Players on April 10, and as Watterson expressed a desire to know me, John Phillips introduced me to him.

"He is old, old and white-haired, and, like Falstaff, glories in being an unrepentant sinner. He confessed that he had been corrupted by an offer of thirty thousand dollars for his autobiography. 'I have resigned from the *Courier Journal*,' he said. 'I am now a man of letters and leisure, but I have waited too long to write my story. It will not measure up to Lorimer's expectations.' "

When I next met Albert Bigelow Paine, he told me a very funny story of himself in relation to Watterson. It ran something like this:

"Henry sent word one day that he wanted to talk to me about his book; and so I made an appointment to meet him. During our talk the old man drank, drank a good deal. In fact he got mellow. 'Now let's call on some of my friends,' he said. In calling on his friends he drank more, but I threw mine away whenever possible. At two A.M. he was tottering, but I was able to take him to his hotel. I got to my own room about three.

"When I woke at nine I felt bad, very bad, and I thought, 'That man Watterson is probably dead.' I was afraid to look in the papers for fear of seeing his death notice. Trembling with apprehension I went over to his hotel and asked the clerk if he had seen anything of Colonel Watterson. 'Oh, yes,' he replied, 'he came down about two hours ago. He has gone for a walk. Left right after breakfast.'

" 'Breakfast! Did that old man eat *breakfast?* You must be mistaken. He couldn't eat so early as that!'

"The clerk sent for the old man's bill—it spoke of chops, rolls, coffee, and hot cakes. I was astounded. Soon afterward, Watterson came in. 'Hello, Albert,' he shouted, 'how you feelin'?'

" 'Bad—very bad,' I answered. Whereupon the old devil looked me over and said gravely, 'Albert, long ago I found out that when I had enough—'twas time to quit!' "

Early on April 12, Albert called me up. "Can you go to Redding?" And at ten we were packing food into his car at Bronxville. At three we were in his bungalow. I was again cook and bottle washer, while he acted as plumber and chauffeur. The country was lovely and we sat out on the porch like crickets absorbing the sunshine.

"Albert is the most fearless thinker of all my friends except Henry Fuller. He is both humorous and sad, and the quaintly colloquial style of his books springs from his conversational method. He pretends to nothing in the way of faith, but lives nevertheless a decent, orderly life and faces the future without concern. I am the richer for knowing him."

Percy MacKaye, who was at the club April 18, told me much of his career as a dramatist. " 'I am always doing the impracticable thing,' he confessed. 'Just now I am working on the words of an opera based on "Rip Van Winkle." '

"He looks pale and worn. Much sickness in his family has worried him, interrupting his writing, but he keeps to his high level. 'How *do* people succeed by writing?' he asked with humorous inflection, almost helpless in the face of his problem. 'I wonder at it myself,' I replied.

"His idealism, his desire to do worthy, original work keeps him from doing profitable work. His 'Washington' had profoundly moving passages and should have been successful, but as a pageant filled with dances and ballads, the form which he loves, was only another success of esteem, like his 'Scarecrow,' which I greatly enjoyed.

The testimonial dinner to Markham came on April 23. My seat at the speakers' table was between Iyanaga, the Japanese consul, and Howard Kyle, the actor.

"Many of the guests I knew, but the meeting was not especially literary, and the speechmaking rather perfunctory. It was helpful, however. Markham, like MacKaye, is out of key with the journalistic chorus. He is a scholar of the New England type, nobly studious, conscientious, and loyal to the best traditions. What can he do in an age of newspaper demigods who decry all that he stands for? Our great cities are filled with lately arrived European aliens to whom the continuing tradition of American scholarship has no appeal."

CHAPTER NINETEEN

"TRAIL-MAKERS OF THE MIDDLE BORDER"

I

WITH my daughters beside me, I sat on a Fifth Avenue reviewing stand for nearly five hours on May fifth, watching a parade of our belated machinery of war, a most impressive spectacle. Cannons, tanks, flying machines, trench mortars, anti-aircraft guns, kitchens, machine shops, field hospitals, supply trains—all the marvelous agencies which this war has developed unrolled before us. Gas warfare, air warfare, trench warfare, submarine warfare—all these new and terrible methods of destruction were shown or suggested. Science has made battle a swift game, chemistry has made it an inhuman game.

"The marching men had the look of veterans, an orderly array of powerful, resolute, and amiable animals, marvelously graceful and efficient. Their officers were strikingly handsome. Diet and drill are the compensations of war. Military discipline gives physical grace, precision, and self-reliance.

"At night as we walked up the slope to the reservoir in the park, we confronted a picture of such contrasting beauty that it will stay in our minds as long as we live. Across the water, in the pale blue mists of coming dusk, the city, softened to ethereal beauty, rose like a dream city, exquisitely lovely. Greed and vice and war were hidden by its mists."

The Whitman celebration which came on May 9 was a sparse and gloomy meeting in the Brooklyn Academy of Music. "Our auditors (as seen from the stage) were all elderly and sat in silence in the dim, cold hall, peering up at us with listlessly expectant gaze. John Burroughs and Thomas Harned came on the stage together. Harned looked old and feeble, but Burroughs walked well and was in good spirits. Samuel Crothers spoke too long, and so did Markham. Harned who followed me mildly reproved me for the candor of my story revealing Whitman's poverty. I had given my honest impression of the house in Mickle Street, Camden. The meeting was a melancholy hour. We were like a group of survivors mourning for a dead comrade."

My daughter's part in a performance of "Everyman" at George Grey Barnard's "Cloisters" led me up there.

"Barnard, looking very handsome, met me in the court and we had a short talk. He referred to his 'Lincoln,' which has been so criticized, and freely confessed that he had suffered under its rejection by London. I can well believe this. All the same, I am willing that it should stand in Manchester and not Westminster Abbey, for it does not entirely please me. It has a noble head, but the feet are clumsy and the attitude of the gaunt body repellent. It is in fact a theoretic Lincoln, a great Liberator growing out of the soil, whereas the real man was in appearance a blend of preacher and county judge. The bent, painfully awkward position of the body, Barnard argued, was characteristic of Lincoln on the platform.

This led me to say, 'Why be realistic on the pose of the body and theoretic as to the shoes?'

"The truth is, Barnard is a poet and a philosopher as well as a great sculptor. He is an artist of amazing power and versatility, but theories sometimes carry him into dim, mysterious deeps where his friends cannot follow. I like him and admire him—he is a genius—but I cannot advocate his 'Lincoln' as a whole; the head, I repeat, is superb.

"Barnard has been most successful in discovering, assembling, and selling pieces of medieval French sculpture and architectural ornaments, and with amazing pertinacity and skill he has built these beautiful 'cloisters' on a bare height overlooking this flimsy upper city. It is all as incredible, as sharply in contrast with its surroundings as he is with his neighbors. It is his creation, his work of art, his dream. It has nothing to do with this age, this city of unthinking personalities, and to me it is grateful because of its historic appeal. It is dependent on him, however, and will not, I fear, last beyond him."

Carl Akeley dined with us on May 12, and told us the tragic story of a woman he knew who had developed an insane jealousy of her husband. "She writes anonymous letters to him, accusing herself and accusing him. She reports telephone conversations with imaginary women. She telephones the husbands, charging their wives with infidelities. She seems to think of nothing else at times. Yesterday she left her husband, taking everything of value. The pitiful part is that this husband and this wife have had a past of great happiness. He cannot realize her estrangement. The memory of what they have been to each other and the victories they have won together in the happy past make his present life a torture."

It was a piteous tale. A few days later he came to a birthday supper which my wife and daughters had prepared for him. "He is a sorrowful soul, notwithstanding his success in pleasing the Roosevelt family with his monumental lion, and we did our best to lighten his mood. His stories have a wondrous fascination for my little daughters. He tells them badly, from my point of view, but he has done the work!—that is the main consideration in their eyes and mine."

Dr. Edward Jones, who lunched the following day with me, related many amusing stories of the oil boom in Texas. "Ragged farmers have been made millionaires overnight. Cities of canvas have arisen with no liquor and no guns. I saw nothing of the madness which used to come from drink. A man to be bestial or devilish in these towns must act that way without whisky. He must go against law and decency deliberately. Liquor can no longer be used as excuse or excitant."

"May 15. This is the record of a writer's career, and as one who is counted among 'established authors'. I here set down the fact that my income does not suffice to relieve my wife of household toil or enable me to enjoy a comfortable study. It is not easy for a man to maintain a high opinion of himself when his best efforts count for so little. All that I have gained seems at times illusory. Other authors have houses, cars, offices as evidences of their ability. At its best, mine is but a poor showing."

At dinner with Mrs. John P. Jones, we met Frederick MacMonnies, whom my wife had known many years ago in Paris, and with whom we had both kept up an intermittent acquaintance during the last twenty years. We had a lively discussion of President Wilson, and my wife was rather overwhelmed by MacMonnies' arguments against the President's acting without authority of the Senate.

"He was looking young and vigorous, almost unchanged from the man he was when I visited him in Giverney, but he is living a most secluded life. 'My work leaves me so tired at the end of the day,' he said by way of excuse for his unsocial habits, 'that I have no wish to go out.' He is never seen in any of the literary or esthetic circles in which I have a place, and hence seems to have diminished in power and influence."

George Arliss and his wife were guests of honor at a dinner given Anne and Frank Shinn on May 21, and we spent a delightful evening with them all.

"Arliss is a slender, dark-complexioned man, slow-spoken and keenly intelligent. His physical endurance is an amazement; where it all comes from I cannot imagine, for his body seems a fragile engine, and yet he keeps going and is making large plans for next year. 'I have been here seventeen years and feel quite American,' he said. 'My ambition, like those of all actors, involves me in a struggle to hold a place in the New York theaters—the dream of every actor.'

"I recall my first sight of Arliss on the stage. It was in 'The Darling of the Gods,' wherein he played the part of a remorseless Oriental despot so wily, so cultured, and so cruel that he remains in my memory as the chief figure of the play. Now I think of him as 'Disraeli,' a marvelous characterization.

"He is an actor whose eyes never betray him. He is

always, every instant, the man portrayed. He wears a single eyeglass, and his diction is clean-cut English-American like all of our best English actors. He has a wide reputation in England, but is living here very modestly. He, too, is feeling the pressure of these transition times. The moving-picture hero is now king of the dramatic world."

For the first time in many years I took no part in Decoration Day. My mind was filled with memories of the West, and of the graves I had left behind me there.

"My sister Harriet is buried at Osage, Jessie somewhere in Dakota, while father, mother, and all my grandparents rest in Wisconsin soil. It is an appalling line, or would be appalling if I permitted myself to dwell upon it. Nothing is gained by mourning the irreparable. My duty is to my wife and daughters, to write as best I can is my only ambition. I must not lose for an instant my hold upon my literary concerns.

"In looking back for a moment upon other Decoration Days, I remember my daughters and their close-clasping little hands. Year by year they saw the parade first in Chicago, later here. They will have great memories of Grant Park, Fifth Avenue, and Riverside Drive, but never again shall I go out to see these wavering lines of gray-haired veterans passing to their graves."

II

"Onteora, June 3. I was awake at five-thirty this morning, and in the beautiful stillness of the Jones home, I drank my thermos bottle of coffee and was in our own cabin at six-thirty. The living room was packed with crates of furniture from our Wisconsin home and I set to work with hammer and screw driver to open these crates, toiling harder and longer than I have been able to do for five years. Amazed at my endurance, I kept at work, and by sunset things were pretty well arranged. This shipment of furniture completes our separation from Wisconsin. We shall never again live in West Salem. Each year will see us more embedded here.

"Each morning I write, each afternoon I paint, hammer, or saw. Each night I go to my bed so tired that I can hardly wag a leg, but I am much stronger than last year and can well afford the ache which comes with physical labor."

In addition to my carpenter work I had taken over a certain care of Juliet Wilbor Tompkins' garden. "She is my nearest literary neighbor and is experimenting for the first time in her life with peas, beans, and onions. She bought the place last autumn 'sight unseen' as the children say, and I, knowing her methods of work, had said to her, 'Turn in and write a story of your purchase and detail your garden aspirations. Such a story will pay for it.' She took my suggestion. She wrote 'Joanna Builds a Nest' which had done precisely what I predicted; it has paid for the house and also for seeds and tools for the garden.

"It is not a large garden, but sometimes as I am hoeing it, it appears to be as wide as a farm. Juliet has lost some of her early enthusiasms about radishes and berries. She now 'cusses out' radishes, peas, and other non-fulfilling plants with a venom which has a certain pathos. She *was* so hopeful last year! It is this intensity of interest in life which makes her stories so successful. She writes deftly, with understanding and humor, and is one of the best paid of women writers."

It was raining hard when I awoke on June 9, but I made ready to return to town with Edward Wheeler. We got away at seven-thirty and for nearly three hours traveled in the rain. We reached Riverby, John Burroughs' Hudson valley home, at eleven-thirty.

"Uncle John was out in the garden hoeing, or rather leaning on a hoe while watching a bird. His hair and beard, white as wool, and the fixity of his pose gave him the appearance of a statue. His attitude was highly characteristic, but as he turned to greet us he seemed so frail and bloodless that I was shocked. He is able to leap up and kick his heels together, however, and did so just to show us that he still retained his agility.

"Taking us to his little bark study which stood on the bank above his garden, he showed us many of his treasured books and pictures. In that small, impermanent pavilion on the river bank are hundreds of autographed books, valuable photographs, and letters from all over the world. He has had small contact with artists, but his correspondence with men of science and poets has been large. He works surrounded by a confused welter of print. He said, 'I am writing on "Accepting the Universe." We can now accept God as an equal. He is as good as we are!'

"As we rode away I said to Wheeler, 'Did you notice the dust and dampness of that pavilion?' It is filled with precious literary material, but it is all decaying. That flimsy little structure is in danger of springing a leak or burning up. All John's other homes are equally impermanent. 'Slabsides' is a mere shack and 'Woodchuck

Lodge' a cheap little farmhouse. None of his treasures are in his stone homestead."

(Burroughs' remark about God being as good as we are revealed that he belonged to a generation which took God seriously. In this regard he failed of Whitman's advice, "Argue not concerning God.")

III

James Gannon of *Everybody's Magazine* had asked me to do an article on Roosevelt for him, and early in June I had sent it in to his office. On arrival at the club June 10 I found a note saying, "We are greatly pleased by your article and shall make it a leading feature of the October number. We intend to give it ten pages of the magazine."

In my reply I suggested that the illustrations delineate Roosevelt as if he were a character in a story. Gannon was struck by this suggestion, but on inquiry found that the illustrations had already been ordered. "Next time," he said, "we will take your advice on this matter."

Gannon was a most attractive young editor, not the kind of editor Howells was or that Gilder was, but suited to his time. "Editing a popular magazine to-day is almost wholly a business," he said. "Literature is only an alluring side show to the circus."

Carl Akeley, who called on me, admitted that he was a lonely man. "I see nothing ahead of me save the possibility of doing the Roosevelt monument," he said.

"He is a singular combination, this sculptor-explorer-inventor-naturalist. He is confident that his gigantic Roosevelt lion will be accepted, and if it is, it will carry his name throughout the world and down to many future generations. His design varies from week to week and is not precisely what I had imagined it to be. He is not the artist I would have selected; and yet he is quite as worthy in his way as Herbert Adams, Hermon MacNeil, or Dan French. His other interests tend to dominate his work as a sculptor."

I returned to Onteora on June 15 and set to work again on my Wisconsin narrative, "The Trail-Makers."

"As I motor about this region I take deep satisfaction in it. It is a colorful hillscape now. Slopes of white daisies, meadows of yellow buttercups, and ridges of burnt-orange snakeweed present wide splashes of pigment which unite to make an inexpressibly radiant foreground over which the blue hills rise in glorious contrast.

"These are good working days, not too cold, not too hot, and I am getting ahead on my story. At night I read Burroughs to the girls while they toast marshmallows at the open fire. It is all finely ancestral, this hour beside the rude old fireplace."

IV

Another of the many enterprises with which I had been concerned was the development of Edward MacDowell's summer home into a colony for composers, authors, and artists of one kind or another. The plan which Mac-Dowell himself suggested, or at least had sanctioned during his illness, was taken up after his death by the Mac-Dowell Memorial Association, which assumed the care of the homestead and arranged for its support. Naturally Mrs. MacDowell had retained her rights in the homestead and logically became its manager.

It had prospered amazingly. Clubs in distant cities had raised funds to build studios and establish scholarships;

and when Mrs. MacDowell wrote me informing me that a convention of women's clubs was about to meet in Peterboro and that she wished me to address them, I at once accepted.

"Peterboro, July 1. I found Marian MacDowell at the open-air theater on the hillside, the center of a confused and confusing swirl of excited actors, musicians, and visitors. She was supervising all, deciding all, directing all, a quaint little figure in a gingham gown and straw helmet, carrying a crutch on her arm. She used to hobble about on two crutches; now she forgets the one she has.

"At four the pageant came off and the fact that its actors were nearly all citizens of the village interested me. It was directed, of course, by skilled hands, but no professional actors were in the cast. Some of the scenes were very impressive. After it was all over, I walked down Edward's path toward the sunset while a thrush sang his requiem."

"Peterboro, July 2. I awoke in a cool, sweet room at a neighboring farmhouse, hearing the purr of a mowing machine and the cackle of barnyard fowls—a delightful symphony. At eleven I set out to visit Edward's grave. I do not know why it was dug in that particular piece of ground, for it is remote from the colony; but it is an impressive burial place. Over the low stone walls the roses nodded and in the fields the timothy waved in the wind. Afar the hills rose clothed in mist. I cannot believe that Edward MacDowell is under that mound, but I feel him in the air as I sit here."

CHAPTER TWENTY

ANOTHER SUMMER IN ONTEORA

I

ALONG about the middle of July, my wife and daughters, on the invitation of Mrs. Ira Nelson Morris, made a return visit to Wyoming to a summer camp in the Big Horn Mountains, leaving me alone in my Catskill cabin still at work on "Trail-Makers of the Middle Border." That I was not entirely happy in my seclusion is evident from the following entry in my diary:

"This has been a dismal week for me. My situation here is absurd. I should have a home nearer New York, and a comfortable study such as every literary man should own. Here I am keeping house in a cabin which is neither country place nor hunter's lodge. To some it would appear a most inglorious and incongruous end to an ambitious career. Burroughs in his ugly little Roxbury cabin is at least living on home acres, whilst my hillside hut is not only alien but accidentally chosen. There is no fundamental reason for my being here.

"In getting back to work on my story of early Wisconsin, it seems likely to run along the lines of depicting Grant as my father's hero. I shall let it go that way, although the Vicksburg campaign may divide the interest in some degree."

In the midst of my depression, Alan Sullivan, a Canadian engineer with a literary turn of mind who was spending the summer in Onteora, came to call.

"Sullivan interests me. It appears that he once spent several years in Sault Ste. Marie and that he has a wide knowledge of all that northern country. He promises to be a congenial companion."

A part of my dissatisfaction was due to the irritating presence of a woman whom Juliet Tompkins had brought to Onteora as her housekeeper and whom she had turned over to us.

"She is supposed to cook for me, but I find her a nuisance. I dislike her intensely but cannot send her away, for she says that she has no place to go. She is a strange person in many ways. She professes to have seen better days. 'I am trying to write stories,' she said; and in fact she drums on my typewriter so much of the time that the cabin has fallen into disorder. There is something unpleasant about the woman. I cannot endure her."

Alan Sullivan called for me with his car July 24, and drove me over to Woodchuck Lodge. "We found Burroughs in process of being motion-pictured. 'I'm getting pretty tired of it,' he said. 'I'm going on Sunday to join Edison and Ford on their annual outing, this time in the Adirondacks. I am too old to go on such a trip, but I've promised to do it and I can't very well get out of it.'

"I urged him to quit the party when he became tired of it.

" 'That I shall do,' he declared. 'And they must keep regular meal hours, also. I can't stand a break-up in my routine.'

"He was a good subject for the camera with his shaggy head, brown shirt, and baggy trousers. 'How inescapably rustic he is,' I said to Sullivan. 'But looking as he does at this moment, he still writes in the way of a master. His style as a writer has no relationship to his everyday speech or everyday dress.'

"With the reserve of an Englishman, Sullivan gave no reply, or, if he did, I gained no clear concept of his impression of the old naturalist who was carrying on the Emersonian tradition of simple living and high thinking."

Late in August (23), my wife and daughters returned, bringing a "poor little rich girl" with them. As the daughter of wealthy people this girl was inclined to a vague sort of socialism, like others of her class. She resented luxury yet clung to it. She wanted to work and she took pleasure in helping cook and wash dishes.

"This is only a pose, or at best a mood. It can't last. She says, 'Money is unimportant,' but she says it because she has it. Her association with my daughters is helpful. I joke her about her radicalism. 'What you need is hard work and plain fare,' I say to her. 'You need to be ordered about by a man.' She looks at me with wide eyes, a faint smile on her lips, as if she were trying to discover my underlying motive. She dresses with exaggerated simplicity and strides about in wide shoes with flat heels. She pretends to a dislike of the society her mother offers and hates the luxury of splendid hotels, whose waste (I agree) is criminal in times like these."

On learning that Bliss Carman was booked for a reading at the Alexander studio, in Onteora, I walked up the hill to hear him.

"He was looking very well, but not as picturesque as usual. His hair was more nearly conventional in cut than I had ever seen it, and his tie was neutral in color. At the request of the committee I introduced him to his audience. He read his verses very quietly, tastefully, but without much force. Mrs. King who followed him recited with fervor and skill. Altogether we recorded another literary event in the history of Onteora.

II

On my return to New York, September 3, I attended the Roosevelt Memorial meeting which seemed to me rather futile. It met and did nothing. Colonel Thompson read a report and then everybody talked. It was adopted by a listless vote. No enthusiasm was in the proceedings. The members present were mostly distinguished politicians from various states.

"Carl Akeley, Frank Chapman, Hermann Hagedorn, Lawrence Abbott, and I formed the esthetic section. I fear the artistic and literary world lies outside Colonel Thompson's survey. Hagedorn, who acted as secretary, was almost as deeply chagrined as I over the way in which the vote ran. He feels, as I do, that the quicker we act the richer the response. America has such a short memory!"

"Onteora, September 17. To-day was sunny and the color wildly glorious. We dined at night at Alan Sullivan's cottage, and one of his visitors, an Englishwoman, betrayed to us something of the bitterness which England holds toward America. She reflected it in her temper and in her worn, alert face, and she succeeded, at last, in rousing gentle Irving Bacheller.

"While she was in the midst of attacking Americans, accusing us of greed, he rose, walked slowly and calmly to the fireplace, picked up the poker, stirred the logs skillfully, then turned and faced our critic. His voice remained low and his manner kindly, but when he had finished she had no rejoinder.

"I think our host sympathized with us in our resentment of the imputations which involved us all. We excused the woman because of the war atmosphere from which she had only just escaped, but there is no justice in her charge which bore upon all America."

"New York, September 30. With strikes all over the nation and lynchings in Omaha and Georgia, with food prices going up and help becoming scarcer and scarcer, we find ourselves in the midst of the war's dread aftermath. To-day a decree was issued suspending 152 periodicals. What the issue of this strike will be no one knows. It may mean the ruin of many magazines. It is all a part of the vast reconstruction program announced by labor leaders. So long as it moves in accordance with law and order I have no complaint to make; but when it advocates the creation of a proletarian dictatorship, I become a conservative. At fifty-nine, one is less tolerant of such leadership.

"Lily Morris, who came to dinner, read us a part of the records of her social experiences as wife of the Swedish ambassador; and for an hour or two our little apartment was filled with kings and queens, diplomats, conspirators, generals, spies, and newspaper correspondents. It was a vivid and intimate picture of what went on in that neutral country during the war."

On invitation from Mrs. Eva Ingersoll Brown, my wife and I took the train for Dobbs Ferry. We were met at the station and driven to Robert Ingersoll's old home, a lovely estate with huge oaks, grassy slopes, clumps of vivid salvia, and glimpses of blue hills along the west bank of the Hudson River. In the midst of the ample grounds stood the mansion built of gray stone, and resembling a German castle.

"Mrs. Brown, glowing with welcome, received us at the door. Her other guests were Dr. Albertens, a handsome Spaniard, connected with the Cuban government, and our old friends Ernest and Grace Seton. At two we sat down to an informal luncheon.

"The house is filled with fading mementoes of Ingersoll—photos, letters, and portraits. It is a mansion with a history, delightfully remote from our present day. It was not difficult for me to imagine the life and times of its owner, the great agnostic. In those days this was a remote estate. As we walked about the grounds, I thought of it as the scene of a novel, and I came away from it as if returning to the present from the past."

III

The coming of Cardinal Mercier in early October was our city sensation. Every one was eager to see him, and as President Butler sent us cards to his reception we gladly availed ourselves of the privilege.

"On reaching the door, we found a continuous line of motors coming and going. Many of our friends were there. The cardinal, an ideal pontifical figure—tall, thin, kindly, and remote—was encircled by his admirers. He embodied my concept of a Pope. His red robe and his various insignia made a very inspiring bit of color in the midst of the company, and when he came out of the house a little later, a crowd of peasant mothers with their little children cheered him shrilly, a sincere tribute. To them he was greater than a king. On all their faces was a look of mingled awe and adoration."

The death of Henry M. Alden, October 7, removed another of America's literary landmarks.

"For over sixty years he was connected with *Harper's Magazine,* and for over forty years he sat in his dusty office, a plain little room, hardly more than a stall, with the ceaseless grind and jar of the elevated road filling his ears. He seemed not to mind this tumult, but his visitors found it deafening. Now he is in silence.

"At his funeral, I saw only a few of my friends. Minna Smith, whom I had not seen for many years, came in and took a seat beside me. John Kendrick Bangs was there seated near Robert Underwood Johnson. I saw no others that I knew. How slight, after all, was Alden's hold on the world of to-day, or even of yesterday. He had very little concern with his neighbors, especially in these later years. As a writer he was not significant. He was not even a great editor; but he was a noble citizen. He stood for all that was most characteristic with us and his judgments profoundly influenced our fiction—that is indisputable."

CHAPTER TWENTY–ONE

ELECTION TO THE CENTURY CLUB

I

My election to membership in the Century Club, in 1919, produced a radical change in my daily routine. For over twenty years the Players Club had been my home in New York City, and to resign from it was a wrench.

"These are uncertain times with me, and as I am now a Centurion I seldom get as far south as Twentieth Street. The world to which I belong and which used to seem so stable is breaking up. Few of the men at the Players remember Edwin Booth or care to perpetuate his memory."

One day at the club (October 15) Albert Paine came up to me and smilingly inquired, "Notice anything strange about me?"

I thought for a moment. "Why, yes, you don't stammer as much as usual."

"That's it!" he replied. "I've been cured!"—and went on speaking rhythmically, volubly, easily. It was amazing.

"I am like the dumb wife who recovered her speech," he said, "I want to talk all the time! I want to spread the good news. I feel it my duty."

I could not blame him for his loquacity. All his life he had suffered the handicap of a stammer which not only made public speaking impossible, but cut him off from full and free association with his fellows. It was a constant source of embarrassment in ordinary conversation, for while he spoke with comparative freedom to his most intimate friends, the slightest excitement made him helpless. Phoning was a chore. Now here he was announcing his good fortune to all his friends, running on as smoothly as any one.

I said, "I shall call upon you for a speech at the Book Show on Wednesday night."

"Better not. I'll talk for an hour and a half," he replied. I did call upon him and for the first time in his life he made a public speech.

On October 16, I received an invitation from the Lewisohn sisters to attend a performance of the Neighborhood Theater on the lower East Side. "We are producing three of Lord Dunsany's plays," they wrote, and I decided to go. I had already heard several of his short pieces and was profoundly interested in them. At eight o'clock I found myself seated amid a throng of strange people, waiting for the curtain to go up. Witter Bynner, Padraic Colum, and Louis Untermeyer were the only writers I knew.

"At my left not far away was seated a tall, blond, boyish man of pleasant expression upon whom many curious glances were directed. This I inferred was Dunsany, and this inference turned out to be right, for at the close of the first play, calls of 'Author, author' rose throughout the audience. In response to these demands he rose and went forward.

"Backing up against the footlights, he stood for a moment in very evident embarrassment, swinging one hand back and forth behind him as if he were scraping the dust off the stage. Gaining composure at last he made a modest and charming speech in which he confessed that this was the first time he had ever seen a performance of these plays—a statement which astonished me as it did others in the audience. He said (as I recall it), 'Your performance to-night has been a revelation to me. I did not know this play could be so impressive.'

"There was something quite charming in his voice and bearing, and when he returned to his seat he was besieged by eager autograph seekers who thrust their programs up at him and begged for his signature. That he was willing to stand there and patiently sign these programs, is evidence of something kindly and youthful in his character."

(I did not meet him on this occasion, but a few days later I attended the MacDowell Club reception to him. The room was thronged, and when I reached him he was seated on the edge of the platform shaking hands with a continuous and apparently endless stream of admiring and curious women. His habit of sitting down to rest had been much remarked upon, and it occurred to me as I met him that one reason for it lay in the great disparity between his tall form and the stature of those who mostly made up his throng of admirers. By sitting he came more nearly on a level with them. As we met him, my wife said, "Aren't you tired of all this?" and he answered, "No, my body gets tired but my soul does not. After a writer has suffered total neglect in his own country for fifteen years, as I have done, he doesn't mind a little—or even a good deal of—appreciation.")

I attended the Roosevelt meeting in Carnegie Hall

late in October, and my record is again one of disappointment.

"The audience was large and fairly enthusiastic but
noticeably middle-aged. It is a bit shocking to find the
'Rough Riders' a group of gray-haired men. General
Wood spoke and spoke well, clearly, forcibly, but without a particle of feeling. In truth no one spoke with emotion—no one but Corinne Robinson. She was effective.
The assembly needed a natural-born orator to stir it
into life—and none appeared.

"I went away, saying to Akeley, 'Whatever is done for
the Roosevelt Memorial must be done now or it will not
be done at all. A wave of receding enthusiasm is not easy
to recover. Roosevelt, like Grant and Lincoln, is certain
to pass through a valley of depreciation. No man, the
greatest of men, can avoid this recession of interest, due
to the effect of reiteration and the need of change.' In
this, Akeley agreed."

One afternoon we all went down to see the Prizma
Pictures which Captain Stone had made of John Burroughs at Woodchuck Lodge. "The scenes were very
lovely, but the reel is too short. It was hardly started
before it was over; but it presented Uncle John in the
manner in which he lived, walking about his breezy
native hills exactly as I have seen him do. It is good to
know that an imperishable record in color and motion of
this fine American figure has been made. John sat beside
me and I wondered what was passing in his mind as he
saw his shadow self upon the screen and realized how
soon he must pass into history."

On October 24, as a part of the Roosevelt Memorial
campaign, I spoke for the Rotary Club in Elmira, Mark

Twain's old town; and afterward Jarvis Langdon, a nephew of Mrs. Clemens', took me to "Quarry Farm" in which Mark had lived, and also to his grave in the Langdon burial lot. My record reads:

"It seems to me incongruous that the body of this Missouri printer, this historian of the Mississippi River and the Wild West, should be buried here in a conventional Eastern town. The house at Quarry Farm remains about as it was when he lived there, filled with mahogany furniture and small pieces of bric-à-brac. Its windows look out over the valley and its yard is pleasant, but it is by no means as beautiful or as spacious as I had imagined it to be. It is not in the least like the fictionist of the great Mississippi Valley. I doubt if it ever represented his taste or that of his wife."

While speaking in the campaign for money to build a Roosevelt Memorial, I found my audiences disappointingly small. "The one at Poughkeepsie was not only small, but middle-aged and funereal in character. Part of this lack of enthusiasm is due to me—I am an unknown advocate—but much of it, I fear, is due to failing interest; but a resurgence of his fame is sure. This campaign is a mistake and yet I am glad to have a part in it. It will yield results in patriotism and a clearer understanding of Roosevelt's work, no matter how small the fund."

II

At the Poetry Society, October 20, Lord Dunsany and John Drinkwater were the guests of honor and each spoke for a few minutes.

"Dunsany, who came in with his agent, young Pond,

was curiously shy and awkward. He had the air of not knowing exactly what it was all about, and his address was rambling and aimless. Drinkwater, however, was entirely at ease. With the air of the practiced orator he expressed himself gracefully, with precision and judgment. He read some of his verses, and very good verses they were, rich in suggestion and musical in tone. Altogether he and Dunsany made a most engaging pair. It was interesting and amusing to see their lecture agent shepherding them, protecting them, and finally leading them away.

"Other English poets and dramatists are announced. They are all after our dollars, but so long as they give *quid pro quo* (as Drinkwater and Dunsany do) no American writer can object. I must admit that most of these visitors are worth while. They are all especially grateful just now when England is so poor and cold and depressed. 'To come here is an escape into sunshine and prosperity,' one of them said."

"Albany, November 1. I spoke in the noble hall of the Educational Building to-day and I am spending the night with John Finley, who, as Commissioner of Education, invited me here. During dinner he told me much of his recent visit to Palestine and expressed unqualified admiration for Allenby. 'He is a great man as well as a great soldier,' he declared. His picture of Allenby's army on the plains of Armageddon was very impressive, and his account of walking by night from Dan to Beersheba was highly characteristic of him. From any one else it would have been an incredible tale, but I knew him to be a walker of credit and renown.

"It is a regrettable fact that he has published no book which fully represents him. He has written many poems, but he is too busy to compose a volume worthy of him. He fills a large place in many organizations, but it is as orator, educator, and publicist rather than as author. His writings reflect his character, but not adequately, for he is one of the finest men I know. He should be our ambassador to England."

III

On my way to Cincinnati, I stopped in Washington, November 4.

"An early morning walk led me to the Lincoln Memorial. The park is beautiful and so is the building— but why a Greek temple? It is an alien object here in the midst of a flat Southern landscape. I grant that it is exquisite, but it is a classical derivation wholly without New World originality or national significance. Relating plain Abraham Lincoln to a marble temple is essentially absurd. It is like putting Walt Whitman's bust in a Gothic chapel."

After my talk to a group of women in Cincinnati, on the afternoon of November 6, Mrs. Collier, one of the committee, drove me out to call upon Mary Watts, the author of "Nathan Burke," a novel which had interested me.

"I found her a quaint, elderly, reticent person who met me guardedly as though she had never heard my name and feared I might be some sort of agent or salesman. It was all rather comical. I praised her books somewhat extravagantly in expectation of getting behind her guard—all to no effect. I came away with a sense of having put myself in a false position."

At Columbus, Ohio, I was met by Professor Joseph V.

Denney, head of the Literature Department; and in dining with some ten or twelve of his associates, I lost all sense of being in an inland town, so entirely congenial was the group.

"We had much talk and good talk on literary and social matters. Andrews and Denney were especially pleasing. To be in such a hotel and in such company after a week of mixed trains and village accommodations is a pleasure. These men are cosmopolitan in feeling. They read and they travel. They are entirely untouched by the cheap journalism of their local press.

"Denney took me to the university chapel, where I was greeted as a man of letters and also—I am sorry to say— as a man of years. My auditors convinced me that there are still parts of America in which New England literary traditions survive. The national note which I sounded met with swift response. My talk dealt with Howells, Clemens, Miller, Harte, Burroughs, Riley, and others of the makers of American literature whom I knew personally; and the fact that many of my hearers were students made the applause especially significant and grateful to me. It may be that quite aside from the money consideration, these lecture trips are not a waste of time and energy. I miss my desk, my mail, and my books—but I shall persist."

(Here in Columbus Howells is remembered, and the places where he lived some sixty years ago are pointed out to the visitor. He often spoke to me of the simple, kindly life of Columbus in 1860, and as I contrasted his picture of it and the present city, I doubted some of its claims to progress.)

CHAPTER TWENTY-TWO

LORD DUNSANY AND OTHER POETS

I

SOON after my return from Ohio I learned that Howells was in the city. I called at once to tell him of my experiences in Columbus. He was but a wraith of the man I had known so long—but he was still able to jest. In speaking of "The Quality of Mercy," he said: "Laffan of the *Sun* bought it for ten thousand dollars and then advertised it as 'The Prize Novel.' I resented the publicity then—I'm not so sensitive now." A little later he said, "I am starting in to write the second part of my autobiography"—here again he smiled—"and if I last long enough I will do my *later* life!"

I said: "You've no conception how stupendous that ten thousand dollar check seemed to me when I read of it."

He replied: "It was not altogether despicable even to me—but I hated the lying announcement of it." He was on his way South.

"November 15. For the first time I entered the door of the Century Club with an air of proprietorship. As a member in good standing I not only commanded the instant attendance of clerks and waiters; I was greeted by many of my distinguished fellows. It chanced to be a special evening, a reception to the English actor, Forbes-

267

Robertson, who was scheduled to give an address in the library, and by nine o'clock the room was filled with gray-haired men. It was decidedly a session of the senators.

"The lecturer while not an old man is on the retired list and naturally called out the veterans. He read beautifully, but his talk was not especially valuable. He looks like a man ill-nourished, but his voice is as rich as ever and his diction almost flawlessly perfect. Frank Chapman, Jesse Lynch Williams, Carl Akeley, and I drew together as a group of 'the brown-haired younger fellows.' I do not regret joining this very dignified club, but I find its membership less vigorous than I had thought it. It is a club of old men."

Ibáñez the Spanish novelist was one of the guests at the National Arts Club November 16 and as I entered I found him tormented—baited, one might say—by a ring of curious spectators. "He is not a handsome figure even when happy. He is said to be an idealist, willing to go to prison for his Socialist theories, but he has not the appearance of a martyr. Rough-hewn, dark, and stern, he displayed power but not grace in his actions. As I was led up to him he was plainly on the point of breaking out of his ring like a tormented bull. Not being able to exchange a single word with him, I hastily backed away, giving way to my wife, who might have spoken to him in French, but she, too, was intimidated and passed on. . . . The man who had him in charge was not unlike the youthful proprietor of a performing bear, one which needed careful watching.

"Literary America is at this moment reading and discussing the savage novels of this Spaniard, but I am not drawn to them. After seeing him I am less inclined to read them. He is to me another of the prepared 'booms' of which New York is suffering in continual procession."

On November 24, my daughter Mary Isabel and I went down to see Augustus Thomas' play, "Palmy Days," and we both greatly enjoyed it.

"While not strictly new at any point, it is interesting from start to finish, and was exceedingly well done in all its technical details. It was valuable also for the picture it drew of dramatic life in the days of Edwin Forrest and the Christy minstrels. I enjoyed it as a lesson in the art of play-writing as it was practiced some thirty years ago.

"It is better done than most of the jack-boot plays of that period. The writing is very good indeed—correct, vigorous, but lacking something essential—something which has gone out of Augustus just as it has gone out of me. The play has all the taste and skill of the master, but lacks the vital flame. I fear it will not find lasting support."

Mrs. Lillian Sabine having sent me tickets for her play based on "Silas Lapham," Mary Isabel and I again enjoyed (November 25) a dramatic afternoon. We were a bit disappointed.

"The lines lacked the clear strength of Howells' dialogue. The play was a bit confused in outline and the last act an anticlimax; but it put me 'away back there!'—in Boston. The costumes were interesting and charming, and Wilton Lackaye in the title part was very good indeed until he got into the 'gol durn' stage of the last act, which seemed to me entirely out of character. My daughter delighted especially in the quaint gowns which the women wore. To her they were comically remote, but to me they were beautiful, for they brought back very vividly the lovely women I knew as a youth in Boston. The production cannot succeed, of course, but it is a praiseworthy effort. I am grateful to Mrs. Sabine and her players."

Early in December, W. D. Moffat, the editor of *The Mentor* (a kind of loose-leaf magazine), who had asked me to write a sketch of Roosevelt's life and character, wrote to say that the article which I had sent in was acceptable, but added, "I fear it may provoke a riot among those of my readers who are admirers of Woodrow Wilson."

To this I replied, "My intention was to make this sketch as impersonal and as detached as though I were speaking for posterity. I have no wish to shock any of your readers, and if certain of my lines are offensive, soften them down. My own personal bias is strongly anti-Wilson; but that should not enter into the article."

A dinner in honor of Lord Dunsany was scheduled at the National Arts Club and as one of the speakers I perched on one of the camp chairs at the head table, confronting a crowded dining room. It was hot and the air was bad and Dunsany was troubled by it, but he made an eloquent, modest, and candid speech.

Lady Dunsany, who sat opposite Mrs. Garland, was very happy. She frankly said, "I am grateful for all that is being done for my husband."

Stuart Walker and Irving Bacheller both spoke warmly in praise of Dunsany's plays, and I, in turn, touched upon two points which had not been emphasized: "The beauty and precision of his English delight me. His plays are unlike any others of our day. Their interest is not dependent upon the struggle of two men for a woman or of two women for a man. To me they are a keen joy because they are neither historical nor concerned with the world we know."

There was much gossip of his "boorishness" going about the city, but I saw nothing of that. He appeared boyishly impulsive to me and a genial, likable character.

A week later I saw him at a reception in Orlando Rouland's studio. He was sitting sprawled out on a couch, surrounded by a group of admiring women. Although plainly bored, he was answering their questions civilly. Soon after I entered he came over to me as if seeking refuge from feminine inquisitors. "He referred gratefully to the astonishing welcome he had received in America and spoke again with even greater candor of his books. 'No one reads me in England or in Ireland—not even in my own county. I have written twenty-two plays and many short stories, but no one in Great Britain knows or cares. I doubt if six copies of my books could be found in my town. The people of my county are delighted to see a lord riding to hounds in pursuit of a fox, but they resent his writing plays. What business has a lord with pen and ink?'

"He was distinctly humorous in his description of his position among his 'constituents'—as a politician might say. He touched upon his failure as a lecturer and said, 'I'm stopping all that. I can't endure the lack of air in your sleeping cars and your hotels; especially your dining rooms are insufferably hot.'

"I liked him, although he lacked something of Galsworthy's tact and patience. I was sorry when our conversation had ended.

"At Mrs. Rouland's request he consented to read something from his book of fables, and as he thumbed the leaves of his book I called out, 'Read "The Flight of the Hen"; I think that a delightful little satire.'

"My suggestion pleased him. He turned to the story of the hen who, having watched the migratory birds flying south in November and their returning flight in April, became desirous of a similar pilgrimage. After once more hearing the birds sing of the seas they had crossed, and the flowery isles they had visited, she said, 'I, too, will migrate,' and so one day in great excitement she spread her wings and sailed away southward over the garden wall and far down into a strange field beyond the brook. After several days of bewildered wandering, she found her way back to the farmyard—and thereafter she, too, boasted of the waters she had crossed and the strange lands she had seen.

"Dunsany read the lines well, with rich and charming voice, and we all applauded him so heartily that he read several others of his delicious fables. I carried away a very charming picture of him. Hereafter I shall defend him from unjust criticism. I found him delightfully unaffected and manly."

II

"Like many others of the early members of the Players, Brander Matthews was seldom seen there during the war. He came in on December 15 and I had a short talk with him. He is a tragic figure to me—all the more tragic for the reason that he keeps up a brave show of jesting at his

infirmities. His legs are almost lifeless from the knees
down and he is hardly able to hobble up the stairs. He
knows his time is short and his work finished. 'I don't
want to do anything,' he said, 'and I don't want anything
to be done for me. I don't want a doctor to cure me.
What's the use?' He uttered these despairing sentences
with a smile, but I was not deceived. He is jesting with
a relentless antagonist."

"December 18. Bacheller, who is still in the midst of
his novel 'A Man for the Ages,' gave a luncheon at
the Century Club to-day in honor of John Drinkwater,
whose play 'Abraham Lincoln' has profoundly interested
us all. A finely representative group of men came together. John Finley, Barton Hepburn, Cass Gilbert,
Augustus Thomas, James Gannon of *Everybody's*, Alex.
Grossett, and Don Seitz were the guests. Drinkwater, a
handsome young man, carried himself with dignity and
won us all. Irving presented his plan for a huge pageant
of democratic significance and was eloquent in the stating of it; and yet I could not believe in its working out.

"My seat was next to Cass Gilbert, and Drinkwater,
addressing us both, spoke with boyish enthusiasm of
Lincoln, 'I enjoyed a keen thrill as I saw the White House
for the first time.' He admitted that he got his inspiration
from Lord Charnwood's life of Lincoln; and this explained its inaccuracy in small affairs. I found the play
curiously, almost ludicrously, wrong in detail but it is
a most moving drama nevertheless. Knowing little of
our political or domestic life, he succeeded in presenting
the tragic life of Lincoln!"

CHAPTER TWENTY-THREE

ANOTHER SOUTHERN TOUR

I

I BEGAN the year 1920 as a guest at Frank Seaman's beautiful Yama Farms Inn, along with Eugene Heffley and Dr. Hamerschlag, the head of the Carnegie Institute in Pittsburgh. Toward dusk Heffley and I took a long walk out into the country, a walk which brought my youth back to me. Boys were coasting down the hill and out over the pond, and a group of girls around a bonfire completed a pleasant picture. We met farmers on bobsleds, their horses smelling acridly of sweat and trotting to the tinkle of bells. The dusky coverts, the snow covered with rabbit tracks, the purple hills, and the song of the icy river all united with magical effect. Inwardly I was a youth; actually, a gray old cripple.

"At night I talked psychics again. Dr. Hamerschlag was especially interested. My hearers were all friendly and I hastened to assure them that I did not habitually talk psychic research. 'Spiritual problems are in the air,' I explained. 'Everybody is more than usually concerned about immortality. The bereavements of the war have created an interest so intense that it leads to credulity. Books on spirit return multiply, but most of them are of no lasting value. Many writers ignore the physical side of these manifestations, but I am never weary of weighing and measuring the forces and agencies employed. It is not a question of faith with me. I am eager to understand the mechanics of the "direct voice," the "independent writing." The smallest mark under test conditions is as significant as the fall of a mountain. If levitation be a fact—as I believe it is—we must account for it on some physical basis, for we live in a physical world and the spirits of the dead must manifest—if they do manifest—in accordance with the laws which govern matter. All these manifestations, whatever their character, are in harmony with natural laws. They belong to unexplored biology.' "

The evening was spent in discussing these points, to no definite agreement, however. Hamerschlag spoke of the lectures of Sir Oliver Lodge whose coming had been announced and asked me if I thought his book "Raymond" valuable. I replied by saying, "The proofs submitted in the book do not satisfy me. The phenomena, while supernormal, are so mixed with the thinking of the psychic and the sitters as to remain unconvincing to me."

On my return to New York I found a note from John Cosgrave of the Sunday *World* asking me to lunch with him.

"I have some work for you. *McClure's Magazine* has again changed hands without change of name and I am its advisory editor."

At this luncheon on December 5 he outlined his plan. "The coming of Sir Oliver Lodge is sure to revive interest in psychical matters and we want to make use of your wide experience in our magazine. We must meet the increasing demand for information on psychic research. I have suggested that *McClure's* commission you to write an article bringing the subject up to date, making it a sequel to the series of 'Shadow World' articles which you wrote for *Everybody's Magazine*. Will you do it?"

Without hesitation I accepted this commission. "In my philosophy there are no 'supernatural events.' The return of the dead, if a fact, can be proved; and as one fact is as natural as any other fact, I have no patience with those who speak of psychic phenomena as happenings outside physical law. I will write such an article with interest and pleasure."

(I set to work at once upon this essay and it was published in March, as I recall it.)

"Leland Summers came to dinner last night (January 10) and talked long and entertainingly of the great personalities of the Peace Conference. He described the changes which the war had made in the shape of shells and instanced the tremendous gain in the range of cannon. He described an appalling charge of armored tanks. He gave us intimate pictures of Lloyd George, Clemenceau, and Wilson. As Baruch's right-hand man, he served as chairman on several most important occasions.

"He told us how it happened that he presided over the actual signing of the peace papers. 'The Germans were an odd lot, not a representative body of men at all. They stalled sullenly along till Baruch, who was in the chair, turned the gavel over to me and left the room. I decided to take a chance. Banging on the desk, I rose. "Gentlemen," I said, "I am going to declare a recess of fifteen minutes. I shall leave the room to you. When I return, I shall expect you to sign these papers." With that I banged the desk again and walked out. When I returned they were ready to sign. They knew that we would not stand for any further debate.' "

Here is the historic fact substantially as Summers smilingly stated it. Baruch, who represented President Wilson, wearied and disgusted with the German delegates, turned the gavel over to his private adviser, Leland Summers, and left the room. Thereupon Summers, an American engineer, acting without title, without official honor, and without pay, was for the moment dictator of the Allied policies. I do not pretend to give Lee's precise words, but only as I set them down the following morning.

Another similar story he told with a laugh in his fine eyes. "One day in Paris Baruch said to me, 'Buster, President Wilson wants me to write an article on the present general situation. I'm too busy to do the job. I want you to sketch out something for me.' He was my boss and his wish a command. Calling in my stenographer, I set to work. With very little time to spare, I dictated the paper, walking up and down the room as I did so, trusting Baruch to go over it before showing it to the President. 'All I need to do is rough it out,' I said. I did just that. I set down exactly what I thought and sent it to Baruch. On the following morning I was astounded to find this article in all the newspapers under huge headings: 'The Tiger Shows His Claws,' and signed 'Clemenceau'! Baruch had turned it over to Clemenceau exactly as I had sent it in and Clemenceau had given it to the press."

"As a man who made history, you do not appear in the records at all."

He replied with a laugh, "Not in *public* records. I was only Baruch's adviser." (At a later luncheon with Baruch, after Lee's death, I mentioned some of these incidents and Baruch confirmed them and spoke with affection of his unassuming aid.)

At a reception at the Cosmopolitan Club given by George B. McCutcheon and Julian Street, I came upon Albert Bigelow Paine looking very well and happy. "My stammer has almost entirely disappeared and I am giving much of my time to celebrating the clinic in which I was cured," he glibly declared. I saw several other old friends, George Pierce Baker, John Cosgrave, and Leroy Scott; but on the whole it proved a rather futile hour.

"My memory for names is now so poor that meeting people in mass is a trial. They mostly have to reintroduce themselves to me. I do not know what has caused this weakness, perhaps my many receptions, for often at the close of an address I am called upon to shake hands with scores of my auditors, men and women whose faces and names mean little to me at the time and hence leave no lasting impression. The casual quality of all this, like reading a newspaper, weakens my memory, for I make no distinct effort to remember faces and I seldom hear the names."

At the National Institute dinner on the 17th. "We elected eight or ten new members, among them Irving Bacheller and Ray Stannard Baker, whose names went through with a good margin. In Irving's case the vote was unanimous. It was a pleasant meeting, but the dinner not worth the four dollars we had paid for it."

A week later, taking my "Grant" under my arm, I went down to see Marsh of Macmillan's. I said to him: "This book seems to me too good a piece of work to be left out of print. I put two good years into it and some careful writing. As I own the plates and all rights, a new edition is a simple matter. It will not sell many copies, but it should pay for itself. I want you to publish it."

To this he agreed. I then went over to see Moffat of *The Mentor,* who promised to make it the basis of an issue of his magazine and to speak of it editorially.

On February 6, some one sent me a clipping from a Dakota paper which stated that the house which I had helped my father build near Ordway, Brown County, in 1881 had burned to the ground. "It was a flimsy little cabin on a bleak ridge, but it held precious memories of my mother and my little sister Jessie. On its door-stone I wrote 'Color in the Wheat,' and in the little bedroom in 1887 I began 'Mrs. Ripley's Trip.' Mother toiled there for nearly twenty years. Yesterday it seemed an immeasurable distance from my New York apartment. To-night it is so near and the memory of my mother so vivid that my heart aches with remembered pain."

II

Early in February I went South on another lecture tour with another invitation to visit Irving Bacheller in Winter Park.

"Columbia, South Carolina, February 10. I reached here at noon. I have a handsome room in the Jefferson Hotel and I am feeling very much at home. Dr. Currell, President of the State University, came in at three to arrange hours for a series of lectures and later I visited the statehouse, which I found most untidy. The halls were littered with papers and its chambers spotted with spittoons. The street leading to it was filled with dust and blowing refuse. The whole town is drab and unkempt, but the air is springlike and the hotel quite civilized.

"I dined with Dr. Currell, and during the evening he said: 'We have a colored school here, a kind of normal college, and the pupils would like to have you address them. They can't pay anything and your going will not endear you to some of our citizens, but it will be a Christian charity if you can find it in your heart to go. I speak for them occasionally.'

"To this I replied, 'I am quite willing to go. I leave the arrangements in your hands.'"

In this mood I visited the Negro College the following day. It was a pathetically dusty, bleak, and comfortless place. The buildings were like barns, the yards barren, and the schoolrooms mere barracks; but the faces of the young people were intelligent and serious. They sang for me two or three really beautiful old negro songs, among them, "Were You There When They Crucified My Lord?"—and in return I gave one or two of the Middle Border ballads, which greatly amused and interested them. Their eyes rolled and their white teeth lightened their dark faces with laughter. Whatever their motives may be, their persistence as students is highly significant.

Knowing that Howells was spending the winter in Savannah I had bought my ticket that way. "On arrival I hurried at once to the hotel to inquire about him. Mildred came down to meet me, looking tired and worn. 'My father is very weak and in great pain,' she said. 'He is under the influence of morphine now and cannot see you. He has been in bed for a month.'"

I went to my room with a feeling that I should never see him again. I met my Indianapolis friends, John and Mary Judah, in the dining room, and learned that they had seen much of Howells and had been of service to him.

"At breakfast this morning [February 19] I sat with John Howells who had arrived during the night and reported that his father was much better. This relieved me greatly. The wind was cold, so cold that we could not walk the streets, so we sat and talked. John commented upon the architecture of the city, which is interesting—in bits. He spoke of the lovely doorways and of the small parks, impressing me once again as a clear thinker and a graceful talker. His English is exceptionally good."

As I could do nothing to aid, and Howells was not able to see me, I went on to Winter Park, Florida.

"Winter Park, February 21. Bacheller and I took a walk through the forest between the lakes, finding the day warm enough to go without coats; and as we walked I talked of Howells. 'He is, I fear, on his deathbed.'

"All about us rose great oaks, and as we paced their dim aisles roofed with moss, the dry leaves under our feet suggested a carpet. One lake, covered with water hyacinths, presented a solid surface like a meadow, a most deceptive sward. The weather was glorious summer, the mocking birds in song, and the orchards heavy with fruit."

Just before leaving New York I had promised Carl Van Doren to write the introduction for a new edition of "The Life of Davy Crockett," and he had supplied me with a bundle of books, among which were copies of several other Crockett lives. I now set to work to read and compare these various versions.

"It is not merely the writing of a preface," Van Doren had written. "It is a critical job. We'd like you to go over all these biographies and autobiographies and compare them, and put your conclusions into your introduction."

I attacked the problem with zest, for Crockett, who had been one of my father's heroes, was of interest to me. I gladly gave my mornings to this work and before I left Florida I was able to send to Van Doren the results of my study.

"March 5, Greensboro, North Carolina. I am now in the 'O. Henry country,' in the O. Henry hotel. Soon after my arrival, Miss Alexander, one of the high-school teachers, came in, accompanied by a genial business man named Hunt, who told me much of the novelist whose fame the town is disposed to capitalize. Miss Alexander loaned me a biography of Porter which I read during the evening. I found it interesting but rather too enthusiastic.

"Porter's stories pall on me. They are so essentially tricky. Many of them are hasty, without logic or continuity. All have humor and some display invention and power, but read in sequence they leave a sense of satiety like eating dishes all highly flavored with the same spice. He is genetically the newspaper comic. I recall only one meeting with him. It was at a reception in New York City. He was a short, stolid man, so reserved in expression as to seem furtive. He made but a vague impression upon me. His success was just beginning at that time. He is now a precious memory in Greensboro and I have no wish to lessen their pride in him."

On March 10, just as I was about to leave the hotel, I met Vachel Lindsay coming in. "He has grown a little older since our last meeting, but is not much different from the man he was when I brought him to the Cliff Dwellers in Chicago ten years ago. He is making considerable noise in the world with his chantings, but I do not greatly value his 'Congo' or any other of his jazz performances. As a shrewd showman he realizes the drawing power of these antics. They make talk."

(In a letter to me just before his death he referred to my criticism. He wrote: "I have almost had fist fights to keep from being mobbed into reciting poems like the 'Congo' and 'General Booth.' Six years ago in the preface to my collected poems, I swore off reciting those two songs. You have saved me from being 'Congoed' into permanent fury. Your praise of the 'Village Magazine' is a stream in the desert."

(As I read his collected poems, I find the mystical lyrical note persisting, but many of his later verses are hasty, lacking that finality of phrase which his earlier compositions possessed. He was forced into the market place and his bizarre chants displaced the poems which in my opinion best represented him.)

CHAPTER TWENTY-FOUR

THE DEATH OF HOWELLS

I

REACHING home in time for breakfast on March 17, I got at my correspondence and cleared away a part of it. "At night I saw Eugene O'Neill's 'Beyond the Horizon,' a singularly original play. It is a New England tragedy, the kind of thing you would say could not succeed, and yet is drawing paying audiences. Nevertheless, it is of doubtful value to me. Its agony is a little too obviously constructed, arranged for. It is as if the author said, 'I *will* be abrupt and different. I *will* end my play with a vengeful oath.' It is New England seen through purple—dark purple—glasses."

Dining with Charles R. Crane, March 30, I met Frederick White, an Englishman, a superb specimen, one of the most attractive men I have met in years, a man of power, tact, and fairness. In presenting him, Crane said, "Mr. White has spent seven months studying America, lecturing in our colleges. He is one of the editors of *Europe*—a man to be counted upon."

Herbert Hoover was one of the guests and presented himself in a surprisingly critical mood. I could not learn the cause of his dissatisfaction, and I cannot recall anything that he said at the dinner, but as we came out into the cloak room together he asked, "Where do you live?"

I told him. He then said, "I am going up that way. I'll take you home."

Thus it came about that we had a half hour's talk with him, and my wife, with a woman's privilege, remarked upon a call for him to lead the Republicans to victory.

He laughed and replied, "It never was a *loud* call. It has declined to a husky whisper. When it gets a little weaker I'll kill it."

All the way up to our door he talked with delightful freedom, alternately joking and growling, and after we reached home I remarked to my wife, "He is too literary, too temperamental, too much 'our kind' to be President. He seems more like a novelist than a politician; but I'd like a chance to vote for him. He can't be nominated; he's too sincere and fine. Some politician is certain to crowd him out."

A lecture at Bowdoin College, March 22, carried me into deep winter. "The town is smothered in snow with no sidewalks cleared, but the president's house is bright with sun, and our breakfast was delicious. The day came on warm and the snow melted so fast that the gutters were brooks. I succeeded, however, in visiting the college library, which has many noble traditions. It is rich in records of Hawthorne, Longfellow, Lowell, Whittier, and many others of the noble New England group. The sky was glorious, but such floods I never saw before. The sun poured down in glory, and the streets were knee-deep with 'posh,' as Whitman calls it."

My daughter Isabel was with me on this trip and on the way back we stopped off at old Salem to see "The House of the Seven Gables," which was of especial interest to her, for I had handed on to her some part of my admiration for the work of Nathaniel Hawthorne. We found it in good repair, serving as shrine and memorial, and my enjoyment of the tinkling bells above the side door and the secret stairway behind the huge fireplace was doubled by my daughter's rapturous delight in them. We have few places in America with equal charm as survivals of Colonial life and literature.

In Boston we called on Margaret Deland, who was most gracious to my daughter, but eager to talk of the Boston we both knew in the early nineties. I held her books in high esteem, and while I had met her occasionally, this was the first opportunity I had ever had to talk with her at leisure. She told me that her "Chester" was a real town, but that it had been swept away or buried by the march of a huge sooty city. I said to her, "Your short stories of Chester people will be known long after the site of the actual town has been forgotten."

"New York, March 31. Luncheon with the associate editor of *The People's Magazine* and a call upon Siddall of *The American Magazine* produced in me a feeling of amazement mingled with disgust. *The American,* with fifteen hundred thousand circulation, and *The People's* with a million, are both (like dozens of others) swamped with advertising, dominated by advertising. 'We are handing one another money these days,' said Siddall; and that is exactly what it looks like. There is something factitious about this prosperity. The worker is wildly spending and giving poor service to his employer. Our periodicals are more and more appealing to the unthinking and the sensual. They have no standards but those which make for circulation."

II

"Yama Farms Inn, April 3. This was John Burroughs' birthday and it came in glorious with sunshine and appropriately joyous with the voices of robins and bluebirds. The Inn is filled with Uncle John's friends, guests of Frank Seaman. Among the ceremonies was the boiling of a kettle of maple sap. This John supervised; then he and I, for purposes of photography, planted a tree in the lawn. After a walk in the woods came the dinner with poems and a speech by the guest of honor, 'the first I ever made' he declared. It was a short speech but expressed his pleasure in the hour. It was a happy combination of poetry, good-fellowship, and hospitality."

I wrote of him that night, "He fitly represents our indigenous literature. His figure lends itself to such a celebration. He photographs well and his face is friendly. Howells could not have lent himself to such an occasion. He is too shy, too remote, too urban. Burroughs is at home with everybody. Although deeply touched by this dinner he was not maudlin. He glowed, but never for a moment lost his native dignity."

(In commenting on something I said at this dinner or elsewhere, Mark Sullivan printed in the editorial column of *Collier's Weekly* the following lines which sum up very well the Burroughs appeal:

"The above passage is worth quoting, not only for its bearing upon the high qualities of John Burroughs, but because it illustrates a type of personality often found in American life and in these feverish days too seldom recognized. That Burroughs gained the broad and growing reputation which is his was probably due to that mastery of English of which Mr. Garland speaks, which was a more or less accidental accompaniment of his other gifts. In other words, he was doubtless one of many such philosophers in American life of whom only a few ever become articulate. Those who have lived long in the back country or, better yet, have been reared on farms, know that the austerity, the patience, and the intellectual grasp upon the fundamentals of life which belonged to Burroughs were not his alone, but inhered among the people of the remotest and least urban countrysides.")

"New York, April 10. At the office of *The Mentor* this afternoon I met Johan Bojer, the Norwegian novelist, a slender, blond, attractive man of fifty-five. He speaks English with difficulty, but I could understand him. He said, 'I have been commissioned to secure and translate fifteen American novels, and when Mr. Moffat suggested you as one of the authors to be represented, I seized upon the idea.'

"He asked me to send him one of my books and this I agreed to do, naming 'The Captain of the Gray Horse Troop' and 'Main-Travelled Roads' as those most representative. He is to send me his book 'Hunger.' He seemed a fine, serious individual—refined rather than rugged, a preacher type, widely different from Ibáñez, who looks like a warrior and is, I am told, a disturber of the peace of Spain."

A few days later Moffat called up and asked me to join a luncheon party in honor of Bojer. This brought me into the Players after a long absence.

I regretted the fact that I was no longer a member, so strong were its associations. Percy MacKaye, Alexander

Black, and I were the literary guests in support of Moffat, who was our host.

"Bojer got along very well despite his hesitant English. He was greatly interested in what I told him of the lecture business. Like all our foreign lecturers, he hopes for large fees. He is a thoughtful, refined type of Norwegian and made a good impression on us all. The fact that my youth was spent in a country where Scandinavians were numerous helped me to understand his speech and his point of view."

The American Academy, at this stage of its development, was very poor in places to meet, and notwithstanding the fact that Maurice Egan, Brander Matthews, and I were scheduled to speak on April 15, a very small audience assembled to hear us in a hall on Forty-second Street.

"Egan, as became a former ambassador, was in conventional dress—frock coat, patent shoes, and high collar. The audience, what there was of it, was cordial, subdued in temper like a thinly attended funeral. My paper on James Whitcomb Riley was applauded, but how feebly! More and more I sense the changes which the war has made—and is still making."

"April 22. Howells being reported at the St. Hubert, I went to call on him, but did not see him. I saw only Mildred, who was plainly disheartened. She did not say so, but her face indicated that his death is near."

"April 24. A bitter wind has blown all day and I have not been out of the house. I am snared in the city and the chances of escape are less each year—and yet I stay! I doubt if any other place in winter would be as satisfactory. It may be that as I get older I shall willingly retire to a suburb, but just now there is not sufficient allurement in the country to compensate me for the loss of what the city offers.

"I am working at the 'Trail-Makers' and at times glimpse a worth-while theme in it. For the most part, however, my interest remains with 'A Daughter of the Middle Border,' which is nearly ready for the printer."

On April 26 I returned to my domestic problem. "Outwardly a moderately successful author and the head of a happy family, I am, after all, enslaved to my conditions. In spite of all my efforts, we live in this little flat—like tenement dwellers. My wife is still a household drudge, for the reason that I cannot afford to have adequate help. Going to the country would not better her condition. Domestic help is scarcer in the country than here. Truth is, the dignified life of other days was based on an over-supply of servants, a condition which no longer holds. I am afraid we must 'worrit along' as we now are and hope for lower rents."

My lecture at Teachers College, April 27, cheered me momentarily. "The aisles were filled and the doorways jammed with students who stood for an hour and a half. The diversity of nationalities in my audience interested me. The man who was about to introduce me said, 'Men and women from South Africa, Liberia, Iceland, Manitoba, England, Cuba, and Mexico, and from nearly every state in the Union, are among your auditors.' At the reception afterward I met many of them and all expressed interest. As an indication of change toward me and my work, the experience was heartening. Most of my auditors were country-born and could understand my elliptical descriptions of farm life."

One evening (April 28) W. D. Moffat, editor of *The*

Mentor, called me on the phone and said, "I am coming for you at four-thirty." He was most mysterious about his plan, but warned me to wear a dinner suit.

"On reaching the car I found William Hornaday, Dan Beard, and Gilmore Brown, all in tuxedo jackets notwithstanding the early hour of the evening. No one explained what it was all about, but we ended up at a country club in Hackensack, where we were the honored guests at a large dinner. Moffat presided gracefully and well. Beard responded aptly, Gilmore Brown told an astounding tale of an earthquake in Mount McKinley Park, and Hornaday vividly described a battle between two grizzly bears in his zoo. It was a long program, but the people seemed pleased."

On the way home together, Hornaday, at my urging, told more stories of bears, tigers, and wolves, and so enthralled us that our return trip was shortened by half. It was an extraordinarily interesting evening with a group of fine, earnest men. "It is in such hours that I find compensation for the close confinement of a city flat."

"April 29. At the meeting of the Academy this morning, I saw George W. Cable wandering about, half blind, confused, and feeble. 'I cannot find my way upstairs,' he said plaintively. His condition gave me a shock. He is old, old!—a tremulous ghost. He will not last long. My mind goes back to the days when he shared the lecture platform with Mark Twain. I can hear again his small, clear voice as he sang his Creole songs—and now!"

Carl Akeley came round in his new car the morning of May 2, and took us for a ride. The sky was sunny and the spring foliage lovely, but the wind was so cold that we did not have the picnic dinner we had planned. We came home and broiled our steak in the oven!

"Akeley seems to have adopted us. He said, 'I bought this bigger car so that I could take all the Garlands to Onteora—or anywhere else they want to go.' In his present unhappy domestic situation he finds comfort in us. He comes in almost daily—whenever he feels lonesome."

At Macmillan's, May 3, I talked with Latham, who had read the manuscript of "A Daughter of the Middle Border." "He likes it—is indeed quite emphatic about it—predicting a wider reading for it than for the first volume; all of which is deeply gratifying. I came away half resolved to forgo serialization, trusting to the added sales to carry it beyond the ordinary returns of serial rights."

At eight that night we all went down to see Joe Lincoln's play, "Shavings," and enjoyed it thoroughly. "It is the best New England comedy on the stage. Winslow is a real creation, ranking with the Music Master and Herne's Uncle Nat as an acting part."

In calling on some friends, May 4, we were again brought face to face with the labor question. "Although these friends are rich and living in a beautiful great apartment, the husband has been doing the cooking for a week. 'Our servants have all left us,' he said. His wife was ill, but that seems not to have softened the hearts of the domestics. They demanded what seemed to her an exorbitant wage and she refused to pay it.

"The situation is simple. Jobs clamor for men, and so long as that condition continues labor will continue to hold its head high. All this is right and fine, provided workmen are loyal to their contracts and do not obstruct and destroy. I sympathize in a large degree with the wage earners' present sense of mastery, but I am out of sympathy with any hasty and violent change, because such change brings suffering."

(I am revising this entry in my diary at a time when labor is humbly asking for a chance to earn its daily bread. The change is so great as to be appalling, and yet, thus far, we have had no violence.)

Dining with Frank Seaman at the Lotos Club May 6, I met George Broadhurst, a small, wiry, intense man, of some reputation as a dramatist, who took us to see "Smilin' Through," a rather thin English comedy with some good acting by Jane Cowl. "Seaman went soundly to sleep in the midst of it and I could not blame him. Some of it was pretty dull."

A walk in the park the following Sunday profoundly disquieted me. The day was beautiful, but the walks and meadows swarmed with strange people, all speaking unknown tongues. As I studied them I saw them as utterly alien to me and all I revered. "Not one among them knows what Lincoln or Grant or Roosevelt meant to this country. They are like flies, concerned only with the heat and cold of the present. They have no love of country. Many of them belong to the Balkan or Slavonic tribes who have no national unity, and they have not yet taken on a love of their new home. To most of them America means only the crowded tenements of New York City. They are sensual, hot-tempered, illogical. Of such people a mob could be made in a moment.

"Our problems are not all worked out in this country; they are increasing in complexity. We need a great President for the next eight years, and New York needs a mayor who can be firm as well as magnanimous in his dealings. These late immigrants have had very little training in law and order. They are careless and impudent. They litter the walks and meadows of the park with rubbish. They are well dressed, extravagantly dressed, but they have no pride in keeping public places clean. As voters they defy the city authorities to arrest them for fouling the parks. Few people of my acquaintance are ever seen here. For two days afterward the walks are repulsive with refuse. The sons and daughters of this generation may take a different attitude. Let us hope so."

III

"May 11. William Dean Howells is dead. To write that sentence is to write an end to the longest and most important friendship of my life. Knowing that he was very feeble, I was not surprised when the news of his death was given out at eleven o'clock. At two I called on John and Mildred, who told me that he had been unconscious for nearly a week.

"As I came away in the glittering sunshine, facing the multitudinous throngs of the city, I thought of his keen delight in it. Although he hated some of its physical aspects, he loved New York and was always coming back to it. Fifty-ninth Street and Fifty-seventh Street were his chosen places of residence. He wished to be near the park and often walked therein. He was interested in every phase of New York's 'scene,' and one of the last pages he wrote was in comment on the collection of Henry James' letters. His preëminence was earned by exquisite craftsmanship, humor, insight, social sympathy, and an almost unequaled knowledge of our social life."

His funeral was held the following afternoon in a small church on lower Fifth Avenue and some eight or ten members of the Academy were in their seats when I entered. The pews were filled with those who knew and loved Howells; and as I stood looking down at the casket, I found it difficult to believe that it contained his body. It was so small!—and his fame so great. I thought of his keen glance, his quick smile, and his humorous outlook on life and wondered what his comment on the service would have been. It was highly traditional and he was not that. We had never talked philosophy or religious faiths but I knew that he was inclined to that of Swedenborg.

"Elihu Root, who sat beside me, was deeply moved, as I was, by the singing of the choir. John Howells, looking thin and gray, sat with his little sons. Mildred was in black, deeply veiled, but John was in business dress. At the end we all went out leaving the body in the hands of strangers who will take it to the flames. So ends the material part of my great friend."

(No death since that of my father had so deeply affected me. Howells was more than an elder brother; he was a spiritual guide, an arbiter in many cases of dispute. My attitude toward him was like that of Mark Twain. I revered his tact, his taste, his sense of what was fine and right. When I went to him for advice he gave it in a few lines, sometimes in a single sentence. He never talked at random, never felt about for a word. Often he aided my decisions by two words—"Why not?" In all my intercourse with him I never knew him to utter more than a short paragraph. He never monologued as Clemens loved to do. Without the slightest pedantry he spoke as he wrote, with exquisite precision, without stereotyped expressions, and I often came away from his study in despair of attaining in my writing the precision of his speech. For several years after his death I often dreamed of sitting with him in his library, discussing books and men just as we used to do in life.)

IV

"May 13. As spring comes on I detest this noisy little apartment. I hate to see my wife and daughters living among shabby furniture. I cannot write here and yet I stay. We endure our flat for the sake of our friends. The vision of a lovely old New England homestead allures us, as an ideal, but after we had lived in it for a few months—what then? Would we not all feel its restricted winter life and long for the city?

"My daughters say, 'You should have taken us back to Wisconsin two years ago'; and in this lies a revelation of the change of attitude which the city has already produced in them. They now realize that they idealized West Salem and that if they were to go back now they would find it sadly changed. Its charm is in their childish memories of it.

"We cannot retain that charm in memory, and so I am putting some part of it into 'A Daughter of the Middle Border,' and there it will endure as a record of the happiest time of my life, a time when my children fancied me a 'king' and worshiped their mother as a 'queen'; our homestead, ugly as it really was, shall go into my chronicle as a house of magic."

"May 14. Chamberlin of *The Transcript* has just wired me asking me to come over to Boston. 'We want you to do a special article on "Howells in Boston," at once,' he wrote. I replied, 'I accept with pleasure.' I see in this an opportunity to write something in honor of the man whose life was an inspiration to me for nearly forty years. Furthermore, I am eager to learn more exactly the conditions of his early life in Cambridge. I shall go on the 17th."

CHAPTER TWENTY–FIVE

HOWELLS' EARLY LIFE IN CAMBRIDGE

I

THE commission to write an article on "Howells in Boston" was not important commercially, but I was willing to undertake it not only as an opportunity for a further tribute to my friend, but also for the reason that I was interested to know more of his life in that vicinity.

"Boston, May 17. Arriving at the Parker House at seven-thirty this morning, I saw Chamberlin at nine and arranged to search out all of the Howells homes in the city. In calling on Thomas Sergeant Perry, one of the oldest and closest of Howells' friends, I found him feeble and slow of movement, but able to give me much valuable information. He first led me to 184 Commonwealth Avenue, where in 1890 I had lunched with Howells and James A. Herne; then to 302 Beacon Street, which is the scene of 'Silas Lapham.' Chamberlin then joined us, and in a car we started in search of the three houses in which Howells had lived while in Cambridge."

Howells was the son of a scholarly country editor in Ohio. He had no collegiate training, but he was natively studious. In his youth he read and practiced the art of writing to the detriment of his health, for he was small and frail. "What I lacked in stature I made up in gravity of demeanor," he wrote of his early youth. At nineteen he had risen to the rank of newspaper correspondent in

Columbus, the state capital of Ohio, and at twenty-two he became the editor of *The State Journal*. At twenty-three he published, in connection with John J. Piatt, a volume of poems, and in 1860 he wrote a campaign life of Abraham Lincoln. This book, slight as it was, secured for him the appointment of consul to Venice, a most important honor, for it fixed upon him for all time a love for Italy and made of him a faithful student of her language and literature. His third book dealt, naturally, with his "Venetian Days," a delightful record of his four-year exile. In 1865 he returned to America.

Nothing could have been farther from Venice than the outskirts of Boston when Howells decided to make his home there. "Two reasons combined to make me a resident of Cambridge," he once said to me. "It was cheap and it contained Longfellow and Harvard University." And so it happened that he began to write in a bare little box of a house on Berkeley Street, about as spacious as an ordinary carpenter of that time would build for himself.

After some search we found this house, and as we entered it Perry said, "I remember the reception which Howells gave John Hay on his wedding journey, and also the 'Welcome East' party which he gave to Bret Harte"; and as I looked into that small sitting room I was able to gauge the Spartan simplicity of life in Cambridge in 1870.

On entering the tiny room on the north side of the house in which Howells began to write (a room hardly larger than a closet which had no heat and no sunlight), Perry remarked, "Conditions didn't matter to Howells. He could write in an ice box. He began 'Venetian Days,' his first important book, in this room."

His second home, on Concord Avenue, was uglier still and stood in those days on the dusty side of a country road, and I could well understand the homesick mood in which he wrote his poem on the oriole, dreaming of "the blue Miami flowing down the dusty Concord road."

His third home was on Sacramento Street and was, in itself, the worst of the lot, a fact which I cannot understand, for he had been made assistant editor of *The Atlantic* and his income must have increased—slightly. "It is certain that he had no money to waste on extra rooms or luxuries of any sort," I said to Perry, who smiled and replied, "None of us had."

From these most depressing literary shrines we drove to Belmont, where "Red Top," his first real home, which still stands just above the Belmont station almost precisely as he left it except in so far as time has exalted the shade trees and washed the paint from the roof.

"It was a complete and delightful home," said Perry, "the result of the combined thought of Howells, his wife, and her architect brother, William R. Mead."

He was not only happy in this lovely home but rightly circumstanced, for in it he wrote "Dr. Breen's Practice," "The Undiscovered Country," "A Woman's Reason," "A Modern Instance," and "The Minister's Charge." No doubt he considered it his permanent residence; certainly he loved it, for the owners of the place showed me a letter written to them in which he calls it "the prettiest place I ever saw," and lovingly adds, "It may interest you to know that I planted every tree on the place and watered them all one summer with my own hands." In another letter he writes of two mulberry trees "which we called 'Elinor' and 'William' after my wife and myself."

"Why did he ever leave this lovely place?" I asked Perry.

"It is easy to answer that. It was a remote spot in those days. His wife was not strong, and in winter she was imprisoned here. Then one of his children became ill, and the distance from medical aid became alarming. His only connection with Boston was an occasional train and the climb up the hill in January was a chore. Whatever his reasons, in 1881, just three years after he had put the date of its building above the fireplace, Howells left it to become a householder in Boston. He found No. 4 Louisburg Square a safer and much more convenient home."

My next task was to visit this square, which Perry said was the "Nankeen Square" of Howells' novel. He did not live here long. In 1885 he built a house at 302 Beacon Street (just as the family of Silas Lapham planned to do) and was living here next door to Oliver Wendell Holmes on "the water side of Beacon" when I went to Boston. In this spacious house he wrote "Indian Summer," "Silas Lapham," "The Minister's Charge," and "Annie Kilburn."

Aided by Perry I gained permission to enter the study which overlooks the Back Bay. Here he wrote for *Harper's Magazine* the articles which made his "Editor's Study" a vital influence in American literature. He had become not only a distinguished citizen of Boston, but the most cultivated, humorous, and characteristic of our novelists. I did not know him while he owned this house, and I had never before entered its door, although I had many times passed it, with awe of its owner.

II

When I went to Boston in 1884, Marcia Gaylord, Helen Harkness, and other of "Howells' women" were subjects of debate. "Why does he always depict foolish or unpleasant women? Has he no acquaintanceship with noble women?" some of his critics demanded.

It is amusing to recall the questions which poured in on me as a teacher of literature—questions glowing with indignation at the injustice he was doing to the women of New England. In reply I said, "You are all wrong. Howells is the most chivalrous of men—chivalrous, not gallant—there is a difference. Furthermore he is just as hard on men. He does not spare the lover in 'April Hopes' nor the clergyman in 'The Minister's Charge.' He employs the same method in dealing with Marcia Gaylord that he uses in the setting for Silas Lapham. He is a genial philosopher—not a lover. You will not find in all the range of his work a bitter or cynical word or phrase."

No writer was more in the public mind and less in the range of public observation than he at that time. He hated publicity. He loved to "poke about" unnoticed, and once he said to me with a sigh of regret, "I wish I could come and go as you do, but alas! I cannot. People are all facing the camera when I come near them now. I used to be able to live unnoticed at hotels and boarding houses; now I cannot."

He was in truth a "personage." The old masters were passing. Longfellow, Whittier, Emerson were gone. Holmes was aging and Lowell failing in health, therefore we all turned to Howells as the dominant personality.

That he was our chief man in fiction was conceded, and yet he continued to move about quietly and modestly. Few ever saw him.

His championship of the cause of realism made him friends as well as enemies, for he was most generous in his praise of those who brought to their writing a love of the near-at-hand, a desire to create in the image of life. He praised Howe's "Story of a Country Town" and he applauded the work of Alice French, George W. Cable, Joel Chandler Harris, Madison Cawein, James Whitcomb Riley, Sarah Orne Jewett, Mary E. Wilkins, and many others of the local color school.

All of these memories came back to me as I sat in that spacious room looking out on "the Back Bay" which was, in 1886, the symbol of wealth and exclusiveness to me.

"I never for one moment dreamed of entering his door or the door of Oliver Wendell Holmes. I had only one pair of shoes and a suit and a half of clothes in those days," I said to Perry, who smiled understandingly, although he never had felt the need of pinching a dime.

I came back to Chamberlin's for supper after a hurried but profitable dip into the past; and at midnight took the train for New York.

"New York, May 18. I was awake early this morning and at work on my Howells material. It was a very interesting trip, and I shall do an article which will convey information not widely known. It is disheartening to realize that Boston has almost forgotten Howells, and that few remain who knew him in Cambridge. Perry is the only one I could find, and he is old and will write no more. I am glad of this chance to do my bit."

(*The Transcript* gave a full page to the article with

several illustrations, and so, in our way, Chamberlin and I paid tribute to our beloved author.)

"To-day, May 20, I met Marsh and Latham and discussed the new book. They are to give a judgment as to what can be done about publication next fall. Coming around by way of *The Mentor* office, I suggested a Hawthorne-Howells number for the first-of-the-year publication. Later I called on Akeley at the Museum of Natural History and saw his sketch of a group for the African Hall—negroes spearing lions. It promises well. 'It is a real commission,' said Akeley, 'and relieves me of want for two years.'"

"Onteora, May 21. Akeley brought his car around at ten A.M. and we had a gorgeous trip coming by way of Napanoch. The spring is at its most perfect stage of life and bloom. We reached our cabin in time for dinner and to put things in order. A jolly party, including Dr. Jones and a Dr. Bryan, a zoölogist from Honolulu."

I worked all day (the 22d) mending the road, dusting the cabin, and clearing out the spring. "Juliet Wilbor Tompkins gave a costume dinner party—a quaint affair. I have never seen a more absurd group. Bryan went as a mandarin. His hat was a lamp shade, his pigtails a green veil twisted. He wore pajamas and carried a fan, a veritable Chinaman. Akeley came as a country girl and was a newspaper comic. I represented Buffalo Bill."

On the way down to the city next morning I stopped in to see John Burroughs. I found him in the "Nest" sitting in an armchair. He had been ill for a week and his nurse, Dr. Barrus, was worried about him. "A slight indiscretion now would carry him away," she said.

He spoke of Howells and said with deep feeling, "How

that man could write! No man of modern times could do it better. That article of his on death in the last numbers of *Harper's* is perfect. Where is he now? Where has he gone? I can't think of him as nonexistent!"

He was close to the fire and covered with a thick gray rug, but on every hand were the evidences of his literary labor and his wide interest in books. "It was a scholar's environment. His books looked like books in use. His table was a worktable. His papers, clippings, notebooks all indicated industry, as though we had interrupted him in the midst of a pressing task—and he is eighty-three!"

He said, "I ran my car up to Slabsides the other day and expect to go again soon," but Dr. Barrus was not so certain.

"June 1. After working intently all the morning, I concluded to let the publication of my book go over for another year. I am too old to be hurried and worried by insistent publishers. I have no quiet place to work in Onteora. Sometimes I am disheartened with it all, especially when I think of my daughters' viewpoint. They will soon see me as a worried, irritable old man, where once I was their 'king.' It is hard for a writer to maintain a lovely spirit in an unquiet study. I must arrange something better for next year. The girls are too old to live cooped up in a small flat and yet we cannot afford to live differently."

"At the *Mentor* office, June 10, I was able to correct the 'Grant' proof and make an important ending to the article which presents in condensed form the great man's epic career. The new edition of my Grant biography is going through at Macmillan's. This pleases me. I consider this one of my best books."

At the Century Club I met Melville Stone looking to
be, as he is, a rosy octogenarian. He said, "I'm taking a
vacation for the first time in twenty-seven years," and
by this he meant (I inferred) something much more serious than a vacation. He is retiring.

"It is a melancholy hour in the life of any busy man
when he discovers that he is no longer necessary. Stone
and his fellows have been forces, each in his groove, but
they are now over seventy and are being superseded by
younger men. Melville has been a just man as well as a
kindly man. I knew him first in Chicago when he was
one of a highly honorable group of city builders. I was
a novelist of very slender income living in a single room
on the North Side, but my poverty did not dismay Melville, who often asked me to dine at his palatial club. I
recall meeting Scott, Ryerson, Hutchinson, Kohlsaat,
and many others in this way. Eugene Field was often
a guest."

"June 12. Akeley came in his car this morning and we
had another glorious ride up the Hudson to Onteora.
I found the Elmers, Mary Antin and her little girl all
taking dinner with my wife and daughters. I had never
met Mary Antin before. What a strange, intense Oriental
type she is!"

"Onteora, June 19. I find the Elmer cottage across
the road a refuge from too much company and too much
telephone. I quite understand John Burroughs' reasons
for retiring to his barn or to Slabsides. Ideal as our camp
is for my wife and daughters, it is not a good place in
which to write. It is only a shack and every footfall is
heard from top to bottom. I am writing here in a neighbor's empty cabin, in quiet, but not with any sense of

appropriateness or comfort. I have made a worktable by setting three small square tables together. The room is fairly large, but has only studio lighting, and I feel the lack of sunlight. At times I work in the kitchen. It has no telephone, however, and I am free from interruption. My routine is already established. I am up at six, get my coffee, and march across to this cottage, where I write— or try to write—till eleven when the mail comes. I then read the newspapers, answer my letters, work in the garden, or play with our Ford car.

"In the effort to conquer its mechanism I went out on the highway to-day. After much fuss and noise and backing and filling, I brought it back in better shape than it went out. I found out how to mix the air and gas in proper proportions and I came in strong. My family laughed at me for being so pleased with myself. 'It is such a meek little car,' Mary Isabel said, and as there are some millions of men, women, and children all over the world confidently driving similar machines, my triumph is not as notable to others as it is to me. Although a ludicrous figure in the eyes of the people on the road, the problem was a serious one to me.

"After three years of disability I find myself playing tennis, sprinting after the ball with a vigor that I had not expected to regain. My daughter drives me to the court in our car, the 'Spook,' which is a source of joy and pride to us all. It carries us up the hill to the tennis court in ten minutes."

On July 16 Carl Akeley wired that he was coming with some friends, and as the night was cool we had a fire for them when they arrived. To our surprise his friends turned out to be Bessie and Robert Vonnoh, old friends of ours. "We came through in fine style, no delay of any sort," they said in praise of Akeley's driving.

On Sunday, in our customary way we had our picnic at the pool on Dr. Jones' farm and I, as usual, did the cooking for the party; that is to say, I broiled the steak, warmed up the creamed potatoes, brewed the coffee, and roasted the sweet corn, while Akeley busied himself gathering ground pines. Dr. Turck collected polliwogs.

"After our dishes were packed, I read aloud Ingersoll's famous lecture, 'The Mistakes of Moses,' which most of the picnickers, I found, enjoyed. The English of this lecture is crisp and telling. It has lasting qualities. We came home by a road new to me, a lovely mountain road which made me feel more deeply than ever the beauty of our summer home. Turck told funny stories for the girls, imitating a drawn cork, bubbling champagne, and the buzz of a fly—stunts which amused them highly."

"In reading Joe Lincoln's 'Roscoe Paine' I am inclined to think him our best delineator of New England; better in some ways than Mary E. Wilkins, because he is never bitter or despairing. His New England is not a decaying New England; it is only a changing New England."

"The Elmer Cottage, August 19. The manuscript of my book lies in a heap at my right hand. Shifting it to my left I begin to go through it again, always in the hope of bettering it. As I returned to it this morning I felt its significance as social history and shall try to deepen that significance. I worked mainly on the chapters which refer to Chicago. In the spirit of erring on the side of mercy, I softened some of the lines which dealt with the grime and squalor of the town which is, I hope, bettering these conditions."

On August 22 Dr. Jones drove me over to Roxbury to visit John Burroughs, whose long silence had alarmed me. It was a glorious day, crisp and cool like September, and the ride was delightful. The lodge looked deserted, but at my knock, Clara Barrus came to the door. Her face broke into a smile and she called, "It's all right, Uncle John. It isn't a sightseer; it's some one you know."

Following her into a back room I found John lying on a couch. "Why, it's Garland!" he shouted joyfully, and rose to meet me.

He looked smaller and feebler than I had ever known him to be, and he said, "I never before have had anything the matter with my head, but a few days ago I suddenly got dizzy and fell in a heap on the floor. Dr. Barrus thought I was dead, but I remained conscious all the time. The world was whirling, however. Since then, I've kept away from people."

Dr. Barrus explained, "He can't stand the flood of curious visitors. They swarm on Sundays. They overflow the porch."

Although mentally alert, John kept his chair, greeting my friends without apology. When I asked him to visit us he said, "I'd like to do so. I get tired of sitting here looking at the same scene day after day. I can still run my car, but Dr. Barrus is afraid to ride with me."

This she admitted. "He might be taken with a fit of dizziness," she said.

I came away in melancholy mood. Thinking of the grand old philosopher sitting there alone, except for troops of careless visitors, attended by one not of his kin, waiting for the Death Angel, whose visit could not long be postponed, filled me with sadness.

"The death of Howells has profoundly affected him. His cottage, which he calls 'Woodchuck Lodge,' is a cheerless place on a rainy day. It has no open fire, no pleasing colors, no glowing pictures, no ornaments. It is, in truth, a bare and mean habitation. It has not even the picturesque poverty of a cabin. It displays the poverty of a poor farmhouse. Its couches are rickety and its chairs worn and cheap. His noble presence makes it a literary shrine, but it has no charm. No wonder he gets tired of it and is glad to get away. If he only had an open fire!"

Professor Richard Jones' interest in my "Daughter of the Middle Border" manuscript was most helpful. "He has read the first half of the manuscript and wants to see the remainder. As I listened to him this evening (August 25), I almost believed in the book. 'It is history, intimate history, and it has charm,' he said. Curiously remote from my period, he is studying it as if it were the product of a poet or dramatist in the time of Dryden. This detachment gives his estimate a singular interest to me. He said, 'I am studying you as a writer of the past in the future.'

"At the same times that this critic interests me, he provokes me to revision. As I gain place as a social historian, I suffer a keener sense of responsibility and a deeper appreciation of my shortcomings in matters of style and proportion. I have *lived* this history, and if I can write it worthily it will make a significant book."

One night Dr. Jones and his niece Alice Benedict came down to call; and as we sat in the firelight Alice played the violin for us. It was a charming hour. "The voices of the strings in the darkness were of deep appeal. They reminded me of the time when Uncle David made his fiddle sing for me as I lay before the fire. This scene cannot possibly mean as much to my children as David's violin and that fire in a Wisconsin log cabin meant to me. There is no mystery here—no strange shadow, no wild forest near at hand. All is clear, poetic, charming; but not mystical, not magical."

At two o'clock, August 28, Dr. Jones came with his car and carried me over to Roxbury to get Burroughs. We found him ready and eager to come. We loaded him in with all that he needed for two or three days' visit and he made the journey to my camp in perfect comfort. "We spent the evening before the fire, talking quietly. He made a great picture as he sat in the firelight, listening while we sang our old songs. He was like a piece of granite sculpture as he dreamed in the glow of the embers. It was a sweet and noble hour, one we shall long remember. His memory is failing and his thought is slightly inert, but he talks well and is interested in many things. He alluded quite calmly to his shortening span of life. 'I do not shrink from death,' he said quietly. 'I've lived my life. I've done my work. I'd like to do three more books—two are nearly done. They will end my writing.' "

On the following morning, after we had eaten breakfast, John and I went out to examine into the work of a skunk who had been at our garbage. My theory that a skunk can produce a cloud of scent as a signal or a lure without leaving any trace of it on the grass or the ground, interested John. "It must be a different sort of scent from that which he sends out when attacked," he said. He dug up the sod in an attempt to discover what small animal had made certain round holes in the path.

"All this is in character with Uncle John's writings, but I observe that he no longer cares to walk. He slept much during the day, which is a sign of approaching death. He makes rules for his diet and then breaks them on the impulse of the moment. He gets away from home with relief and then becomes childishly eager to return. All of which is amusing to some people, but of tragic import to me. These peculiarities are certain evidence of decline. With all his philosophy, there is in him the soul of a New England farmer. He is eccentric but in a gentle way, not in any mean or ignoble way.

"One of his first acts after we got him back to Woodchuck Lodge was to see if the boys had delivered any woodchuck skins. He is intent on getting enough to make two more overcoats. He gives a great deal of time to the tanning of these woodchuck pelts. He removes the skins and prepares them for dressing—a trivial task for a philosopher, it seems to me."

CHAPTER TWENTY–SIX

THRONGS OF FRIENDLY WITNESSES

I

ONE day in late September (1920) as I entered the Century Club, I saw Cass Gilbert, president of the National Institute of Arts and Letters, and Dr. Fletcher, its secretary, dining together.

"At Gilbert's invitation I joined them to discuss the program for a joint meeting in November. Gilbert is unquestionably one of our big architects, and yet I cannot rid myself of a feeling that the head of the Institute should be an author."

When Ray Stannard Baker came to call on me the following day, I questioned him on the Peace Conference.

"He is still a stalwart partisan of President Wilson, and smiled when speaking of the 'shipload of experts' which the President had taken with him to Europe, but refused to comment on its absurd features. He is an able writer and a most congenial companion. His work as 'David Grayson' has charm and a lasting appeal. He is at work on the sixth book of the series, and I imagine he finds it a pleasant relief from his journalistic drudgery."

"Dining at Carl Akeley's, we met Mr. and Mrs. Roy Chapman Andrews who are just back [October 3] from the Gobi Desert and planning to return there in February. Roy is a tall, bald, keen-faced young man of pleasing manner. With his bald spot covered he looks like a boy, but he is in fact nearing forty. He is Western born, a graduate of Beloit College, and has already made a high place for himself as a naturalist. He is now organizing an expedition which is to explore Central Asia seeking remains of prehistoric man. 'It is to extend over a period of at least five years and maybe longer,' he said.

"He is genial in manner and makes no assumption of learning, and yet he has been able to finance this expedition among those who recognize the value of scientific attainment. His wife, a pretty little thing, will go with him. They have a baby boy whom they plan to leave at Peking while they are in the desert. His descriptions of Gobi and his experiences there were absorbingly interesting."

Katharine Gerould had been at Onteora in the summer of 1919, and my interest in her work was quickened.

"I have just read her 'Change of Air' and a book of short stories called 'The Great Tradition.' They are distinctly not of the 'woman's journal' type. They belong rather with the work of Henry James and Edith Wharton. They deal almost entirely with subtle reactions between married people, seldom with lovers of the passionate age. They are, like their author, highly critical and remorseless. They are fragmentary, which is also against the popular magazine rule. Her essays are less valuable to me than her stories, although the same keen discernment makes itself felt in them. She is an intellectual aristocrat, one who declines to compromise with simpletons. She picks up certain strands of life here and there, scrutinizes them keenly, pitilessly, and then lets them drop. I put her books down with a mood of depression, but their artistry pleases me."

In going over the straw vote which I had suggested to decide on possible candidates for the presidency of the Academy, I was forced to acknowledge that few of the men suggested were of the purely literary character which Howells maintained to the end. "He was the logical head of the organization while he lived and it is not easy to fill his place. It may be that men like Sloane and Butler, classed as educators rather than as creative men of letters, are the best types for president and chancellor. The Academy is in its formative stage and needs careful handling; vigorous officers are more necessary to it than poets and novelists. It should have the authority which the high character of its membership indicates. Nothing is gained by half-hearted action."

As acting secretary I met Chancellor Sloane and Dr. Butler, October 5, to discuss our plan for the Howells Memorial meeting. After some talk I stated that the informal vote of the members indicated Sloane for the presidency and Butler as chancellor. This announcement took them by surprise, but neither of them declined to serve. I said, "It is a question of getting something done and we need men of your standing to do it. Our members feel that we particularly need a chancellor of administrative ability who can, and will, attend meetings."

Sloane, who had just returned from the Old World, reported that the Europe he once knew existed no longer. "There is no France or Belgium or Italy—as I once knew them," he declared.

II

One of my most loyal advocates at this time was Dr. Benjamin Shambaugh, professor of political science at the State University of Iowa, and during the early autumn I had received from him an invitation to address a convention of Middle West historians. "They all recognize the value of your contribution to Western history and wish to honor you," he had written.

As I had been receiving many letters from teachers of history I had been sufficiently interested to say, "I will come"; but now as the date for my entraining came on, I dreaded the journey and duties demanded of me. Among other engagements which I had been led to make was an afternoon at the "Book Fair" in Marshall Field's Chicago store, to sign copies of my books for the public.

"It was hot when I reached the city, October 8, and in the Book Fair on October 8 I found a throng of buyers awaiting me. The Macmillan booth was crowded and for two hours and a half I signed my name as rapidly as I could make my pen work. The interest in my border books was extremely gratifying. Not since my 'Captain of the Gray Horse Troop' have I been so confident of success."

On October 28 I was guest of honor at a dinner given by Professor Shambaugh at his house in Iowa City.

"It was one of the most tasteful and amusing dinners ever given to me. At each plate were comical little effigies whose heads were eggs. Their bodies were ears of corn and husks served as skirts. Some of them had hats made of acorns and tiny volumes marked 'Main-Travelled Roads' served as souvenirs. Quaint little brownies, each holding 'A Son of the Middle Border' in one hand and a garland in the other, were perched upon the ice cream. Chains of squash seeds hung from the chandelier, and pumpkins held candles like stalks of corn.

All this was the work of Mrs. Shambaugh, whose eyes shone with humor as she pointed out to me the significance of each decoration. It was worth a poem or a most adroit speech, but alas! I could only express my gratitude without wit or poetry."

"Chicago, November 5. The total effect of three social affairs to-day is a sense of depression. At the Cliff Dwellers I was told that its literary group is diminishing. At the Little Room I saw no new members. 'All of us are aging,' said Henry Fuller, 'and no young writers or artists are being brought into the organization.'

"At the Cliff Dwellers I lunched with William Goodman and Charles Hutchinson. Goodman, a lumber dealer, was chairman of the club, and the men at the other tables were mainly music teachers and architects.

"At the Caxton Club I met several survivors of the pioneer era: Glessner, Ryerson, Burley, Hamill—all men of early Chicago—men of whom I once stood a little in awe, by reason of their wealth. Hutchinson showed me through the Art Institute of which he was so largely the creator. 'I am eager to get the new building built before I go,' he explained, and his voice, trembling with age, denoted an eager haste. I sensed in his decay the passing of a marvelous era."

III

A lecture at the Indiana State University, November 10, brought about a meeting with Theodore Steele whom I had known for many years and whose beautiful landscape paintings I admired. He came for me at the university and took me out into the country to see his home and studio, some twenty miles away. The weather was mild and the foliage glorious. In half an hour we entered a hilly country, a land of winding roads and rail fences which reminded me of pioneer days in Wisconsin.

At last we reached his home on a high ridge covered with noble oaks and elms. It was a lonely spot, but there he lived and painted all the year round, and looking about me I saw many of the scenes he had put on canvas. As he displayed the work in his studio, I honored him for his devotion to his state. I said to him, "The work you have done is beautiful and absolutely American."

"There is something large and brave in this man's action," I made record at the time. "He withdrew from dinners, receptions, gave up teaching and portrait painting, and came here to live among the hills he loved and wished to fix upon canvas. In his quiet way he is a master —as true to the Mid-West as Gardner Symons and Willard Metcalf were to their Eastern hills and streams. He is a lone pioneer, toiling on without adequate recompense and growing old in his toil. His hand is tremulous, but it has not lost its cunning."

We were awake at six o'clock the following morning and I saw Steele's landscape at dawn. It was glorious! The autumn foliage was richly toned and the grass, covered with frost, was an exquisite silver carpet. On every side a noble composition allured. Mrs. Steele, heroic soul, rose early and made our breakfast, and as we walked down to the highway bus, Steele paid a tribute to his wife. "She upholds me in all my doings," he said. "I don't mind living here, but it is lonely for her."

On my way to the railway I thought of this fine old artist going back to his brush, eager to catch some part of the ineffable beauty of the morning while his brave wife washed the breakfast dishes!

My journey to the East involved a return to Indianapolis and I could not fail of a visit to my faithful friends John and Mary Judah, who still lived in the big old house on Massachusetts Street. I lunched with them that day and told them of Steele, whom they understood and admired. "Indiana has come to honor him," they assured me.

Mary spoke of Howells and of his last illness in Savannah. "We were able to be of service to him during his illness. John helped carry him to the train. He was deeply grateful, and though he said little he smiled with such sweetness that we knew he had come to love and rely upon us."

IV

Soon after my return to New York (November 21), Hermann Hagedorn came in for a little while and talked of his collection of Roosevelt data. "He is so intense, so full of hope and good cheer, that his face is a benediction. He and Percy MacKaye are two of the most aspiring of all our young literary men, although, as he said, 'We are no longer boys.'"

At the MacDowell Club, a week later, I acted as host, a little under compulsion.

"Winston Churchill came in, tall, brown, lean, and manly and we had some talk about his work. I introduced him to Carl Akeley. There were very few other 'celebrities' in the group. Although a reception to certain dramatists, few of them presented themselves. Several actresses came, among them Mary Shaw, looking her age but as intellectually gay as ever. She insisted that I should lunch with her at the Professional Women's League and speak. I was not able to refuse."

On my way down to the Century Club, the following afternoon, I dropped in on Augustus Thomas to show him some of Schrenck-Notzing's ectoplasmic photographs and we had an hour of psychic talk. As usual he delighted me with his wit, his keen insight, and his command of English.

"He is genuinely interested in psychic research and I enjoy discussing it with him. I find him a most engaging host. He is swift to understand my thought; indeed his mind frequently outruns mine, perhaps because I hesitate a little over my phraseology. From his house I went to Macmillan's, where I definitely agreed to publish 'A Daughter of the Middle Border' in the spring list. This will mean a crowded and worrisome December for me, but it must be done."

On December 1 came the dinner to Tagore, the Hindu poet, one of our temporary American enthusiasms, which would be funny if they were not so revealing. As I saw this long-bearded Indian philosopher expounding the "eternal verities" to a throng of women, naked almost to the waist and swollen with rich food, I said, "What a farce! How can he discuss his ascetic philosophy with such auditors?" Edward Wheeler and Samuel Ratcliffe (who preceded Tagore), each tried hard, but did not succeed in saying anything worth recording, clever as they both were.

Tagore had much to say of the differences between the materialistic philosophy of the West and the interior calm of the Oriental sage, but admitted that American dollars would be of the greatest aid in building up his school. Most of his hearers were aware that he had come to America as a lecturer and that he charged large fees, but that did not matter provided he amused them. To most of us he was just another speaker harvesting American dollars. "I don't complain of it," I said to Wheeler, "I'd do the same if I were in his place."

At the "Ends of the Earth" dinner, December 3, I found George Bird Grinnell, Frederick Dellenbaugh, Carl Akeley, Poultney Bigelow, Roy Andrews, and many others whom I knew. Bigelow presided in a quaint, rambling fashion and his wit provoked controversy.

"General Pershing, looking very handsome, came in late. I had never seen him before, and I studied him with care. He is a finer figure than I had imagined him to be, but he is a very poor speaker. His words gave me a better understanding of the reasons why he is not put forward as a candidate for President. He is a gallant commander, but not a thinking man in the degree that Wood is. Wood gives the impression of power, of clarity, of sincere conviction. Pershing gives the impression of a soldier whose range is narrow. His limitation is not a mere inability to speak; it is a far deeper inhibition."

Lunching next day with Señor Lobo, the Brazilian consul, I was interested to learn that he held the thirteenth chair in the Brazilian Academy and that he had been commissioned to get in touch with our Academy. I found him altogether charming, and assured him that I would do all I could to assist him. He asked minutely about my own work. "I intend to write of you for the Brazilian papers," he explained.

Later, I joined Augustus Thomas' party. "He was

giving a luncheon to Channing Pollock, who is about to set out for a trip abroad. Childe Hassam was there, also Zogbaum the artist—a pleasant group. These two meetings are typical of my life in New York. As I said to Lobo, 'New York is not a city; it is a group of cities.' He replied, 'It is a world. My wife is in love with it and frankly says she intends to stay here.' "

At Juliet Wilbor Tompkins' dinner, December 5, I met Rachel Crothers, a quiet, self-contained, middle-aged woman, and Sydnor Harrison, a small, blond man of fifty or more. The Garlands and Ralph Clarkson of Chicago completed the group.

"Miss Crothers is not the lively kind, but she is most intelligent and sympathetic. She is like her plays, wholesome and kindly. Harrison was humorous, and almost as deft as Fuller but less keen. Although a Virginian, his accent is not typically of the South. It is curiously flat in tone and nippy. The *a*'s and *o*'s are pinched in his mouth. He told me something of Cabell who is also a Virginian. He said, 'Cabell works at night and for years has lived in seclusion, a fact which his books make evident.' Harrison is a pleasant dinner companion, capable of humorous give-and-take in the studio manner. He is a writer of insight and skill."

"December 6. In reading *The Bookman* to-day I discovered a sense of disgust at the whole business of authorship and book publishing. These 'blurbs,' as they are called by the publishers themselves, are so obviously insincere and the books so unworthy, for the most part, that I wonder at the good men who consent to such advertising.

"The moving picture sets the pace for fake drama, as

it sets the pace for magazine editing, and our raw, half-educated readers and auditors are the game for which publishers are mostly gunning. A throng of young people to whom academic standards are of no value has risen to authority in the market place. The public buys what it likes, as the ox rushes to his corn. This cheapening of art will go on until this generation has exhausted its desire for sensual suggestion, and then another and possibly nobler generation will arise to take its place in the sun. In such wise the waves of life rush on!"

At the Gamut Club, December 7, a woman's club somewhat like the Players, I was the speaker guest. "Mary Shaw presided very gracefully and well and there were several good talks by women. A Miss Blank, a plump, humorous woman, told of 'playing second' to a goose in a film drama. Mary Shaw, whom I have known for more than twenty years, is near seventy, but her mind is keen and her laugh musical. Life has been a battle for her, but she has taken an Irishwoman's unfailing delight in it."

The Academy directors met at noon, December 8, and elected Brander Matthews chancellor for the coming year. Afterward President Sloane, Fletcher, the secretary of the Institute, and I went to the Century Club and completed plans for the Howells Memorial meeting. "It must be a worthy memorial," I urged, "for he was not only our president but our most distinguished man of letters."

V

One morning in December (the 11th) Frank Seaman again phoned me from Yama Farms inviting me to come up for the week-end. "Baron Rosen is coming up," he added, "and as he doesn't know the way, I wish you would go to his hotel and escort him to the train. I'll phone him and tell him you are coming for him at noon."

Baron Rosen was a vague personality to me. I associated him with the pre-war Russian Embassy and I had read one or two articles by him; but beyond the fact that he was living in New York City in exile I knew very little of his history. The cloud of association which came with his name did not personalize him in my thinking and I went down to the hotel and sent up my name, wondering just what sort of English-speaking Russo-German I was about to meet.

As I stood in the lobby, waiting, he came running down the broad stairway, a short, dark man wearing a fur cap and a heavy overcoat.

Speaking easily but with an accent, he apologized for his delay. "The truth is, I am only just out of bed."

I took charge of him as Seaman had ordered and we were soon in a taxi and on our way to Weehawken. On the way he said, "I hope there is a dining car on the train; I have had no breakfast."

This troubled me a little, for there was no diner on this train, and with but a few moments to spare in the station, his only chance for a snack was at the lunch counter, and somehow I could not quite figure a Russian noble and diplomat perching on a revolving stool before a careless waitress. However, I explained the situation and said, "While I am securing our tickets you'll have ten minutes for a roll and a cup of coffee. I hope you don't mind the informality."

"Not at all," he heartily rejoined. Leading him to an empty stool, I waited a moment to see that he was waited upon. A calm and somewhat acid waitress approached. The baron lifted a finger. "One hot dog and a cup of black coffee—lively, my dear!"

I was enlightened. The baron knew all about lunch counters and waiters. I left him with a sense of relief. Nobility of this adaptive sort promised amusement on our three hours' ride.

When I returned to fetch him to the train I found him in conversation with his waitress, who was smiling down at him with a wondering look in her eyes as if to say, "You're a queer old duck, but I kinda like you."

No sooner were we settled in our seats than I began, "Baron Rosen, I wish you'd tell me what is going on in Russia."

His face shadowed. "I never talk about Russia, it is too painful." Then as if to head off any more questions, he turned on me. "Seaman said you were a writer— what have you written?"

"Oh, a lot of novels and short stories and some history."

He caught at the word "history." "What history?"

I mentioned my "Life of General Grant."

"Did you write a life of Grant? I knew Grant. I liked him and admired him."

My memory began to bring up facts connected with this early experience in the baron's official life. "You have been in America before?"

"Many times. I have lived in America nearly forty years."

I laughed. "No wonder you knew what to order from a lunch-room stool."

We were now on the best possible terms, and he went on to talk of Grant and other of the men who were my boyhood admiration, and at last, as if as an expression of confidence, he told of his escape from Russia.

"We had but an hour's warning—my wife and daughters and I. We got out just in time, but we saved nothing except a small bag of jewels which my wife carried in her hand. She and my daughters are living on those jewels now, in Paris, whilst I am earning my living as a journalist. The Bolsheviki confiscated all I had, houses, lands, money—everything. I don't know what I should have done without the interest of Lorimer of *The Saturday Evening Post*. He has taken several of my articles and paid me well for them. He wants another and I must hit upon a subject."

His attitude toward the lunch-room counter suggested a theme. "Why don't you do an article in which your life as an exile should furnish humorous episodes?" I can't remember now my precise notion, but it pleased him.

"I see it!" he replied. "I see an article in the suggestion."

That night, as we sat about the fire in the beautiful lounge of Yama Farms Inn, Frank Seaman got the baron to talking of his exile. He expressed no bitterness, no hatred; on the contrary, he presented the situation from Lenin's side. "They are fanatics, Lenin and Trotsky and all their ruthless gang. Bolshevism is their religion. With them, individuals are merely pawns in a great game, insects in whom they see material for social experiment. They had nothing against me personally. I was only another aristocrat to be despoiled. Theirs is a theoretic organization. They have no gold except that which they confiscate. They have no goods. They dig nothing out of the ground and the peasants produce only what they can swallow. They have no desire to give their meal and grain in exchange for the worthless money of the towns—" Stopping abruptly, he dismissed the subject with a gesture. "I speak no more of Russia; it is too sorrowful. I am an American."

He was an old man, a brave, pitiful survivor of the world he had loved—a world which could not return to him or his descendants. His courage in face of his years and his need was magnificent.

Just before Christmas I met President Sloane and Chancellor Matthews at the office of the Academy. They were both highly elated, and Sloane at once said, "The Academy is to have a magnificent new building on West One Hundred and Fifty-fifth Street. The matter is settled and plans are being drawn."

"What a superb Christmas present!" I exclaimed. "What a noble piece of news!"

Sloane shook his head. "It must be kept secret; the donor dislikes publicity."

I thought this a mistake and strongly urged giving out the news. "Here is a gift which concerns every man of letters in the nation," I said, "a gift which will give dignity and power to the Academy. I believe in making the fullest use of it while it *is* news."

On Christmas Eve Carl Akeley came in, carrying in his arms the plaster cast of a lion. It was a copy of one of the small models of his Roosevelt lion. "Here is my present to the Garland family," he said.

I indicated the mantel over the gas log, and he placed it there facing the light from the window. "It was made for the place, wasn't it?"

(It remained there till we moved. It rests to-day in lonely silence over our smoke-blackened fireplace in Onteora, a memorial to both Roosevelt and Akeley.)

Again upon the invitation of Frank Seaman, we left New York (two days after Christmas) with its sloshy streets, and rode away into a lovely winter landscape.

"At half-past four we had tea with lovely Olive Sarre. At dinner we sat at Seaman's table with Carl Lumholz, Baron Rosen, and Siekich the pianist. Seaman said, 'This is our international table!' Tagore and his son were in the dining room, but sat apart from us. Whether this was from choice or from a suspicion that they were not entirely acceptable to the other guests, I cannot say. Later I saw the tall, turbaned poet talking to a group of women, but the men were not inclined to listen.

"To Seaman I said, 'The luxury of your hospitality is dangerous; but after fifty years of hard labor and rigid economy, I think I can share it without being enfeebled.'"

VI

On the way down to the city the following day I had much talk with Tagore and his son. "I found young Tagore rather more congenial than his father. The poet's voice is too soft, his manner too benevolent, to be convincing. To my mind he is unnaturally smiling and gentle. Once or twice he betrayed his sterner side. He and his son are both nationalists. 'England has not played entirely fair with us,' they charged with some bitterness. 'She made the fullest use of India during the war but has not given us anything in return.' There is some truth in this, but the question is, what would happen to India if England withdrew her forces? Young Tagore was more outspoken than his father. He considered English rule a tyranny."

CHAPTER TWENTY-SEVEN

"A DAUGHTER OF THE MIDDLE BORDER"

I

ZONA GALE had been my neighbor in Wisconsin and I had followed her progress with sincere interest. I had read her Friendship Village stories with delight, although they were, at times, unduly sentimental; and I had followed her as (in her novel "Birth") she swung toward the starkly realistic method, and now, in the first week of January, 1921, I was called upon to judge her play, "Miss Lulu Bett," which was being played at the Belmont Theater, for I was serving as one of the advisory committee for the Pulitzer Prize award. I would have seen the play in any case, for Miss Gale was in the city and had invited my wife and daughters to the performance.

I found it most amusing with many exquisite touches of characterization, but I came away with a sense of disappointment. It didn't quite carry all the way through. In trying for success, the dramatist—or the manager—had fumbled about for a "happy ending." The acting was admirable in almost every rôle, but the most original character in the play was "Granma," a testy old woman whose defective hearing left her outside the family conversation. She carried on her own lines of thought, however, and her occasional interruptive remarks were curiously and amusingly out of key.

"She is one of the most original characters in our present-day drama and Louise Closser Hale played her with gusto and understanding. Lulu, the household drudge, was equally original in conception. In fact this whole family is of a sort never before seen in our theater. This play is Zona Gale at her best—skillfully concise, caustic, yet never cruel, an admirable report of a commonplace Wisconsin family moving in the deep rut of a small-town routine. It is well worth considering as a claimant for the Pulitzer Prize."

William Allen White was in the audience, plump and smiling. "I am delighted with the play," he said, and during one of the intermissions we all met the author and her manager. Zona seemed rather subdued, but I saw no reason for being discouraged. I said to her, "Your novel is well advertised and while this play may not prove a money success, it is a good start. It is amazingly unconventional in phrasing and characterization."

The Roosevelt House corner-stone laying on the 6th was most successfully carried out.

"Although the sky was bright the wind was keen and I shivered in a drafty place for nearly two hours, listening to a dozen speeches, some of them very good indeed. General Wood towered as usual, a big personality, and Corinne Roosevelt Robinson gave a succinct and eloquent address. Nevertheless as I looked around at the near-by towering buildings and considered this attempt to rebuild something vanishing, creating a monument in the path of commerce, it all seemed a mistake. Year by year these thirty-story towers of commercial New York have been assembling here. How can a few brave women hope to preserve a poetic monument in the shadow of these cliffs of trade?"

On the 8th, at Mrs. Morris' invitation, the Garland family saw "Mary Rose," Barrie's new piece, and a most heart-searching experience it was for all of us. I have seldom been more moved than by this play, which was at once a dream and a fairy story. We left the theater in a mood of wonder and sadness, and for an hour or more we moved silently as if our minds were elsewhere. Happily my daughters did not see in it the baffling mystery of time and the tragedy of all human relationships, as I saw them in this story. "I felt once more the amazing originality of this small Scot. He lays hold upon certain subconscious sources of power, an unfailing well of inspiration over which other writers have no control. This drama makes our own plays seem thin and cheap by contrast. Our commercial stage is vulgar and flip. Our men are writing down, seeking swift returns in money. Barrie writes as a man assured. He is about my own age, and as I contrast my achievements with his I am disheartened.

"As a man of sixty-one, I find it hard to set up new lines of thought or action. Whether this is a perfectly logical stage of my life, or whether it is a sign of premature ossification, I cannot determine. Some days I have a disgust of routine. I hate shaving and changing my shoes. I can only sit at my desk and revise my records; while Barrie, at the same age, retains his imagination and initiative to a challenging degree. I cannot pretend to any fictive interest. Like most men of my age, I am fighting decay. Irving, Augustus, Albert—all of us are doing our best to keep going a few years longer. What is it all for? Why tramp in the ghastly procession? Mark Twain was right; it all seems a futility—at times—but my daughters are happy. To them the world is very wonderful and worth while. They are links in the endless chain as I have been. . . . To what end?"

Immediately after seeing Barrie's play I wrote him a letter which expressed my feeling at the time:

"I have just returned from seeing your 'Mary Rose' and I have seldom been so moved, so filled with the all-pervading tragedy of life. Whether my daughters felt the same pathos, the heartbreak of its message, I cannot say. I hope they didn't, for at sixty we look at such visions with different eyes to those we owned in youth. Furthermore as a student of psychic phenomena I found myself responding to the suggestion of it all.

"I am at work on the second volume of my 'Middle Border' and the question I ask at the end is precisely that which I find in your play—'What is the meaning of the dream we call life?' There was an intolerable pathos in your play. It was an exquisitely cruel conception—that of bringing the young wife back to a family which had grown old! It is hard to say just why it moved me so. I came away wearied with the tension it put upon my imagination.

"The scene on the island brought back to me the curious fact that at our luncheon in London, many years ago, your other guest was an inspector of schools in the Hebrides. Do you recall him—a black-bearded man he was then—and our talk? He invited me to make the rounds with him and now I wish that I had accepted. Your play would have meant all the more to me.

"Shall you ever come to America again? If you do, I hope you will let me know, for I would like you to dine with me and meet my wife and daughters. In summer we are near neighbors to Maude Adams in Onteora and the tradition is that you have been up there at least once. I often speak of you and of our pleasant meetings when we were still on the sunny side of forty. I see all your plays as they come and I read them after they are printed with wonder of your imaginative freshness. Sometimes I think you must have the help of 'The Invisible Ones.'

"With sincerest admiration."

As the manuscript of "A Daughter of the Middle Border" reached its seventh revision, I felt a little more secure about it.

"At times I say, 'What does criticism matter? The book is history, not the story of my family alone, but of thousands of other families. My experiences are representative. Ten years from now it will *all* be impersonal and I shall be remote.'"

One afternoon, just to test out the latest developments in the motion-picture industry, I visited three theaters. "In each I saw the same tawdry sex melodrama, the same huge, flat, ghastly white faces, the same heaving bosoms of absurd heroines, the same wooden-visaged heroes except in the case of George Arliss—and even he was inexpressive, for the light took the fine lines out of his face. In all the theaters I visited I found the same listless crowd sitting in darkness while flickering shadows played on their viscous brains. Not one of the stories showed any originality or imagination and only one had any scenes of normal repose or normal action. As in the novels of the moment, the stock ingredients are embezzlement, seduction, rape, adultery, incest, and a cheapening of womanly virtues. Normal human life seems not to interest publishers or play producers.

"On one stage I found a vile compound garnished with music, a parade of nakedness. The program was a hodge-podge of real events, travel notes, coarse comedy, and suggestive lines. It was so nauseating that I got up and went out. The audience was mainly women; they must like this stuff or they would not pay for it."

In going up to call on Archer Huntington at his museum, January 21, I rode on top of the bus, so mild was the air. Huntington not only showed me the lots he had given to the Academy, but spoke of "your building" in a way which indicated that its construction was assured.

"I never before realized the man's height. Beside him I seemed small. He is only fifty and yet I think of him as my elder. 'I've had a good time,' he said. 'I wonder if you've had as much fun as I have?' To this I replied, 'I will send you a copy of my chronicle which will tell the story.' Speaking of getting fat, I said, 'I have to fight it with exercise.' To this he answered, 'I never exercise,' and smilingly extended his arm for me to grip. It was hard as wood. 'How do you keep it so?' I asked. 'Oh, I walk a little,' he replied."

January 22 was the date of my address at the Century Club, an address arranged by my good friend, Frederick Dellenbaugh, and as I entered the library I found it filled with gray-haired men. I had been announced to speak on "Personal Reminiscences of the Makers of American Literature"; and it came over me with chilling effect that I, so long known as one of the younger writers, was now a graybeard talking to other graybeards about authors soon to be forgotten. Most of the writers in my audience were sixty or more, and all but one of the authors I spoke about were dead. "Only Burroughs is still alive and he is nearly eighty-four."

Aside from this fact, my talk made literary history for me. The room was filled and the close of my lecture heartily cheered, which was a gratification, for at the beginning I met with a frosty silence. My auditors had heard many speakers and were naturally critical, and I was somewhat in doubt as to their endorsement of me in the rôle of literary historian.

"Altogether it was a fairly successful venture," said loyal Dellenbaugh, who had introduced me. "It was a pleasant introduction to your fellow members."

At the request of my lecture bureau, I consented to present Gilbert Chesterton to his first audience in the Times Square Theater on the 23d; and on reaching the dressing room I was amused by the excited and elaborate stage directions which the English "impresario" furnished me! I was to do this and to avoid that—"and, above all, do not take up Chesterton's time." Chesterton, a big, awkward, physically gross man of middle age, met me with remote and formal glance. My name meant nothing to him. I don't know what he thought of the arrangement, but he impressed me as a patient and slightly bewildered college dean.

"He read his lecture slowly and rather feebly to a silent and wondering audience. It was a labored essay and not important from any point of view. Except for its occasional humorous paradoxes, I found it dull. At its close I could not remember a single phrase. I observed that all through his talk he busied himself with picking lint from the cloth cover of his reading desk and piling it in little heaps at one corner. My mind was thus divided between two tasks."

From here I went to the Town Hall, where I heard the end of Vice President Coolidge's talk, and the record reads thus: "He is a clear-cut, forceful, and at times epigrammatic speaker, but his accent is old-school Yankee. In truth it is almost comically nasal. Toward the end of his oration he became really fine. The general impression which I carried away was that of a self-contained, honest, and able New England country lawyer."

Edwin H. Winter came to dinner on the 24th and we got him talking of J. J. Hill of St. Paul.

"Hill never had any railway experience before he took hold of that little piece of Great Northern track," he said. "It was in the hands of a receiver and its bonds and stocks were mostly in Holland. Jim saw the possibilities of this road and hounded every man he met to buy it for him. He just about pulled all the buttons off the coats of his friends. At last we all dodged when we saw him coming. He was a coal dealer at the time, and known to be a visionary, so no one put any faith in what he said. He knew that northern country, however, and believed in it. That faith made him a power.

"He was a developer—not a great railroad man. Although a man of native good taste, he had no knowledge of art. He was cruel on impulse and generous on impulse. He used men and threw them away. His biographer has made a ridiculous book. It would have been enormously more valuable if he had made Hill the human being that he was."

II

On my way to Rochester to deliver a lecture, January 31, I found time to read Sinclair Lewis' "Main Street" which was being widely discussed.

"It is a disturbing and depressing book. It is true, amazingly true, up to a certain point, but it fails to convince simply because the writer is not quite large enough, not quite generous enough, to fuse the minute, distressing details into something noble. The characters are too much like puppets, types rather than persons. In the more individualized figures the author fails to convince, for the reason that he does not hold to the lines of his characters. As for the town, the same methods applied to any country would yield a similar result. There is also something bitter in this writing, something vengeful. The author appears to be 'taking it out' of his native town. It left me irritated rather than convicted. I liked his earlier books, but I do not like this! As William Allen White says, 'it is the shady side of Main Street.' "

A visit to Philadelphia soon after this brought me into an embittered group of city dwellers. Harrison Morris, Joseph Pennell, Herbert Welsh, and Agnes Repplier all had much to say in criticism of their town. Pennell was especially savage.

"It was all disturbing, but I sat on the side lines and listened, feeling beneath it all a love for Philadelphia. They saw its decay, political corruption, and took it out in overstatement of its faults. Philadelphia, like many other of our cities, is in the possession of a raw mob of immigrant voters, a fact which intellectuals naturally resent."

My talk and reading which I gave at Red Bank, February 4, was much more serious than I had intended it to be. My audience remained intent and solemn throughout. They gazed at me sadly, as though I had taken something away from them. A few spoke of it as a pleasure, but many wept as I read "David and His Violin." I think they realized that I represented their dying race. "They are the Eastern cousins of my people, the McClintocks and the Garlands. Are we to pass? Are the peasants of southeastern Europe to possess America?"

John and Mildred Howells came to Sunday night supper, February 6, and we discussed the question of an exhibit of Howells' manuscripts. Mildred, a gray-haired woman, was charming and John made a keen, clear-cut impression on us all.

"If they have planned any life of their illustrious father, I do not know of it. They are both highly individual and will hardly be persuaded to any other course than that which they have already decided upon. It was a pleasure to have them with us and I shall take joy in helping them collect and print Howells' letters, which were always graceful and significant. A volume of them will be of distinct literary as well as historical value. To me and to all the writers of my generation he meant much; but to the young of to-day he is not even a name, so swiftly do the tides of life go rolling on. Unless the record is made now, it will not be made at all."

Zona Gale came to dinner February 11 and took us all down to see her play again.

"She goes to every performance and studies each scene with desperate intentness. I cannot blame her; to have it 'go' will mean so much to her. To have it fail would be a disaster, hence her maternal anxiety. 'Miss Lulu Bett' is an interesting slice of life, but too light, I fear, to win a prize, although it is highly original and well done."

We saw Shaw's "Heartbreak House" on the 17th and found it both diverting and puzzling. "It is, I suppose, a parable, but I did not succeed in getting a clear notion of its meaning.

"At Mrs. Cosgrave's dinner I touched the opposite pole of my world. There I found a dozen or more of my friends: Lawrence Gilman, Will Irwin, Julian Street, Henry Canby, and Irvin Cobb. I had some talk with Canby, who has come on from Yale to take charge of the *Literary Review* of the *Post*. He is a small, refined, attractive man of about forty, a man I should like to neighbor with. Gilman is almost as handsome as ever, and I took pleasure in meeting him again. He should occupy a much higher position than he has attained. I suspect the struggle to make a living has consumed his energies—and his time—keeping him the journalist."

"February 27. At five Mrs. Walston Brown, Robert Ingersoll's daughter, sent her car for us, and on the way we picked up Helen Gardener at the Cosmopolitan Club. I had not seen her for twenty years and I should not have known her. She is now a Civil Service Commissioner and lives in Washington. She was full of amusing stories of her work and seemed gay and secure and happy. She did not recognize me at first, but when she did we began to talk of Boston. It was her book, 'An Unofficial Patriot,' which furnished James A. Herne with the theme for his play, 'Griffith Davenport.' She was a fairly well-known radical in the early nineties, but never a literary figure. Her work was always of a reformative cast."

Only eight men assembled at the Academy luncheon, February 28, but it was a pleasant meeting. Lorado Taft and Childe Hassam were present and took part in the discussion. The reception to President Sloane was well attended. It was a lovely party in all respects. The guests were mainly from New York families of literary tradition.

"Our academic spirit is still weak. In this great welter of America, where half our population is illiterate and two-thirds of the other half indifferent to the past and careless of the future, an Academy is needed much more than in France or England, just *because* our enormous population is diverse, ignorant, and slovenly. If the Academy is to function, it must concern itself with popular magazines and motion pictures. It should ignore these present-day agencies which have no standards and no traditions."

III

The Howells Memorial meeting at the Public Library, upon which I had been working for so long, came off March 1. The beautiful hall was comfortably filled and the speakers kept well within their allotted time. The audience was deeply impressed and apparently pleased. Many spoke to me in praise of the program. It was in no sense a season of mourning; on the contrary it was an expression of appreciation of the author who stood for the best in American life and letters.

"Howells lived his life fully, happily, honorably, and we are emphasizing these qualities of his work which

America should know and keep in mind," said Sloane, in effect.

"John Howells was present, but asked to be 'ignored' and in accordance with his wishes we made no reference to his coming and going. I suspect that the head men at Harper & Bros. were surprised by the interest and enthusiasm of this meeting, which showed the hold Howells still has on people of middle age."

In coming past the Plaza Theater one afternoon I saw the sign "Charlie Chaplin in 'The Kid.'" Hopping off the car, I went in and for two hours studied this popular "picture."

"It was thin stuff! The story was banal, the action childish. It consisted for the most part of comedy fights, wild chases through dark alleys and over housetops, with now and again a touch of something human. The 'kid' and the infant were delightful, but most of the action was not worth any one's staying."

Robert Frost phoned about five on March 8, saying that he would like to call. Although we had a houseful of guests, I was eager to see him and told him to come at eight, which he did. Minded to know him better, I drew him out as fully as possible. He pleased us all by his quiet humor, his rugged honesty, and his common sense.

He told of suddenly pulling up stakes on his New Hampshire farm and taking his family to England. He described his chance meeting with Ezra Pound, "the high priest" of the English "young rebels" in London. "I knew 'the wild bunch' there as well as in New York," he said, and indicated a good-natured contempt for their assertions. Speaking of his plans, he added, "I've given up my work at Amherst College. It was too rigid for me,

too analytical. It took all my energy. I could not compose. I am back on a farm in South Shaftsbury, Vermont.
I bought it for the benefit of my eighteen-year-old boy,
who is not very strong and needs the country life. My
wife sanctions all my quixotic moves, and so we are
back just about where we were when we sailed for England. I had fifty cents in my pocket when I settled in
Franconia before the war and I've got about that amount
now!"

I asked him if he had ever tried prose. "Yes," he said,
"I went to England to write a novel, but I never did."

I was greatly taken with him. I rejoiced in his rugged
sincerity and humor. "He has a curiously attractive, dry,
philosophic wit. He is taller than I had thought him to be,
a blond, gray-eyed New England type. He would look
well as the judge in a court of law."

CHAPTER TWENTY–EIGHT

DEATH OF JOHN BURROUGHS

I

THE meeting of the directors of the Academy, March 9, was a happy one. Matters of far-reaching importance were brought forward and decided upon. First, Archer M. Huntington presented a check from his mother for two hundred thousand dollars and followed this up by saying "I will subscribe two hundred thousand more." Then at Sloane's request, the office of secretary to the president was created.

"At my suggestion a committee was appointed to overhaul the constitution and by-laws, which had never been closely scanned. 'Now that we have the money for an Academy building, our organization must be perfected. We should strive to widen interest and responsibility, but this is not an easy task. Few of our members are willing or able to serve on committees, and those who would be most valuable are nonresidents, prevented by distance from attending meetings."

Down at the *Century* office I had a talk with its new editor, Glenn Frank, who said, "I still await a verdict on your Middle Border manuscript. I don't know just how much I can use or in what form." On my way back I called on Hermann Hagedorn, whose study is in the tower of the Metropolitan Building. He was busy on Roosevelt's

early life. "My story of Roosevelt in the Bad Lands is
ready for the market—or nearly so," he said. He has organized a research bureau and will get together every
scrap of Roosevelt history. It is a happy chance which
has brought this vivid young poet to the task of collecting
material for a biography of Roosevelt.

On March 14, Glenn Frank and his wife came to dinner. "It is a singular and very significant fact that this
new editor of the *Century*, a Missourian by birth, is a
sociologist, and not at all a literary man. It is a far cry
from Gilder to Frank, but he is able and filled with the
brave spirit of the true American. He candidly admits
his lack of literary contact. His tone and his phrases are
Mid-Western. He is handsome, clear-eyed, and aspiring
and will readily take on culture. He has a superb opportunity and means to revive the magazine by using the best
writing he can get, and his ideas for its make-up are engaging. 'I have a free hand,' he said, 'and if I fail to make
a success of it, the fault is mine.'"

In an errand to the West Side, I found myself near
Brander Matthews on the 18th, and decided to call upon
him. "He came stumping down the stairs to meet me,
clinging to the banister like a man with two entirely dead
legs—a pitiful figure. 'I am alone in this big house with
my ailing wife,' he explained. 'She has not been out of
doors for a year and a half and is going blind.' His situation is tragic, and yet he gave little expression to his dismay. He spoke of his devotion, but only briefly and
shyly. After a few minutes' chat he rose. 'My wife is
calling. I must return to her. She depends upon me
entirely now.'

"I came away contrasting the gay intellectuality of

his former Sundays at home with his condition now. He can not last long in this house. He is failing for lack of air and exercise—and cheer."

On March 19, still in pursuit of information concerning the moving picture, I spent three hours in a West Side theater endeavoring to discover what it was that people found entertaining. Four dreadful vaudeville acts preceded the play, and to be quite fair, the other spectators, I suspect, were as bored as I. They, too, had come to see "The Inside of the Cup" and merely *endured* the "acts."

"This play which was based on Churchill's novel is, in some ways, the best argument for the motion picture I have yet seen. Parts of it are genuinely moving, but it is so obviously a thesis and its men so lacking in character that it may fail of success. The faces of the actors when seen in 'close up' were ghastly white and without lines of expression. Some of the outdoor groups were charming and the scenes in the church admirably done. It was a threshing of old straw, but it was fine and manly in content. It tells a story and was in direct contrast to the low appeal of the entertainment which preceded it."

At the MacDowell Club that night I sat beside Rachel Crothers, whose play "Nice People" was running rather successfully just then. She made a good speech and so did Effie Shannon. They both spoke to the point and quit at just the right moment, which is not always the case with men. I remarked upon this to Miss Crothers, who explained this brevity by saying, "We are so new to this speech-making business that we are fearful of boring our audience."

"March 21. Each day, at least each forenoon, is now given to another revision of 'A Daughter of the Middle

Border.' I have taken to the habit of revising while in my bed, or rather *on* my bed. I find that I can more easily concentrate in this way, but it is only revision, after all. It is very difficult to compose in this little apartment which vibrates with noises from without as well as from sounds within. My mornings are all spent in grinding away at the manuscript, changing a word here, building up a paragraph there. It is not inspiring work, but it is the kind of work that counted in the other book. At night, Mary Isabel and I went down to see 'Nice People,' Miss Crothers' play. We liked most of it very well indeed. It hit hard and might have hit harder. 'It makes one think,' Mary Isabel said as we came away."

On March 22, I saw "Rollo's Wild Oat" by Clare Kummer. I had never before seen any of her work, and while I found this piece amusing, it is too light to be anything more than passing entertainment. "Like most of our drama to-day it is mere froth. It has no literary significance. It is all done for a transient public with cynical managers as purveyors."

In the course of my reading of novels entered for the Pulitzer Prize contest, I read "The Book of Susan" by Wilson Dodd. It disappointed me, although there is much good work in it. I found it rather formless. The author's grip on me loosened many times during the body of the book and he lost me altogether at the end. It is in the manner of the English two-volume novels, those of De Morgan or Samuel Butler. It rambles, comments, anticipates, and retraces in an irritating way. As a candidate for the Pulitzer Prize, it failed to win my vote. I have no knowledge of Dodd, but I imagine him a Yale man. All the novels I have read recently are lacking in style, in workmanship. I cannot vote a prize to any of them."

"March 27. My daughters and I took part in the Easter parade on Fifth Avenue, and a sad mixture of Jew and Gentile it turned out to be—graceless immodesty in short skirts, brainless pretension wearing bunches of orchids. Dark skins and dark eyes predominated. The tall, gray-eyed, straight-nosed aristocrats of other years are gone. It was a parade of the sons and daughters of all the races of the south of Europe with a few Nordic onlookers like myself. Manhattan is no longer American as in the days when the Knickerbocker families were its social rulers. It is American only in the other and less grateful sense of being a hodge-podge of individuals of no dignity or consequence; peasants in newly acquired finery—ancestors of the future."

II

"March 29. Word has just come in that John Burroughs died on the train last night while coming through Ohio. His body will arrive—a cold, outworn shell instead of the living man I had planned to greet. I hope he died in his sleep. With his passing, there are few figures of his dignity left in our literature. Whitlock, Tarkington, Frost, and Robinson have something which Howells and Burroughs had. It is not so much what men come up through as what they bring with them. Burroughs thought less of his market and more of the quality of his work than our later men. He was not so tempted. In his day magazines were less like advertising bulletins, less involved in 'business.'

"At night I attended a meeting of the Poetry Society,

a motley collection of verse writers. All the poems read
were short, some of them were real, but none were important. The fact is, we are all living on the surface of
life, so dominated by the daily papers and the moving
pictures that deep, quiet thinking is almost lost out of
our world.

"In the vote for the medal of the National Institute
last year, no poet was considered worthy; and I see no
commanding figures on the horizon to-day. We have
many who write with precision and grace, but no one
who can command larger forms. We are gaining in
workmanship but not in power."

At ten o'clock on the morning of April 2, I started for
Poughkeepsie and West Park to take part in the burial
services of Burroughs at Riverby. At Highland I waited
for the train, sitting by a rushing stream in the warm sun.
The day was glorious spring, but not many birds were
astir.

"In the yard at Riverby I found many carriages, and at
'the Nest' I was met by Dr. Barrus, Julian Burroughs,
and Grace Vanamee, Secretary to the President of the
American Academy. Edison was sitting in an armchair,
alone and silent, for his deafness makes conversation with
him difficult. He looked very old and white and sad.
Henry Ford was in the background, a shy, ascetic
figure.

"The company assembling was non-literary. Julian's
family and his friends, Dr. Barrus' family and friends, a
few of Burroughs' neighbors, made up the group. Dallas
Lore Sharp, Frank Chapman, and I were the literary representatives. I was the only member of the Academy in
attendance. A beautiful wreath bound by purple and

gold, the colors of the Academy, had been sent by the directors as a symbol of their regard.

"The services began with the playing by a small phonograph of a melody which the dead man especially loved. A minister then read a formal prayer. This was followed by the reading of some verses which Burroughs is said to have valued for their philosophical content. At this point I read some verses which had been handed to me. Frank Chapman, who had known Burroughs for many years and understood the value of his contribution to bird lore and general literature, was in the room and should have been called up. However, we had been told that another ceremony had been arranged for the next day at the grave on the hillside farm at Roxbury."

As Dr. Barrus could not care for the men at "the Nest," five of us were invited to spend the night at a small monastery next door.

"Rising at six, April 3, we ate our breakfast in silence, waited upon by silent monks. To find such an institution next door to the Burroughs home was an amazement to me. At half-past eight we started for Roxbury in seven motor cars. The burial was to be at Woodchuck Lodge, and when we reached the gate, the grave beside the rock in the pasture was already surrounded by a throng. It was a glorious April day, Uncle John's eighty-fourth birthday, with a few birds piping. The people assembled were mostly neighbors or friends from the village."

"The ceremony was similar to that which had been presented at 'the Nest.' Not one of Burroughs' scientific or literary friends were called upon to speak. Mrs. Vanamee and I again read some verses, the phonograph plaintively piped its little tune, a parson made a short prayer,

and then the mourners were invited to take their last
look at the face of their friend. After the coffin was
lowered and an armful of green fir branches dropped
down upon it, I plucked a leaf from the wreath which the
Academy had sent and tossed it into the grave as a fare-
well tribute to the man I had known so long."

It was a fitting place for the burial of John Burroughs.
Born here on this hillside, he had returned to it after
eighty-four years of wandering, to be mixed with the
soil of his home acres. These men and women, whose
faces were lined by years of care, were neighbors, life-
long friends and relatives. Work-worn, gaunt and gray,
they stood in silence till they were given permission to
take the flowers which remained; then one by one they
approached, selected a blossom, and went away.

It was a tender neighborly ceremony, but it did not
satisfy those of us who knew Burroughs as a scholar, a
man of many books, and a philosopher of wide appeal.
"A memorial meeting by his fellow Academicians should
come later," I said to the president of the Academy.
"This ceremony on the hill is significant in its homely
way, but it was not adequate in a national way. The entire Academy should participate in a public meeting in
the city."

In this judgment all the directors agreed.

CHAPTER TWENTY-NINE

HOUSING THE AMERICAN ACADEMY

I

Up to April, 1921, the American Academy (of which I was still acting secretary in the absence of Robert Underwood Johnson) had no home. It possessed only an office at 347 Madison Avenue. Its meetings still took place at the Century Club, either in a small side room on the first floor or at a table in the dining room. It was at luncheon on April 4 that I listened with surprise and pleasure to an important announcement by President Sloane: "I have in my pocket a letter from Archer M. Huntington in which he offers to lend us the building on West Eighty-first Street, a handsome three-story structure, which he has been using as an office."

Huntington had already given us two lots on West One Hundred and Fifty-fifth Street and half a million dollars and his further munificence stunned me. "We have no way of meeting the cost of such a home," I said to Sloane. However, I joined in a resolution of acceptance which carried a vote of thanks, and when Sloane asked me to go up and look at the premises, I planned to do so that afternoon.

"Huntington received me with a quizzical smile and showed me all the resources of the building, which is ideally located for our purposes. He gave me the impression that he made very little use of it and that we would be doing him a favor by taking it off his hands. I said, 'It is just what we need. It will provide library space, workshop, and assembly rooms, but I don't know how we can provide for its upkeep.'

"There was something elusively humorous in his attitude and yet he was quite serious underneath it all. 'America needs such an organization as yours. You should have a home. I think you'll find some one to help in its upkeep.'

"As I stood in the doorway looking out on the square in which the Natural History Museum stood, and across the avenue to Central Park, I thought it exactly the location for the Academy. I felt deeply grateful to this art lover and poet, who was minded to use his wealth for the advancement of American arts and letters, but was careful not to say so!"

In my report to Sloane, I said, "Our organization, eminent as its membership is, lacks the weight and power which a stately home alone can give. Here is a building which can be made the center of all our activities. Its library can be our lecture hall and its offices our archives. We can set about collecting the books of our members at once."

President Sloane, quite elated by the possibilities which the occupancy of this building suggested, authorized me to prepare and print a letter inviting a gift of books and manuscripts by members of the Academy. We now had space for a library and also for a hall in which to hold our public lectures. In a single day we passed from the narrow confines of a small office to the possession of a three-story building overlooking Central Park, and by great good fortune the donor of this building was a man of letters, a poet, and a patron of art. I was deeply impressed by the beautiful library which he at once planned to remove in order to give place to us.

On April 5, in accordance with a promise I had made to Margaret Widdemer, I shared an Authors' Reading held in the home of Adolph Lewisohn. "Cosmo Hamilton presided. Inez Gillmore Irwin read a story, so did Dorothy Canfield. Marguerite Wilkinson recited a fine poem and I, after a short talk, read a dialect poem. The audience was small, the air chill, and the performers rather melancholy. I had a few moments' conversation with Dorothy Canfield Fisher, a small, thin woman with a pleasing face. When I spoke of her 'Hillsboro People,' praising their apparent fidelity to Vermont types, she smilingly admitted that they were all composite portraits of her neighbors and relatives."

(Since this note was written, Mrs. Fisher has moved on to higher ground. Her novels dealing with the social reactions of the Great War, especially "The Deepening Stream" and "The Brimming Cup," have placed her, in my judgment, among the very best of our fictionists. Her own life has been a deepening stream but with nothing turbid in its depths. There is something unaccountable in the brain of this small woman, as there is in that of Zona Gale. With finer skill and nobler courage than most of their men contemporaries, they seize upon the distinctive and the essential in the life of their time.)

"April 8. Lunching at the Museum of Natural History with Frank Chapman, Carl Akeley, and Clyde Fisher, I helped formulate a plan for the John Burroughs Memorial Association. We wrote and signed a short notice to be given out to the press. Fisher reported that Dr. Barrus and Julian Burroughs were ready, even eager, to have us take over the care of both Riverby and Slabsides. I voted for this. I said: 'I am especially anxious to secure the old stone house at Riverby, for it is a solid, enduring structure. I am hoping that some good friend will buy it and endow it. Slabsides is but a shack and will rot down in a few years. Riverby is rugged. It *looks* like John Burroughs.'

"The other members of the committee were cool to my argument. 'The truth is,' they replied, 'John did very little writing in the stone house. He never liked it. He built the bark study and Slabsides to get away from it. He regarded that as his wife's domain.' I persisted. 'Nevertheless, it should be made a permanent shrine. The public does not know that it was not his study.' "

On April 18, as a guest and speaker, I dined with the Indiana Society.

"This was not a very dignified or inspiring experience. A jazz band was whooping it up in an adjoining hall and my audience was small and visibly distracted. I struggled for a time against the orchestra, then gave it up and read some verses which proved only mildly amusing to my auditors.

"At the close of the program many came up to say, 'I knew Riley,' but they were not pleased with my address. I had said, 'Riley is our Indiana minstrel. He is the Burns of the Mid-West. No other state has a vernacular poet of his rank. He fills the sky out there.' It was evident that some of my auditors deprecated his dialect. 'We don't talk Hoosier these days,' they said. I had never met this resentment before and it took me by surprise."

On April 19, the Academy moved into its new building on Eighty-first Street.

"When I reached the door I found the van unloading our files while Huntington's men were still at work clearing out his effects. As I came in he smilingly said, 'I am being put out. You and Mrs. Vanamee are what I call "insistent hustlers." I never *would* have gotten out of here if it hadn't been for you.' "

Three days later, while Sloane and I were inspecting the building, Huntington came in, a smiling giant. Taking a seat in our office, he proceeded to discuss our plans and needs. I had told him of our timidity in matters of expenditure, and the results of my talk were amusing as well as far-reaching. With humorous intonation, he said, 'I've been lying awake nights looking over your situation and I have decided that you need more money for furniture. I am here to confer with you and to add two thousand dollars to my allowance—but you, Dr. Sloane, must not get your hands on it,' he added with a smile. 'You'd put it into your general fund.'

"Sloane was amused by his attitude, but consented to the arrangement. Huntington, in the midst of making out the check, suddenly exclaimed, 'There! I don't know what's the matter with me! I've made it out for three thousand instead of two!' He hesitated a moment, then said, 'Well, let it go! I can't change it now,' and handed the check to Sloane."

I met the Burroughs Memorial Committee, on the 25th, and helped to push its organization a little farther forward.

"Mrs. Henry Ford was present at the meeting and appeared interested. Once or twice she hinted that she would contribute something, but our chairman was out-lining a plan which involved calling upon the children of the nation to contribute to the fund. 'Millions will contribute their pennies,' he declared. This I doubt. I cannot see an immense outpouring of coppers. I hope Ford and Edison will take over all the Burroughs homes and endow them."

Joe Lincoln and his wife were spending the winter at the La Salle Hotel, and dining with them one evening, we had several hours of friendly talk. "I like him more than ever. He is neither brilliant nor profound, but he is hearty, wholesome, humorous, and thoroughly American. We were greatly taken by his pretty little wife and rejoiced in the good things coming to her. Lincoln is prosperous these days. His play 'Shavings' and his novel 'The Portygee' are notably successful. Although not disposed to lavishness (like myself he has been schooled in economy) he is enjoying life. Some critics find him commonplace, but I value his Yankee good sense and his kindly humor. He says nothing brilliant, nothing that is quotable, but he is a delightful companion."

The spring was in full leaf on May 10 and a walk in the park presented moments of transcendent beauty, but *only* at moments. "The grass was littered with strange types of recent immigrants. I should have rejoiced in their being there, but my spirits sank as I remembered their influence as voters. All of our larger cities are filled with voters like these, and I have moods when I fear the future. My only gleam of hope comes from seeing their sons playing baseball on the green. Our sports may Americanize them."

President Sloane called me up on May 11, asking me to

meet with the directors. "We need you to make a quorum," he said.

"The result of this meeting was rather important. During the session I suggested that the number of directors be raised to nine and that Archer M. Huntington be elected to our board. 'He is not only a patron of arts; he is a poet and a scholar,' I said in making the nomination. My motion was adopted and Cass Gilbert was also added to the board of directors. Sloane was delighted. 'This will not only bring Huntington into closer contact with us but enable us to make use of Gilbert's skill and judgment as an architect,' he said.

"Each day strengthens the Academy's position. We have a home, a place for our books, and I am authorized to carry on a campaign for the collection of memorabilia of the members."

II

The annual outing of the Poetry Society at the Untermyer place came on May 14, but when I went to the train (which was scheduled to leave at three) I was surprised by the smallness of the waiting group. Six cars had been chartered, but one would have sufficed to carry all the visitors. There was no eager mob at the gates this time.

On my arrival at the Greystone station, I walked up the hill alone. The house, which resembled a German castle, was unchanged, but its grounds were lovelier than ever. The formal gardens, with their brilliant blooms, graveled walks, fountains, and classic columns, were like those of some Old World castle. The sculptured seats, the statuary, the theater, all were of imperial magnitude.

"By what magic has this son of a small Jewish shop-keeper attained this splendor?" I asked of Wheeler. "Is it right? Is it American? Is there not something wrong in a social organization which permits such individual efflorescence?" Wheeler smiled as he replied, "You and I would do the same if we could."

"For over twenty years this powerful attorney has lived in this magnificence. Since my first meeting with him, he has gone forward in developing this home. In the midst of the war, in the midst of labor's menace, his hedges have flourished, his fountains have played, his flowers have bloomed. He has known nothing of econ-omy. I confess that this magnificence troubles me. It is said that a million dollars has gone into the making of this garden. Is it justified? I grant this man's great ability but I question whether such grandeur can endure."

In calling at Macmillan's a few days later I found the editors enthusiastic about "A Daughter of the Middle Border."

"It begins to look like a 'go.' It is to be published on my sixty-first birthday. I feel the need of haste. My readers are elderly. Each year they drop away. My daughters wish me to share the honor—if there is to be any—of this new volume, and my publishers believe that it will be as successful as the other and so, now, while we are all together and well and happy, it seems best to bring it out." With the manuscript again before me I set to work on a final revise.

The unveiling of the tablet to Mark Twain in the Hall of Fame at New York University led me to accept an invitation to attend the ceremonies which came on May 21. The chancellor of the university had requested me to read the formal address while the Clemens memorial was being unveiled, and President William M. Sloane of the Academy of Arts and Letters spoke for Saint Gaudens. The colonnade in which several statues were already set was semicircular in form, and after a formal luncheon, the officials, speakers, and distinguished guests formed in line and marched slowly round this narrow hall, pausing for a few minutes before each newly placed tablet. "As I stood waiting my turn, I reflected upon the curious fact that I, the son of a Wisconsin farmer, had been delegated to read an address to the chancellor of New York University announcing the unveiling of a tablet to a printer from Missouri whose place in the Hall of Fame was won by his humor and by his descriptions of the Mississippi River and the mountain West. As he had made history in his large way, so I, in my small way, was adding significance to this ceremony by acting as spokesman for the West.

"The day was quite perfect and the audience, while not large, was of the character which determines scholarship and rewards lasting achievement. Professor Sloane and Dr. Henry van Dyke both spoke and spoke well, with notable precision of phrase. The Academy and the Institute were both well represented in the audience."

CHAPTER THIRTY

LITERARY LIFE AT ONTEORA

I

RETURNING to my cabin in the Catskills, I set to work on the manuscript of "A Daughter of the Middle Border" and worked till June 20, when, being invited to a seat in Mrs. John Alexander's car, I returned to the city.

On the way she told me many stories of her illustrious husband. One that was especially amusing described his masquerade in preparation for a visit from the Swedish painter, Anders Zorn.

"Zorn was given to loud neckties and resounding waist-coats," said Mrs. Alexander, "and so, anticipating his visit, John got out an old light gray suit and painted huge checks upon it, using bright pink and green pastels. In addition he bought a deep scarlet tie. When fully attired, he was amazing, but he met Zorn at the door with such gravity and was so matter of fact in all ways that his visitor was puzzled. Zorn hadn't a very keen sense of humor. At last he perceived the joke and began to laugh. I was relieved; I was afraid he might be angry."

I asked her about Sargent. She replied, "We knew Sargent and liked him although he was not an ingratiating personality. We have not seen him recently. He makes his home in London."

During my stay in the city I lunched with Huntington

at his big Fifth Avenue house and went deeply into some of the vital points concerning the Academy.

"He seemed especially pleased by my report of progress in collecting books and memorabilia. I told him frankly that I did not intend to ask him for another dollar. 'It seems to me others should now come in.' As he gave me his hand in parting, he said, 'I'm with you whole-heartedly in this work. We'll make it a big institution.' I came away with the feeling that with a home and an endowment, the Academy should be an educative force in American art."

In returning to Onteora, I took the Hudson River boat. "This trip is always restful, and to-day on the way I read 'The Heart of Midlothian,' which I found to be a diffuse and surprisingly artless book, full of fine characters but without careful selection. Many pages of it were so dull that my attention wandered. The story is obvious at every point and the characters are switched about by the author without apparent reason. Would it be successful if published in this form to-day?"

"Onteora, June 29. After working with a young local carpenter for a week, I learned to-day that he served in our army overseas as a gunner in the light field artillery and that he had taken part in seven 'drives,' one of which lasted for twenty-one days. 'I fired for twelve hours in one battle while wearing a gas mask and I was wounded in the knee,' he said quietly. He had served in England, France, Italy, and Germany, and yet he only mentioned his war experience in response to my questioning. He is the son of a neighboring farmer named Speenberg.

"He is a type of hundreds of thousands of men all over America, who had survived an epic overseas war experience and had returned to humdrum life in their native villages, merging, without a particle of boasting, in their neighborhood activities. They now find themselves in the process of being ignored. In a sense they are silenced, benumbed by their return to the commonplace. No one asks about their service and they themselves seldom talk of it. Perhaps they will recount their battles when they are farther away from the majesty and the horror of them. Words are inadequate now. They understate it when they speak of it, minimizing rather than expanding. Such men as young Speenberg will never be able to express themselves on these themes."

In a volume entitled "The Lore of the Wanderer," I came upon an essay by an author named E. A. Thomas which got deep under my acceptance of conventional life in New York.

"We are all slaves to routine, to comfort, to small things which we regard as necessities," I set down in my diary. "I am being subdued, worn out, sapped, by life in a flat. My feet hardly ever touch the earth, and yet only in the city can I do my work in the world. Sometimes I wonder whether any of my work, any part of my life, is worth the effort to maintain it. Per contra, is not the normal man the one who takes only comfortable thought of the future, living his routine from day to day?"

On a hot railway ride to the city, July 19, I read Leon's "Son of the Hidalgos" and Robert Grant's "Unleavened Bread."

"Both are good books, each with a sociologic significance. The one is a picture of the dying régime in Spain, the other a picture of slaving, aspiring America. Leon's book has much to do with religious experiences and did not hold my interest throughout; but his descriptions of life in a remote Spanish village are exquisite. In the original they are no doubt almost lyrical in their expression. Grant's book lacks the grace of Leon's book, but is true and broad-minded. As a study of certain types of social climbers, Selma is very much worth while."

After a meeting of the Academy, July 20, Sloane, Thomas, and I lunched with Huntington in his superb library, an amazing place.

"His house has an entrance on Fifth Avenue and another on Eighty-ninth Street; and in reaching his dining room we passed through an enormous hall of the English type, on the walls of which hung splendid Spanish paintings. He seemed to enjoy having us with him, and expressed his entire agreement with our plans."

"Onteora, July 28. Following Emerson's example and as a matter of literary and social history, I here state that I often rise at six to wash and wipe the dishes left by the previous night's party. My daughters protest but do not actually intervene. I console them by saying, 'Roosevelt would have done it,' and he would—and did. His training on the trail and on the ranch gave him not only the skill but the mind to do it.

"In my case, practice in the art of washing dishes goes back to the days of my childhood when I used to help my sister Hattie. From a conventional point of view it is a sad spectacle, but there is no more disgrace to it than greasing a harness or currying a horse. In reading Emerson's journals I am astonished by his domesticity. He and Hawthorne were both quite capable of cleaning out the barn or washing a shirt. It is only fair that I should share the burden of our entertaining."

Lunching at Mrs. Gray's on Onteora Mountain, I met Carr Van Anda, the managing editor of *The New York Times,* and later called upon him at his home at the bottom of the hill.

"In our talk I discovered that he is from Georgetown, Ohio. Here again is a marvelous story. How did this Ohio village boy come to be managing editor of the greatest newspaper in America? There is a romance in this. I spoke of Ulysses Grant's life in Georgetown, and he said banteringly, 'You should be the orator at the Grant Centennial next year.' Van Anda is a keen, remorseless news gatherer. He believes in publishing the facts of the world's happenings uncolored by prejudice."

"August 29. I am rereading Howells' 'World of Chance.' In the presence of labor and its rewards to-day and in the light of the communistic attempt in Russia, his statements seem almost as far away from the present as those of Charles Reade or George Eliot, and yet he faithfully represents what we were all saying and thinking in 1890. I know, for I was one of the reformers he has delineated. Radicals of to-day may bring about a higher civilization than my generation imagined, but I see no signs of it. I see only deterioration.

"In rereading 'Lin McLean' by Owen Wister, I am again reminded that few books bear rereading. This one does, but it has obvious faults. It is all too plainly a series of short stories depicting the life of a cowboy, yet it holds up surprisingly well.

"Seeing my niece, Emily Taft, going about her work in the city's heat reminds me of the time when I, too, ignored the weather. In those days, when I had anything to do I did it, giving no heed to wind or sun. Now I am waiting, longing to get back to my cool cabin in the hills. My life here in the city is a process of endurance. In torture, I exist, hoping each hour for a change of air.

"I marvel at the patience of the poor who sleep crowded into close-packed, fetid dens night after night with no hope of anything better, and yet I doubt if any improvement would come by way of a proletarian dictatorship. To give these folk power would unchain strange beasts. Improvement must come by evolution, not by edict."

Late in the day on September 12, the page proof of "A Daughter of the Middle Border" came to me and I put in more than eight hours' work upon it, finishing it just before midnight.

"I found many places which I would like to rewrite, but it is too late to do that. As it is, so it must take its chances. It is a record of fact, and when I get away from its transitory personal aspects, it takes on something of the quality of history. Whether it is noble or trivial will depend upon the reader. Some will find it unduly personal. Others will wish the revelation had been more complete. So far as I am concerned, I wish its words were better. Not all of it has that final unchangeable order for which I am always striving and which another year's labor might have won. I am never satisfied with a manuscript."

II

As the time for laying the cornerstone of our new building on West One Hundred and Fifty-fifth Street approached, I began to urge that it be made an important

occasion. "We should invite the heads of all the Old
World academies and we should bring together as many
men distinguished in the arts as would add to the representative significance of the event," I urged upon Sloane,
who agreed, but was not well enough to come from
Princeton as often as we needed his advice. I was still
acting secretary.

One afternoon I came upon Elihu Root at the Century
Club. He was lunching with Hermann Hagedorn, who
was consulting him on some of the points in his Roosevelt biography. Knowing how highly Sloane and Matthews valued Senator Root's judgments, I seized the opportunity to outline my program for the laying of the
cornerstone of our new building. "We should have official
recognition from Washington," I said. He agreed and
promised to take the matter up with the State Department and also with the President.

"October 2. Reading the papers to-day threw me into
a mood of doubt regarding the future of our nation. We
are at a time where religion no longer guides and decency
is in contempt. Family life is sacrificed to the café, the
automobile, the theater, and the dance hall. We are taking
on the worst phases of European life. The pursuit of
pleasure, not happiness, leads to increasingly frequent
divorce, and 'escapades' (as they are delicately called)
fill the newspapers. It is the fashion for women to drink,
smoke, and swear. Roadhouse manners are 'smart.'

"How much of this is due to the rising tide of feminism
is a question. Without doubt a large part of it springs
from deliberate intention on the part of women. License is in the air and motion pictures publish it to the
world. Young girls sense it and express it in naïve ways.

I am just old-fashioned enough to be saddened and dismayed by this reversal to barnyard morality. It is a return to a lower level of social life."

(As I revise this paragraph ten years later and bring to mind the novels, plays, and histories of "loose women" which have won success and of the actresses whose nudity and lewd posturing have won them fame and fortune, I am in agreement with the biologists who prophesy a complete overturn of society.

(These salacious books, plays, and songs are bought by women. The audiences which support these road-house "shows" are predominantly feminine. Every "spicy" divorce trial is besieged by women. Illicit love affairs appear to be irresistibly attractive to old and young. It may be that this is a normal appetite and that I am all wrong in thinking it destructive of modesty, womanly virtue, and the higher life. No protest by men can check this tendency; reform must come from the women themselves.)

"October 3. A part of my depression these days is due to my surroundings. All the morning I have been trying to write while the bell of the dumb-waiter, the whine of the vacuum cleaner, the call of the garbage man, and the whir of the telephone bell have been beating in upon my brain, interrupting my train of thought, destroying all hope of a peaceful forenoon. For five years I have endured these interruptions. Whatever I have written has been composed under these conditions. In winter my little study is often cold and in summer it is almost intolerable by reason of its heat and the clamor of my neighbors in the area.

"I set these facts down so that my readers may know

in what circumstances my books were written. I am aware that newspaper men work uncomplainingly under worse conditions than these, but I suspect they are less worried about the quality of their manuscript. It is all very foolish in me, but I am trying to do something abiding, and all that hinders this aim irritates me. I do not complain; I merely state the facts."

"Augustus Thomas and I had an hour's talk to-day concerning autobiographies in general and the reminiscences which he is writing for *The Saturday Evening Post*. His career is as typical of America as that of any man I know. From my point of view he is a successful man, although of late his plays have fallen short of the applause which he desired and which some of them deserved. Like many another man, he has been driven too hard. The result has been plays not quite at his best level."

"November 3. I have been on jury duty for two weeks, and I find myself going to the courtroom as if to my office, so quickly do I respond to its routine. The attendants know me and greet me. The clerk is most considerate and the members of the jury friendly. To-day we were empaneled in another room and the jurors 'joshed' one another as their names were called. One man proposed a pool so that the one drawn next should get four dollars. Altogether this jury experience has deepened my conviction that our law procedure needs to be entirely reformed. Much of it is farcical and some of it is corrupt."

On November 4, Carl Van Doren and his wife, and Marguerite Wilkinson and her husband came to dinner.

"I value them all. Van Doren is an especially admirable type, vigorous in mind and body, sanely sympathetic in his judgment, and wholly American in his point of view. I don't know a young man who interests me more at this time than he, and I say this without taking into account what he has written of me. His grandfather was an Illinois pioneer. He is in the prime of life and working intensely. His book, 'The American Novel,' is just out and he is at work on 'Contemporary Novelists.' He is literary editor of *The Nation,* professor of literature at Columbia University, and is, withal, a delightful companion. That he will come to high honor I have no doubt.

"The Wilkinsons are a joyous team. Marguerite is a poet, a very real poet, and he a lover of the woods and streams. They are both hardened campers. They have just returned from a tricycle trip through England. Marguerite's book, 'The Dingbat of Arcady,' tells the story of their outing in the Northwest."

On November 7 I was one of the speakers at a meeting in memory of Stephen Crane, held in a fine old church in Newark.

"Crane was born in Newark, and the citizens have placed a tablet on the front of the library to perpetuate the name of their most illustrious poet and novelist—a handsome thing to do. I was glad to assist. It was a curious meeting. It opened with prayer and was presided over by a man who is neither literary nor a personal friend of Crane. It had a little the air of a church service or a funeral. A clergyman spoke at some length and a local lawyer read a long article. My own contribution to the meeting was slight. Time did not allow of retelling the story of my early meetings with Crane, but I was able to picture him as he appeared while a reporter for lectures at the Sea Side Assembly in Avon-by-the-Sea in the summer of 1889 and later when he brought to my New York apartment the manuscript of 'The Red Badge of Courage,' his first successful book."

(In "Roadside Meetings" I have recorded at some length my experiences with Crane as poet and novelist. To quote my address in Newark would be but a repetition of a chapter in that book.)

CHAPTER THIRTY-ONE

BURIAL OF THE UNKNOWN SOLDIER

I

THE ceremonies connected with the burial of the Unknown Soldier in Washington on November 10 interested me; and when Mark Sullivan invited me to visit him, I dropped my writing and went over to the capital a day or two in advance of the entombment.

Washington appealed to me more strongly than ever, so gracious, so reposeful, and so American did it seem in contrast with New York. I said to Sullivan, "It is the logical place of residence for a man of letters; and yet I doubt if I could remain contented here."

The burial of the Unknown Soldier had filled the city with distinguished Old World guests and visitors from other cities. "The body, which has been lying in state at the capitol, was brought out at eight o'clock. Attended by the President and members of Congress, and escorted by admirals and generals, the casket was carried up the avenue and over to Arlington, where a most impressive ceremony was held.

"Mark Sullivan, with whom I am staying, procured me a seat from which I saw the street procession, and Postmaster-General Will Hays gave me a ticket for a chair in the amphitheater. After the procession had passed, Mark and I set out for Arlington in a taxi; but the road became so jammed with cars that we were forced to abandon our cab and walk. Fortunately Postmaster Hays (whose office gave him passage) came along and took us in his car. In this way we reached the amphitheater in time for the speeches. Here for the first time I heard the loud-speaker mechanism which made every word of the service audible a quarter of a mile from the stand. It was incredible! I could only echo the old lady's remark, 'What won't men do next?' "

"November 11. The Sullivans and I dined with Secretary and Mrs. Hoover who live only a block away. Mark said, 'I consider Hoover the biggest man walkin' around these parts,' and I am inclined to agree. The secretary is grown into a most impressive figure. He is far less youthful in appearance than when I saw him last, and the lines of care on his bulging brow offset the boyish lines of his face. He is a very serious man, but he chuckled occasionally over some remark which seemed humorous to him. We talked of the Middle West and Mrs. Hoover spoke of my work with interest. She is more 'bookish' than he, but he is also a reader, as his handsome library shows. He is widely experienced in commercial matters and his judgment should be valued."

II

On my way back from Washington, November 14, I read Hagedorn's "Roosevelt in the Bad Lands," and so shortened my journey by half. "It is a fine book. Hagedorn has pictured Roosevelt's ranch life with amazing skill. He has so recreated it that I am able to relive it, for I experienced much the same sort of life in 1882. It is a book which few men could have written, and Hagedorn could not have done it so vividly without visiting the actual locality. His boyish enthusiasm never flags and he has a stirring command of poetic prose. His zest is keen and his point of view tolerant. Without doubt his frank and smiling face won the confidence of the Medora citizens to his cause and led them to talk freely of their youthful experiences. For all time the story of Roosevelt's ranching days is secure. It is recorded here in fuller detail than in any other book."

On November 16 I dined at the National Arts Club with H. H. Howland of the Century Company.

"Frederick O'Brien, author of several South Sea books, was there—a compact, handsome little man, lively and intelligent. To me he is merely a high-class reporter and his talk, like his writing, lacks distinction, but he is bright and amusing. His speech at the hall made a fine impression on the audience and he quite won me by admitting that the 'South Sea' of his books exists only in a state of mind. My 'lay,' he said, 'is to depict an idyllic savagery.' This he has done to the acceptance of a smart city public who talk of 'returning to nature.'"

As acting secretary of the Academy, I was concerned for a month or more with preparation for its annual meeting on the 18th of November, a meeting of especial interest, for it included a memorial to John Burroughs and the laying of the cornerstone of a new building. Marshal Foch, as representing the French Government and the French Academy, had consented to be the chief figure in the ceremony.

The tributes to Burroughs were spoken on the afternoon of the 18th in the small auditorium of the Academy on West Eighty-first Street, and several hundred of his friends and guests of the Academy came and went during the afternoon. As a long-time friend of Burroughs I had been chosen to make a short address. A fine bust of him by Hermon MacNeil was on a stand beside the platform and in my tribute I called attention to it by saying, "When I met John Burroughs first he looked like that, a handsome, brown-bearded man of fifty."

Weather conditions were favorable for the cornerstone ceremony next day, and when I reached the terrace which led to the foundations of our new building, I found a throng of people eagerly awaiting the coming of the illustrious French soldier.

"Robert Underwood Johnson, who had only just returned from Italy, had marshaled a reception committee composed of Augustus Thomas, Owen Wister, Maurice F. Egan, and Gari Melchers; and they were standing at the entrance when quite unexpectedly (half an hour in advance of the time set) Marshal Foch and his escort suddenly appeared. The buglers greeted him with a rapid fanfare and we all stood with uncovered heads whilst he and his suite remained at salute. President Sloane, Chancellor Matthews, and Bishop Manning then led the way to the building preceded by the buglers.

"At the door of the Numismatic Society we halted while the marshal received a medal. This afforded our members full opportunity to see him. Taking position close to the stone, he listened while Secretary Johnson read a poem and Sloane made a brief address. Chancellor Matthews then deposited the box of records and one of the workmen cemented the copper box and another spread the mortar. At last, when all was prepared, Marshal Foch raised the trowel. Slowly the great stone swung to its place. Foch then tapped it with a maul and the bugles announced the task was done! The marshal instantly withdrew, much to the disappointment of those who wished to meet him."

III

As Chairman of the Literature Committee of the MacDowell Club I presided at an evening meeting on November 22 in which Henry S. Canby of the *Literary Review*, Mr. Bishop of *Vanity Fair*, and Gilbert Seldes of *The Dial* were the speakers.

"Canby spoke solidly, learnedly, and well, but Bishop and Seldes were less at ease. Seldes voiced the 'remorseless criticism' of *The Dial* and was almost comically solemn about it. He patronized Howells and all the rest of the 'older school,' except Henry James, and lauded *The Dial's* plan for giving youth full opportunity for experiment. It was all very youthful and very 'destructive' in the way of our literary Bolsheviki. It was all amusing, but I regretted giving time and strength to the discussion."

(It may interest the reader to know that this journal of "mercilessly destructive criticism" was subsidized and that when its subsidizer withdrew support, it vanished.)

At Gertrude Hogan's studio the following afternoon, I had a talk with Zona Gale. "I am here for a few days' visit," she said. She was slightly heavier than I had ever seen her and quite radiant with health and happiness. She spoke appreciatively of the Pulitzer Prize Committee award for her "Miss Lulu Bett," and I assured her that it was unanimous.

"We dined at the Plaza Hotel with Dr. Norman Bridge

and his partner, Edward Doheny, head of one of the largest oil companies in Mexico.

"Dr. Bridge, whom I have known for thirty years, is nearly eighty years of age, but is still a handsome figure. Doheny and Walker (his attorney) interested me keenly. Unquestionably men of shrewdness and power, they are making a fight against the Mexican President who is demanding a larger share of the oil which is being drawn from the soil of the state. Doheny calls this action 'confiscation,' but I do not. I understand Obregón's position. He feels that Americans are draining Mexico of its wealth without adequately paying for the privilege. 'He may not be going about it in exactly the right way, but there is justice in his plea,' I said to Bridge, who is a broadminded thinker."

"November 25. The tea in honor of Zona Gale, aside from her presence, was of small interest to me. The young writers I saw there may be the literary giants of the future, but I have no way of knowing it.

"Miss Gale is a most extraordinary little lady. Starting from Portage, Wisconsin, some twenty years ago, a pale, slight, unknown girl, she has reached a reasonable affluence and a highly honorable position in American fiction. In this race she has had nothing to aid her but good work and a lovely character. With no powerful family connections to make things easy for her, she has toiled incessantly, and this industry (added to her personal charm) has made her what she is. Her stories of 'Friendship Village' gave her vogue with the women's magazines and she has gained steadily in skill and insight.

"Edwin Markham was present, looking neater and rather more regulated than usual. His vigor continues unabated. Notwithstanding his years, he still lectures and reads. Travel seems not to daunt or subdue him. He is one of the few scholars of the old type remaining in New York. He talks books, quotes books, and lives books."

Dining with Charles R. Crane on November 30, I met a man whom Crane introduced as "Paul Miliukof, the greatest living Russian." He was a sturdy, white-haired man with a gentle and very sad face. His voice was low and in all his talk I could detect no bitterness, no hate, and yet Crane said, "He has been through hell's tortures for the past five years."

He told us that he got out of Russia just half an hour before Lenin gave orders for his arrest. What he intends to do here in America I did not ask. He was to have been the first president of the Russian Republic, but instead he is in exile, with no hope of ever returning to his home.

His reluctance to talk forced Crane into action. He described in some detail his first trip to Java on a sailing vessel. "I went as a kind of companion to the captain," he said, "but I became a real sailor. I stood tricks at the wheel and studied the charts and sextant till I could run the vessel. The captain offered to make me a mate, but I concluded not. I had other plans."

He went to Japan and China and later to Palestine. He told us much of Faisal, the prince of Damascus, whose friendship he had won, "a really wonderful character."

Miliukof listened gravely, giving me the impression of a polite and kindly listener who was carrying on an entirely private line of thought. He was gentle, abstracted, and somber. As I studied him I recalled my enthusiasm for the Russian Revolution when it seemed that he or some one like him would be its ruler. I began to understand his failure.

"He is not an executive, but a dreamer," I afterward said to Crane. "He is too gentle to deal with ruthless adversaries."

IV

Ellen Glasgow and Mrs. Duke were guests with us at Edwin Winter's apartment on December 5. I had not seen Ellen for several years and I rather dreaded the meeting, for she was reported to be very deaf. She looked extremely well, but the moment she spoke I perceived that her hearing was less acute than when I had seen her last. She managed her sounding box very cleverly, however, and shared in the conversation quite fully. "She is a powerful personality, a brave thinker, one of the best in the South."

A few days later, Constance Skinner, a daughter of the far Northwest, came to dinner with us and told us of her life in British Columbia.

"My father was a Hudson's Bay trader in Quesnel, and I spent my childhood at this trading post. My girlhood was spent in Victoria. At sixteen I was a reporter on a paper there, and two years later became its dramatic editor."

From Victoria she worked her way to Los Angeles to a place on *The Times,* then went to *The Examiner* in San Francisco. When this editor was transferred, she went to Chicago. From Chicago she came to New York and was doing special historical writing for the Yale Press.

"She is making a brave fight. Her career has been essentially masculine. She has adventured as a boy would do and she has made a place for herself. It is an amazing story, typical of the New World and the New Woman. It could not have happened twenty years ago. She represents a small army of girls who have marched upon New York."

Lorado Taft and Will Stefansson took dinner with us December 20.

"We talked—or Stefansson talked—till midnight, while Taft alternately dozed and smiled. Stefansson's story of his life in Dakota was absorbingly interesting. His defense of 'the friendly Arctic' was amusing. He pictured (as he does more fully in his books) the vivid contrasts of the North, insisting that it is not only habitable but a place of peace and plenty—'for those who understand it and know how to use it.' Tall, blond, blue-eyed, he resembled a rugged Norwegian farmer as he confronted us, and his speech had the flat, crackling intonation of the Norsk, so familiar to me. 'I am planning to go back,' he declared, 'not as a seeker for the North Pole but as a geographer and ethnologist. There is a mighty world up there, a vast field of exploration and settlement.'

"He smilingly admitted that in Dakota he was known as 'Willy Stevenson,' but that his Icelandic name was Stefansson. He had much to say on the subject of diet and asserted (as he does in his book) that the eating of raw fish prevents scurvy. 'I can live indefinitely on a meat diet, as the Sioux once did,' he declared.

(He remains in my mind as I saw him that night—confident, successful. In proof of his theory he actually lived for a year on meat alone.)

George Seymour and his wife Flora, editors of *The Stepladder*, came to tea December 21.

"Seymour is a big, blond, slow-spoken youth with a remarkably good use of English. He is an expert accountant on a salary, but he and his alert little wife are doing a notable work in building up The Order of Bookfellows. Their home is in Chicago and *The Stepladder* is their organ. They are a bravely idealistic pair, insisting on the value of books in an age of radio, motion pictures, and jazz."

At seven my wife and I set out for Brooklyn, where I had agreed to read for the patrons of the Child's Museum. I arrived at the place chilled to the marrow and morose, but the institution cheered and interested me. The people in charge, a kindly lot of elderly women, met me with expressions of gratitude and presented me to the other volunteer readers, Leonora Speyer, John Farrar, and John Weaver.

"Farrar, boyish and shy and awkward, made a hit with his children's poems, and Weaver read some verse in the vernacular of present-day Brooklyn. As we were going out he said to me, 'We younger fellows are just "doing stunts." Our stuff isn't literature.' His frankness was engaging. I agreed with him but did not say so."

For some reason, perhaps because of my chill that night, I got up the next morning feeling very old and weak and poor—which I was.

"This is one of the days when I do not attempt to deceive myself. To live at all I must assume to be well and happy, and to succeed I must believe in myself and in my work. Occasionally I come down to earth and realize that I am a sixty-year-old machine, in danger of going to pieces at any moment. On such days, the small sale of my books, the narrow circle of my fame, and the uncertainty of my future combine to crush the spirit out of me. However I shall probably bob up to-morrow."

CHAPTER THIRTY-TWO

POETS AND POETRY WEEK

I

SHORTLY after the holidays I paid a visit to Macmillan's and there discovered with most disheartening completeness that "A Daughter of the Middle Border" had failed to interest the critics and the public.

"Although it has been on the market three months, only a half dozen reviews of it have come in, and these were written by my personal friends. The whole outlook is humiliatingly dark. Interest in my work appears to have entirely evaporated. In spite of the acclaim of 'A Son of the Middle Border,' its sequel is of no value even to the readers of the first volume. I strongly feel that the use of photographs was a mistake. They took away from the historic value of the text. All the illustrations should have been pen drawings like those in Volume I."

Although I did not set it down at the time, the cause of this book's failure ran deeper than the effect of its illustrations. In a year when women wore skirts above their knees and young girls danced cheek to cheek with their partners, when road-house anecdotes were heard in drawing-rooms, and sexual promiscuity was openly advocated, what chance had my quiet story of a pioneer wife and mother?

In the midst of this period of self-questioning, I

lunched at the Century Club with Carl Van Doren and John Farrar and listened in on a discussion concerning the work of the literary come-outers. Van Doren's judgment, while quite reasonable in some respects, failed of my agreement in others.

"I have no sympathy with this present-day literature of revolt," I said.

To this he retorted, "It is the same sort of revolt which you shared in '93."

To this I replied at some length and to this general effect: "To me there is a vital difference. The writers whom you have named seem to me abnormally concerned with the sexual side of life. Love in their books is raw animalism, instant in its demands. Their lack of restraint, their insistence on dissolute heroines, is not American but European. My interest is not in them, but in the man or woman who creates *new* characters and *new* themes. I honor a writer who discovers new relationships in human life—relationships which spring from our life as Americans.

"There is nothing distinctive in this literature of incest, adultery, and other forms of sexual lawlessness. It does not appeal to me as new or important. Much of it is based on records of the police courts. We are not making progress by publishing the doings of the brothel. I despise the motive which underlies the use of such material. The theories which I put into 'Crumbling Idols,' to which you refer, distinctly led away from such themes. 'All that the past was not, the future will be,' I quoted at that time, and in saying this I had in mind Emerson and Whitman rather than the French naturalists."

(We parted amicably but with no marked change of

opinion on their side or on mine. Ten years have passed since then and the pornographic school is losing power. The weakness of a "shocking" literature lies in the diminishing sensitiveness of the reader and the necessity for finding new ways of outraging decency. Once I despaired of living long enough to see the lady come back. To-day women's gowns are charmingly feminine. Grandmothers are again in evidence. True we have the pajama craze, but its ugliness only enhances the beauty of the cloaks and gowns of evening wear. With this change of costume has come a change in psychology. What will happen next year no man can tell; but I hasten to record my pleasure in the passing of the women who assumed the vices of men.)

On January 19, Ellen Glasgow came to dinner with us. "She was very gay, but her deafness made conversation somewhat formal. She was good-humored about it, however. Candidly adjusting herself to the situation, she put her little telephone box on the table before her as I put on my glasses to carve the roast; and she got on very well except when talk became general. Although she is gay of spirit on the surface, she is, I suspect, still fundamentally the scientist. She was a disciple of Herbert Spencer when I knew her first in 1898, and I cannot believe she has grown less logical with the years. She is one of the strongest of the Southern novelists and has kept a high level in all she has written."

II

The last week in January was "Poetry Week," and verse writers had assembled from every direction. As one who wrote an occasional rhyme, I was permitted to share in the various receptions and dinners, indeed I was called upon to preside over a meeting at the MacDowell Club. My record concerning this program is not lacking in definition:

"The poets on the program were neither amusing nor impressive. Some of the reading was good, but the verse had no vital significance. Much of it was bookish and artificial, in no sense distinctive of American conditions or American thought. It was the kind of verse a young college man would write. As speakers, they were bungling. One man used the word 'awfully' three times in the first sentence of his address, and his voice lacked quality. It was amusing to find these hypercritical youngsters so fumbling and crude in their oratory. I was pleased when Arthur Guiterman came on, for he read his humorous verse delightfully. Anna Hempstead Branch was charming."

January 25 was another day of life among the poets. In the library of a great house I joined in another program of readings by Arthur Guiterman, Edwin Markham, Amy Lowell, and Margaret Widdemer.

"Amy Lowell, who bustled in late, was authoritative and outspokenly critical of those who read too long. She carries herself now with the aplomb of a leader; the field marshal of the free-verse cohorts.

"At night I was a guest at a dinner which (as a close to 'Poetry Week') brought together a throng of poets of all ages and both sexes. Witter Bynner, who presided gracefully, was too kind in introducing his speakers, but Amy Lowell again expressed herself with forceful clarity. The hit of the evening, however, was the address of Dr. Chang, a visiting Chinese scholar, who spoke with depth, beauty, and power. His mellow culture, distinction of phrase, and beauty of tone made the provincialism of several preceding speakers almost ludicrous.

"Arthur Ficke was also admirable. He spoke as a man of comparative knowledge, with dignity and taste. Amy Lowell, for all her claims to subtlety in *vers libre,* was baldly prosaic—a kind of New England schoolmistress speaking her mind to her pupils. The long cigars which she smoked were indicative of her state of mind."

III

Meeting Edward Wheeler at the club the following noon, I started a discussion by saying, "Your Poetry Society has built up a huge claque for verse writing, but has it produced any real poets?"

He replied, "Thus far the outcome hardly justifies the organization." With a rueful smile, he added, "The program of last night went on for another hour after you left. You didn't miss much. I am glad you escaped. Some of our members have almost no sense of values and they nearly all lack cultivation. The society is not a failure, but our output of verse is disappointing. The promise for a real poet is less definite now than it was five years ago. The war seems to have unhinged things generally. We have had an emotional debauch and it may be years before the young poets of the nation recover from it."

"It is not so much the war," I replied; "it is a lack of culture, of background. The spirit of journalism is in all we do. Our writers are just off the farm, or from the small town. Amy Lowell's free verse is a fad, a phase. It has nothing stable, nothing quotable in it. You can't hand on a wreath of smoke to another generation. It offers nothing solid. It is too easy, too theoretic in its technique. It is all of a piece with cubism, imagism, vorticism, and other artistic vagaries where sound scholarship and cultural background count for nothing.

"Why attempt to deceive ourselves? Most of the writers of to-day are educated in newspaper offices or by the editors of commercial magazines. Others are graduates of schools of journalism—they start with that ideal. Consider that group last night. What are they in relation to Emerson, Lowell, and Howells? Merely a gang of amiable young journalists experimenting—doing 'stunts,' as one of them said to me. Nothing is gained by 'kidding' them or 'kidding' ourselves. What has 'Poetry Week' produced? Not one writer of sustained power. We have many singers of exquisite little songs, but none of vision and sweep. England isn't much richer—the age just doesn't produce fine poetry."

Wheeler listened gravely, and replied, "You're a little hard on us, but I must admit our verse is scrappy."

(In going over this notation to-day, I am reminded that Amy Lowell has gone, and with her the fad for *vers libre*. It has vanished like smoke. What will follow?)

IV

"January 28. A dinner with Carl Van Doren increased my liking for him. He and his wife are fine types of serious young America. They are students and thinkers. Ellen Glasgow and her sister were the only other guests at the table, and we had a lively discussion of literary theories.

"Van Doren's home is a place of books, but he is not bookish in the old-fashioned way. When I met him first

I took him to be a reporter on the New York *Nation,* for he came to the office of the American Academy to interview me on our building plans. He told me to-night that he is steadily moving away from teaching into editorial work. He is a handsome fellow, quiet and genial. I have confidence in his future."

(If this sounds a bit patronizing, let the reader remember that I was over sixty at this time and Van Doren nearly thirty years my junior. Since then he has built himself into a place of great distinction as editor and critic.)

On January 30, some forty or more of Sam McClure's old friends and authors came together at a dinner in his honor, a meeting of "the Old Guard."

"The spirit of the meeting was entirely 'before the war' in its wholesome American quality. Frank Doubleday presided felicitously and the honored guest made a modest and rather touching speech. He was genuinely moved by this array of loyal friends. 'To be praised like this after so many years of being on the outside of things is consoling.' He spoke of his old magazine as a mirror of the times. 'I hope I can make the new one equally representative of the best in American life of to-day,' he said. His attitude was patriotic, buoyant, and manly.

"I sat beside John Finley and Herbert Houston. Albert Shaw, who was opposite, looked the handsome scholar that he is. He greeted me with affection. 'There are some books which I read fast and others which I read slowly. I am reading *your* Middle Border books slowly,' he said, 'and I am finding them full of the America I knew.'

"I did not stay till the last, but I heard most of the speeches. They were in praise of McClure, who deserves all that was said of him. I cannot believe, however, that

he will fulfill a tenth part of the predictions which arose
in the glow of this feast. His sun, like mine, is setting.

"The question, 'What to do next?' is giving me a great
deal of thought and some worry. My readers are passing
and whatsoever I get out of my manuscripts while I am
alive is so much secured. That I am now a veteran limping off the stage, giving place to younger men, is evident.
Many of these men are writing in a way repellent to
me. As Howells whimsically said, 'I hate young men';
by which he meant a certain kind of thirty-five-year-old
'youth' generated by the war, cynical, sex-obsessed, and
greedy. They have only contempt for me and the literature I represent. Our differences are irreconcilable."

A plan for a summer in England was taking shape in
my mind, but I had not committed myself to it. I agreed
with my wife that it was a wild extravagance, but I began nevertheless to collect steamship folders and detailed information as to hotels and railway fare. I spent
hours studying advertisements in the English magazines
and in calculating the cost of a flat in London.

In dining with Professor Charles Downer Hazen on
the 7th, I again met Gerald Stanley Lee, a picturesque
figure.

"Lee interests me. His remarks are always apt and his
phrases pleasingly concise. Although a thinker of unusual clarity who has written some meaty books, he has
not yet won a distinct place in our literature, perhaps
because his writings have not been placeable. They are
hard to characterize. They are neither essays, sermons,
nor histories; they are in truth 'jars of mixed pickles'—
comments on men and affairs of a sociologic nature. They
are sententious, incisive in diction, but lacking in *tissue*.

'Crowds' is an admirable book in some ways, but I doubt if it has the quality of permanence. It is too chaotic. The author wears a stock in his writing as in daily life and belongs to the Emerson-Thoreau group of thinkers. He is a tall, thin, plain man, with blond hair and gray eyes, always alert and smiling."

At Elon Hooker's on the 8th I had more talk with Lee. Glenn Frank was in the group, and the talk was largely on France and her present demands. No two of us agreed on any point. Hooker was all for combating the propaganda against France, but I was not ready to enter upon such a campaign.

"England is fighting for her existence," I argued. "She can't go much farther without revolution of an economic sort. She needs support." Lee agreed with me that the workers of Germany had had enough of war. "They can't be led against France or any other nation." He recalled that one of his projects during the war was to drop bulletins and pamphlets from airplanes in order to let the German soldiers know what was going on.

At Mrs. Riggs' reception, February 9, I was presented to Geraldine Farrar, a colorful, vigorous woman of middle age to whom a circle of men were paying homage.

"She was 'made up' theatrically, but seemed, nevertheless, a wholesome person, frankly American in accent. I had no talk with her—in truth I had nothing to say to her except that I had heard her sing many times, which was banal enough to put me among her worshipers.

"A dramatic critic was in the group, and I was amused to hear her say, 'He is a person to be placated.' Such indeed was his attitude. I've no doubt there are singers and

playwrights who court the favor of such writers, but to
me he was just a pleasant young fellow earning a precarious living in a world of daily excitement. This was
made evident by an altercation with another dramatic
writer, during which they pleasantly promised to punch
each other's faces. I could hardly believe them in earnest as they stood uttering these threats in quiet voices.
What it was all about I did not learn; but it must have
been something very vital to them both."

V

In an earlier chapter I have recorded my meetings with
Mrs. Curran, the writer whose spirit guide was "Patience
Worth," an English maid of Shakespeare's time. When
I had my first sitting with her she used a kind of ouija
board, but at later meetings, while she still held the board
in her lap, she spelled the words of the poems which she
composed instantly to the order of her sitter.

"February 16. At Mrs. Robert Franks' to-night I met
Mrs. Curran again. She looked thinner and much older
than when I saw her last. She said, 'My husband is ill—
hopelessly so.' With regard to her 'phase' she explained,
'I have moved on to a point where I no longer use the
ouija board or spell out words. I hear the words and
repeat them as I hear them.'

"Some thirty or forty guests were seated in the music
room and we were all invited to name subjects for poems.
Various subjects were named, and Mrs. Curran, standing
before us with her eyes on the ceiling, reeled off yards
of verse dealing with each title—all remarkably graceful
and apt, but all running (it seemed to me) just below the
level of acceptable verse. Her mind appeared to creak

a bit on the subjects I suggested. With John Burroughs for a subject she was less happy than when dealing with Keats and Shelley."

She was clever—amazingly so, and later I said to Edwin Winter: "I couldn't write one of those poems with a week to do it in. Her composition is a subconscious stunt, a skill developed by years of intense application. She has a certain phraseology on which she relies to produce her effects at a moment's notice."

She complained at the close of her performance of a critical element in her audience. She especially felt my scepticism, for by closing my eyes and listening critically I sensed her repetitions, gropings, and fumblings. Her mind worked swiftly, consciously. It was not all based on subliminal action. However, it was mysterious enough. I know of no other writer capable of similar rapidity of performance."

VI

Having accepted an invitation to address the Y.M.C.A. of Yale University on February 19, I began to worry about it.

"I have no wish to instruct anybody. No student wants to hear me preach and I certainly have no desire to do so. Let others exhort. The world is full of those who believe they are ordained for such work. Once I felt important. To-day I am content to let the world wag on as it will.

"I have a natural desire to linger a little longer on the stage, but this desire is not strong enough to lead me into new relationships or along new paths of endeavor. My interests are now almost entirely in the past. I find myself returning to my middle period with relief from the jazz and the rampant vulgarity of to-day. No doubt this, too, is a phase, a period of transition; but I don't like it, whatever it is called. However, my likes or dislikes are of no weight to any one."

On the date of my lecture, Dr. Turck and I went to Yale and spent the day there. Fenton Turck, who had arranged for my coming, met us at the train and took us to see the beautiful Harkness tower. Later we all had luncheon with William Lyon Phelps.

"Phelps owns a spacious house of Colonial pattern through whose doorway literary students come and go with joyous freedom. He is a charming speaker and one of the most popular instructors in the university. At dinner President Angell and Allen Johnson, the historian, joined our party and were pleasing guests. I had never met Johnson before.

"He is a slender, refined man of scholarly type. After he had expressed interest in my chronicle of Middle Border home life, I told him that I was at work on a manuscript which described a family taking the back trail from Wisconsin to Massachusetts. He asked, 'How long has it been since you visited London?' . . . 'Sixteen years.' . . . 'That is too long to be away from your ancestral home,' he remarked. 'I know it is, but I have not found myself able to go. I am secretly planning to go this summer and take my wife and daughters.' To this he responded, 'Do so, by all means. It will be of the greatest value in the work you are doing. I value your chronicle and hope you will bring it down to date. Why not take it to England as an extension of your back-trailing?' This suggestion was of great value to me."

Two days later, in discussing Johnson's suggestion with

Marsh, I said quite confidently, "My plan is to present the reverse of the pioneer movement. Allen Johnson's suggestion that I go to England and complete the book there appeals to me. I already have a dim notion of how it should work out. I am planning to sail for England in June at the end of my daughters' school term."

At the invitation of Glenn Frank I lunched at the Players, February 23. Dr. Jones of the State University of Missouri, Ray Stannard Baker, and Edward J. Wheeler were the other guests, a fine group of men.

"Baker was very grave of mood and rather worn of temper. He is one of the few men who are permitted to see Woodrow Wilson, who is a very sick man. Baker said, 'He is improving in health, but is in no condition to write. His mind does not initiate anything now.' Baker, highly valued by Wilson, is examining his papers. He will ultimately write Wilson's life. He admitted that the ex-President's condition is hopeless."

In calling on Eva Ingersoll Brown, I met John Lane, the London publisher, who talked of bringing out my later books in England. I assured him that it would give me pleasure to have them sold there, but that I anticipated no demand for them. "If you can sell two thousand copies you will be doing very well." He was interested in my plan for spending the summer in England, and offered to present me to the literary groups with which he was affiliated.

CHAPTER THIRTY-THREE

A NEW EDITION OF MY BOOKS

I

EARLY in 1922—on January 3d to be exact—Henry Hoyns and Edward Marsh, representing Harper & Bros., met me at the Century Club to discuss a plan for a twelve-volume uniform edition of my fiction. I had long desired such a group of my books, and as I was nearing sixty-two years of age and planning to spend a long vacation in England, my publishers were disposed to meet my wishes—with certain provisos. Having placed the editorial decisions in the hands of Marsh, the firm asked me to do three things: first, accept a smaller royalty; second, write a new preface for each volume, and third, assemble the material for a new book, one which should bring together all my stories of the American Indian. To these provisos I gave consent and at once set to work selecting the fiction to be included.

The plan involved a revaluation of my work, not only by my friends and certain amiable critics but by myself. I found myself in the position of a parent forced to inspect his children and put several of them out of doors. "All my books have their good points," I urged. "They resemble me in their faults as well as in their virtues—and they number more than thirty, big and little. However, I'll do my best to value and arrange them."

I began with "Jason Edwards," my first born, and decided against it. "It is too short, too sour of temper, too drab of clothing, too preachy." Then my second novel, "A Spoil of Office," was set on the doorstep. "Its characters are too largely political reformers. The story starts well, and has much of my youthful idealism in it. It presents a vivid picture of my prairie world, but it needs an entire remaking in order to enter the select circle. I hate to say this, for Bradley Talcott has his fine moments, but he lacks tact and cultivation."

I started the list with "Main-Travelled Roads" and "Boy-Life on the Prairie," for these were demanded by my publishers, and so were "Rose of Dutcher's Coolly" (child of my early maturity) and "The Eagle's Heart," my first successful romance, a story full of faults but having wide appeal.

"The Captain of the Gray Horse Troop," which had been my most successful book, was included, and so was "Hesper," my second "best seller." One was based upon the three-cornered contest between a band of settlers and a tribe of red hunters with the soldiers as peacemakers, and the other chronicled a dramatic struggle above the clouds between organized labor and organized capital with the free miner as the party of the third part. These books could not be left out. "Cavanagh," which was based on my life among the forest rangers, went in, but my only humorous romance, "Her Mountain Lover," and "Witches' Gold" both lost my approval and were left out as being merely long short stories. So were "The Moccasin Ranch," "The Light of the Star," and "The Forester's Daughter," but "The Tyranny of the Dark" was a full-sized novel and contained many of my experiences in the twilight zone of psychic research. However, it gave place to "Money Magic," the study of a Colorado girl's loyalty to her gambler husband.

Despite the fact that many of the books excluded had pages which I highly valued, I was in substantial agreement with my editors, who wished the set to be a worthy representation of my Western fiction. We decided to call it "The Border Edition."

Having written a new preface for each of the selected volumes, I began to assemble all my stories of the American Indian and turned them over to Marsh.

In truth the first quarter of 1922 was a stock-taking time for me. "How much have I accomplished? What is the value of my output?" I asked myself, and, to secure a new valuation, Marsh, in his capacity as editor, sent a set of these books to a list of my fellow craftsmen asking for a critical review of the work I had thus far published.

Among those who were interested enough to comply, I particularly valued the judgment of Brand Whitlock, William Allen White, Zona Gale, Carl Van Doren, and Henry Fuller, all of whom dwelt long on the two volumes of "Main-Travelled Roads," then skipped rapidly over the novels leading up to "A Son of the Middle Border" and its sequel, "A Daughter of the Middle Border." Although I was not at all sure they had all read these intervening pages, I could not protest. In a moment of friendly banter I said to Van Doren, "I don't agree with your estimate of my 'Captain of the Gray Horse Troop.'" To this he replied thoughtfully, "I am inclined to think I did rather less than justice to that book."

None of the critics save Fuller had read "The Silent

Eaters," which went into print for the first time as the concluding narrative of "The Book of the American Indian," and few of them had read "They of the High Trails" and "Mart Haney."

To Fuller I said, "I admit to a sag in the quality of my production from 1906 to 1912, but I do not think the critics are justified in slighting all that I wrote between 1893 and 1917. I had no opportunity of revising any of these plates. They are reprinted with all the faults and blunders of the original editions. As for my stories of Colorado, Montana, and Wyoming, they contain pictures and experiences which were a joy to me then and are remembered joys as I reread them. I hate to see them go into the discard. Furthermore, it is only fair to me to say that there are no rotten spots in any of these books. Some of them were written for the magazines in order that my wife and children might be fed and sheltered and clothed. I do not offer this as an apology, but as an explanation. I know the weaknesses of my books, but I am not ashamed of them. If I could rewrite 'A Spoil of Office' I could make it a worthy picture of a stirring era in Western settlement, but to remake the plates would not pay the publisher. So of several others. They are condemned to go, carrying with them much that is of value."

Fuller brought up another subject. "What are you going to do with all those field notebooks?"

"I don't know. They, too, have much that I value—pictures, scenes, incidents, and sketches of characters, but they cannot be published as they are and I have not the time to rewrite them. They will go into the files of the Academy—perhaps to be destroyed when I am a little farther away from the experiences which gave them form."

II

For years I had been urging Lorado Taft to exhibit his work in New York and to accept every opportunity to lecture there. "It is possible to achieve a national reputation without the endorsement of Manhattan, but it will be a slower and more difficult process," I argued. "To deny the influence of New York City is as absurd as it would be for the artists of Lyons or Marseilles to deny the weight and power of Paris. Your high place in the Middle West is all very well as a stage in your progress; but you should move on to a position more commanding."

My arguments had been of some effect; he came more often to speak for this or that organization in or near New York and took pleasure in the meetings with his fellows which the Century Club afforded. Each visit was a bit longer and honors of one kind or another convinced him that the East was disposed to consider him something more than a local celebrity. His loyalty to Chicago was considered an amiable weakness.

One of the aspiring institutions of the lower East Side was the Neighborhood Playhouse to which I have several times alluded. It was (as its name implies) a community recreational center with a stage, a workshop, and a restaurant connected, all established and supported by the Lewisohn sisters, two public-spirited women of wealth and cultivation. I had met them several times and knew in a general way what their organization had accomplished, and when Alice Lewisohn wrote me late in February, saying, "We are soon to produce an indoor pageant based on Whitman's 'Salut au Monde,' and we would like to have you come down and tell us about old Walt," I quite willingly consented. The idea of the pageant interested me.

On receiving my note, she wrote again, saying, "You must dine with us and see our young people at their work," and on March 2 I ate in the café with the players and their friends and later (introduced by Miss Arthur, the manager of the theater), I spoke to some sixty or seventy of the volunteer actors, artists, and workers of the theater.

My theme was "Whitman as I Saw Him," and the respect, almost veneration, which some of the faces expressed, arose not from anything I had written but from the amazing fact that I had actually seen and talked with a poet who was almost a myth to these young sons and daughters of Jewish immigrants. My white hair and mustache related me to the Mark Twain and Whitman age. When I had finished they made no comment, but resumed their work on the costumes and scenery which the play demanded.

Alice Lewisohn, a pale, slight woman, appeared all too frail to assume the care and responsibility which the management of this social center involved; but her friends assured me that she not only directed the plays, but took important rôles in them. "I am not in the next one," she said, "but you must come down and see it." This I promised to do.

III

Winston Churchill, of whom I had heard little for several years, sent me an invitation to his lecture at the

Plaza Hotel, March 3; and as his address was on a psychical subject, I accepted with some curiosity. I had not known that he was interested in such matters.

"A fairly good audience of his readers and literary friends were seated in the ballroom as I entered, and I saw many familiar faces. Some one—I have forgotten who —told me that Churchill had ceased to write fiction and that he was giving his time almost entirely to the study of the subconscious mind.

"He was heartily greeted as he came in with his manuscript under his arm, but his lecture was hard to follow. He was analytic and his method unemotional. He offered little by way of illustration. As the work of a popular novelist, it was a surprisingly analytic essay.

"It appears that for two years he has been experimenting with automatic writing. 'This lecture is the outcome of my researches,' he said, and if I understood him correctly he does not accept the spirit hypothesis but relates all his messages to 'the primitive mind' and 'the creative mind.' The audience sat through it most patiently and applauded him handsomely at the close, evidence of the appeal his essentially fine character had made on each of his auditors. Even those who could not understand his conclusions praised him for his frank and manly attitude."

As members of the Pulitzer committee, William Lyon Phelps, Jesse Lynch Williams, and I met at the Yale Club March 4 to compare judgments concerning the prize play.

"Phelps and Williams argued that 'Anna Christie,' O'Neill's play, has more power than any other this year, and I am to see it as a possible choice. Thus far I have kept clear of it. The story of it does not attract me. During luncheon the talk fell upon the spring invasion of English poets and the tales which Phelps told were highly amusing.

"They quarter themselves on certain of our good-humored folk, and with the hides of hippos resist all hints to leave," he declared. He told of one man (I forget which one) who stayed on month after month at the home of a rich Long Island family until at last in desperation the owner announced that he had decided to close the house and go to Florida. "How jolly!" exclaimed the Englishman. "I've always wanted to see Florida."

My wife and I accepted seats in a box at the opera on March 11, and as a result I saw "La Traviata" for the first time. Up to this moment I had successfully avoided it.

"Well as I knew some of its arias, I had very little idea of the piece, which impressed me as an incredible mixture of 'patter' and lovely melody. The scenes were all set in a gorgeously hued land of make-believe, with symbols of trees and pasteboard walls of castles. Nothing proceeded as it naturally should. Retainers illogically came and went, gypsies in gay, untarnished clothing reclined on colorful rocks at the foot of great cliffs. Men gestured and shouted while women waved their arms or clawed their breasts, and yet now and again the scenes achieved beauty and significance. Three or four times the music actually moved me; but for the most part I saw in it the originals of Gilbert and Sullivan's burlesques."

The Town Hall luncheon in honor of Lorado Taft came off March 15 with about a hundred guests. "A few artists were present, but only a few. We met half a dozen editors and writers, personal friends of mine; the others were a hit-or-miss lot, it appeared to me. Ely was most enthusiastic in his welcome and Lorado happy in his brief reply. On the whole, it made a snappy end to his two weeks' stay with us. 'I begin to like New York,' he confessed."

That night my wife and I saw O'Neill's "First Man," a painful, depressing, but original and powerful play. "The author rides his theme hard but it is his own. This is not a carpentered piece. It is written—like a short story. Strange to say it does not seem theatrical, although perfectly adapted to acting."

IV

In a visit to Washington toward the end of March (23), I dined with Senator Lodge at his home.

"I was saddened to find him an old man and in a certain sense a lonely man. He is nearing the sunset. He will win his fight in the Senate to-morrow, but he is not ready to quit in the hour of his triumph. His friends all say, 'He persists in standing for renomination and we fear his defeat. If he would only resign his political ambitions now!' That his powers are slowing down is evident. His mind acts slowly. His words come hesitatingly. He is interested only in political affairs. He talked of nothing else. He lives in an atmosphere of political maneuverings. He was dignified and kindly in manner, but it was evident that his thoughts were centered upon holding his place in the Senate for at least another term. To meet defeat now means death."

When he learned that I was going to England, he gave me a note of introduction to the Secretary of State, saying, "Ask him for a formal letter to our ambassadors in England and France," and then (more important than all), he gave me a note to Lord Balfour for whom he expressed a high admiration. "I saw much of Balfour while he was here. He is a scholar as well as a statesman."

I went away with a feeling of regret, sensing the end of a most distinguished career. I wrote:

"Our rough-and-ready representatives from the West and South pretend to despise Lodge and some of them actually hate him; but he has my respect and admiration. His quiet dignity, his clear-cut, scholarly phrases are in pleasing contrast to the blundering, blatant oratory so often heard on the floor of the Senate as well as in the House. To say that he is, like Arthur Balfour, a gentleman and a scholar as well as a statesman would only add to the dislike which certain political leaders openly profess. The older I grow the less virtue I find in log-rolling, back-country politicians. It is time for America to grow up in this regard as in others."

This letter from Senator Lodge and the one from the State Department definitely committed me to the carrying out of the plan so tremendously exciting to my wife and daughters as well as to me.

"It is unjustifiable, extravagant, hazardous," I said to Mark Sullivan, "but I'm going to do it." He smiled and replied, "Not so bad as all that. I'm going over myself, next year."

On my way back to New York, I finished reading "If Winter Comes," by Hutchinson, which wearied me while it interested me. "There is something irritating about its style. I admit its fine qualities, but it is sadly jumbled at the end by the introduction of another man to tell the story of 'Mark Sabre,' a device which to my thinking breaks up the unity of the book. To me it is an over-rated work and I wonder at its wide reading over here. In England it has had but a very moderate sale—so I am told."

(No one speaks of the book now. It lasted only a year or two, but it had an enormous sale.)

Professor Throop's meeting on Sunday, March 26, turned out to be a "Hamlin Garland Day" in very truth.

"As I entered the room, Throop motioned me to come forward, but I shook my head and took a seat at the end of the hall. To sit there as an auditor to my summing up was a bit like listening to my obituary; but my daughters, who sat beside me, were as enthralled as if they had never heard of 'The Middle Border' before. Afterward, as I went up the aisle, the entire audience rose as a sign of respect for my gray hairs.

"George Grey Barnard made a friendly speech and so did May Riley Smith. At the close I was pressed upon by those who wished to shake hands, an American desire, and I met all who came, although it is always an awkward thing to do. What can one say?"

At Professor Seligman's dinner, March 27, I met Professor Michael Pupin, the electrical expert, now a professor at Columbia. "He is a big man, German in appearance. Although born in Serbia he is proudly American—a handsome, jovial, attractive personality. I should like to know him better. His career shows how quickly an American can be made."

On the following day, at the urgent request of Wilson Irvine of Chicago, I went to the studio of Wayman Adams, an Indiana artist, and sat for a portrait.

"Adams gave six hours of close attention to the job, and succeeded in painting a powerful and rather grim likeness of me. I recognize its truth, but it will not please my wife nor my daughters."

"April 6. David Jayne Hill's address at the Academy was a scholarly and eloquent analysis of our diplomatic service. His fine voice, his colloquial style, and the humor of his phraseology delighted his audience. His English was quite faultless and his manner logical in arrangement. At no point was his expression conventional. We all congratulated him.

"At the close of the session, Maurice Egan came up to me and said with a smile, 'I am naming no names, but before you sail for England I shall have some good news for you.' This leads me to suspect that the Pulitzer Committee, of which he is a member, has voted a prize for my chronicle of the Middle Border."

That night I shared the secret with my wife. "If Egan's report is true there is all the more warrant for our summer in London."

I was further encouraged when an editor on *The Popular Science Monthly* called me up and asked for an article on "Doyle and Psychic Research" and suggested that he could use other articles from England. "All this is heartening. Macmillan's are advertising a new edition of my 'Grant' as a part of the celebration of his birthday.

"When one has had poverty for a daily companion in early life, one has need of the sustaining power of luxury, honor, and sympathetic companions. It is so easy to slip back into the worn grooves of humility and doubt. When I get away from the people who know me and value me, back into local trains and ratty hotels, I am like one who has slipped into familiar pits of poverty. My fame, my hard-won comforts, and my dignities are all illusory. It is this experience now and then which keeps me from wasting any of my substance. I must prepare for sickness and age. No doubt much of the penuriousness of certain men of great wealth arises from this early deep-laid sense of insecurity."

V

Having learned that my friend Conan Doyle was at the Ambassador Hotel, April 10, my wife and I were moved to call on him. "We found Sir Arthur surrounded by three sturdy children shepherded by his wife. He seemed much the same as when I saw him last, somewhat heavier in face and figure but not much grayer. He is a bit hard of hearing and kept his good ear toward me. He was very frank in his expression of pleasure in my coming to see him. 'It means so much to meet an old friend,' he said. He spoke of the time when I 'buzzed' the ball to him. By 'buzz' he meant curve, I suppose. It was hot in the hotel and he looked rather parboiled. 'I am besieged by swarms of reporters and photographers,' he said. 'It has been a hectic day for us all.'

"His lecture managers having asked me to present him to his first audience, I naturally asked, 'What shall I say?' He replied, 'My dear fellow, I leave it all to you. I am delighted to share the platform with you.' "

"April 12. As I came on the platform of Carnegie Hall preceding Doyle's address, I faced an enormous audience. I was intimidated by these faces, but Doyle, though very tense, was exalted by his opportunity. Every seat in the auditorium was taken. It seemed a vast and lofty cavern

walled with pink tiles, each tile a countenance. I had no
perception of individuals except so far as the floor seats
and near-by boxes were concerned. My introduction was
very short and sympathetic—just a few words to prepare
for his greeting.

"His speech was not a scientific exegesis; it was a plea,
an exhortation. He had the spirit of the evangelist and
his manly voice profoundly affected his auditors. Even
those who did not agree with him granted his sincerity
and applauded the nobility of his purpose."

"April 17. A college student from Wisconsin called
to see me this afternoon preparatory to a study of my
work, which is to be the subject of her thesis next year,
when she hopes to gain a master's degree. As we sat discussing the literary history of the Middle West, I saw
myself as a part of something in motion! Here is this girl
(she seemed hardly older than my daughter, Mary Isabel)
using my work as the subject of a careful historical mono-
graph, precisely as though I were a personage in English
literature. I have suddenly become a veteran—almost
a venerable person! It is hard for me to accept that
view of myself and my work. I have so long been a
'promising writer.'"

The meeting of the American Branch of the P. E. N.
Club on the 19th was pleasant but not important. Some
thirty-five people assembled, some of established reputation; others were youngsters like Farrar, Nathan, and
Frank. S. S. McClure and I were the oldest men present.

"Alexander Black presided in so far as there was any
presiding. He and Mrs. Riggs appear to be the principal
organizers here. What the test of membership is I cannot
discover; but as I am only an honorary member I have

no responsibilities in the matter. The idea of the club, as I understand it, is to bring about personal meetings and a better understanding among authors throughout the world."

On April 21, Finley phoned that he liked my article on Grant and saw no necessity for any changes in it. This set me free to go to the office of Harper's and discuss the question of a collection of my stories of the American Indian.

All along my way from 1887 to 1922, I had been doing an occasional study of the red man. The Sioux and Cheyenne could not be left out of my picture of the Northwest. In my two volumes of "Main-Travelled Roads" I had delineated certain types of the settlers with whom I had grown up, and in "They of the High Trails" I had characterized some of the trailers with whom I had camped and prospected; and now my sketches of the men dispossessed and destroyed by the settler and the mountaineer were about to go into a volume which should be at once an interpretation and a tribute.

My title for this collection had been "The Red Pioneer" and I had thought to make it a companion volume uniform with my other books of short stories, but my publishers, Harper & Brothers, argued that a volume of that sort would not sell. "Our plan is to make a large book of a distinctly impressive type, illustrate it with pictures by Frederic Remington, who did a number of illustrations for your stories which have appeared in *Harper's Weekly*, and sell it for six dollars."

To this I agreed, although I could not see any of my readers paying so much money for one of my books, and as I was about to sail for England I turned over to their

editor, Edward Marsh, all my stories of red men and
women, among them my most ambitious narrative which
I called "The Silent Eaters," a manuscript of some sixty
thousand words. This was in truth a defense of Sitting Bull, the most renowned of Sioux chieftains, made
from the standpoint of a young Sioux who had been educated among the white people. Originally I had called it
"My Chief, the Sitting Bull," as a young Scot might have
written of his chief, "The Bruce."

All of these stories were faithful to my impressions of
the many red villages I had studied. They were all written without the settler's bias. I had the artist's point of
view. I took the red man as I found him. To me he was
a product of his environment, like the eagle or the mountain lion. To call him a fiend, a devil, was unscientific.
The question of his origin, the basis of his customs should
not be clouded by racial or religious prejudice, nor confused by the hate of those who desired the lands he
occupied. In short the red people were to me human
beings who had come up along another line of civilization
from ours. Although in some ways our inferiors, they
possessed certain singularly noble traits.

In each of my stories I had attempted the delineation
of a type, "Hippy the Dare Devil," "Rising Wolf the
Ghost Dancer," "White Weasel the Dandy," and the like.

My design was directly opposite to that of Remington,
who carried to the study of these hunters all the contempt, all the conventional notions of a hard and rather
prosaic illustrator. He never got the wilderness point of
view. His white hunters were all ragged, bearded, narrow
between the eyes, and his red men stringy, gross of feature, and cruel. I recognized no harmony between his

drawings and my text, but as I was poor and my publishers agreed that they could not publish the book as I wished to have it done, I laid all my manuscript on their editorial desk and went away.

(It may interest the reader to know that the editors were right and that they have sold more than ten times the number of copies I had anticipated.)

Doyle's third lecture drew another enormous throng of good-looking folk, mostly middle-aged.

"There is a deep and growing interest in the subject. Never was spiritualism so respectable as now. Doyle, who is a crusader, has raised a new wave of faith. No advocate up to this time has ever had such vogue. His auditors, well-dressed and intelligent, were serious but not solemn. They applauded his manly directness. But to me his talk presented no convincing proof of spirit return. It was a most valuable presentation of phenomena, but I could not agree with his interpretations."

"April 22. It happened that my daughter Constance was the one to see the Whitman pageant with me and her appreciation of it helped me to value it. It was a very moving spectacle indeed. 'Old Walt,' throned at one side of the stage, commented like the seer that he was, whilst a great circular window (according to the lighting), allowed the audience to look out upon a globe swinging in infinite space. On this globe, across this space, moved vague mists and cloudy forms, pictures of Greece, Rome, and India. Scenes of joy and sorrow, types of ancient men and women drifted by, so studied, so presented that the procession made a cumulative appeal to the spectator while the music aided in suggesting the primeval and the vast. The postures of the dancers, archaic and moving, were often beautiful, and the close, with lines from the poet read majestically by Ian Maclaren, was a true climax.

"Altogether it was a performance such as Whitman himself would have enjoyed."

April 24 was the date of the American Academy's welcome to the French delegates.

"At four-thirty we were in our seats. At last the doors were opened and President Sloane led Messieurs Donnay and Chevrillon into our presence. We received them standing. The president then spoke a few words explaining the situation and presented Chancellor Nicholas Murray Butler, who made a polished and tactful speech, in which he emphasized the fact that the American Academy rejoiced in receiving in its own home, in executive session, delegates of the French Academy."

At seven-thirty that night I took my wife and daughters to the Ritz where, as guests of the Academy, they shared a splendid banquet in honor of the French Academicians.

"It was a brilliant assembly but the speaking was dull. Sloane not only read his paper but could not be heard, and only part of us understood the Frenchmen.

"Although genial citizens and men of learning they were not allowed to speak in English, and their long papers were exceedingly trying to those who, like myself, could not follow them. Many went to sleep, but all were patient and nothing marred the good feeling of the hour. Joffre slept also, a peaceful Titan, big, blond, and shaggy of eyebrow. His was a kindly face to my thinking—not that of a great warrior."

The meeting in honor of Grant's one hundredth birthday, April 27, was successful. My daughter Isabel pleased the audience with her reading of two war-time poems, and my hearers applauded when I said of Grant, "Whatever his limitations he (under Lincoln) saved this Union."

"A few veterans of the Grand Army were present and their gray heads and tremulous lips added a touch of pathos to the celebration. Joffre, who was expected, did not come and in an hour of waiting the meeting sang itself out in a sad anticlimax. However, it added one more to the many celebrations which the country gave this day as evidence of the gratitude in which it still holds the man who fought it out all summer and all winter in a year of national despair."

CHAPTER THIRTY-FOUR

LONDON HOMES AND ENGLISH AUTHORS

I

(In taking up the story of my third summer in England, I was disposed to leave out all those notes and diary entries which had been used in "Back Trailers of the Middle Border," but my publishers argued against this. They said, "You are now writing a purely literary and personal narrative, a statement of facts, and you must make use, in fullest detail, of all your records which bear upon writers and books. 'Back-Trailers' is a part of your family history. This volume is presented from a different angle. Furthermore, you cannot assume that the readers of 'My Friendly Contemporaries' are familiar with the story of your family outing."

With this explanation of the situation, I proceed, trusting that those familiar with my previous books will pardon any repetitious pages.)

As the date of my sailing approached, the task of getting away increased in complexity. I had times of paralyzing doubt. "Why take such a risk at your time of life and with your slender resources?" I asked myself; and at my boldest I answered, "Because it is essentially expedient. You have not seen London since 1906. A summer there will freshen you up in a literary way, and your agent is sure it will make your next season's lectures more attractive."

In the midst of this debate, which I fear the reader will find rather comical, I received official notification of the fact that my Middle Border chronicle had won the Pulitzer Prize "for the best autobiography during 1921."

On May 23, I acknowledged this award. "It comes opportunely—as Egan said it would. It gives me courage to set aside the money necessary for a summer in England. This thousand-dollar check is like something found in the grass. It permits, at least, a five thousand dollar extravagance. Each time I buy a ticket I shall say, 'I can afford this, for there *is* that thousand-dollar check found in the grass!' "

In writing to one of the committee I said, "I infer that in reaching your judgment you took into account the first volume, considering 'A Daughter of the Middle Border' the direct sequel of 'A Son of the Middle Border'; and I hope this is true, for they form one continuous narrative."

To this he replied, "Yes, we took the first volume into account."

The reader must not overestimate the money value of this award. It made very little difference in the sales of either volume, although it revived my publishers' interest in them. My books had no news value. To a public eager for sexual abnormalities set forth with the oaths and indecencies of the road house my books were dull fare indeed. My readers were quiet people, mostly elderly, who had lived through somewhat similar conditions. It will not do to say that these two volumes were undeserving the prize, for to do so would bring into question the judgment of those who had publicly endorsed them; but I realized then, and more fully now, how unimportant this award appeared in the eyes of the millions who read the "snappy stories" in the daily papers. A few friends sent congratulations, a somewhat larger number said with careless intonation, "I see you got the Pulitzer Prize"—and passed on.

"There is only one way to make this award count, and that is to take my two daughters to London and give them a kind of postgraduate course in English history."

Our plans were now arranged. I was to sail in advance and by way of Quebec in order to avoid as much of the sea as possible, and my wife and daughters were to follow two weeks later. At dinner on the day of my departure, I remained quite unconvinced that my extravagant adventure was about to begin.

To leave our flat, our dog, and our camp in the Catskills was madness. But my daughters, who had lost none of their confidence in my wonder-working powers, had no doubts. They were willing to follow where I led.

All this excitement, this doubt and fear, will seem absurd to those of my readers who go to Europe frequently; but to those who have never been able to afford such an extravagance, I look for sympathy and understanding.

"In some such spirit of dubiety I imagine Emerson and Hawthorne sailing for Liverpool. According to their own record, they had less assurance of the future than I. They, too, went from small, careful households, taking berths in ships of second-class fare, as I am doing, seeking, as I am seeking, the center of the English-speaking world.

I shall not say they went humbly, but that they went inconspicuously is certain, for few knew or cared when or in what guise they set forth."

"Montreal, May 29. Here I am in the railway station waiting the train for Quebec. The ride up the Hudson and through Saratoga past Lake George and Lake Champlain was very lovely, and I reached here in good condition. This big new station is crowded with Scotch and Irish immigrants trooping through on their way to Manitoba, an alert, expectant, and cheerful procession, reminding me of the Dakota land seekers in '81. The attendants are all Scotch or French. I go on to Quebec at ten. While waiting I am finishing a rereading of Hardy's 'Under the Greenwood Tree' which appeals to me now as a very slight but pleasant performance, of value only for its characterizations and for its record of primitive customs in an English village."

Quebec was in sight as I looked out of my sleeping-car window the following morning and I reached the *Empress of Scotland* in time for breakfast, a very bad breakfast, and for the remainder of the forenoon, till we sailed, I labored to pass the time.

"My fellow passengers in the second-class cabin are a mixed lot, mainly rough-hewn Canadian ranchers, shopkeepers, clerks, and the like, on their way back to the 'old country' for a visit. They are plain folk, all very far from the dress-suit belt. At four-thirty we set off down the river and a noble course it is. The majestic flood is gold and blue under the sunset sky, with stern mountains to the north, and rocky islands or wooded points giving them charm to the near-at-hand shore. It is magnificent in color as well as in grandeur of line. This is the kind of sailing I enjoy!"

II

"Gower Street, London, June 7. After a noisy final night on board our ship, we had an early breakfast and then (as the boat was approaching Southampton) we all lined up in the lounge to pass the immigration officers. The war has made this inspection something of an ordeal, but I passed safely and at eleven got away in the queer little train which is the special steamship train for London.

"Almost at once I was in the midst of a land of lush meadows, smooth pastures, slow-moving streams, and thatched cottages—the England of my ancestors. I am 'in chambers' on Gower Street, writing on a bare pine table in a room of such monastic plainness, with furnishings so primitive and so uncomfortable, that I can scarcely believe it to be one of the rooms of the University of London Club."

That night my Gower Street cell was so intolerably noisy that I moved the following day to a huge hotel on the Strand, where, strange to say, I found a delightfully quiet room.

"My deeply ingrained habits of economy make me uneasy as I calculate the expense of living here, but I could not stand the motor horns of Gower Street," I wrote to my Chicago friend, Henry Fuller. "The crowds in the Strand appear so universally seedy of dress that I have made no attempt to change from my American costume. I am going about in a soft hat and gray suit. The men on the streets are distinctly less formal, in dress, than in 1906. The tall hat and the frock coat which even the clerks and shopkeepers then wore are gone. A widespread democratization in manners is in progress."

One of the men I most wished to see was Barrie, and, in taking a note round to his door, I was surprised to find Adelphi Terrace House as an office building served by a small mechanical elevator. Sir James, I discovered, lived on the top floor. On the way I passed Bernard Shaw's home in one of the Adelphi Terrace houses—the corner one. I had already written to Shaw and was awaiting his reply.

The Sunday following my arrival was an almost perfect summer day, without a cloud in the sky, but so cool that I could sit in the sun, which I did for several hours in Kensington Gardens, thus gaining a new concept of English weather. The glorious old oaks of the park and the kindly, leisurely throng of men and women with their flocks of lovely, blue-eyed, flaxen-haired children gave me a sense of peace and security. "What a change from New York and Central Park!"

In my diary I find this note: "One of England's illusions is a belief that her people speak the English language handsomely and correctly, and so they do—some of them. But as for the English I hear on the street and in the shops it is a foreign tongue. I can scarcely understand it. The lack of *h*'s is not so general as it was when I was here before, but the high, faint voices of the women and the nipping enunciation of the men, along with an almost universal use of *i* for *a* (as in 'great' which becomes 'grite' and 'way' which is pronounced 'wiy') is disconcerting. It is dangerous to generalize, but with one of Shaw's essays to back me up I can say, 'There *is* no English accent.' Each shire has its peculiar pronunciation as well as its distinctive speech tune. The accent which most Americans consider typically English is that of the Oxford men.

"London voices are lower-toned than ours. The hotels, banks, ticket offices are much less clamorous. We have no such decorum in our parks. Think of sitting at tea in Central Park with gangs of hoodlums screaming around you, and groups of Slavonian peasants (once-removed from dirt floors) lolling on the benches. Here the people gather at four of the afternoon as quietly and as harmoniously as if on a private lawn."

"June 12. For many years Barrie has lived at the top of Adelphi Terrace House and there I found him to-day. I was met at the door by a small, middle-aged servitor who ushered me into a large room which was at once sitting room and study. Barrie rose from his seat behind a desk and came to meet me with outstretched hand. He had grown old, but seemed vigorous—in his measure. He was never a strong man. His face was strange, sad, almost grim in repose, but his profile was unchanged. I at once began to speak of the room. 'What a central place you have here.'

"He showed me the views which his windows commanded. 'To the east I can see St. Paul's, to the south the bishop's palace in Lambeth, and to the west Waterloo Bridge and the Houses of Parliament.'

" 'You are at the very heart of London,' I said.

" 'As near as I could get,' he replied.

"He took the seat at his desk, but did not remain there long. As he talked he moved up and down the room, smoking his pipe. He spoke in snatches, with long pauses between. He confessed his hermit life. 'Although I live at the heart of a city of seven million people, I see almost no one.'

" 'Do you know Lord Balfour?' I asked.

" 'Very well,' he replied. 'I've just been at the seashore with him.'

"I confessed that I had a letter to him from Senator Cabot Lodge, but that I was in doubt about presenting it.

" 'Why not?' said Barrie. 'He'll be glad to see you. He's most approachable, especially so to Americans. He never reads a paper—he'd be quite surprised if you said to him, "We had an earthquake last night"—but he enjoys getting news of the States by word of mouth. Present your letter at once.'

"Apropos of the tobacco jar on his desk, I said, 'I suppose that is "the Arcadian mixture." I hope you made a great deal of money out of its sale.'

"With a faint smile he replied, 'I *imagined* that mixture, but another man patented it and made millions out of it—so I am told. The truth is I did not smoke at all when I wrote "My Lady Nicotine." I was led to begin this deplorable habit by the charm of my own description of it.' He said this with a comic gleam in his eyes."

Throughout our talk his humor was indirectly expressed. It escaped as through a chink in the serious mask of his face. He used an occasional Scotch word or phrase and his accent was Scotch. He said "gude" for "good." His face remained inexpressive, but his eyes now and then filled with light. His mood was somber.

Naturally we discussed his fellow craftsmen and the men I wished to see. His opinions were generous. He spoke highly of Galsworthy, Masefield, Drinkwater, and Shaw. "I like Shaw. He was perversely pro-German dur-

gave it to me. His last words were a gentle command. "Present your note to Balfour."

III

At eight o'clock that night I found myself at a dinner in the Lyceum Club, a woman's club in Piccadilly West. As one of the guests of honor, I was placed at the speakers' table among people unknown to me.

"Two seats down, on my left, sat a small man with large glasses whom I recognized as Hutchinson, whose novel, 'If Winter Comes,' was one of the commercial successes of the day. He was a quaint little man from whom one would not expect much, but when called upon for a speech he carried through to the end a rather clever analogy. He said, 'In trying to account for the large sale of my book, I have decided that it was due to the fact that the public considered it a treatise on the weather!' Dwelling wittily upon this explanation, he left a very good impression on his auditors.

"Upon being called upon myself, I decided to do that which would most certainly interest them. I gave them the story of my first meeting with Mark Twain, reproducing for them his distinctive drawl. The incident which Clemens had enlarged upon related to the publication of Grant's 'Memoirs.' My version of it amused my auditors, and after we left the tables a group of them drew me into another room with intent, I suspect, to secure another equally characteristic anecdote. But I had shot my bolt, I had nothing more to offer. How I came to be a guest of the club, I never knew."

Just before sailing for England, I had received notice from the P. E. N. Club that at John Galsworthy's sug-

gestion I had been selected as the first name on the list
of American honorary members; and in a letter written
at about the same time he had said, "Let me know your
address immediately upon arrival in London." This I had
done, and had received, almost by return mail, an invitation to dine at his house in Hampstead.

On June 13, he sent his beautiful car to bring me to his
house which is called "Grove Lodge," and stands at the
end of a short street in a section known as "The Grove."

My note reads thus: "It is a tasteful, delightful,
scholarly home, comfortable in the American sense, well
warmed and cheerful in its furnishings. On the walls are
portraits of his literary friends and the big dining room,
where we sat at a long refectory table, was warmed by
an open fire. Altogether he made me feel among friends.
I had no sense of being in London at the moment. As one
of the leading men of letters in England, he is less solitary
of habit than Kipling, Conrad, and others of his fellows.
He is willing to join things now and again, and to help
out in ways which are civic as well as literary."

Lunching next day with some newspaper men, I had
a taste of the fare, the smells, the steam, and the smoke
of "Grooms," a very curious restaurant on the Strand,
a place so tiny that to reach the upper rooms we were
obliged to pass through the kitchen. "It is hardly more
than eight feet wide and yet it is said that Thackeray and
his fellows used to take their coffee here, and that it was
a meeting place of the literary men of that time. It is all
well enough for once, but I should not care to lunch there
habitually. Its air is too bad and its quarters too crowded."

From "Grooms" I went almost immediately to Israel
Zangwill's apartment in the Temple. I found him waiting for me. "He is plainer than ever, more careless of

habit than he used to be, and more and more the Jew. Nevertheless, we instantly renewed our friendship. He sparkled with wit and glowed with his familiar, quaint humor. 'I am working on the Zionist plan quite as zealously as when you were here sixteen years ago,' he said, still unaware of the hopelessness of the whole scheme."

"Zangwill," I said seriously, "the only New Jerusalem your people really hope to reach is New York City. A few may go to rebuild Zion, but the millions dream of America. One of your leaders in New York said to me that without an immigration law, there would not be ships enough to bring the Jews of Europe to our ports. You are wasting time which should go to the writing of books and plays."

This led to his saying, "I am coming to America next year. I hope with another play."

He explained that he had given up his quarters in the Temple. "This apartment belongs to my brother Louis. I am living on the coast near Brighton."

(He came to America in 1923 but had a most unhappy time. He started wrong by severely criticizing our import rules and immigrant officials and ended by arousing the opposition of all the newspaper paragraphers and dramatic critics. I saw him at his home in a lovely village on the beach near Brighton, but in a sadly broken state of mind and body. "They have destroyed my market in America," he said of the newspaper critics. I did my best to cheer him up but could not bring a smile to his face. It was a pitiful figure that I left behind me that lovely day in that charming garden. He never regained his place in the American literary world and died in less than two years after my interview with him.)

CHAPTER THIRTY-FIVE

RENEWING LITERARY FRIENDSHIPS

I

As Emerson in his first trip to England had Thomas Carlyle most in mind, and Howells in later time sought Thomas Hardy, so I desired to renew acquaintance with Rudyard Kipling, James Barrie, Bernard Shaw, and others of my own generation and somewhat of my own way of thinking. In saying this I do not mean to rank myself with Howells or compare Kipling and Shaw with Carlyle or Hardy; I merely wish to relate my pilgrimage with the pilgrimages of other sons and daughters of English emigrants, readers who have from time to time returned to the homes of their beloved poets and novelists, authors of books which had made their names magical.

"My years are a barrier between me and the young writers, if they exist," I said to Galsworthy. "I am told that the war has swept away one whole generation of writers."

"That is true," he replied. "We can never know what genius the war destroyed."

As in 1899 and again in 1906, Bernard Shaw had been one of the men to whom I had immediately addressed a letter, so now I wrote announcing my arrival in London. By return mail came an invitation to call. It was a postcard on which in addition to specific directions (written in violet ink) he had drawn a diagram with a line of arrows pointing the way from my hotel to his door. As it happened, I did not need this map, but I valued it for its characteristic humor.

A metal door plate on the corner house of Adelphi Terrace directed me to the second floor. Mounting a narrow flight of stairs, I came to a small semicircular iron gate with an arched row of pointed palings. Beside it was a bell pull. I rang. A maid came down, opened the gate, and conducted me to the hall above and to a reception room on the same level. There a tall, ruddy-cheeked, white-haired man came to meet me. It was Shaw!

For a moment I was silenced by the change which sixteen years had wrought, but he greeted me as if we had parted only last week and the humor which sparkled in his blue eyes reassured me. Although his hair was perfectly white, he carried himself alertly.

Mrs. Shaw (less changed) greeted me pleasantly and introduced another guest, William Archer, who said, "I know Mr. Garland. We have met in America."

Shaw returned to his seat in a deeply cushioned chair, crossed his long legs and studied me—as I studied him—noting, no doubt, the sad changes in me. He was still the Scotchman (not the Irishman) to me. His speech was as I remembered it, delightfully fluent and humorous and his manner frank and kindly.

The talk fell almost immediately upon the war, and all three told stories of the air raids through which this particular street had passed, corroborating Barrie's statement that the Terrace had suffered under more than a hundred such attacks. "The Germans were after the bridges but their aim was bad," said Shaw. He humorously confessed to a blue funk into which the shells threw him, but added a characteristic comment: "However, I became too lazy to get up out of my bed and go down into the cellar."

Mrs. Shaw spoke of standing for ten minutes on one occasion, expecting each instant to be smashed. "Every moment seemed our last," she said. "About this time the servants came to us and asked if they might not serve dinner. They wanted something to do. They felt that the habitual action would relieve the tension."

"Yes," said Shaw, "and I noticed that the waitress' hand did not shake as she passed the vegetables." He then added with humorous inflection, "I thought of having my roof painted white with large black letters saying, 'Herein dwells Herr G. Bernard Shaw,' in the hope of influencing the official bomber." (This was a reference to the fact that he had been called pro-German during the war.) "I didn't mind the shelling at Ypres," he explained, "for there I was walking about; but to lie in my bed while the bang-bang of the aircraft guns was going on was a test of endurance."

As he talked I noticed once again how North of Ireland his accent is. It is more Scotch than Irish, not at all English. I observed also that his voice was still musical, powerful, and flexible. He did not monopolize the talk, however. He is a good listener—at times. He was dressed in gray, his white beard was somewhat ragged and his hair ruffled; but he was a handsome old man.

I spoke of "Heartbreak House," and he answered with candid interest, "I think it a rather good piece, myself, but it only had a short run here. It drew exactly two thousand dollars per week and as it cost over three thousand to produce it, the manager cannot be blamed for

taking it off. It was very curious—quite inexplicable—
that it should play to precisely two thousand dollars, no
more and no less. Our 'Back to Methuselah' production
just about broke even. The war and certain other dramatic matters occupied the public."

He asked, "What are you writing?" I replied, naming
my two Middle Border chronicles, saying, "I am going to
send them to you, but you needn't read them. They are
not fiction; they are autobiographic studies of Western
life." He remarked, "That's what's the matter with
them." I did not defend them.

He took a keener interest in the transfer of my little
family from New York to London, and said, "We shall
be glad to see them at our summer home."

I asked, "Where is your summer home?"

"Near Welwyn." And he alluded to my previous visit
to him in that neighborhood. I recalled our wandering
about his garden at night, hoping to hear the nightingales
who refused to utter a note, and he smilingly retorted,
"It's all very well to hear a nightingale sing once, but
when, like a German prima donna's, the bird's voice gets
worse and worse, night by night, till it is hardly more than
a croak, he becomes a nuisance."

No writer could have been more unaffected than he in
talking of his plays. There was no restraint in his manner, no trace of that cold reserve with which Englishmen
are so often charged. "What will you show your daughters first?" he asked. And when I replied, "The Horse
Guards," he laughed, and Mrs. Shaw exclaimed, "Oh,
you republicans! Your keenest interest is in kings and
queens!"

"Naturally," I said. "The scarlet and gold of monarchy

interests us—as a show. It is a kind of fairy world. I wish democracy had a little more of its color."

A little later, Shaw, speaking of the difference between the allied armies, said, "It is the English soldier's sheeplike habit of obedience which made him invincible. You say to a British soldier, 'Drive close to that curb,' and he will go within an inch of it. Command a Belgian to do the same, and he will venture within two feet of it—a Frenchman will allow three feet. But an American ordered to do the same thing, will reply, 'Go to hell! I'll drive where I please!' " He said this with humorous intent, but there is a fundamental truth in it.

"His knowledge of American social conditions is astonishing. How he gets this knowledge I do not know, for he does not read the American papers. I bantered him about some recent photographs in which he was posed as a wood chopper, and he cheerfully admitted the imposture. 'I had some difficulty in knowing which end of the ax to take hold upon.'

"As I was leaving he went with me into the hall and at the stairway gave me his private telephone number. 'Call me after your wife and daughters arrive,' he said, 'and we'll arrange a luncheon.' Altogether he was delightfully informal, quite as I remembered him. His great fame has not changed his relationship to me, however much it has increased the disparity between his wealth and mine."

II

On June 16 I lunched with Kipling at Brown's Hotel in the same room where we ate in 1906.

"As I entered the door I saw him in the hall. I recog-

nized him instantly, although he is more sadly changed
than either Shaw or Barrie. He has grown quite bald, but
his eyebrows, bushy and very thick, are still almost black.
His hair has grown gray."

He met me, however, with something of the youthful
enthusiasm with which he used to bubble—for the moment I represented something of his youth in America.
No doubt I brought back to him many memories, associations running over a period of thirty years or more.
With a familiar boyish smile he said, "How long is it since
we first met?"

I replied, "Almost a third of a century."

He protested, "Why plumb those abysses?" and beneath his banter I perceived that he meant it, so much of
sorrow has come to him in these later years. The camera
had done him an injustice, however. He was not as old as
he had been pictured.

As we took our seats at a small table in a quiet corner
of the dining room, he became the frank, cordial host,
interested in my plans for a summer in England. He
spoke of the drought on his farm and of the rains which
came just in time to save his wheat; and when I exclaimed,
"Wheat! Do you raise wheat?" he said, "Yes, Mrs. Kipling and I own three hundred acres of land which we till,
not by proxy, but personally. We worry over the
weather and crops like regular farmers."

When I told him that I expected to have a flat in London and to make daily excursions from it, he made many
helpful suggestions as to what we should see. "You must
bring your wife and daughters down to my farm. I can
show them a magnificent Norman ruin near by—Bodiam
Castle."

That he kept in close touch with American affairs was evident. He spoke of the changes which were taking place in our population. "You are experiencing a Smyrnian invasion," he said. "I was amazed by the number of South-of-Europe types among your soldiers as they marched through the streets of London. Many of them were not American as I knew the type."

I admitted that so far as New York and other of our larger cities were concerned we had taken in an enormous mass of indigestible material from southeastern Europe; and we discussed the cheap magazine, the blatant newspaper, and the pornographic motion pictures which this citizenry demands. I alluded to the decay of noble personalities in the present-day literature, and in reference to this complaint he laughingly said, "My dear fellow, that discontent is a disease of our years."

Admitting the truth of this, I replied: "I suppose the old fellows felt the same about our generation. Nevertheless there *is* a difference."

He talked of Howells, of Brander Matthews, of Riley, and many others of the men he had known, but he was not greatly interested in the younger writers. During this hour we were both reliving our youth, a time which the war had rendered remote and very sweet, and his face recovered some of its youthful lines, and his voice regained some of its familiar inflections. We deliberately avoided battle grounds and finished our luncheon in the spirit in which we had begun.

I can not pretend to any special literary significance in this meeting. The fault is my own, no doubt. Had I carried to it something of the quality which Emerson brought to his dinners with Carlyle, I might have drawn from my host something to compare with the great Scotchman's fiery eloquence, but even so, all would have been dependent upon my memory. I can only report the impression which Kipling made upon me, with a very imperfect record of his words.

After my return to my hotel I set down some of the sentences I remembered, careful to retain at least their kindly intent, although I could only reproduce now and then a phrase. I trust that he and others of my English friends will pardon any failure to record their precise words.

CHAPTER THIRTY-SIX

A LUNCHEON AT BALFOUR'S

I

"LONDON, June 17. With some misgivings I signed, this morning, the lease for No. 60 in one of the Albert Hall Mansions, a group of seven-story apartment buildings; and when my wife and daughters arrive, I shall have a home for them. The fact is, I intend to move in myself on the 22d, four days before their boat lands. It is an extravagance to have this spacious flat, but I want my girls to enjoy their stay in London and they might not do so if they were called upon to live in a Bloomsbury boarding house.

"It is Sunday and the Strand is amazingly quiet. These channels which run bank-full of traffic on other days are empty and silent to-day. It is as if the waters of civilization had suddenly been drawn off. The wind is cold and I am wearing my overcoat indoors and out. The clubs are all chilly and I can find no place to get warm, a fact which makes me all the more resigned to the extravagance of possessing a flat where I can regulate the heat. All my friends are out of town and the air being raw I have kept indoors for the most part.

"Along about noon, as I was passing Westminster Abbey, the bells of the cathedral began to chime. Those of the Parliament buildings joined in, and at this precise

instant the sun came out, flooding the city with pale
gold light. It was a glorious moment. The historic value
of the square as well as the beauty of its buildings rushed
upon me. 'After all,' I said, 'these are my inheritances.
Beautiful in themselves, they are rich in poetic association such as no European buildings can arouse."

Lunching with Sir Gilbert Parker on Monday, I found
him living in a spacious four-story house overlooking one
of the leafy parks in the West City. He received me in
his study, whose windows gave on a noisy street and a
square enclosed by a high fence.

"His wife was away and we ate alone, served in formal
English fashion. He is less changed than any of my old-
time friends, but he shows his years. He is a little grayer
and a little heavier than when we met in Chicago, a few
years before. I saw little of his home other than its library
and dining room, which were somewhat gloomily Victorian.

"We had a long talk, part of the time on books, part of
the time on old friends in Boston, and our first meeting
in the office of the *Arena*. He showed a deep interest in
the post-war political and economic conditions in America. As a member of Parliament, he belongs to the Imperialist Party, but represents the Colonial point of view.
As a member of the small group of legislators who understand the growing power of Canada, New Zealand, and
Australia, he was honored by King Edward. All his later
novels reflect his views along these lines."

The Authors' Club was a place of refuge for me during
these days of waiting and I fell into the habit of lunching
there.

"Some of the men are known to me by their works,

but they take no interest in me. The secretary of the club is kind, and so is a fine old lawyer-author, a Mr. David Graham, who confided to me that he had written a book on the legal aspects of the case against Mary Queen of Scots. No one could be more un-English than this man. His speech, his outlook on life, are entirely Scotch."

As we sat at lunch one day, Mr. Rose (the secretary) related a number of amusing stories concerning the bombing raids. One of those especially illuminating concerned his aged aunt, who took occasion to visit him in the midst of the airship campaign.

"She was eighty-seven years of age, and owned a perfectly safe and comfortable home in the mid-country; but she decided to come down to the city—'to see the show,' she said. We passed through a period of dreadful anxiety, for the old lady was determined to look out of the door. We had a chair placed for her against a solid brick wall, and whenever the bombing was going on, we ordered her to take her seat in this chair and to remain there until everything was quiet. Did she stay there? She did not! She was at the window the entire time and would have had her head out of it had we not held her back by force.

"At the end of several weeks of this anxiety—of which she apparently realized nothing—she reported herself satisfied. 'I have had a lovely time,' she said, 'I have seen it all and heard it all and now I am ready to go home' —and home she went!"

One of the men who had accompanied Lord Northcliffe to America during the disarmament conference was Wickham Steed, editor of the London *Times*; and Mark Sullivan, who thought Steed might be interested in me, had given me a letter of introduction to him. "You'll like Steed," he said. "He is a scholarly fellow and his position on the *Times* puts him in touch with everything that is going on all over the world."

Steed replied to my note with cordial promptness, inviting me to lunch with him on the 22d. This was my day for getting into my apartment, but I paused in the process of moving long enough to walk across the park and eat a one-o'clock meal with this very distinguished editor. My record reads:

"I found Steed (a tall, fine-featured man with a small pointed beard) living in a handsome apartment north of Kensington Gardens. He was cosmopolitan in speech and manner and most congenial. He reminded me of John W. Alexander, graceful, genial, and scholarly. The only other guest was a young Scot whose name I did not catch.

"Steed did most of the talking. He told me much of his chief, Lord Northcliffe. He knows America very well, and while keenly critical, is friendly. He admitted that the future is ours. 'I know your great country,' he said. 'I've traveled there, but my chief interest is in Europe. Poland, Russia, the Balkans—these are the storm centers.' As he talked, I felt myself in the midst of world affairs. He brought me home in his beautiful car on his way to the *Times*.

"I am making these notes at a desk in my own handsome sitting room in a quiet as profound as if I were in my Onteora camp. I do not hear a sound outside or within, except the clock in the hall."

My flat was so peaceful and so quiet that night that I slept in it, as Dickens said of the lawyers in the Temple, "like a worm in a nut." My family was still on the ocean, but I had discovered a housekeeper who had put the place to rights. She was a trained English servant, the mother of a family, intelligent and reliable, just what we required. "I was a lady's maid before my marriage," she said with a note of pride in her voice.

"She addresses me in the third person, but is a self-respecting individual nevertheless. I arranged with her to have the flat in perfect order with dinner on the table when my wife and daughters arrive. I have this moment posted a letter to Lord Balfour enclosing Senator Lodge's note of introduction, and await a reply with something more than interest. He is one of the busiest men in England and but for Barrie's urging I would not have sent the note."

Sunday was a test of the English railway system, and so far as I was concerned, it failed. All day I tried vainly to find out just when the boat train from Liverpool would arrive at Euston Station. At nine o'clock I was at the terminal for the third time. All the offices, even the telegraph offices, were closed, and as I waited, the lights went out, one by one, until at eleven o'clock even the ticket offices became dark. There were no lights in bookstalls or restaurants.

Finding it impossible to remain in the cold and gloomy station, I went to one of the connecting railway hotels but soon found myself regarded as an unwelcome intruder. Walking across the yard, I spent a half hour in a dirty tea house, the only one open. On my way back I met a policeman. To him I said, "Is it possible that this great terminal has no place for people who are awaiting passengers on an incoming train?"

He sympathized with my predicament. "I regret to say we have only a small emergency waiting room. I fear you'll find it very uncomfortable."

I did. It was about sixteen feet square and had no seats other than three wide, oak benches entirely without backs; and yet this was one of the greatest terminals in London. To me it was a dank, dirty, grimy collection of sheds. It had no information bureau concerning trains. The station master's small den was the only place with a light, and at last, unable to get from him any definite news of the latest train from Liverpool, I gave up and returned to my flat. It was then long after midnight.

At nine next morning I returned to the station and waited all the forenoon, meeting train after train. "I *must* meet my family here," I explained to the officials. "My wife does not know my address and unless I meet her here, she won't know where to find me."

At last they came, and bundling them into a cab I carried them away on a trip which must have been profoundly exciting to them. As we rolled along, I said, "Now, children, I have done the best I could. This is going to be a very expensive summer, and you must make the most of everything. I have found a home and you mustn't mind if it is a long way out and over a cigar store." Although a bit dashed by my talk, they bravely said, "It doesn't matter. Whatever you have done is all right for us."

As we turned into the towering buildings which form the group of Albert Hall flats, my wife thought (so she told me afterward) that I had taken lodgings in some sort of apartment hotel; and when the porter led us to the elevator and carried us up to the fourth floor, she still thought that I had secured board with some impoverished flat owner who was taking in lodgers.

Inserting a key in the door, I opened it with a flourish. "Enter!" I commanded. "This is our home in London."

It was a larger and far more quiet flat than the one we had in New York, and that night as we took our seats at our own London table in precisely the same positions which we occupied in New York, I said, "I told you I intended to transfer you from Ninety-second Street, Manhattan, to a flat in London, and I have done it. We are at home in Kensington."

II

With no expectation of an early reply from Lord Balfour, I was greatly surprised, on the second morning after my wife's arrival, to receive a cordial note from his sister, inviting us to luncheon on the following day, and on my way to the bank, I turned in upon Carlton Terrace and left a note of acceptance.

It would be absurd in me to assume indifference to the honor involved in this invitation, for Arthur Balfour was at this time one of the best known and most valued men in the English government. He was indeed filling two important positions, and his house was the official residence of the Secretary of State. On its front wall was a tablet stating that it had been the residence of Lord Palmerston. But Balfour was much more than a Cabinet member. He was a polished orator, a scholar, and a man of letters. He had earned his title by the nobility of his character and by his achievements. He was known and greatly admired by many Americans who had met him in Washington.

I did not deceive myself. I knew that this kindly courtesy was due not to anything I had done but to the influence of three men: Theodore Roosevelt, Senator Henry Cabot Lodge, and Sir James Barrie. I was certain that Barrie had spoken to him about me and had led him to expect the letter of introduction which I held. I did not for one moment ascribe this luncheon invitation to any personal interest in me. To him I was merely an American writer sponsored by certain highly valued friends. Nevertheless, I was glad of the opportunity to meet him, for I regarded him as one of the most interesting men in English politics. His speeches at the disarmament congress had filled me with admiration. Polished, tactful, scholarly, they confirmed all that I had heard of him.

At one o'clock, June 28, my wife and I drove to the historic Palmerston mansion, a large, plain brownstone structure. After removing our outer garments in the broad entrance hall, we mounted two flights of broad stairs to a long reception room on the north side of the hall. "Here Miss Balfour received us and introduced us to her other guests. She is a gray, bent, middle-aged woman of a type familiar to me, a Scotch gudewife, cordial, unassuming, and shrewd."

The first of those to whom we were presented was Lady Salisbury, a lovely person, and the second was Lord David Cecil, a pale, slender boy who appeared too young for the weight of his hereditary title. The third was a red-haired, lively young woman whom Miss Balfour called "my niece." Her husband's name was Lascelles, and as they were both alertly literary we got on very well, comparing English and American books and authors.

In the midst of our talk, Barrie came walking in, seemingly very much at home. Miss Balfour immediately introduced him to my wife, but as she had never seen him before and did not catch his name, she remained unaware of her good fortune till some time after taking her seat beside him at the table.

Just as we went out to lunch, Lord Lee of Fareham was announced and a handsome, graceful, dark-eyed man entered and was greeted by all the guests. As he took my hand I said, "Lord Lee, I have two letters of introduction to you."

He smiled and said, "Why haven't you presented them?"

I confessed that I was in awe of a sea lord who lived in Admiralty House. "We are both concerned with the final edition of Roosevelt's works, however, and that is an introduction. You are to write a preface to 'The War of 1812,' I am told, and I am doing one for 'The Winning of the West.'"

"That certainly establishes a bond," he replied. "Roosevelt was my friend for many years. Those of us who are writing these introductions should be a kind of fraternity."

Balfour, looking gray and weary, entered at this moment and in greeting me explained that he had been detained by official business. "I am doing two men's work these days and have almost no time for meeting my friends." His manner was surprisingly direct and unofficial. He spoke of Senator Lodge, of Roosevelt, and other of our mutual friends. We had but a moment's interchange, however, for luncheon had been announced. He led the way with Lady Salisbury and Mrs. Garland, and Miss Balfour and I brought up the rear.

"My place at the table was at Miss Balfour's right and next to her niece, whilst my wife was seated between our host and Barrie at the far end of the table, which I deeply regretted, for I especially wished to hear what these two distinguished Scots would say.

"Mrs. Lascelles, Lord Cecil, and I at our end of the table argued the need of a better understanding of the present-day literature of the two countries. 'We exchange too many sensational, distorted studies of our social groups,' I said. To this they both agreed. 'We have no teachers of American literature in our schools, while all yours have chairs of English. We get our notions of your writers from haphazard reading.' "

Late in the meal we all listened while Barrie told how he came to write his play, "Shall We Join the Ladies?" He admitted that it was the first act of a three-act play. "I have thought out the two remaining acts, but I doubt if I ever write them." Balfour jocularly suggested that he bring out an act each year, "or better yet, at the close of the run of each preceding act." It was all jolly and informal, quite like a literary luncheon in a New York home. Titles counted for little in this company of congenial spirits to whom books and paintings were subjects of conversation.

As we rose from the table, Balfour invited my wife and me to a closer view of the paintings on the walls of the dining room. "They are all by Burne-Jones," he said. "I ordered them when a young man. Some of them, as you see, are unfinished."

He showed us also several other landscapes, some of them Scottish, and as we were looking at one of these he said, "The war has laid enormous burdens upon our landed estates. Taxes are eating us up. I may be obliged to sell my country place in order to maintain my London house." He did not say this with bitterness; he expressed only a philosophic resignation.

In this half hour I got at his quality. "He is, as Barrie had said, 'a man of letters.' He is an intellectual aristocrat, a man of discernment. His title is an earned title, like Barrie's. I am willing to take off my hat to lords of this character."

He accompanied us down the stairway to the entrance hall in the most democratic and kindly fashion and then said, "Is there anything I can do for you?"

To this I replied, "Like all other Americans, we hope to see the House of Lords in action."

Calling his secretary to him he said, "Please see that cards of admission to the gallery of the House are sent to Mr. and Mrs. Garland," and with kindly smile and warm clasp of hand, he sent us on our way.

(I never saw him again. When I returned to England in 1923, he was ill and in retirement. The change of administration had brought his resignation from office. He was over seventy and while he partially recovered his health, he dropped out of active political life. He died a few years later. He was, as the English say, a great scholar and a great gentleman.)

CHAPTER THIRTY-SEVEN

KIPLING'S HOME AND BODIAM CASTLE

I

ON June 29, I recorded my observations concerning the literary situation in London:

"Conditions here are very much the same as those in New York. Scores of publishers are 'blurbing' for sales and hundreds of authors are clamoring for notice. The magazines and the literary pages of the daily papers are filled with blaring announcements of new books, each more 'important' and 'greater' than the other. Fleet Street and Fifth Avenue are quite the same in appeal, and this literary logrolling is so confusing that I can only cling to familiar names in order to keep my bearings.

"Naturally, as a result of sensational novelists each striving to outdo the other, there is a deliberate attempt at shocking the public—a studied use of the woman libertine is prevalent. Sexual promiscuity is excused if not advocated. Furthermore, each new author is playing frankly for the American market. One man said, 'I write for the New York magazines, not for ours.' America is the El Dorado of the English novelists.

"No young poet looms high above his fellows. Every one appears to be writing 'daring' fiction. I meet 'distinguished novelists' whose books are entirely unknown to me. How these authors get their books published is a mystery. *Somebody* must believe in them. Sales are said to be very small: one thousand copies is the usual edition, I am told. One publisher said, 'Most novels fail to sell more than five hundred copies, which is just enough to pay for the expense of production.'

"The truth is the book-buying public in England is small as compared with ours. One fairly successful woman writer confessed that her books paid her less than three hundred dollars each. In poetry, the same thing holds true. No man or woman under thirty-five is recognized as the genius of the moment. Masefield, Yeats, Noyes are all drawing toward middle age. The outstanding figures in England are not verse writers but dramatists, men like Shaw, Barrie, Galsworthy, and Milne. Kipling is writing very little now, and Hardy, a great figure, lingers on the edge of the horizon, soon to disappear."

II

June 30 was the day of our visit to Kipling, and we took an early train for Etchingham, his station in Sussex. Elsie Kipling, a handsome, dark-eyed girl, met us at the train. "My father," she explained, "is attending a meeting in the village and I am to take you for a drive to Bodiam and bring you home to tea."

The Kipling car was spacious enough to carry us all inside, but I elected to sit with the driver, who explained that the ruin was several miles away to the south and east. The day was characteristically English; that is to say, one shower followed another with intervals of pale sunlight. Fortunately, just as we reached the stile leading into the castle grounds (a lovely stretch of pasture land), the sun came out and we set forth across the wet grass toward a grove of trees.

Suddenly, out of a screen of oaks, the towers of a great gray castle loomed. Around its base at the edge of the moat in which it stood, a dog was driving a flock of sheep, and over its turrets, rooks wheeled and dipped, a glorious picture of a Norman fortress set in an English landscape.

As we approached the drawbridge of the castle we discovered it to be, as Kipling had described it, a noble survival of feudal architecture. Its towers were almost intact and the moat and its retaining walls were still in place. To me of the Mid-West there was something deeply stirring in the fact that this structure, standing in the midst of a lovely mead, had lived through eight hundred years of storm and sun. It enabled me to visualize some part of the Norman invasion to which it belonged. I imagined it built in an opening of the forest, as a refuge of the Norman peasants, much as our stockaded forts in Kentucky were for the protection of our settlers in time of war with Iroquois and Delaware.

"Interiorly the castle is a ruin," I wrote at the time. "Its floors are gone and so are most of its stairways; but we were able to climb to the towers and look down upon the moat and out over the valley which it defended. We were able also to trace the ancient dining hall and kitchen and the places where the horses were kept. My daughters were especially interested in the rooms set apart for the ladies and sought to reconstruct some part of the life of that time. But the sky darkened and we hurried back to the car, eager to see Kipling. Half an hour later we turned in at his gate.

"Bateman's" (which is the name of Kipling's house),

appealed to me at first glance as one of the most complete and interesting examples of sixteenth century domestic architecture I had ever seen; and as we entered it we found its walls and ceilings practically unchanged. All the furniture was in keeping. It was the home of a poet.

Kipling came running down the stairs to meet us, alert as a boy. His unusually bushy eyebrows gave him the look of an old man, but there was something inextinguishably youthful in his smile as he welcomed us. That he had suffered from the loss of his son was evident, but he made no mention of his personal griefs.

Almost immediately he asked, "Shall you visit France?" and when my wife answered, "No, I think we shall spend the entire summer in England," he urged us not to neglect the battlefields. "In no other way can you understand how the French people saved the world from the Germans."

He then passed into a statement in explanation of the French attitude, which was being much discussed in the press at this time. "You cannot blame them for keeping up their armies. They must be prepared to defend themselves. If a man has been attacked by the same bulldog twice you can't convince him of the harmlessness of that particular animal." A little later he spoke of Rheims as a "dead city," and paid tribute to the millions of men who had fallen and many of them without burial. "Go and see those fields," he repeated. "It is your duty."

He, too, alluded to the London air raids, and one of the stories he told was grimly humorous. It appears that a bomb had fallen into the courtyard of a club to which he belonged.

The shell did not explode and one of the officers of

the club, an archbishop, appointed two of the scientific members as a committee to have the bomb removed. Neither of these professors of physics would touch the thing. The president of the club then appealed to the heads of the War Office, but they refused to be bothered. "It is not of sufficient importance to warrant action," they said. The club then phoned certain generals imploring aid—all in vain. At last after much excited suggestion, argument, and prayer, some one called the attention of the club's gardener to the shell. He came and took it away in a wheelbarrow. "This," observed Kipling, "was one of the comic reliefs of a frightful time."

As he showed us about the house he assured us that he had made no structural changes in it, and we noted with pleasure that its furniture was all in harmony with its beautiful old paneling. "It's the most perfect literary home I know. How did you happen to obtain it?" I asked.

He replied to this effect: "I knew this country as a boy. I used to come down this way to visit my aunt, Lady Burne-Jones; so when I reached the point where I could own a permanent home in England, I naturally drifted to this region. That was about twenty years ago. On hearing that this place, a fine old sixteenth century house, was for sale, I came to see it. I found it singularly unchanged from its original shape.

"This is an iron country. They used to have iron foundries all through Sussex and this house was built in 1640 by an ironmaster who had made a fortune in smelting iron, and I may say in parenthesis that a large part of his fortune came from making cannons for the Spanish. The house which had been held by his family for several generations gradually declined to the status of a farmhouse, which was fortunate, for the farmer who bought it could not afford to make it over into something modern.

"It happened that I made my first inspection of it riding in an American automobile, a ramshackle affair; and after I had secured the place, I asked the owner why he had been moved to sell. He was quite frank to say that the roads were too hard on his horses. 'You'll find the hill between here and the village a barrier.' . . . 'But,' I said to him, 'I don't intend to use horses.' He looked at my car and laughed. 'You can't depend on those motors. They'll never work.' Some years later when I met him he said ruefully, 'If I'd known as much about motors then as I do now I wouldn't have sold you that place at any price.'"

We had our tea and cakes in the beautiful dining room, quite unchanged from its original design and filled with appropriate furniture.

"While seated at the table, Elsie occupied a high-backed chair at one end of the long refectory table, and my daughter Constance, a similar chair at the opposite end. The two girls were in charming contrast. There was something Celtic in Elsie's dark beauty, while Constance, with her gray eyes, fair complexion, and long yellow hair, was entirely Nordic. I observed Kipling watching her out of the corner of his eye, and when a little later the girls left the table, he turned to my wife and said with a gesture toward the chair in which Constance had sat, 'That one looks like a Saxon princess.'"

After our tea we went out into the gardens. I use the word in the plural, for he showed us a flower garden, a walled garden—and a large vegetable garden. He told us that he was having difficulty this year in harvesting his crops, on account of the rain.

"The gardens, the fields, the terraces, all in perfect order, formed a lovely combination of farm and country seat. To find a story writer and poet in such surroundings gave me a sense of satisfaction. 'Although the house has been inhabited for three hundred years,' Kipling said, 'it has no ghost. It is not in the smuggler zone. All the old houses in the smuggler zone have ghosts.'

"He pointed out a mansion on a distant ridge. 'That is another ironmaster's house, older than mine. It hasn't a nail in it.' Returning to the subject of his farm, he said, 'I *almost* make it pay! But unless we have some protection against Canadian and other overseas beef we stock farmers cannot survive.'"

"This was a note which I had heard other Englishmen sound. 'England to be self-sustaining must have a protective tariff,' they argued. 'An import duty would raise the price of meat and bread to the consumer, but it would help our farmers. Free trade is all very well in time of peace, but in time of war it is a source of weakness. England should raise more of her own food.'

"This is Kipling's permanent home; and while it seems remote to me it is only two hours' run from London. It is difficult to explain the building of a beautiful house on such a site. It has no water other than a small brook, and no special outlook. It is rich in human association, however. Its beauty lies in its walls and furniture, in its completeness. Its mellow charm, its dignity, make it notable even in a land abounding in historic homes."

In speaking of historic places, Kipling said, "Don't fail to see Knolle, one of the finest survivals of the seventeenth century in all England," and we marked this in our itinerary.

I did not ask him what he was writing, for I had heard that he was no longer interested in writing. But toward the end of our talk he told us that he was at work on a history of the Irish Lancers, in which his son was an officer. This was the only reference he made to his son's death, and I did not ask him to tell me more. I had no wish to bring back those tragic days.

He told me something which I had never before realized: "I was forced to face life unaided while my father was a resident of India, but I am glad of that experience. It was of enormous benefit to me. I am grateful for the fact that I did not have everything smoothed out for me in my boyhood. My lack of a college education forced me into newspaper work at an early age."

To this I replied, "And yet we both are disposed to save our children from a similar experience."

In the glow of his friendly confidence I quite forgot his world-wide reputation. We had been young together. We had known each other for more than thirty years, and now, gray and saddened, we were nearing the end of our life work. Something of the realization of these facts was in our talk this day.

One of the small incidents which I most vividly recall was Kipling's action in whipping out a penknife to clip a flower for Constance. A little later he plucked some rosemary and quoted, "This for remembrance," and Mary Isabel said, "We shall put this in our memory book and keep it forever."

His beautiful car was waiting for us, and in this we rode away to catch an express train for the city. In a few minutes we had left this charming country behind, a country not unlike our native Wisconsin with its wooded hills and lovely meadows. It possesses a thousand years of historic record, but it is known all over the world as the home of the great English poet, Rudyard Kipling.

"In this tea with Kipling, as in many other meetings which I am enjoying here in England, I am carrying forward in my obscure way the work which Emerson, Hawthorne, and Howells wrought, each in his turn. Masefield's fame is as wide to-day as Tennyson's was in 1880. It is possible that Carlyle at the time of his greatest reputation was less known and less honored than Galsworthy. Masefield's beardlessness, Barrie's close-cut hair, and Kipling's alert, boyish manner are all opposed to the popular notion of great literary men. Kipling is not literary in the sense that Tennyson was literary. No one is, these days. Something has gone out of our men of letters or else something has gone out of us who read about them.

"The truth is, there is something of the super-journalist in Kipling. Much of his writing has been for the newspapers in some form or other. Fine as his earlier poems are, they are lacking in reflective quality. Power and originality they have, but they are lacking in qualities which Tennyson had, which Emerson had—which is to say, they are representative of another age. The walls of his home, mellow with the dusk of centuries, have no relation to his work. He is of a later England.

"It is evident, however, that he intends to end his days at Bateman's, and there is dignity in the plan; but a certain melancholy comes over me with the thought. He is so vital, and his wanderings have been so world-wide, that this valley home takes on the character of a last stand. That his career is near its end must be admitted. His work, like that of Hardy, Barrie, and Shaw, is nearly done. Something went out of him during the war. The subconscious faculties which made his early work so marvelous can never regain their power. 'All of which is a disease of our years,' to repeat his own words."

(He is still alive as I write these lines and still writing but I seldom hear from him. Now and again I see a newspaper portrait of him and it becomes increasingly difficult for me to discover in these pictures the vivid, powerful young man with whom James Whitcomb Riley and I dined nearly forty years ago.)

CHAPTER THIRTY-EIGHT

LITERARY LIFE IN KENSINGTON

I

ALL through June the winds had been chill to me and on July 3 I still carried an overcoat. There were compensations, however. "There are no flies, no mosquitoes, and almost no dust blowing. The entire city is astonishingly well cared for. True, the marble buildings are dark with soot, but the streets, even the alleys, are clean. It is an ugly city, but a marvelous summer place for Americans. Its many side streets and retired small parks offer inexpensive homes. Its quiet amazes us. Vast as it is, it is far less noisy than New York or Chicago. The Thames is muddy and its banks are as repulsive as the water front of Jersey City. The Authors' Club makes much of its view of this turbid river covered with coal barges and lined with drab warehouses, but to me it is ugly. The Parliament buildings, glorious as they are, sit low on the bank of what was once a marsh.

"Drab as Kensington is, it offers many surprises. We are constantly discovering picturesque survivals of ancient lanes, parish halls, and village gardens. Last night we wandered out after dinner and happened into a walled country churchyard not ten minutes' walk from Albert Hall. Brompton, once a village, is now lost in the spread of the city, and this silent square is very alluring. Each

457

day is filled with similar discoveries. All about us are the
homes of writers and artists. Thackeray, Dickens,
Browning, Carlyle, all had homes in Kensington or Chelsea. I have come to hate the Strand. Its fakers, beggars,
foxy shopkeepers, newsboys, cheap restaurants, and
thronging buses weary me—and yet only a few yards
away from this aisle of traffic are the remains of a Roman
bath! Ten minutes' walk will discover the grave of
Templars—eight hundred years old. The Staple Inn
and the Temple provide escape from the commonplaces
of the modern city. It is only in such places that I regain
my feeling of veneration for London, my sense of its
history and its power.

"At the Authors' Club, where I spend an occasional
hour, an almost funereal air of quiet reigns. Only now
and then does a man enter or leave the lounge, generally
without a word to a soul. None of the members take the
slightest account of me. I go in, read the newspapers, and
eat my lunch without speaking to any one but the
waiters. The Savile Club is almost equally quiet, and so
I have fallen into the habit of lunching at the Savage
Club, which is rather more companionable and has the
further interest of presenting pleasant reminders of
hunting and boating in far lands and seas. Like all the
others I have seen, it is plain and small. Alan Sullivan,
my sponsor here, often gathers a group together for a
friendly chat.

"As I come and go in the clubs which used to seem in-
accessible, I wonder if something has not gone out of
them. Has the war broken down their walls—or made
their gates less forbidding? Surely none of those I have
entered can be called formal or formidable. They are

reserved, but they are not exclusive or aristocratic—as they are made to appear in novels. They are filled with hard-working professionals of one kind or another.

"Lunching to-day at the Reform Club with William Archer, I renewed my pleasure in his acquaintance. I have always found him a manly critic with a genuine understanding and admiration of America. He is not a man of humor. His talk is never witty, but his judgments are logical and just. He knows the whole field of the English-speaking stage and is respected by its leaders."

II

"The Fourth of July reception at the embassy was a 'jam.' Our ambassador, Colonel George Harvey, is so seldom in the city that the counselor, the Honorable Post Wheeler (whom I knew many years ago in Chicago) is acting ambassador most of the time. I was in the line waiting to greet Harvey, when Wheeler, a small, dark, bright-eyed man, darted across the hall to greet me. He was in charge of the function, but kept modestly in the background. His wife, whom I had also met at the Little Room and elsewhere, is Hallie Rives, a novelist from the South, like her famous cousin, Amélie Rives. She gave us the number of their house on the Chelsea Embankment and asked us to luncheon.

"Wheeler, a scholarly and able lawyer, who has been in the diplomatic service in Japan and in Italy for many years, is now in a position of great social power."

The Fourth of July was also the date chosen for the international dinner of the P. E. N. Club, and my wife and I, as representatives of the American membership, went down to the restaurant near Piccadilly Circus in which the meeting was to be held.

My first disappointment was in not finding Galsworthy in charge of the program, and besides this I was disappointed in the personnel. No doubt there were distinguished authors in attendance, but those at my table appeared to be largely "part time" writers.

"Cunninghame-Graham, the presiding officer of the evening, who sat at the end of the long table, was a stranger to me. I had never read a line of his writing. Directly opposite me sat a plump, bullet-headed man with a thin, high, falsetto voice. This was H. G. Wells, who civilly offered to share his bottle of wine with me. I thanked him and explained that I seldom drank wine. He then attempted to talk with me, but his weak, husky pipe failed to reach me. I could not hear half his words. He spoke of Stonehenge and urged me to see another ruin far older than Stonehenge. I failed to catch even the name of this ruin.

"In response to some remark of mine, he alluded to himself humorously as 'a kind of Vesuvius,' perhaps in reference to the amount of work he is pouring forth. He seemed friendly, but as I could not follow his sentences, no real interchange took place. In fact I had nothing to say to him. I like his earlier work, but all his later books are repellent."

At the close of the dinner, I found my wife talking with an East Indian, a superb figure in a robe of embroidered satin and wearing a snowy turban, in the center of which blazed a glorious diamond. My wife introduced him to me in Western fashion as "His Royal Highness the Maharajah of Jhalawar," and he, in smiling acceptance of her republican lack of ceremony, greeted me as one man of letters greets another.

In graceful English he explained that he was living in Oxford while his son pursued a course in agriculture. "I am myself working for a doctor's degree," he explained. "I am writing a thesis on the ancient laws of India."

In the course of our conversation I spoke of the mystery which shrouds the use and significance of Stonehenge, and then said, "But these ancient Western monuments are young compared to those in your country."

He smiled. "Yes, we go back many thousands of years beyond Stonehenge. You must come to visit me in Jhalawar."

My wife asked, "Will you let us ride on an elephant?"

"I will meet you at the boundary with a *herd* of elephants," he replied, "but meanwhile come to me at Oxford. I shall be glad to send my car for you."

It was impossible for me to take his royalty seriously, but his visiting card gave his full title, and this I carefully preserved for use in case I wished to write him. He was distinctly the most interesting personality at this dinner.

While talking with him I observed a small, quaint, badly dressed woman wandering around, so blond, so rural in appearance that I wondered who she might be. She suggested a New England village poetess—small and plain and ill at ease. There was something almost pathetic in her uneasiness. "She is the country relative of some of these writers and is here by special favor," I decided. On being presented, I learned with amazement that she was May Sinclair! It was quite impossible to fuse this little woman with the author of "The Divine Fire." Nothing of the passion and eloquence of that book could be detected in this frail person. She recalled the case of Emily Brontë. She and H. G. Wells were to me the two best known figures at the dinner, and yet their personal peculiarities had never before been brought to my attention.

(This dinner, I afterward learned, was managed almost entirely by Mrs. Dawson Scott and her daughter, indeed Mrs. Scott was the leading spirit in forming this international literary organization. She was a novelist and poet from Devonshire, making a somewhat precarious living in London as a writer, and a much more assured income, she candidly stated, by building houses in her native town. I came to know her very well during the month and to respect her abilities and her courage.)

In a luncheon at Lady Willert's home two days later, I met John C. Squire, editor of the *Mercury* and author of a powerful poem on the Chicago stockyards.

"He is a rough-hewn individual, not attractive at first glance, but a man of power. I know very little of his writing other than that poem with its appalling indictment of meat-eating. It is all there, the brutalizing labor, the stench, the blood, the cruelty. On reading it I admitted that if I were forced to kill animals and prepare their flesh for cooking, I would never eat meat again." (I have gone on eating meat—and the stockyards still exist!)

III

"July 14. How easily routine grips a man of sixty-two! I have been in this apartment less than a month and yet I am as deep-sunk in a groove as if I had been here a year.

I rise at half past six—as I am accustomed to doing in New York—I go to the kitchen and make my coffee. I toast a roll, open the back door for the milk bottle and the front door for the newspaper, and then settle to work just as in my study on Ninety-second Street, oblivious to the fact that the British Museum with all its records is only thirty minutes away and that the telephone directory at my elbow contains the addresses of all the great ones in British art and British literature. For the most part I wait. Things come to me. No doubt I am missing things—but then things are missing me. I am now a fatalist. I am not striving. I am not expectant. I could become feverish with anxiety over the opportunities which offer, but routine comes in to soothe and revalue.

"I dreamed last night that Edward Wheeler was dead and that he had come to me through a medium. Let us see if this will prove another 'coincidence.' " (It did not. He did not die "at that instant, allowing for differences in time.")

"We lunched on this day, the 17th, with Sir Arthur Conan Doyle and his wife. They have lately returned from their American tour and are lyrical in praise of the cities they have seen and the people they have met. They invited us all to their place in Crowborough and we shall go down at their convenience. Doyle is one of the happiest, most fortunate men of my acquaintance and fully acknowledges that he owes most of his good fortune to his vast American public."

IV

"Our luncheon at Admiralty House on the 18th was surprisingly informal. Lord Lee, who is First Lord of the

Admiralty, was genial and unofficial, and Lady Lee, at whose right I sat, put me at ease by saying, 'I come from your state,' to which I replied with a question, 'Do you mean Wisconsin?' She corrected herself. 'I should have said your father's state. I was born in Maine, but I spent many years in Washington. I met my husband there, a military attaché.' She went on to say that she knew many of the men and women I had mentioned in my books. I forgot that I was in Admiralty House, so candid and friendly were they both."

One of the men whom my daughter Isabel wished to meet—a desire which I shared—was Maurice Hewlett, and one morning, a dark and rainy morning, we took the train for Salisbury near which he lived.

An hour and a half through lovely rolling farm country brought us to Salisbury station and ten minutes' walk set us face to face with its glorious cathedral. My first impression was of its repose and the harmony of its color. "Built of yellowish green-gray stone, unmarred by time, it rose out of a lovely lawn like the chapel in a college campus with nothing to break its serene majesty. It was entirely satisfying. What devoted and learned architects existed in the midst of the poor and ignorant of that time! Skill and judgment and taste combined to build to this plan—no matter where the plan came from."

A ride of half an hour by motor from Salisbury brought us to Broad Chalke, a tiny village hardly more than a cluster of farmhouses. After some wandering we came to a farmhouse on the hillside, a narrow building surrounded by a wall and presenting its eastern end to the visitor. We walked slowly into the yard unable to believe that we should find the author of 'Richard Yea-and-Nay' living in such a humble little home. It was hardly more than a gardener's cottage, surrounded by walls protected by thatches of straw. Two men were at work in the garden, and one of these at once started up the hill to meet us.

"This was Hewlett. I knew him at once, although he had grown gray and thin. He is smaller than I had expected him to be and less formal in manner. He greeted us with quiet hospitality and gave us seats in curious canvas chairs, each with a small awning.

"There was in him little of the remoteness I had expected to find, and nothing austere. He was entirely detached from the quality of his books. His face is rather thin and his brow high. His eyes are a blue-gray and his glance candid and friendly. He was dressed in a plain, well-worn dark suit and his speech was very like that of a cultured American.

"To relate this small, sad man with the richly woven tapestries of his medieval romances was not easy. His manner was that of a literary editor who refuses to talk shop. That he was interested and somewhat embarrassed was evident. Few Americans seek him out and he was curious to know the reasons for our coming.

" 'An American lecture agent came to see me last week,' he said. 'He wanted me to make a tour of the States, but I am afraid Americans consider me an extinct volcano. No one reads my books now.'

"His cottage is charming, but not in the least the kind of home I had expected to find him occupying. It is very small, quaint, and dainty, but without modern conveniences. It is in effect the haven of a scholar grown elderly, one who has visited with kings. In answer to my question he replied, 'Yes, I live here all the year round. In fact I seldom go to London. I belong to none of its clubs. I hate the city.' "

As he said this I wondered what companionship he could find here, in this tiny, remote village. "It is not my native village," he said, "that is more than twenty miles away." He did not say how he came to settle in Broad Chalke, but when he said, "I have lived here twenty years but only one year in this house," I began to understand. He went on, "My home for nineteen years was in the rectory of that little church over there, a lovely old place dating from the year 1350."

"Can we see your old home and study?" I asked. "My daughter will not be quite content without a glimpse of it."

"Oh, yes. I'll give you a card to the present owner who will gladly open it for you."

My daughter voiced her love for his "Richard Yea-and-Nay," and this appeared to please him. He said, "Broadly speaking, the story is true. It is based on an intensive reading of the records. Of course there is a great deal of fictive matter in the detail, but mainly it is a faithful picture of Richard and his time."

"Your estimate of the king was rather shocking to some of us," I said, and to this he smilingly replied, "I suppose you expected my book to come out like Scott's 'Talisman.' " I confessed that I had expected to find Richard a little more idealized.

Of "The Forest Lovers" he said, "I began that book as a joke. I wrote the first sentences on a sheet of blotting paper and laid it aside and forgot it. Some years later I happened across it and the theme seized upon me. It was my first book, published in 1898."

He expressed a special liking for "The Queen's Quair":

"I delved among records for two years in preparation for the writing of that book," he said, and gave us the impression that he regarded it as his best book. As to the scene of "The Forest Lovers," he confessed that he was a bit vague as to what forest he had in mind. "It is a mixture of Fontainebleau and England, I suspect."

As we sat conversing slowly and at ease, looking out over the lovely, smooth rolling hills, a cowbell hung above the door jangled a call to tea.

At a gayly decorated table in the tiny dining room, Hewlett took the place of hostess. No woman was in sight. "My wife and daughter live in London," he briefly explained. "There is hardly room for three in this cottage." (I could understand that his wife and daughter prefer London to this village.) "I only go to London to meet the editors of the magazines. I make my living now by writing essays and reviews. I am told that my books are still read in American university circles and that I could find bookings for lectures in college towns. I am tempted to try it."

He reverted to his youth. "I was educated for the bar and I was thirty-four when I began to write. Farnol, Cabell, and Doyle are my followers, not to say imitators. I like Doyle as a man, but he is 'dotty' on spiritualism. I have no high opinion of Hutchinson, but I value young Milne. I sometimes wonder if he is a growing man." He spoke highly of De la Mare, also of Robert Graves. "I consider Graves a better man than Nichols."

Of Conrad he said, "I find him hard reading. He cannot tell a story. I cannot name any poet who is doing sustained work." He spoke slightingly of Locke, but considered Galsworthy a big man. "Wells is a man of power and a good fellow, but his 'Outline of History,' very good in the early part, is weak in the Greek section." In speaking of Kipling's fine old home, he said, "I tried to get that house once, just before Kipling saw it."

In answer to my daughter's question, he said, " 'The Queen's Quair' was written in the old rectory; but 'The Forest Lovers' was not." He confessed his need of keeping at work: "There's nothing else for men of our age and habit to do." Which recalled a similar remark of Howells, who, when criticized for writing too much, ruefully replied, "What can an old fellow do but write?"

Close beside the little old church we found the rectory, whose garden runs back to the little stream which flows between Hewlett's beloved home and his cottage. He had not offered to go with us and I think I understood his feeling. To my daughter I said, "Here is the home of the author of 'Richard Yea-and-Nay' and 'The Queen's Quair.' " An old woman answered our bell and listened closely while we explained our presence. At the end of it she bade us enter. The interior was as perfect (in its simpler way) as Kipling's home, so English, so vine-clad, so filled with memories, and when at last we were ushered into the great beamed library where Hewlett had wrought for so many years, I said: "Here is the proper 'atmosphere' for a writer of medieval romance. To give this up must have been a painful wrench. I wish we could have seen our author in it with his own books and furniture around him."

This room, like his work, typifies the England of castles and cathedrals with its romance of horses and knights and halls. His closely woven tapestried prose, the primitive savagery of his tales, their piety, their grotesque monks, and their noble knights, are all coeval with the Templars' Chapel in the ancient City of London. This quiet old rectory, which had held human beings for six hundred years, was in harmony with his tales. Here he sat and dreamed of the past, till the Great War reached in and shook him from his dream.

"He is growing old. A new generation of readers has sprung up, a generation with new heroes and new prophets, and he is forgotten. Nevertheless, as the figures of the horseman and the lamb, the shield and the lion, will continue to adorn the pavements of England's temples, so for many years the story of 'Richard Yea-and-Nay' and 'The Queen's Quair' will remain a part of English literary history.

"Hewlett typifies a noble group of writers—a stately generation of thinkers and poets. They are being superseded; and yet, like Hawthorne and Howells, they will not pass; they will remain long after the journalistic fictionists of to-day are done."

V

July 17. In a walk along the Chelsea Embankment one afternoon I came upon a statue of Thomas Carlyle, one that I had never seen before. It stands in a small park not far from the Cheyne Row house in which he lived for so many years. The figure is very realistic and placed on a low pedestal. It represents him as a small, frail, sorrowful old man. There is nothing of the thunderer, nothing of the dour old Scotch warrior in this portrait. With thin legs covered by a shawl, with wistful eyes staring out into eternal dark, he sits at the end of his journey. Standing before this statue, my notions of the great Northern sage, the merciless critic, were transformed. I saw him a man entirely human and lovable.

From here I went directly to his home, which is maintained as a memorial to him and his work.

"To enter the door of this house is like entering a village home of 1860, and to find on its walls snapshot photographs of its owner was a bit surprising. Although it is less than forty years since Carlyle left this house, he is so remote as to be incredible to us of to-day.

"The house is small and bare with a minute garden at the back. In Carlyle's time it had no bathrooms, no gas, no plumbing—no conveniences of any kind. The family procured its water from a pump in the kitchen, and the old philosopher must have bathed in a tin tub after carrying the water up three flights of stairs. The kitchen is below the street level, a cellar in fact; and yet it was in this room that Carlyle and Tennyson sat all one evening, smoking busily, and without saying a word except that, as Tennyson was leaving, Carlyle removed his pipe from his mouth and said, 'Alfred, we've had a glorious time. Come again.'

"The bedrooms are hardly more than closets and have very poor ventilation. Ventilation, I fear, was an unconsidered trifle in those days. The whole house is as primitive as a New England farmhouse. Chelsea in Carlyle's time was a village suburb; and he lived here very much as the farmers and mechanics around him lived, in daily discomfort."

There is something superbly dramatic in the fact that from this drab little tenement Carlyle visited the great ones of the earth and that they in turn came here to pay homage. Emerson slept in the "spare room," a room which the bed nearly filled. And on the wall of the library is a letter written by Prime Minister Beaconsfield offering Carlyle a baronetcy and a pension. Near it is Carlyle's reply declining both the honor and the money. In a case near by is a copy of his noble letter telling of the tragic loss of his manuscript, the first book of his "French Revolution."

As I walked up and down these worn stairways and confronted the well-scoured tables in that basement kitchen, I was able to reconstruct the life of the family. I perceived in it the frugality of my own Scotch forbears, a frugality for which Scotland is famous. I could hear old Tammas creaking and grumbling up the stairs with a bucket of water in each hand whilst down below Jane Welsh was putting the kitchen to rights. No doubt they ate down there, except on certain state occasions, for it was not easy to get food and dishes up the narrow stairway to the dining room. So far as I know they did not employ a servant. The whole effect of their life was like that of their cousins on the plains of Iowa.

Emerson who came to visit the great Scotchman was not surprised by his poverty, for he kept house in very much the same simplicity at Concord. His home, although more spacious than Carlyle's, was almost as bare of superficialities. Hawthorne had even less.

"All my life I have known of this house in Cheyne Row, but no one has ever given me to understand that it was only a poor, bare, little rented house with a cellar kitchen and a pump in the sink. In fear of demoting Carlyle, writers have concealed the humbleness of his home. They have omitted to describe its discomforts. What must its rooms have been during the cold and fog and rain of the English winter? No doubt the only really comfortable place to sit was in the kitchen. It is on record that Carlyle complained of the chill of his study; and with my knowledge of English climate I can well believe not only that the whole house was as dank as a refrigerator but that it smelled like a musty cellar. All houses heated by small coal grate fires are icy in the corners and full of stagnant air. Carlyle's house was no exception.

"Nevertheless in that bare attic, double-walled to shut out neighborhood noises, some of his noblest prose was written. All of the 'French Revolution' and all of 'Frederick the Great' were composed here. Here stands the flat, hair-clothed sofa on which the historian reclined, and here is preserved the rug which he used to pull up over his knees. Here are casts of his hands, gnarled and gaunt, and a death mask (which does not in the least resemble the man of legend—the dour, scoffing, roaring critic of God and His universe) pictures a rough-hewn, kindly, sorrowful visage. I left this house with a better understanding of Carlyle."

CHAPTER THIRTY-NINE

CONAN DOYLE AND BATTLE ABBEY

I

In discussing with Barrie the younger writers and dramatists, I had frankly confessed my distaste for much of their work, "but," I said, "there must be those who are not entirely given over to the dirty side of life and I should like to know one or two who might be considered representative."

In reply, he had named A. A. Milne as one whose plays were original and skillfully written. "He is a fine young fellow who carries his success well. He lives on Mallord Street in Chelsea not far from you. He will be delighted to meet you and you will like him."

We had already seen two of his plays in New York, where they had been most successful, and at this time two of his plays were on the boards in London. He was at that moment the most successful young playwright in England and my daughters were eager to meet the author of "Mr. Pim Passes By" and "The Dover Road."

In my letter to him I said, "I have your address from Sir James Barrie," thinking that he needed some sort of assurance concerning me, and went on to say that my daughters were keenly interested in his work and that we should be delighted to have him and Mrs. Milne to luncheon at our home. After posting the letter I said to my wife, "Milne will probably set us down as another strange American family lion-hunting in London. He will come—if he comes!—wondering what we are like, as I am wondering what he is like. I haven't the slightest notion of his character. I only know that he is a little above thirty years of age—but Barrie's word is all the assurance I need."

I had written, "It will be a family luncheon, for we want to talk with you." The date of their coming was July 25 and I made a brief record of it.

"Milne and his wife came in about one. He is a long, lean young fellow, very blond and shy, quite unspoiled by success. He flushed when I praised his work, and modestly disclaimed great merit. He said, 'I owe my start entirely to Barrie. He was my highest admiration and I ventured to send him one of my plays. He read it and turned it over to a manager with a note advising its production. I was only a hard-working magazinist before the war. My military service made a big hole in my life, but it started me on my career as a dramatist.'

"His wife, a very happy young person, confirmed this. Openly adoring her husband and enjoying his success to the full, she spoke of their present freedom from care in contrast with the time when he was away in the trenches. 'He wrote his first play while on invalid leave suffering from trench fever,' she explained. 'He'd been a writer on *Punch* for some years and was assistant editor when the war began.'

"As she talked and he sat regarding my daughters, I studied him. He wore a neat new suit—vividly blue—with socks to match and he carried a handkerchief of the same color in his sleeve. His hair, a sandy red, was brushed away from his high brow in the present boy's mode. He was charmingly young and happy with something finely sensitive in face and voice. He was more Scotch than English. I conceived that he had come to luncheon quite as curious about the Garlands as we were about him.

"His work interests me for the reason that, like Barrie, he has won his enormous public without playing down to the animal appetites of men and women. There is not a lewd situation in his plays. They are humorous, quick of changing mood, and entirely free of degrading suggestion. He is boyish, but his blue eyes are keen. He came through the war without losing faith in the wholesome average of human life."

He told us that he had in hand a play based on Kenneth Grahame's "Wind in the Willows" and that he had an intense admiration for the book. "In all my other plays the themes are my own, but in this case I am using a tale which, as a boy, I adored."

His first play was read by a friend who suggested that he send it to Barrie. Barrie passed it on to Boucicault with the word, "Produce this!" Success came—"not tumultuously," he said with a smile, "but it came."

This explains in some degree the likeness of his work to that of Barrie. He belongs to the same school of writers, men who deal with the kindly, normal, humorous side of life. He does not imitate Barrie, but he naturally sees life in somewhat the same fashion.

"It is evident that he does not fully realize the enormous American vogue he has won. With two new plays announced and a third under his pen, he is on the way to becoming Barrie's successor. His talent is for facile and delightful comedy. His dialogue is notably swift and whimsical. He and Barrie both dislike this word, but I can think of none other to take its place. He stands entirely apart from the sex-obsessed youth of his time and I honor him for it."

He sat with us, smoking a pipe like a college man and talking in occasional spurts till nearly four o'clock. As they were leaving, he said, "You must all come over and dine with us," and this we promised to do.

II

Sir Arthur Conan Doyle's invitation to visit him at his home in Crowborough did not come until late in July, for the reason that he had lingered on in America, so great was the demand for his lectures on spiritualistic phenomena; but shortly after his arrival he sent me a note in which he suggested that we come down to Sussex. "Come prepared for a week-end," he said, and added, "What would you like to see ? We'll motor on Saturday." Thinking he had a car and knowing Hastings was not far away, I suggested a trip to Battle Abbey. My record follows:

"Sir Arthur met us at Crowborough Station, looking big and burly and kindly and drove us to his home some miles away on a high ridge to the east. As we neared it, we saw the Stars and Stripes flying from a pole. 'That is in honor of you,' Doyle said. 'I fly it on all suitable occasions, for I love America and am grateful to her people.'

"The house was not an architectural unit; on the contrary it had the effect of four cottages joined roof to roof, but it was new, spacious and heated, all in the New World way, with nothing old or historic. It had no period furniture, no age-old doors or quaint windows, but it offered up-to-date bathrooms, radiator heat, and sunshine. A corps of servants loyal to their employer was in attendance. There was nothing typically English about the place except the domestic service. I have never known a more cheerful, harmonious home. 'I believe in being comfortable,' said Doyle. 'I follow American fashions in heating and lighting.'

"We lunched at a long table covered with flowers. His three children, two boys and a girl, were sturdy youngsters ranging from ten to thirteen years of age. His son by his first wife was killed in the war and it was very largely on his children's account that he had built this lovely sanitary home. It had nothing of the charm of Kipling's ironmaster's mansion, but it insured freedom from chilblains.

" 'I have arranged to visit Battle Abbey,' Doyle said, 'and we are to start immediately after luncheon. We must get back by dinner time.'

"At three, we set out in a big motor car for Battle Abbey—a glorious ride through lovely villages filled with cottages of Shakespeare's time—with mossy roofs, diamond-paned windows, and overhanging second stories. We longed to stop and explore, but Doyle whirled us remorselessly on. 'I have wired Sir Augustus Webster, the owner of the Abbey, and he will be waiting for us,' he said. So the glorious time-worn churches and feudal halls were left behind.

"In the square before the tall Norman gate of the Abbey grounds we found a throng of motor cars and chars-à-bancs filled with sight-seeing folk from many countries; but Doyle's name had magic in it. To the amazement of the tourists, we found the gate no barrier. We were met just inside by a small, gray, dim-eyed, soft-voiced man of sixty. He looked like a kindly janitor, but was in truth Sir Augustus Webster, the hereditary owner of this grand old ruin. Greatly pleased to be host of Conan Doyle, he included the Garlands in his hospitality.

"It soon became evident that he was a careful student of the Abbey and the epoch-making battle which it commemorates. He personally led us about the ruins, explaining in detail the plan of the battle, and describing the buildings of the Abbey as they were in the eleventh century. The abbot's hall, into which he conducted us, is still in good repair. 'For eight generations,' he said with sad intonation, 'this has been the home of my family, but I must give it up. The war has ruined me.' Evidences of this change were visible in the cartloads of furniture which had been moved from the bedchambers out into the great hall ready for the moving van. 'It is to be a girls' school after September 1st,' he explained, and as I looked about the noble old hall hung with beautiful tapestries, portraits, and shields, and compared them with the clutter of cheap chairs and bureaus, I understood the despair of the aristocrat whose world is passing into dust.

"He is alone. His son was killed in the war and his wife drowned herself in a pool on the estate. He has no near relatives and to be relieved of the strain of keeping this historic building he is renting it. He is a type. He represents the passing ancient order which the new order has no intention of maintaining. His seedy clothing, his defensive smile, his wistful voice are all significant of decay. His family strain has faded to a single strand in the web of English history."

(As I shall not touch upon this again, I am moved to record that he only lived a year or two longer. It is not entirely fanciful to say he died of loneliness and sorrow, but he made no complaint.)

At dinner that night, Doyle sketched his own happy and busy life. "I was educated in Edinburgh," he said, "and later studied surgery in Germany and Austria. I became a specialist in diseases of the eye and ear, but I went to Africa during the Boer War as a surgeon. This led to my book on the 'Jameson Raid.'" (This was the book which led to his being knighted.) "My invention of Sherlock Holmes came in the nineties after a number of successful historic romances."

I recalled our meeting in Chicago at the time of the World's Fair. "You were writing for *McClure's Magazine* then."

In speaking of the Great War he said, "I organized the first volunteer regiment and went in as a private. I marched from here to the training camp every day, eight miles each way, with all my accouterments on. One day a young inspector observed a Boer War medal on my breast. 'Well, my man,' he pleasantly remarked, 'you saw service in Africa—did you?' . . . 'Yes, sir,' I replied respectfully. He then said, 'What arm of the service?' . . . 'Surgeon, sir.' . . . 'Ah, that is good,' he remarked with a kindly air, and passed on. Later he spoke to my captain. 'Who is that big fellow with the Boer War medal—that man in the rear rank?' . . . 'That,' said my captain with a grin, 'is Sherlock Holmes.' . . . 'Good

God!' said the young inspector, 'I hope he won't lay my idiotic break up against me.' I didn't."

Naturally we had much talk of psychic research, and he stated very earnestly that he held it his duty to proclaim the truth of spirit return. "No other subject is of equal importance." In this I agreed, although I had not his clear conviction in the matter.

He said, "For the moment, I am giving no thought to anything else." A statement which means much, for he is still in the plenitude of his powers. "I am bringing my children up in this faith. They share many of our séances. I want them to feel that spirit communication is as natural as the telephone."

He showed us a silver plate set in the floor of the sitting room where his dead son had spoken to him, and where messengers from the unseen world had momentarily shown themselves. He has the courage of the crusader, and is bringing all his great fame to bear on the problem of educating the public in these vital beliefs.

"I am glad to record that despite all this psychic propaganda he and his wife remain the most normal of human beings. Their children are wholesome, vigorous, and happy. To have an ectoplasmic form step from a cloud of vapor or to hear a spirit voice sounding from the air are commonplace experiences to them. Several of Doyle's fellows assured me that he was 'a bit mad,' but to me he was not only perfectly sane but humorously able to meet all dissenters. Hewlett, Kipling, Galsworthy, and Barrie spoke of him with affection but with sorrow over his crusade. William Archer put it concisely when he said, 'He has lost standing in England just as Sir Oliver Lodge has sacrificed much of his great fame.'"

We saw the Doyles several times after this. They came to lunch at our table and we lunched with them at a place in the city.

"Conan Doyle is one of the most delightful and generous-minded of all my English author friends and it grieves me that I cannot share his faith."

On September 7 he wrote, "I wish you had a grip on our spiritualist philosophy. It is so vital, while the phenomena, though obviously true, are really of no importance. We have known far greater happiness since we have mastered the facts, and the argument of independent witnesses is so great that it is impossible to doubt their truth. But when you know that you will see your folk even as you knew them and that you will gallop your horse Ladrone down the trails once more, it all becomes natural and beautiful. It is strange to think that the American Indians with their happy hunting grounds were really far nearer to the truth of the facts of the next existence than the missionaries."

To this I could only reply by saying, "My dear Doyle, I wish I could acquire your faith. I grant the existence of the phenomena, but my mind refuses, thus far, to accept your beautiful faith."

(I saw him again in 1923 and seven years later he died. Since then Lady Doyle is reported as declaring that she has had messages from him quite as clear as those he used to have from his son. Of this I know nothing at first hand. If his spirit is aware of what I am writing, I wish him to know that I remember him with affection as well as with admiration for his knowledge and literary skill.)

CHAPTER FORTY

WE VISIT JOSEPH CONRAD

I

Meanwhile I had been carrying on a polite correspondence with the Maharajah of Jhalawar, carefully copying his address from the card which he had given me, and at last arrived at a date convenient for us to visit Oxford and for him to receive us at his house. This, according to my diary, was August 4.

"The maharajah's car met us at the station, and as we rolled grandly up the street the coronet on the radiator top drew a salute from every policeman along the way and I vainly tried to imagine the kind of palace this Indian prince would occupy in this city of college students and professors. It was incredible almost to the point of being fantastic, and when the car drew up at the door of a commonplace little villa such as a university don might own, we were shocked and disappointed. Our notion of Indian princes suffered revision. It held no hint of the Orient in furnishings or procedure for the maharajah met me in the spirit of a fellow scribe. He presented us quite informally to his household, which consisted of his son, a large, dark youth of twenty-one, his counselor, a small, dark man who spoke English perfectly, and to an Englishwoman, the wife of the councillor, wearing Eastern dress. Two tall black, austere, and silent men in the room as his bodyguard were not named. The only other guest was an Irish actor of whom I knew nothing."

The house was plainly a rented house, for its furniture was of the commonplace English sort with no relationship to these dark-skinned Orientals. His Highness, as all his household were careful to call him, was not as impressive as when we saw him at the literary dinner. His English dress, like his English home, lessened his exotic charm. "I am only an English citizen here," he said, and was as cordial and as unassuming as an English gentleman, although his household maintained many of the formalities which they practiced in India.

The son, an intelligent and rather shy, plump youth, was ready to confess his ignorance of American social conditions. "I am studying Western methods of agriculture," he said, "and am preparing to be of use to my people. Some time I shall go to America."

To the maharajah I frankly confessed that I knew nothing of the etiquette involved in writing to him. "I copied your visiting card and now am at a loss as to the proper form in addressing you. I am a plainsman, you know, the son of a pioneer farmer of Wisconsin."

He smiled as he replied, "My family name is Singh. 'Rajah' means ruler and 'maha' signifies superior ruler or high ruler. 'Maharajah' therefore means overlord or super ruler. It does not matter what you call me. For the time being I am a student in this university."

To this I replied, "I have no objection to addressing you in the proper terms. My only hesitancy arises out of ignorance. I do not know what the proper term is. If I blunder, I hope you'll pardon me."

I suspect that he had looked up my record, for he asked me for a list of my books.

The luncheon table presented a singular mixture of black, pink, brown, and gray faces. On my right sat the princess, a shy, little woman, and on my left a young Welsh girl who did much to keep things going, while I studied with some amusement the grim and watchful faces of the guard who sat at the foot of the table. That he disapproved of his ruler's democracy was evident. In the center of the table on a perch just before His Highness sat a parrot squawking for food, and to this bird the supreme ruler of Jhalawar occasionally addressed a word or extended a crust. In consequence our talk was broken and somewhat labored—or at least mine was.

My wife who was seated at the right of our host and beside the prince, appeared to get on fairly well with both men, but I found the timid little princess a conversational problem. I could not draw her out. I talked of America and she listened with interest, for she hoped some time to go there. She was not accustomed to freedom of action on the part of women, and I suspect would have gladly forgone the honor of sitting beside an elderly American novelist.

As soon as we had finished luncheon, the maharajah said, "My car is yours. Use it for the entire afternoon. We dine at seven."

We thanked him and accepted the car and driver with great joy, for they made it possible for us not only to see every part of Oxford but to visit some of the surrounding points of interest.

For several hours we drove from one college to another, alighting before the gateways of lovely quadrangles and the doorways of storied libraries, always with the silent influence of that coroneted radiator working to our honor and privilege, until, surfeited with towers, mullioned windows, stained glass, quaint halls, and lovely gardens, we drove back into the restful commonplace of the maharajah's cottage.

Our dinner was an elaborate series of strange dishes and the talk was mainly of America. Aside from using his title, I treated our host as he asked to be treated—as a man of letters. In describing our great new railway stations and our magnificent high-school buildings I said, "These are the only temples we can show. They are the temples of democracy and they are magnificent," and in saying this I caught myself boasting in the American fashion and instantly stopped with a sense of shame. "It is easy for us to brag of our bigness and newness—we have nothing else!"

On the whole we left Oxford with a feeling of disappointment. Our day had not been worth quite as much as we had anticipated. The maharajah was less interesting than we had expected him to be and Oxford's streets and college interiors had wearied us. "They are interesting as survivals of the past," I said to my wife, "but our universities, with all their bleak and unlovely quadrangles, are better warmed and lighted. Sunny recitation rooms are easier on the student, unesthetic as they may seem to the Old World visitor. Oxford is all very interesting for a few hours or a few days, but I have no desire to live there."

The maharajah inquired about my family, and when he learned that I had my two young daughters with me he said, "You must come again and bring them with you.

My son and his wife have never met an American girl and they would be delighted to know your daughters. Come up and spend the night. I'll send my car to Kensington to fetch you at any time convenient to you."

This we promised to do.

II

It is characteristic of our life in England that on the day following our visit to this Indian prince, we had dinner with the most successful of all the younger playwrights and that we walked to his door through Chelsea. We had no difficulty in finding the Milne door, for it was painted a vivid blue, and on entering the house we found it gay with red and orange hangings and decorations, a charmingly individual and tasteful home. At the back was a tiny garden in which stood a laughing little Italian cherub.

Their small son, a beautiful elf-like creature about two years old, was their chief delight. Milne openly adored his child. He flushed with pleasure when we exclaimed over his son's elfin charm. It amused and touched me to see how he hung over Robin's busy labors with a sofa cushion. I was once such an adoring parent.

He greeted us shyly, his thin, sensitive face showing his uneasiness. When we reached the sitting room he doubled down into a deep chair and looked at us with keen, appraising eyes. I began by saying, "I have reread 'The Wind in the Willows' since your visit to us and I don't see how you can put it into play form. I doubt its success."

"It is a labor of love," he explained.

He told me that he was born in London and that his

father was still alive. "Both my son's grandfathers are alive," he said, in explanation of the readiness with which the exquisite little Robin came to me. "He takes you for another grandfather."

"Milne is a hard man to talk with. He is curiously shy. Talk does not flow from his lips. It comes out in brief gurgles, and only in answer to questions. He volunteers nothing. I suspect that he regarded me as a venerable philosopher, a sage whose years entitled him to deference and precedence. His delightful little home was evidence of the modest estimate he places upon his powers."

I said, "There is a warm welcome awaiting you in America."

"I want to go," he replied, "but I can't bring myself to leave my wife and my son. Later I may go and take them with me."

He was very close-lipped in the matter of passing judgment on his contemporaries. He appeared reserved rather than timid in this regard. Perhaps he felt unfitted to instruct a man of my age and experience. Like Hutchinson, he had the world by the ear.

"The question is, Will he grow? Is he capable of development? Has he anything of Barrie's depth? He can be as big as he pleases. His further success can be won by continuing the same qualities of humor and wholesome sentiment, but he must not repeat his themes."

III

"August 7. After two months of almost continuous rain, or cloudy skies, I am led to wonder if England knows what real sunshine and real moonlight are. I have seen the stars and the moon only at rare intervals. People tell us this is an exceptional summer, but the actions of the workmen and the shopkeepers are significant. They do not mind the rain—or rather, they ignore it. The calm way in which nurses sit out in the park with their baby carriages, and the bricklayers placidly lay brick in the drizzle, proves that they expect continuous rain. As literature takes its figures of speech, its color, and its form from environment, I now understand why the moon has so small a part in the poetry of the British islands. Just as the bloom of the hedges, the velvet texture of the grass, and the beauty of the oaks and beeches constantly appear in English literature, so our brilliant skies, our flooding sunlight, and our vivid moonlight enrich our own verse and prose. As I recall the gorgeous moons and suns of Onteora—or the evening clouds above the roofs of Manhattan—I have a sense of loss. No wealth of historic association can compensate me for the gloom and the cold of an English winter.

"M. Taine's comment on the climate of England takes on deeper significance after two months' life in London. The attitude of the women toward sunlight is comical. At the least hint of it they raise parasols. The fair complexions of the men are seldom touched with tan. They all talk of being 'warm-blooded,' but the truth is their skins are thickened by exposure; the girls are wearing thin gowns whilst I go about in an overcoat."

On August 9th we saw Barrie's short play, "Shall We Join the Ladies?" and Galsworthy's "Loyalties" and greatly enjoyed them both. The Barrie playlet is a mystery play of an amusing tone, but "Loyalties," like all of Galsworthy's work, is an entirely serious study of class and other prejudices. Both were interesting and extremely well done. "These two writers are still in the front rank of English men of letters. Kipling and Conrad are the others most regarded. Bennett is less spoken of and Wells is called a super-reporter—I am inclined to say a superhuman reporter, so continuous is the flow of his ink. He spoke of himself as 'a geyser' and I am content to let it go at that. Who are to come after this great group? No doubt there are young Barries and Shaws and Kip-lings prowling about, but no one can point them out.

"The outstanding figures in present-day English litera-ture, the men who could and should form an Academy, are inclined to flock alone. They do not 'belong' to liter-ary organizations. Wells and Galsworthy, exceptional as they are, are more social, not to say socialistic, in their natures. Doyle and Gosse and Bennett are inclined to help this and that, but the first-class men, unless they are hu-manitarian, are apt to remain in seclusion or strictly within their own circles."

IV

As I went about London I found an almost unanimous agreement regarding Joseph Conrad's position. He was everywhere named with respect even by the youngsters who were supercilious about Barrie and others of his generation. "Conrad's a big man," they reluctantly ad-mitted.

I had never met this writing sailor, although I had been reading him for over twenty years—ever since Stephen Crane had written me in praise of "The Nigger of the Narcissus." He was declared to be an elusive foreigner, one seldom seen in London. "Conrad is only a pen name; his Polish name is long and difficult and he

has Anglicized it—he lives down near Canterbury,"
Barrie said, "in Bishopsbourne," and it was to this address
that I sent a letter telling of my presence in England
and of my desire to see him.

He replied asking me to visit him if I should be coming
to Canterbury and this I promised to do. By great good
fortune Dr. Edward Jones, our neighbor in the Catskills,
turned up at our flat one August morning and invited us
to motor down to Canterbury with him. "We'll follow
the old Roman road," he said, "and lunch in the shadow
of the cathedral." Accepting his offer, I stated my desire to visit Conrad who lived near by. "Very well," he
said, "while we are seeing Canterbury, you can take the
car and call upon him."

This I did, accompanied by my daughter Isabel. My
record, somewhat amplified, reads thus:

"We found Conrad's home to be a suburban cottage
on the edge of a park in Bishopsbourne some six or eight
miles to the eastward. It was a quaint and shapeless structure, one that had just grown from an old cottage into
a modern two-story house. In front of it is a hedge and
a circular lawn, and its doorway is most hospitable. It
has no outlook, however—its seat is in a valley—and I
could not associate Conrad, the sea rover, with it. It is a
quiet, secluded village.

"As for Conrad, I had in mind a rather tall, austere, reserved man, one whose words were few and chosen with
care—and when he came bustling out to meet us, I was
amazed. He is short, broad-shouldered, and gray-haired.
His body radiates energy. His arms fly about like flails.
His face was alight with welcome and his words came
mumbling, tumbling out. He was altogether continental.

He gesticulated like a Polish Jew, but his speech was filled with cockney accents. He said 'trine' for train and 'grite' for great. He was as gallant as a Frenchman as he greeted my daughter. He was swift, unresting, and confused, yet sincerely cordial.

"His volubility and his Polish accent, joined with his cockney pronunciation of words, made him utterly incredible. For a time I could only gaze and listen, struggling to readjust my concepts of him. To complete my confusion he fumbled in his vest pocket and produced a single English eyeglass which he nervously screwed into one eye.

"He seemed moved by our visit. 'It is good of you to come all this way to see me. I have written for years with the thought in my mind, "What will Hamlin Garland think of my books?" but I had given up all hope of seeing you.'

"This remark amazed me. I had never known that he was even aware of my existence. I replied, 'I have read you for more than twenty years—ever since Stephen Crane wrote advising me to read "The Nigger of the Narcissus." I particularly enjoyed "Nostromo." '

"This pleased him, but he confessed that he knew very little of South America. 'I wrote it from material acquired elsewhere.'

"Speaking of his house, he said, 'I have been here only three years, but I have lived in or near Bishopsbourne for thirty years. I am a Kentishman.' As he said this, he expressed himself as an Oriental and not as a Nordic. He made it plain that he, too, is a solitary. 'I know few of my fellow authors. I meet few people of any kind. I seldom go to London; the truth is, I am afraid to go—my doctor warns me that my heart is weak. My wife, poor thing, must needs go along.' This was in reference to her wounded knee which made it necessary for her to sit with her leg outstretched upon a chair. She is a large, fair woman, kindly and watchful. She is the mother of two sons, but Joseph is her unceasing care. She is wholly English, but has no pronounced accent of any kind.

"Conrad talked freely, volubly of his early experiences. He told of going to sea as a common sailor, of being promoted to third officer, of winning command of a merchant ship at the age of twenty-eight. 'I went round the world in these capacities. I traded in Burma, India, and the Congo. I was one of the first to know the Congo. I sailed up the great rivers of the Orient. There's where I got my material for "Almayer's Folly" and "Lord Jim." I began to write while still a sailor. I began "Almayer's Folly" with no thought of its being published. I knew nothing of book publishing. I wrote part of it in a lodging in London and I carried the manuscript with me. I worked on it from time to time on several voyages, but had no hope of its getting into print, till one day in London as I was passing Fisher Unwin's publishing house I saw displayed several small-size volumes. "By Jove," I said, "my book would go into that set." I sent the manuscript to them. Three months went by. Not a word! Then one day a letter came, a typewritten letter, the first I had ever seen. It was from the publishers offering to take the book.'

"After a moment's pause he said with a touch of retrospective emotion, 'The writing of that story gave me more pleasure and satisfaction than anything I have done since. It was a novel experience. I took pleasure in every line;

now, I am tired of writing. I groan and creak and swear as I crowd myself to the task.'

"To lighten the momentary gloom, I asked, 'Aren't you coming to America?'

"He shook his head rather sadly. 'No, I am afraid to go. I am not well enough to stand the strain.' In answer to my statement, 'You have a loyal friend in Doubleday,' he replied sharply, 'He is a good business man. I do not believe in mixing sentiment with business. Doubleday would not publish my books if he did not expect to make money. Publishers do not permit friendship to come into the making of contracts.'

"Returning to 'The Nigger of the Narcissus,' he said, 'America would not buy a book about niggers, so my publishers changed the title to "Children of the Sea." I accepted the change. I was in no situation to object. I had no success with any book till I sold a serial to *Hearst's Magazine*. My friends were shocked, but I had no scruples; I was spoiling the Egyptians. Since then I have lived comfortably, but not, as you see, lavishly.'

"He took us out to see his gardens. 'I have a tree that was a well-grown sapling when Queen Elizabeth visited Canterbury. I go every day to make my devotions to him.'

"It was in truth a noble monument to England's past. As we stood looking at it he said, 'See how he clutches the earth. His roots are like the claws of a colossal lion. I bought this place to please my wife. She loves trees and flowers.'

"I said, 'It seems a singular home for an old sea rover.'

"This he admitted. 'Yes, but it is the only home I shall ever have. My powers are failing—I am fully aware of that. I save myself in every possible way, for I have two or three more books to write. I need the money. One of my sons is still at school and my poor wife is a cripple. She must be provided for. These are the reasons why I seldom leave my house. Nevertheless I am coming to London to see your family.'

"I understood his feeling. He no longer writes with an exultant sense of power. Like all his contemporaries, he is a machine running down. He acknowledged a sense of weakness, of apprehension. 'I feel worked out,' he said, and he is. The world already has the best of him. In explanation of his spoken English, he said, 'While I converse, as you see, without hesitation, I am not, even now, absolutely sure of my English. My writing is based on the dictionary.' To this I replied, 'That is what gives it distinction and charm. It is entirely free from worn-out forms.'

"As he grew more confidential, he confessed that he took no joy in his lovely home. 'It has no outlook, no horizon. It is a hole—for me. My wife loves it and so—I stay. It is no place for a seafaring man. I can see nothing but fields and a wall of woods.'

I spoke of Kipling's valley farm and he retorted, 'Yes, he is in a similar hole.' He shrugged his shoulders in a continental gesture. 'However, I live and write. In imagination I am still on the sea.'

"Like others of us he is going on with fixed purpose, grinding out copy in a last desperate spurt. He calls his trouble 'gout,' but one does not die of gout. His fear of sudden death is due to some organic weakness of his heart."

To hear this rugged old sea dog who had weathered a

thousand storms confess that he dared not spend a night away from his home was pitiful. "I have a horror of falling sick in a hotel," he confessed. There was little of the triumphant novelist about him. He seemed an anxious, hard-working professional man, a man who must keep going no matter how he suffers. This may be a pose, but if so it was most convincing. As Hewlett said, "I am a burned-out volcano," so Conrad was confessing to a similar failure of creative energy. He indicated that he had had several seizures. "I have lost confidence in the old machine," he said.

In several ways he was unmistakably continental. He continually interrupted me, piling his own observations upon the back of mine. It was not precisely discourteous nor was it egoistic; it was in the habit of his race. By contrast with Kipling, Barrie, Galsworthy, Shaw (for Shaw can listen patiently) he was essentially European.

My notes end with this paragraph:

"It is a sorrowful business, this watching a generation of noble writers moving toward the darkened wings of the stage they have held so long. This change is inevitable and naturally brings the question, 'Will the next wave of fiction and the drama have similar dignity and power?' Whatever the qualities of this later work, my relationship to it can never be the same as that I bear to that of my day."

CHAPTER FORTY–ONE

CONRAD COMES TO TOWN

I

DESPITE the democratization of war, the habit of service, of obedience, still persisted in England—at least in domestics above thirty years of age. Householders spoke to me of "insolence" and "disrespect," but I did not meet with either. Perhaps my gray hairs defended me from discourtesy. Whatever the reason, I met only kindness and deference. It is true social life was less formal than before the war, but I did not find it less kindly. The spirit of revolt, if it existed, was not manifest to me. I felt safer about my daughters than in New York.

"Like so many other Americans, I came to England with a feeling that writers and artists (and mechanics) were better off in America—in a new country, and that for their stability of employment Englishmen accepted a much lower wage than Americans demanded. In this thinking I am confirmed, but as the months go by I find my thought changing. Opportunities for wealth and distinction are more numerous than I had imagined them to be. To be condemned to a life of labor with pen or pencil in this small country is not as serious as I had always regarded it. There are compensations. I begin to understand the Briton's intense loyalty to his island. Notwithstanding the chill of its climate, it is a pleasant place to live.

"I am aware that all this reads rather trite, but what I am trying to say is this: As a man from midland America, I still hold the prejudices of the borderland. My sense of safety, born of the developing *new*, is diminished in the midst of the established old. I still have the psychology of the colonist who loves the parent land with its parks, manor houses, castles, and thatched cottages, but is afraid to return to it without adequate and enduring income."

This subject came up when Sir Gilbert Parker dined with us on the 12th.

"Our plain food and homely service threw him into reminiscent mood and during this he gave us a lively account of his youth in Canada and his early education for the ministry. Like nearly all my writer friends, he draws a large part of his royalties from American publishers and candidly admits it. He spoke of his knowledge of both sides of the Colonial problem. 'My novel, "The Weavers," arose out of my experiences in Egypt,' he said. 'America has been good to me. It has bought my books with generous interest.'

"Throughout the evening he talked with freedom of his work as a member of Parliament and as director of 'American publicity' during the war. He had seen all the great ones, and for the time our small dining room was thronged with generals, admirals, lords, and kings. He spoke of Kitchener as a popular idol, but totally unfit to meet the new military conditions. 'Trench warfare was repellent to him. He was too old, too inflexible, and so made way for younger men.'

"As he talked, I understood very well his value in Parliament. He knew the United States, he knew Canada, Australia, and New Zealand. He brought to King Edward the psychology of the New World. He was able to express (as no 'Little Englander,' no stay-at-home Tory, could possibly do) the changing heart of the colonist. He had no small talk, but he was a most responding dinner guest. We held many prejudices and many friends in common, and when he went away I counted happily on seeing him again, for he said, 'I shall winter hereafter in California or Arizona. I cannot stand the English winters.'"

Late in August, my wife took our daughters to Paris, leaving me to go on with my work in the flat. On August 24th, I set down these lines: "I have moments when my presence here in this spacious London flat is an incredible fantasy. With my wife and daughters away, my fire and my regular meals are a willful extravagance. Sitting alone here to-night I find myself deep in the past. From dining with English knights and international diplomats, I revert at times to my boyhood on the Iowa prairie. The farthermost reach of my imagination in those days was Boston. The thought of visiting Faneuil Hall and Bunker Hill was as thrilling to me then as the tales of Aladdin and his wonder-working lamp. Alas, the blue of each mountain wall fades out as I approach it! Here in the midst of London, a householder, I sit with only a faint stir of the wonder with which I first approached this island. Nothing that I see or do is worth writing about to-night. I ate my dinner alone, quite formally, waited upon in true English fashion."

One morning (August 27th) Joseph Conrad telephoned to say that he and Mrs. Conrad were in town. "We want to call on you." I explained that my wife and daughters were away and added, "I'll come down to see you."

I found them in the sitting room of a small hotel off Piccadilly waiting for me. Conrad came to meet me with a rush, his voice vibrant with emotion. There was no English reserve in his expression. In this he was entirely continental.

For some reason we again fell to discussing Stephen Crane, for whom Conrad had a real affection. He said, "Moreton Frewen gave Stephen the free use of an old Elizabethan manor house near Rye. It was in bad repair, almost a ruin, but it was a huge place and part of it habitable. Cora's bedroom was enormous, like a hall, and Steve's study was immensely long and narrow. I didn't visit them often. They were always surrounded by a gang of near-authors and grafters from London."

Mrs. Conrad added her impression. "It was an interesting old house. It had three secret passages and a ghost. Stephen made a good deal of money, but it all went toward keeping up this place which was always filled with what Joseph calls 'free lunchers'—and all the while the poor man was dying!"

Conrad then spoke of the last time he saw Crane. "It was in Dover. He was being carried to the boat on his way to a sanitarium in the Black Forest. He had grown a beard. Can you think of Steve with a beard? But his eyes were the eyes I knew—the eyes of a poet. He went away and I saw him no more. He was greatly honored over here. He often spoke of you with respect and gratitude."

A little later Conrad expressed a distrust of life, of

future social conditions, and I replied, "I feel that. It is a mood which comes to men of threescore and more."

He spoke of his hard-working early life. "It was as strenuous as your own, but on shipboard."

This led me to say, "I don't know just how it happens that I, the son of an Iowa farmer, sit here, a London householder, talking with you, a Pole residing in Kent." To this he quickly retorted, "It's because of something inside your jacket."

I pointed to my head. "You mean here?"

"No. If it were all in your head you wouldn't be here. It isn't a matter of what is under a man's hat. It is a question of vital forces—of feeling, sympathy."

I argued that it was something more mysterious than that. "It is largely a subconscious endowment. When the subconscious fails to work, nothing goes right."

"That's true," he replied, "when my subconscious self fails to work, I'm done."

"You told me once that writing was a torture, a dismal grind. There must be times when you get *some* fun out of it."

He admitted that he took pleasure in the initial stages of a novel—"the frightful grind comes in working out the concept."

He spoke several times of his hard service as a seaman. "It gave me my material."

To this I added, "And what an inexhaustible fund it is."

"Yes," he said, "I am still reshaping it. I can't use the life around me."

In this hour he opened his heart to me, showing nothing of the Englishman's reserve. He was fluent but not distinctive in speech. He had no verbal felicities. His diction was copious, but lacked the biting power of Kipling's phrases and the humorous ease of Shaw. (He is like his work in these respects. He has little humor and his words are lacking in charm.) He sounded 'd' in words which we pronounce with a 't.' He said, 'lik-edd me' instead of 'likt me.' He was a continental who spoke as a cockney, but wrote as a master of dictionary English.

He spoke of getting back to Canterbury. "I have friends coming to see me there," he said, as if this were very important. Once more he said, "I daren't stay in the city overnight. I am in pain most of the time and I feel the creeping weakness of age. I am afraid of being stricken here—in some hotel or on the street."

We fell into a description of our individual methods of work, of the disastrous effects of city life and the like. He asked about my latest book. I described it briefly and said, "I'll send you a copy." He said, "I wish I had it now. I have a few days' leisure to read." I offered to go to my flat and get a copy. He sprang up. "I'll go with you."

As he was too lame to walk, I called a taxi and in a few minutes we were entering my door. "Constance was there, and Conrad took her into his affection at once. He was ornate in his compliments, entirely European. He spoke of her typical American loveliness and was so absorbed in conversation with her that he forgot the book he had come to get. However, he made amends after reading the inscription I had put on the flyleaf. I called him 'King of the Seven Seas' and he was plainly moved thereby. It was a bit disconcerting to find him so demonstrative, and yet he impressed me as essentially noble and trustworthy—a loyal husband and father.

"He bustled away down the hall with a peculiar rolling

gait which he always shows when hurried, leaving an empty, silent place behind him. His is not an amiable personality. He is disturbing, dominant, and unaccountable. That he likes us is evident. 'You must come again to Bishopsbourne—all of you,' he vehemently declared as he left our door."

"He is (as I said in autographing my book) a son of the sea, as I am a son of the plains. All of his work is based on the observations he made as a youthful sailor. Of these he has an inexhaustible supply—a fund on which he is still drawing. 'I cannot use the life around me,' he had said. Sitting in his lovely Kentish home, he turns his gaze inward on wide, remembered waters and from these visions builds his great romances—cloudy, vague, and tragic. It is, however, a kind of self-digestion, a feeding on himself, and it is destroying him, mind and body. His isolation is psychic, a stern self-immolation. He denies himself friends, amusement, and family life in order to continue his re-creation of the life of those lonely, distant isles. This toil is telling upon his brain. But what a brain it is—what an ocean of memories it contains!"

II

My artist daughter, Constance, had manifested from childhood a keen interest in drawing and the illustrator whom she most admired was Arthur Rackham, whose highly imaginative, exquisitely drawn illustrations in her fairy books had made him a king in her world. I shared her admiration for Rackham and set about obtaining an introduction to him. Kipling told us where to find him, and one day late in August we took a bus to Primrose

Hill, near which (he had written to say) his studio was situated.

My notes read: "It is a plain little structure, a combined workroom and cottage, standing on a back street, one of a row of similar artist homes, a singularly suburban colony such as only London can provide. It held no hint of dragons, witches, willow-tree hags, gnomes, fairies, or kings of wind and water.

"He met us at the door, a small, alert, thin man, quite bald, plainly dressed, and speaking like a cultivated Bostonian. He was kindly and unassuming—almost too modest, and his studio, bare and commonplace, offered nothing to indicate the grotesquely beautiful drawings which have made him internationally famous. 'I live here only a part of each month,' he said. 'My home is in Arundel, some fifty miles south of London.'

"He apologized for the bareness of his walls. 'I am sorry, but I have almost nothing to show you. An illustrator's work gets away from him, you know,' he said, appealing to my daughter.

"He took us into his little garden and submitted to a snapshot. 'I have a daughter of my own,' he said as if in explanation of his good nature. He talked with Constance as a teacher might, advising her in matters relating to pen-and-ink illustration, and as I studied him I perceived more clearly than ever that his art was very largely subconscious—something which he had not acquired and could not convey to others. 'He is a genius,' I thought, 'one whose creative processes have little to do with the facts of their world.' "

I think my daughter gradually came to understand that the magic of this artist's pen was due to the transforming magic of his brain. At any rate, we came away with a vivid impression of the man—sincere, kindly, modest, hardly to be associated with his masterly and highly imaginative drawings.

Constance said, "I know he is the Rackham whose work I love, but I cannot realize it."

(He came to New York a few years later, bringing an exhibition of his drawings, and we saw him in the midst of them, a very happy man, for on almost every frame hung a card marked "Sold." He told us also that he had been given a very large commission for a series of magazine illustrations. We congratulated him with sincere pleasure in his success and urged him to come again. So far as I knew, he never did.)

III

At the suggestion of Brander Matthews and other of my fellow Academicians, I had written Edmund Gosse, saying, "I should like to call on you and discuss certain matters concerning the similar organizations with which we are connected."

An invitation to tea came along about the first of September and in acceptance thereof I found my way to his house. It was one of a row of spacious connected dwellings called Hanover Terrace and his windows fronted on Regent's Park. It was distinctly the home of a man of letters and reminded me of Matthews' house on West End Avenue. It was a three-story dwelling filled with books, pictures, manuscripts, and photographs, an ideally perfect literary shrine for those who value the Victorian age, the workshop of one who knew all the great ones of that pre-war period.

"He charmed me at once by the ease and dignity of his

manner. He knew Howells well, also Henry James, William James, and others of my valued friends, and we were soon deep in reminiscences of them. He has a background of culture, travel, and illustrious friendships which so many of the moderns utterly lack. He is no street scavenger. He lives an intellectual life surrounded by those who are equally interested in scholarship. He is considered a 'back number' by the Fleet Street critics, but he is a back number to which it is helpful to refer now and then.

"His home is a center, one of the chief centers of Victorian scholarship and criticism. No other man I have met so clearly represents the literature which is neither new nor old, the writing which endures. Although over seventy years of age, he holds his years well. He is not the purblind recluse. He likes company—as Stedman did —and believes in organization. While not a creative mind, he has been and still is, a critical force. He writes occasional reviews for the *Sunday Times* and for the literary magazines.

"He was greatly interested in what I told him of our Academy. He said, 'We need such a building, but, alas, we have no kindly millionaire to build it and endow it!' As I was going away he autographed for me his small autobiographical volume, in which he deals with the character of his father."

While walking across Hyde park late that afternoon, I felt once again (and more deeply than ever) the magic of green England. The sun suddenly broke its way through the clouds, flooding the gardens with warm light. The trees in their ripening luxuriance, the lawns glistening with raindrops, the riders on the "Row," the slowly moving boats on the Serpentine with the church spires showing above the noble old oaks—all these united to form a rich, deep-toned, and reposeful English scene, over which a mist hung, clothing the trees with silver and resolving every vista into delightful vagueness and mystery.

The view of Kensington Palace across the Round Pond was regal. The stairway appeared to rise from the water's edge and the dusk of evening softened the walls into beauty. Over it the clouds, vast and softly outlined, were lit with deep copper and red. The sheep feeding under the wide-spreading oaks, the boys sailing their boats, the ducks swimming about in small fleets, were all familiar to me now but touched with poetic light. It was such a moment as this which Barrie had seized upon—the hush just before the musical cry "All Out!" which denotes the closing hour. "This small Scot, of all men, has made this English scene magical and enchanting."

On September 4 I made this note: "I am working each morning on the third volume of my Middle Border chronicle which for the moment we are calling 'The Back-Trailers.' There is a certain advantage in being three thousand miles from the scene of my narrative. This is not an easy book to write, for part of it deals with New York City and the London part will run along the beaten track of English travel. All that will save it from being trite will be my contact with distinctive and interesting personalities. English landscapes, English cities, do not greatly change from year to year, but authors and artists do. I shall rough-out the early chapters and revise them in the light of my diaries after my return. Six weeks of our stay remain and they are likely to be richer in experience than any that have gone before."

CHAPTER FORTY-TWO

BERNARD SHAW AND HIS NEIGHBORS

I

ON September 23 I received a card from Shaw with the following directions in his own handwriting:

"Ayot St. Lawrence, Welwyn, Herts. Train leaves Kings Cross terminus (depot) at 11:30. Take tickets to Hatfield, which on this train is the second stop. On emerging from the station you will find somewhere about an ancient and very shabby brown car with B. S. 73 on the number plate. Three persons of reasonable girth will fit into the interior without excessive compression, and one will have to sit beside the chauffeur. The distance by car is seven miles. The old car is weatherproof except for the front sitter, who will need a mackintosh if it rains. If the weather is too bad for anything, you can cry off to another day by telephone. G. B. S."

With these very clear directions, we could not go wrong. We reached the station, identified his brown car, which did not appear shabby to us, and fifteen minutes later entered Ayot St. Lawrence, which was hardly more than a hamlet. As we were running along a pleasant, tree-shadowed lane we overtook a tall, white-haired man in gray knickerbockers who was writing, as he walked, in a small book. It was Shaw, and as we passed him he waved his hand in greeting but did not interrupt our course.

As we entered the house, a comfortable, undistinguished villa, Mrs. Shaw met us and took my wife and daughters in charge while I hastened back to her husband. He was walking along intent on his writing, and after a few words of greeting, I said, "I am curious to know what you are doing. Can you compose while walking?"

He handed to me his notebook filled with writing in small and very neat characters. He explained, "I can write shorthand as I walk along the road, or while riding in a train. I work in the open air whenever possible. In this way I combine exercise with composition. My longhand shows senile decay. My shorthand does not," he added with a laugh in his eyes.

He was looking very well, though a bit too high-colored, and I thought him an extremely handsome old man. His hand was cold, but I sensed the power and music of his voice, a noble organ. "Are you writing a play?" I asked.

He made an expressive gesture of renunciation. "No. I'm through! I shall write no more plays. I am at work just now on a preface to a new edition of my 'Perfect Wagnerite.'"

I remarked once again the Scotch-Irish quality of his speech. It was almost precisely that which the Gilfillans and McClintocks of my native Wisconsin valley used. His declaration, "I am through with plays," I did not take seriously.

His house had no special charm or distinction and there was no alluring outlook from its windows. It was, in truth, rather commonplace, not much better than my own La Crosse country home. It was comfortable, pleasantly situated, but presented nothing to indicate the presence of a world-renowned dramatist. Its interior, while well furnished and comfortable, was not noticeably literary or artistic. It offered no signs of Bernard Shaw. The reception room was dignified, but presented few books. He had no study. "He prefers to write outdoors," Mrs. Shaw stated. "He is not fussy about small things. He can write anywhere." She called him "Geebee." "We own this house, but regard it only as a refuge from London."

Shaw was at his best as he stood with his back to the mantel, delivering a vicious attack on England's system of church benefices, and emphasizing the asinine character of country curates. "You see the law of primogeniture left nothing for the younger sons but the army, the navy, or the church. As the rectories were all built for men with private incomes, real clergymen cannot maintain them. They rent them to successful literary men like me."

All of this was apropos of my visit to him in 1906, when he was living in a rectory surrounded by a charming garden. I listened with joy to his diatribe, refusing to take him seriously. His eyes sparkled with humor, and his phrases made me chuckle. He was amusing us—designedly. Delightfully witty and deliciously funny and with no malice in his assault, he expected us to laugh—and we did laugh.

Here is a good place to interpolate that no reporter is fair to Shaw who does not describe his accompanying smile, his twinkling, watchful, humorous glance, and his mocking pose. There was not a particle of rancor or cynicism in what he said of the church. He merely saw the comic side of buying a living in it, as one would buy a partnership in some genteel business. It was funny to him and he reported it in delightfully humorous phrase. He was not trying to reform an abuse; he was dissecting an amusing English social custom. He laughs while exposing absurd and stupid laws. That is his way of reforming society.

Referring back to his house, he said, "No one comes here except those we want to see. It is in effect a retreat"; and when my wife said, "Aren't you coming to America?" he instantly replied:

"Why should I? All the nice Americans come to England to see me." Here again a failure to convey his humorous glance and inflection would give a wrong impression. There was nothing egotistical in his reply. It was banter. He went on, a thought more seriously, "I've been pressed, many times, to go and now I am too old. No one wants to see men of my age."

He talked of his play, "Back to Methuselah," and said, "I had no thought of its being played as they did it in New York. My intention was to have an intermission for dinner as they do in the Passion Play at Oberammergau." He spoke of it as his last play.

I asked him how long he had been in this house. "Since 1911," he replied. Referring back to his audience in America, he said, "When writing an article I do not consider England, primarily—I address myself to the States. Many of our writers who can't lecture go to America and make their fortunes whilst I, who *can* lecture, remain at home."

He spoke of William Randolph Hearst. "I do not join in the clamor against him, because as a matter of fact he represents a good many of the causes I am advocating."

I alluded to a recent interview in which he had spoken very plainly of the situation in Ireland. He retorted, "Yes, and you noticed, perhaps, that I left Ireland immediately after giving the interview to the press." He was amusing, but less free of bitterness in speaking of America's prohibitory laws. "I have no wish to visit a country where for wearing a red necktie I can be arrested and thrown into prison."

He hesitated for a word now and then—a new development in his speech—"another sign of senile decay," he cheerfully pointed out. He was distinctly less effervescent than in 1906. Speaking of the change in his fortunes, he said, "These copyrights all over the world are a nuisance. They bring in royalty from every country, but they turn a man of letters into an accountant."

Just before luncheon, a handsome, dark-eyed young man came in and Shaw introduced him as "My neighbor, Mr. Cherry-Garrard, who was with the Scott Antarctic Expedition. He is writing a book about it."

(Shaw called him "Cherry," but I learned later that his name was Apsley Cherry-Garrard and that his family had been distinguished not only in Herts but in the city. One of his ancestors had been mayor of London. His bearing indicated an intimate friendship with Shaw, who tried to draw him out for our benefit.)

He tactfully declined to tell his story, but promised to come to dinner soon and submit to questioning. He was nearing forty, a graceful, medium-sized man whose face and form bore no traces of the hardships which Shaw hinted at when he said, "I named Cherry's book 'The Worst Journey in the World' "; on the contrary he appeared too young to have been in Scott's ship.

At the dining table I observed that Shaw ate only eggs, vegetables, nut sandwiches, and fruit. His wife, beside whom I sat, told me that he did not smoke. "He does not drink tea, coffee, or wine of any kind, and he wears a knickerbocker suit habitually," she said. "He is always writing. If he gets cold while working indoors, he walks out along the roads, writing as he goes along."

She did not touch on the matter of evening dress, but Cherry-Garrard said, "The only time I ever knew him to wear even a dinner jacket was at a prize fight." His shoes, I noticed, were sturdy brogans with a flap over the instep. He is a Dublin man, but Scotch in his long body, fair complexion, and blue eyes.

His attitude toward my wife and daughters was understanding as well as kind. His wife said to me, "He is really a shy man; but he has quite opened his heart to your wife and daughters."

The more I considered this home—just an ordinary village rectory seven miles from Hatfield, Shaw's tall figure coming and going along these lanes, busy with his shorthand composition—the more amazing it all seemed. "His house is not as handsome as that of W. W. Jacobs; it is not much better than that of John Masefield, and is equally devoid of literary or historic associations. His London apartment on Adelphi Terrace is understandable, but this cottage is not like him.

"He has no children and so far as I know has no desire to perpetuate his kind. He is facing decay and with relentless honesty acknowledges it. Like Hewlett, Doyle,

Conrad, and Hardy he is soon to leave the stage. But he will go with a jest and a smile. He hates to die—as we all do—but he considers complaint foolish."

His wife told me that he had just written the preface for a book on prison reform, a volume made up of writings by men and women who had been jailed as "conscientious objectors," but that it had been returned to him. "The editors did not like some of the things he had written. It happened, however, that our friends the Sidney Webbs were bringing out a somewhat similar book and so it will appear there."

This led Shaw to speak at some length of an article he had written for *The Manchester Guardian,* one which they had declined to publish. He touched on his correspondence. "I like particularly those people who keep my small checks and frame them. They have the autographs and I have the undisturbed funds in the bank—and so we are all happy. Not all my letters are from admirers. I wrote to one American paper, a Southern paper, saying, 'I decline to go to a country where my wife may at any moment be tarred and feathered.' This brought out a long letter from a Texas woman who said, 'The account of that lynching was exaggerated. The woman was not a lady; she was only a chambermaid, and she was on the balcony where she had no business to be. In fact she was a person of bad character and besides they only poured tar on her head and took her to the edge of town and told her not to come back.' "

This amused Shaw and he emphasized the word "only" with a wicked glint in his eyes. There was nothing for me to say. Our papers at the time were filled with somewhat similar items.

He spoke of his early work as a musical critic and ranged himself on the side of the younger experimenters. He commended Goossens, Bax, and Ireland. "They are adding something new to music. They are writing scores which seem 'crazy,' just as Wagner's compositions at one time did. Your MacDowell did concertos and sonatas well, but he created no new forms." In speaking of one of these modernistic composers, he said, "When I began to play one of his pieces I considered it in the key of A, but it passed into the key of D. Then I discovered that the treble was written in the key of A and the bass in D; and that each hand was supposed to keep to its own key, with sharps and flats coming in anywhere that the composer found them necessary to his meaning."

To this I added, "These men are the cubists and vorticists of music," and he agreed, "Why not?" Then he remarked, "These revolutionary musicians are all Irish or Welsh."

Later he said, "Certain people in America regard me as a kind of god," and his eyes shone with laughter, as if such adoration was incredibly ludicrous; and so it was, seen from the center of his modest home.

"And yet," my written comment reads, "this intellectual worship has its fine side. It is genuine. It is not self-seeking. It springs from the feeling that he is, in many ways, and in a large way, their spokesman. His fearlessness, his frank contempt for certain conventions, and his essentially wholesome outlook on life and art make him a leader. Then, too, his aloofness adds to the charm of his personality. He wears the nimbus of the distant prophet.

"His wife assured me that he never frets over small

things. 'He is so filled with his writing that he doesn't know what is going on around him. He was very unhappy during the war, and as many of our most intimate friends turned against us, we spent a good deal of time out here—but we did not escape the war. An aircraft gun was planted in our yard. Galsworthy remained friendly and so did Barrie. They lunched with Geebee frequently. But Kipling we never saw.' "

In speaking of accent and differences in the use of words, Shaw banteringly said, "In a century or so it will be quite impossible for us to understand one another, and we shall have teachers of the American language just as we now have instructors in French and German." He used the phrase "American language" with comical intent.

From Cherry-Garrard I received confirmation of all my impressions of Shaw. "He's a good neighbor. We all like him. He is genial with everybody."

As he said this I recalled the action of Henry James, who, as he went about Rye with me, smilingly returned the greetings of postmen, grocery boys, and shopkeepers.

Cherry-Garrard said, "No one could have been kinder to a young author than Shaw has been to me. He read my long manuscript with care and encouraged me to finish and publish it. He named it for me and is writing about it to all his friends. I took him to a prize fight once. The tickets cost me twenty pounds. When he found this out he called me on the phone. 'Did you pay twenty guineas for those tickets?' I admitted that I did. 'Very well,' he said, 'I'll write an article and pay for them'— and this he did."

This luncheon with Shaw deepened my understanding

of him as a citizen and increased my liking for him. To find him a genial neighbor and a lover of the countryside was not so much a discovery as a confirmation, for in all our talks I had never heard him utter an unkind or petulant word. His harshest criticisms were spoken without bitterness. Sharply as I disagreed with his judgments at times, I had no feeling of resentment. I did not even try to argue with him. I enjoyed his critical comment on any subject.

Notwithstanding the pleasure I took in his table talk, I was not quite content. I had enjoyed his gay harangues, but I had found little time for an exchange of ideas; and when in parting he said, "You must come out again," I replied, "Do you walk?"

"I walk every day. Come out some afternoon and I'll show you the countryside."

II

"September 30. As our stay in London is almost at an end, I decided to take my walk with Shaw to-day. At the station I asked for a ticket to 'Wheat-hamp-stead' but the ticket seller said, 'You mean Weet'mste'd,' and I let it go at that. This village was only a few miles from Shaw's place and I had planned to visit 'Lamer Park,' Cherry-Garrard's home, as I walked across.

"From Wheathampstead, a little town—some of which is a thousand years old—I took my way on foot up through a huge park belonging to the Cherry-Garrard family, and as I rose I came into a richly typical English landscape. On a smoothly undulating lawn, great oaks, centuries old, spread their majestic arms. Over their tops whirled clouds of rooks. Beyond stood the mansion, a huge, plain, square building. It was as if I were walking into the foreground of an illustration for a novel by Trollope.

"The house appeared deserted. Its windows were shuttered. No smoke rose from its chimneys, but as I approached I detected a solitary figure seated on a bench beside the front door—like a patient in a sanitarium sunning himself for an hour. Superbly set as the mansion was, it suggested loneliness and decay—a condition which the war had brought about."

The man on the bench was the heir and owner of this country seat, Apsley Cherry-Garrard, whose forbears had been mayors of London, and who was the last of his line.

"As he ushered me into his great library, the silence of the room, the absence of attendants, the hushed gloom of the entire house chilled me, depressed me. In some ways it was up to date. It was flecklessly clean and heated and lighted by electricity made on the place, but to me it was a melancholy home. Here in the splendid dining room, a single chair, placed at the end of a long table, was evidence of the owner's solitary luncheon."

He showed me the manuscript of the book which Shaw had named "The Worst Journey in the World" and for which he was writing an introduction. It was a large manuscript and Cherry (as Shaw called him) said that it would make two octavo volumes, and as he said this I wondered if he would succeed in finding a publisher for a story written so long after the date of the expedition.

(This manuscript was published in two volumes under the title, Shaw's title, "The Worst Journey in the World," and I had the pleasure of reading it and writing about it. It is a vivid account of Scott's expedition so far as a subordinate member of the crew could record it, and describes the particular journey which gave the book its title, an expedition undertaken by the writer and a scientist named Wilson, in the cold and darkness of the long midnight in search of the breeding grounds of the emperor penguins. It is an incredible tale of hardship: they froze, they starved, they toiled till they slept on their feet as they pushed and pulled their sledge across the icy, wind-swept, sunless table-lands. They got back to the base camp, but they were walking skeletons when they staggered into the light of the mess hall.

(They had three eggs to show for all their suffering, and Cherry-Garrard ends the book with a quietly ironic note. The director of the natural history museum to whom he presented these eggs in person treated him like an errand boy and did not even thank him!)

After a look about the house, Cherry took me out into the spacious garden, where against high walls fruit trees were spread to get the sunlight; and finally showed me a large room (at the back of the house) which he had turned into an electrical plant. "I cannot afford to hire servants," he explained, "and so I am bringing invention to bear on the housekeeping problem. As the eldest son the estate has fallen to me and I must keep it in repair."

Knowing that I was due at Shaw's house, Cherry volunteered to walk across the fields with me. On the way we talked of his famous neighbor.

"Shaw was out as we entered, but soon came in, looking

very 'nifty' in a light-gray reefer jacket, knee-breeches, and leather puttees.

"While we drank our tea he monologued; first on one subject, then on another—pleasantly, wittily, with an occasional humorous slam-bang paradox. He was tolerant of Mrs. Shaw's interruptions and protests, turning a kindly and patient glance in her direction—for a moment—then proceeded on his way.

"He said to me, 'What do you mean by the Middle Border? Do you mean the line between Canada and Wisconsin?'

"In answering these questions I quoted Augustus Thomas, who said, 'The Middle Border—why, the Middle Border is wherever Hamlin Garland is.' In a sense it does not exist and never did. It was but a vaguely defined region even in my boyhood. It was the line drawn by the plow and, broadly speaking, ran parallel to the upper Mississippi when I was a lad. It lay between the land of the hunter and the harvester.

"This answer seemed to satisfy him and he passed to another subject. 'Can you tell me how you produce and elect so many granitic, imposing public men who haven't an idea in their heads? Most of your Presidents have been of Harding's type, good-looking men of commonplace character.'

"To this I retorted, 'You wouldn't call Theodore Roosevelt commonplace?' This set him off on a long tirade against Roosevelt as a meat-eater, a hunter, and an imperialist. Seeing that I was quite unmoved by his attack he paused suddenly and said in pacific tone, 'You knew him, you admired him. Why?'

"This gave me my inning. I packed into five or ten

minutes all I could recall of Roosevelt's many-sided activities; and when I had finished he remarked meditatively, 'You have given me a new concept of the man.' "
(He had said his say and was tolerant of my defence. In this mood he was wholly admirable and winning.)

He walked with me to the station, and on the way conversed quietly, genially, allowing me full time for rebuttal of the criticisms he made. He was genially companionable, and a surprisingly good listener when interested. (His monologuing, like that of Roosevelt, arises out of the fact that he is absorbingly interesting and no one cares to interrupt him. By sitting open-eared we force him to talk.)

He spoke freely of his war experiences. "I was accused of being a traitor and pro-German; but the English authorities knew all the time what I was doing. Although there was much clamor against me I was not once molested. I wrote pamphlets for the government, papers which were scattered in Morocco, Ireland, and other places to counteract the revolutionary work of enemies there." He made it plain that at the very hour when his fellow citizens were calling for his arrest, he was doing official work. The authorities protected him for this purpose.

He inveighed against "military frontiers." He said, "Such lines are absurd. They cannot hold. Nothing but racial lines can be defended. All those lines drawn by alien 'experts' will be overrun and prove sources of irritation."

I clasped his hand at parting with a deepening sense of the changes which sixteen years had brought about. "His war utterances alienated many thousands of his admirers, and while their judgments have softened, they are still resentful. His loyalty is still questioned and his social theories rejected. It is hard to avoid the conviction that in many cases he is right; and yet his statements continue to shock the English people. Ten years from now most of his article on 'Common Sense About the War' will be accepted by us all. He was right. We *must* live in the same world with the Germans; they cannot be annihilated."

(Many of Shaw's predictions have since been realized. German music, German literature and German art have their place in America as well as in England. War hatreds are dying out. Germany cannot be destroyed; its people are still neighbors of the English and must continue to be so regarded.)

CHAPTER FORTY-THREE

BARRIE COMES TO DINNER

I

BARRIE had been out of the city for six weeks or more, and as we began to see the end of our vacation in the falling leaves and shortening days, I began to fear that I might not see "the Laird of Kensington" again. We had exchanged notes concerning a dinner engagement, and I had said, "Whenever you are in town, let us know. Your convenience is ours."

On September 27, the long-expected note arrived:

"My dear Garland, would it suit you if I came to dinner to-morrow (Wednesday)? I want to see you all. If not we must meet some other day. You might ring me up and tell them here—and the time, if it fits in. I only got back the other day." In a postscript he added, "I feel now the America of your book better than the America I have visited."

In a flutter of excitement, my daughter phoned his secretary to say that we would be most happy to receive Sir James at seven.

(Having treated of this important event at some length in "Back-Trailers from the Middle Border," I hesitated about including it in this volume, but my advisers all declared that it could not be left out, and so with its literary significance emphasized, I take it from my notebooks, trusting that those who chanced to read "The Back-Trailers" will for a moment forget the earlier version and consider this an ineludable part of my English records.)

"September 28. Barrie came to dinner last night, and as the other guests left early we had him to ourselves from nine till after midnight. He talked as I had never heard him talk before, in quiet monotone, deep-sunk in an easy chair, smoking meanwhile a long cigar. As the ash grew on the end of his cigar he handled it with tender care—'bragging,' he called it, taking a boyish satisfaction in seeing how long he could keep it from falling.

"I think he felt in us a definite kinship, for he spoke with the freedom of a man at the fireside of an American. My daughters sat at his feet, quite literally, on cushions, asking innumerable questions, none of which he seemed to resent. He told them what he did and how he felt when the Queen came to have tea with him. He confessed that the King had sent him a key to Kensington Gardens. 'I am the only civilian who can go in or out at will. Occasionally I go in on moonlit nights to see the fairies. They know I am their friend, and sometimes I let mortals out, those who have found themselves locked in.'

"I thrust in a question. 'What are those cries which I hear very early in the morning? They are somewhat like the "All out" warnings at night, but I can never quite distinguish the words.'

"With a look which was at once humorous and tender, he replied, 'That is I, going about warning the fairies of the incoming mortals.'

"When my wife spoke of our home in Onteora and of Maude Adams' secluded home there he said, 'I visited Onteora once with Frohman, but I was there only one night. All I can remember is riding through an interminable forest.' I then recalled an interview which the New York papers printed at the time, and a gleam of fun came into his face. 'Yes, I was besieged by reporters. I told them all to meet me at my hotel the following morning and that I would give them an interview—and so I did. I rose early, wrote out the interview myself, left it with the clerk, and fled!'

"He described his first meeting with Maude Adams. 'She was playing in "Rosemary" and instantly convinced me that she was the girl for Babbie in "The Little Minister," and so I named her to my manager.'

"In answer to my daughter's question, he replied, 'I am not doing anything just now—I am "resting" as the player folk say. I have lost interest in "Shall We Join the Ladies?" I doubt if I ever finish it.'

"My wife asked, 'Is Thrums your native village?'

" 'Yes, but its real name is Kirriemuir. The conditions which I described in all my early books were those surrounding my father and mother—customs which were just passing when I was a lad. Some of the cottages still maintained hand looms, as I described them. I have not put much of my own family into my novels. My mother, who died before my father, I sketched in "Margaret Ogilvy." My experience in Edinburgh and in London went into my work—I couldn't keep them out, and something of my boyhood is in "Tommy." '

"One of the girls recalled the passage which described Margaret Ogilvy counting the words of an article to see that her son was paid for every word, and with a smile he replied, 'That is true. She did just that.'

"He admitted that among all his plays he particularly liked 'Mary Rose,' 'Dear Brutus,' and 'The Admirable Crichton.' Of this last play he said, 'I wrote the last act first.' Of 'What Every Woman Knows' he said, 'I liked the first act, but though I worked hard on the second act, it never pleased me. I wrote the first act in two days, but spent two months on the last act—and at that, it was bad. When I am interested I work fast; when I am not, writing is hard labor.'

"For the most part his face expressed only a reflective sadness, but now and again he uttered a droll phrase which made my daughters laugh. He was entirely frank with them. His life had been so like mine, in its broad phases, that they accepted him as a kind of literary Scotch uncle. His Kirriemuir was my West Salem, his Edinburgh my Boston, his London my New York. While recognizing his immensely greater success, they perceived our essential kinship. I, too, was Scotch—poetic and musical by way of my mother's family, the McClintocks.

"In spite of his occasional flashes of humor and his evident liking for my daughters, he impressed me as a sad and lonely man. I thought, 'He is without wife or child, an aging man like myself. He, too, is letting go. He may do more work and good work, but it will not come out of joyous labor—it will come hard.'

"My daughters were proud of the fact that he stayed on till after midnight, but I became a bit worried for fear that the taxis would all have left our neighborhood. I went down in the lift with him and out to the corner, where luckily we found a cab waiting. As he was about to enter the car he said, 'Let me have your telephone number.' I gave it, and waited while he put it down in his little book. When I reported this action to my daughters they exclaimed joyously, 'That means luncheon or tea. Now we shall see his house!' "

II

This luncheon did not come till just before our sailing date, but I include the entry here. "Barrie met us suffering from a severe cold and we were troubled by the consciousness that he had risen from a sick bed to entertain us. This conviction shortened our stay. He coughed distressingly all through luncheon, but grew a little better as we went back to his fire.

"He did his best to put my daughters at ease concerning him, refusing to admit that his 'hoast' (as he called his cough) was serious. He showed them a manuscript volume, a kind of Swiss Family Robinson story of a trip with his adopted sons. He talked about his boys as he showed the many snap shots which illustrated the chronicle of the expedition. 'One of these lads was killed in the war and another was drowned while swimming,' he said, and his voice faltered as he spoke of them. These pictures spoke eloquently of the comradeship which had existed between him and his boys. He was in each group, a participant in all the sports and a leader in all the heroic games.

"He showed us also a picture of his boyhood home, a tiny cottage, with his father standing at the gate (a sturdy, round-faced man in workingman's clothing who looked more English than Scotch), and he spoke of his sister-in-law as still living in this cottage. It was a humble home, incredibly humble as I considered the honor and wealth which our host had won.

"He showed us a photograph of the Queen on which she had written her name, and my daughters were quite awed by this autograph. His life was to them a fairy story, of which this visit of the Queen was a glorious climax.

We came away deeply concerned about his condition, but a few days later we were reassured by a note from him. I have recorded this luncheon for the reason that it shows the essential kindness of the man. He could very justly have called the luncheon off, but he knew how deeply disappointed my daughters would have been and so went through a meal which he could not share and did his heroic best to interest us all. I never think of it without a feeling of admiration for his courage and a sense of gratitude for his consideration. My girls would have been broken-hearted by a postponement of this visit, for the end of our vacation was near.

III

Earlier in the summer Arnold Bennett had invited me to visit him on his yacht at Southampton, but I had not been able to accept. I wrote asking him to dine with us. Our sailing date was but ten days away when a third letter came from him dated September 29 at his city home in Hanover Square.

"I've been yachting and address-less, but have now come back to town and got your letter. I particularly want to see and hear you and to make the acquaintance of your wife and daughters, *but* I never go out for lunch (for creative reasons) and I don't often dine out. Moreover it is proper, this being in London, that you and your family should come and dine with me. What about Tuesday next, third of October, at eight? Tell me with how many daughters you have enhonored the world. You cannot, I regret to say, meet my wife here, as she is not living with me now. I live alone in the strictest respectability—as always!"

For some reason which I failed to set down, we were unable to dine with him on the date suggested, but we accepted his invitation to tea on October the ninth. Hanover Street is just off the roaring, rushing maelstrom called Piccadilly Circus and as we went exploring this region in search of his door, it seemed quite impossible that we should find it in that maze of narrow streets. I began to wonder if we had not taken the wrong Hanover Street, but we were reassured when the number we sought indicated a large and rather somber house —not an apartment. There was a little square opposite presenting a singularly quiet eddy of the city's flood tide.

"Bennett met us in his spacious drawing-room, a prosperous, genial figure. He was grayer and stouter than when in America, but he had lost nothing of his kindly humor. He was as loquacious in his way as Conrad and almost as gallant. He paid my daughters many compliments and amused them by his sallies and abrupt changes in tone. He asked surprising questions, seeking to disconcert them, studying them all the while, I suspect, as possible material. We all enjoyed his humor. No awkward pauses came while we were there.

"The house was filled with interesting books and pictures, and was designedly Victorian in every detail. The

dining room, which he showed us with pride, was especially pleasing to us, for it was furnished with a huge wal-
nut sideboard, and the silver, the dishes, the chairs were of
1870. 'We have all laughed at the furniture of our grandfather's day,' he said, 'but as these pieces are related
to my childhood, I now find them quaintly charming.'
And so they were. The completeness of the setting was
like that of a stage, arranged by a careful manager, solidly
dignified, richly toned, and harmonious. It was a deeply
satisfying arrangement.

"With a note of humorous pride in his voice, he called
our attention to each feature. 'I have them all, you see,
even the glass dome enclosing a bouquet of wax flowers.
All the things which my grandmother loved are here.
Others of them came from the homes of my relations.
I rejoice in these furnishings. They offer something which
French decoration cannot give me. They create in me
a sense of solidarity with my ancestors.'

"I liked this loyalty to his grandparents and said so.
'We have something analogous to it in America, but we
have only recently come to value it. After all, associations do count.' "

He was admirable in this setting. It was the proper environment for the author of "The Old Wives' Tale,"
"Clayhanger," and "Milestones."

We did not talk much of books, for he was set upon
amusing my daughters. He turned to them, leaving me
free to walk about the room and to examine the books
and pictures. "In its own way his home is as harmonious
with the quality of his books as Hewlett's old rectory
was to his stories of the feudal age. It is a prosperous
middle-class home of 'the Five Towns' set down within

sound of the swarming myriads of Soho Square and Piccadilly Circus."

(Since I began this chapter, Arnold Bennett has laid down his busy pen and critics are now concerned with his place in English fiction. His output is enormous in bulk. Most of his books are inordinately long and the modern reader finds them "slow"—which in truth they are; but in the best of them, the earlier of them, he recorded the growth of an English manufacturing region, and the life of an era undisturbed by war. It is probable that "The Old Wives' Tale" will remain his most accepted work. It is a pleasure to remember him as our host that afternoon.)

CHAPTER FORTY–FOUR
CONRAD, OXFORD, AND MASEFIELD

I

ONE afternoon Maurice Hewlett came in to tea and chatted for an hour.

"He was looking gray and thin and sad, but in the glow of my daughters' interest, became quite animated.

"In all that he said he was the scholar, the student, the thinker." (I never saw him again. He died the following year.)

In making a final call on Wickham Steed one afternoon, I found five or six European journalists assembled. The talk at first was all about the Turkish situation, but finally they fell to discussion of Lord Northcliffe's death and stories were told wherein he was described as an incessant talker and a man of tireless energy. "He was not a profound thinker," said one of the men. "He was neither philosopher nor statesman but he was an enormous force during the war." As they talked I felt once again the dangerous power which such an individual, owner of a daily newspaper, wields. That Northcliffe used his power patriotically, no one appears to doubt.

Joining Wymark Jacobs and his family at the theater the following day, I saw a film version of his story "The Skipper's Wooing."

"It was a pale little drama with pretty moments in it.

531

As we were waiting, Jacobs told me another story of Joseph Conrad's hot-blooded youth. It seems that he had a controversy with a Frenchman who was a deadly pistol shot. A friend said to him, 'Your only hope is to hit your enemy first. Fire instantly on the signal.' Conrad did so and cut a finger from his opponent's right hand. 'The Frenchman was as game as one of your Western desperadoes,' said Jacobs. 'Taking the pistol in his left hand, he fired. His bullet hit Conrad in the side. It struck a rib, glanced out and did no serious damage. This satisfied both parties and ended the war.' "

"Conrad must have been a regular fighting cock in those days," I said.

"According to all accounts he was just that," replied Jacobs.

Jacobs was very amusing also in his description of America as the happy hunting ground of English lecturers. "Men we never hear of in London go to the States and bring back a pot of money. I can not understand your public. It must be very gullible."

"Not many are deceived," I assured him. "Americans are easily bored."

As I rode down to the city, October 2, I met my first London fog. It was not a thick murk, but a luminous haze in which the Strand's ugly buildings were glorified. The roofs vanished in thunderous, vague vistas suggesting a conflagration. The spires and towers were transformed into airy, pale-blue masses against a cloudless, straw-colored sky. The Law Courts loomed like Oriental palaces, and the walls and sculptures of St. Paul's were clothed in delicate beauty. Commonplace figures on cornices and façades soared like appealing angels in the vague heavens. All of London's drab ugliness was transmuted into something mysterious and enchanting, and yet no one else appeared aware of this glorious transformation. The hurrying throngs of shopkeepers and bankers, to all appearance, remained oblivious.

The cause of this poetic effect was prosaic. From a million chimneys the smoke of a million fires held down by the heavy upper air was hanging over the house tops.

On the 4th Joseph Conrad and his wife came to lunch. "All the way from Canterbury," he said, "not to see you but to see your wife and daughters." He was very voluble, very gallant, very French in conversation—much less the Englishman than at any other of our meetings.

"He seemed to enjoy his luncheon. He was very gay and, for the moment, carefree, but his wife told me that he is not at all well. He has lost confidence in the future. He no longer trusts the sturdy frame which has weathered so many storms. He spoke freely of his books. He told again of the inception of his first story, 'Almayer's Folly,' and described his honeymoon on an island off the Breton coast. When I repeated the story of his savage saber duel with another youth in the dark hold of a vessel, he refused to confirm or deny it. He laughed and replied, 'It is not easy to recall those days. Forty-five years is a long time ago.' That he was capable of just such a dare-devil encounter I was assured.

"He was quite ready to talk of his literary struggles. 'My early books were all failures. Each one proved a "frost." But at last my volume of short stories "Between Land and Sea" succeeded so notably that Harper & Bros. took me up. They paid me very well, too, but I had no wide reading till Munsey paid me six thousand dollars

for the magazine rights of "Victory." I have never had
a genuine success. We lived for years in a six-room cottage in Kent. I came to England first when I was nineteen. I loved it, and have counted myself a man of Kent
for many years. America I have never seen. In all my
years of sailing I never entered New York harbor, but
I hope to see it next year. As a mariner, my trade was
all Southern, never with the United States.'

"He was fairly loquacious and was aware of it. 'I go
out so little and I so seldom have an audience like this,'
he indicated my daughters, 'that I can not control my
tongue. Then, too, I have the *habit* of speech—my wife is
the silent one—one of us must be the *pooblic*,' he added
with a self-derisive gleam in his eyes. 'I hardly ever go
out to dinner or luncheon. Strangers bore me, I don't
know what to say to them. My sons are not literary—
they are much more interested in mechanics—and so,
when such an opportunity as this comes, I am disposed to
make the most of it.' This was as near as he came to
humor. He is never comic.

"His wife, a sweet, sunny-dispositioned soul, said little.
I can imagine her remaining calm while he rages. He is
a fiery little man even now. What must he have been
forty years ago! That he was quick to take offence, that
he was warm-hearted and impulsive—and dangerous, I
can well believe.

"We got on well. He does not disconcert me as Shaw
does. Shaw is so ready, so swift, so keenly observant, and
so mercilessly critical. He writes and speaks of what he
sees; Conrad, of what he remembers. All Conrad's books
are based on his experiences as a sailor. He works his seas
as Harte worked his mines.

"Strange to say, he moves me to pity. He is old, ill, and apprehensive. Like all my literary English friends, he is contemplating the end. He hates growing old as I do. Whether he is mistaken about his cardiac weakness or not, I take pleasure in thinking of him as going back to his comfortable home, with an assured income. So much he has won fairly after years of painful effort with his pen." (He was justified in his care of himself. His heart was seriously affected. He died the following summer.)

II

"October 6. I begin to feel the depression of an English autumn. At eight this morning it was still dark. At nine I was unable to read without a lamp. I perceive that I shall rejoice in the sunlight of New York City. Here men are resigned to gloom. If I had no hope of escape from it I should also make the most of dinners in chilly dining rooms, walks beneath dripping skies, and working under almost continuous electric light. How English literature has been able to develop so much variety, cheer, romance in such a climate is a mystery. In their gloomy churches, their clammy castles, along their bleak lanes, and beneath their sodden thatches, English poets and dramatists have wrought heroically. Undismayed by London's ramshackle ugliness, her fogs, her poverty, her turbid, murky rivers, Dickens kindled crackling fires in humble chimneys and set innumerable kettles boiling. He made fireside cheer a duty. I never before realized how far north London is. It is like Labrador with its long winter nights.

"St. John Ervine and his wife came to dinner. He is a handsome, vigorous, North-of-Ireland man and she a Devonshire lass. We liked them both. They are alert and

up to date without taint of bohemian cheapness and vulgarity. By direct questioning I drew out the story of his
war experiences. He described the loss of his leg while in
the trenches. 'I said, "Thank God! This ends lice, mud,
rats, and bursting shells for me. I have had my fill of
war!" and all the fellows felt precisely as I did about
it but dared not admit it.'

"His descriptions of his confused hospital life made us
laugh, but his little wife did not smile. 'It was a ghastly
time for me,' she said, 'and yet,' she went on to admit,
'many Englishwomen, like myself, took a strange pleasure
in war work. We lived in a mood of exaltation which
turned small pleasures into great joys. We had compensations, just as the men did, diversions which enabled us
to live and laugh and work.'

"Ervine is a powerful young fellow, but not at all like
his plays, which are gloomy. His face at times reminds
me of Francis Hackett—keen, tense, smiling. He has a
candid glance and a boyish ingenuousness which quite
won me."

III

Our friend the maharajah had written once or twice to
say that he was expecting us to come again and bring
our daughters. "Come prepared to spend the night," he
repeated, and at last we agreed upon a time. Early in the
forenoon of October 7—a week before our sailing date—
his great car with its coroneted radiator cap came to our
door, much to the delight of our daughters, and took us
all to Oxford by way of Runnymede, Windsor, and
Eton—a glorious panorama of English landscape and
village life.

"Opposite Magna Charta Island, I stopped the car and alighted in order that my feet should touch this storied ground. All I saw, in truth, was a pleasant meadow with a slow stream pulsing through it. Nothing—nothing indicated the history of this spot. The waves of humankind which had washed over these low banks had left no more trace than the grass. I could not visualize it as a battle ground."

In spite of all I had said, my daughters were disappointed to find the maharajah's "castle" an ordinary village home, and the simplicity of his dress and manners was equally disappointing, but they were impressed by the ceremony with which he and his son were treated. All of his family rose when he entered and remained standing till he was seated—a rule which we frequently forgot, I regret to say.

My daughters were also deeply interested in the princess and her small son, who was brought in for them to see, and it was while playing with the child on the floor by the fire that they omitted to rise when the maharajah reentered the room.

This led my wife to say, "What would you do if we neglected these courtesies while in your own country?"

"I should order your immediate decapitation," he smilingly replied.

I was quite touched by the presence of a set of my books, which he had ordered specially bound for his library in India, and I gladly autographed them for him. "They will present a very strange new world to you," I said.

"It is a world which I long to see," was his reply.

Not having room for us in his house, he made us guests

at the hotel, and that night he and his entire official family came down to dine with us in a private dining room. He was handsome in his tuxedo suit and yellow turban lit by a resplendent jewel, and his counselor, Pundit Schrankow, came in a gorgeous robe (his official dress), and the little princess and her attendants wore native gowns with veils looping from their heads to their shoulders. My wife and daughters had put on their prettiest dresses and I was in full uniform. Altogether we created a sensation among the guests and employees of the hotel.

The dinner was not distinctive in any other way and passed off quietly and pleasantly. The talk was on India and America naturally, and our host again urged us to visit his small kingdom. He told us of the library which he was collecting and asked me to name the American authors whom I considered most representative of modern American literature.

At last we rose and at the suggestion of the maharajah stepped out into the street to see the moonlight. "It is a most unusual union of mild air and brilliant moonlight," he said. "Let us walk out and see Oxford under these fortunate conditions."

It must have been nearly ten o'clock as we set forth, bareheaded and in our dinner clothes, the maharajah leading the way with Mrs. Garland. No one was abroad and part of the time we walked in the middle of the street, stopping whenever a particularly beautiful combination of tower and roof line caught our eyes. At times we filed through dark, narrow lanes in order that some garden vista or quadrangle might be seen magically illumined. Surely this was an amazing expedition. Our royal guide, who knew and loved every angle of the college walls, was a noble expositor. What family of Western Americans ever saw Oxford under such a leader, beneath such a moon? It was an incredible yet unforgettable hour.

Early on the following day (October 8) the maharajah (who particularly wished to meet Masefield), his son, my daughters, and I drove to the poet's home at Boar's Hill.

"Self-contained as he was, I could see that he was surprised and embarrassed by this invasion of an American family led by an East Indian potentate, although I had telephoned the number of my party. After some general conversation he drew me aside, 'Come out and see my garden,' he said, and I, hearing in this the promise of a private conversation, followed him along a path which led through bracken standing as high as my shoulders while he explained that this was a part of his estate, a section of the primeval landscape."

This path led to the door of his workshop, a mere box standing on the edge of the hill, a tiny, unheated, littered shack, not unlike the one I had built on my Dakota claim in 1881.

"This is my refuge," he said. "No one comes here uninvited." And as he spoke I was reminded of John Burroughs and his bark pavilion.

On a small workbench at one end of this flimsy workshop stood a block of wood which had already taken shape as the hull of a ship. "This," said Masefield, "is my diversion. I carve these boats for my friends. I built a three-master for Thomas Hardy and after rigging it completely, sent it to him at Max Gate. He wrote me that he loved it and that he displays it on his mantelpiece."

In this handicraft the sailor poet was able to reënjoy some part of his life as a sailor—something which his verse could not express. I saw other signs of this love of ships, but something pathetic came to me in the fact that he was forced to write sea songs in a graceless shack far removed from the sight of waves or the sound of the surf.

Leaving the cabin, we wandered down across the lower end of his plot which consisted of several acres of hill, mostly covered with gorse and bracken. He showed me his vegetable garden, his chickens, his two pigs, and his small car.

To break a silence I said, "I suppose you do all the weeding of your garden yourself?"

With humorous inflection he replied, "No, I am content to take my exercise in other ways—running a car, for instance."

He was altogether charming, sincere, and dignified, with the face of a poet and the tone and bearing of a cultivated man. He told me that he had been led to settle here by the advantages which the university offered.

"Are you connected with it?" I asked.

"No. I was given a degree last June, but I am not connected with any of the colleges—not in any official capacity. Occasionally I speak for some society, however."

He told us that he was born in Ledbury, a town not far away, and that his father was a lawyer in that town. "My home for many years," he said, "was in a very old house with a moat. I sold it, however, to purchase this one. I had many friends in Oxford and I also wanted access to the books which I needed in writing some of my plays and poems."

In all his talk he ignored the two East Indian nobles, and I could not be sure that this was not a racial prejudice.

As I was responsible for bringing them, I was uncomfortable in this situation and hastened my departure.

Masefield went with us to the car, and as he stood talking with us I observed a striking likeness between him and our chauffeur. They were of the same type physically, their accent was the same, and their voices were of precisely the same rich throaty quality. On our way up the driver had said to me, "I think I have met Mr. Masefield," and now as he stood beside the poet, recalling that meeting, they were like twin brothers. Nothing was said about this amazing resemblance, and as I did not see Masefield again, the mystery remains unsolved.

CHAPTER FORTY–FIVE

IN CONCLUSION

FOUR days before our sailing date, Sir Arthur and Lady Conan Doyle came to luncheon. Hearty, wholesome, joyous, and sane, Doyle was in sharp contrast to Hewlett, whose vogue had passed, and to Masefield, who dealt in a commodity for which there was small demand.

He said, "I am eager to see American beauty spots when I go West again, and you are the man to name the places I should show to my children. You know the West as no other man of my acquaintance knows it."

With this request for information I complied and for an hour we talked of rivers, mountain ranges, camps, trails, waterfalls, cañons, and red men and cowboys. I said, "We have no ruins to show except those of the cliff-dwellings, but Colorado and Wyoming can offer snow peaks and rivers running white with speed."

No one listening would have considered either of us in the slightest degree a man of the séance room. He was an athlete, an outdoor man, and so was I in my degree— and a horseman besides.

"October 13. This has been a busy day. Closing up accounts and receiving friends filled every hour. We took one last turn in the park which was very beautiful in the autumn mist. Late in the day Milne came to call. He seemed to enjoy our fire, while my daughters talked of his coming to New York. His gayety, his enthusiasm, his wholesomeness delighted them. Constance said, 'He is next to Barrie.' Just before going he unloaded from his pocket a dozen snap shots of his little son and I liked him all the better for this display of paternal pride. As husband and father he is candidly normal.

"That night as we were sitting before our fire, realizing with a pang of regret that in a few hours we would be on the sea and headed for home, some one rang our bell. It was a messenger with two packages addressed to my daughters. They looked like five-pound boxes of candy, and such indeed they were, and in each was a card, 'With the compliments of James M. Barrie.'

"It was a lovely thought on Barrie's part, one which my daughters will remember all their lives. He has given us just the right ending for the story of our joyous summer in England and of our many walks in Kensington Gardens."

POSTSCRIPT

"At sea, October 14. We rose early this morning in our Kensington home. At nine my wife and daughters went their way to Tilbury Dock and I to Euston Station and Liverpool. It was a glorious morning. London put forth her best graces to detain us, but we were eager to sail. I am writing this in the library of a fine new steamship bound for Montreal with every promise of a smooth and swift passage. The people on the boat are nearly all Canadians and I catch already the spirit of the New World.

"In looking back on my residence in London, I have no regrets for the extravagance of it. I am richer and stronger than when I came. I know now the kind of men Conrad and Milne and Hewlett are. I have visited the homes of Kipling, Shaw, Bennett, Barrie, Masefield, Doyle, and many others of my fellows. Galsworthy, Hope, and Gosse have been my neighbors—each in his kind. London is a well-conned map. I know the streets and the buses which course them. I know Sussex and Kent and Herts. I have wandered along the lanes and across the fields of Surrey. England is something more than a reality; it is a familiar ancestral home. I feel, as Hawthorne did, the deep-laid charm of it and I acknowledge the psychological changes which its landscape and history have wrought.

"I have gained perspective on American life and American literature. I perceive more clearly the shallowness, the lack of background in our writers, but I am more than ever convinced that the future belongs to us. I am more tolerant of Old World criticism—more understanding of the London point of view.

"This trip has been like a return to a remembered field of great trees, all in full leaf but gorgeously hued for decay. My generation of authors is still supreme, but their powers are failing. Their sap no longer streams upward, their vitality is ebbing swiftly toward the earth. But among them, in their shadow, are new growths manifesting, new forces stirring. To what height they will attain, to what nobility of form they will come, only time can tell."

(Ten more volumes of my diaries remain to be edited, and to those interested I am moved to say, "Wind and weather permitting, another log-book will some time be added to the set.")